Empire and Globalisati

Focusing on the great population movement of British emigrants before 1914, this book provides a new perspective on the relationship between empire and globalisation. It shows how distinct structures of economic opportunity developed around the people who settled across a wider British World through the co-ethnic networks they created. Yet these networks could also limit and distort economic growth. The powerful appeal of ethnic identification often made trade and investment with racial 'outsiders' less appealing, thereby skewing economic activities towards communities perceived to be 'British'. By highlighting the importance of these networks to migration, finance and trade, this book contributes to debates about globalisation in the past and present. It reveals how the networks upon which the era of modern globalisation was built quickly turned in on themselves after 1914, converting racial, ethnic and class tensions into protectionism, nationalism and xenophobia. Avoiding such an outcome is a challenge faced today.

GARY B. MAGEE is a professor of Economics at Monash University, Australia. His books include *Productivity and Performance in the Paper Industry: Labour, Capital and Technology in Britain and America* (1997) *Knowledge Generation: Technological Change and Economic Growth in Colonial Australia* (2000).

ANDREW S. THOMPSON is professor of Commonwealth and Imperial History at the School of History, and Pro-Vice-Chancellor for research at the University of Leeds. His previous publications include *The Empire Strikes Back? The Impact of Imperialism on Britain from the Mid-Nineteenth Century* (2005) and *The Impact of the South African War, 1899–1902* (co-edited with D. Omissi, 2002).

Empire and Globalisation

*Networks of People, Goods and Capital
in the British World, c. 1850–1914*

Gary B. Magee
and
Andrew S. Thompson

CAMBRIDGE
UNIVERSITY PRESS

CAMBRIDGE UNIVERSITY PRESS
Cambridge, New York, Melbourne, Madrid, Cape Town, Singapore,
São Paulo, Delhi, Tokyo, Mexico City

Cambridge University Press
The Edinburgh Building, Cambridge CB2 8RU, UK

Published in the United States of America by Cambridge University Press, New York

www.cambridge.org
Information on this title: www.cambridge.org/9780521727587

© Gary B. Magee and Andrew S. Thompson 2010

First published 2010
Reprinted 2011

Printed in the United Kingdom at the University Press, Cambridge

A catalogue record for this publication is available from the British Library

Library of Congress Cataloguing in Publication data
Magee, Gary Bryan, 1965–
　Empire and globalisation : networks of people, goods and capital in the
　British world, c. 1850–1914 / Gary Magee, Andrew S. Thompson.
　　p.　cm.
　ISBN 978-0-521-89889-8 (hardback)
　1. Great Britain–Emigration and immigration–History.　2. Great Britain–
　Commerce–History.　3. British–Foreign countries–History.　I. Thompson,
　Andrew S. (Andrew Stuart), 1968–　II. Title.　III. Title: Empire and globalization.
　JV1011.M343 2010
　304.80941′09034–dc22　　　2009053428

ISBN 978-0-521-89889-8 Hardback
ISBN 978-0-521-72758-7 Paperback

For Annabel, Tasha, Ciaran and Faye

Contents

Figures

Tables

Preface

'Empire' and 'globalisation' are currently two of the most prominent and widely debated discourses in the humanities and social sciences. This book explores the historical relationship between them. We take as our starting-point one of the great global movements of population – the largely voluntary emigration of men, women and children from Europe to the New World between the mid nineteenth century and the First World War. While migration may be 'as old as humanity itself', it was during these years that the world witnessed an unprecedented exodus of 50 million or so Europeans.[1] Britain led the way, supplying approximately 13.5 million migrants, or a quarter of the total. Aided by improvements in transport and communications, arguably no less dramatic in their ability to transform life than those witnessed over the last half-century, the majority of these British people settled across Australia, New Zealand, South Africa, Canada and the United States.[2]

The consequences of this population outflow were profound. On the one hand, emigration was a force for global economic growth – integrating labour, commodity and capital markets to an extent never previously seen. Yet, on the other, this business of white settlement – for that is is was it was, or at least became – led to the widespread dispossession and oppression of indigenous peoples, as well as to a racialisation of the social order, the polarising effects of which were felt powerfully at the time and still resonate today.[3] The outbreak of the First World War

[1] For the different phases of modern migration, see D. S. Massey, J. Arango, G. Hugo, A. Kouaouci, A. Pellegrino and J. Edward Taylor (eds.), *Worlds in Motion: Understanding International Migration at the End of the Millennium* (Oxford: Oxford University Press, 1998), pp. 1–7 (quotation from p. 1).

[2] At least 52 million migrants left Europe for overseas destinations between 1815 and 1930; see D. Baines, *Emigration from Europe, 1815–1930* (Cambridge: Cambridge University Press, 1995), pp. 9–11.

[3] For a history of land-taking and its repercussions across the so-called 'neo-Europes', see for example J. C. Weaver, *The Great Land Rush and the Making of the Modern World, 1650–1900* (Montreal and Kingston: McGill-Queen's University Press, 2003).

effectively put an end to this era of European mass migration, ushering in a period of limited population movements, as well as the passing of a series of restrictive immigration laws. Not until the 1960s did global migration flows increase sharply again, except that from this point onward they were more likely to come *from* developing countries, and to choose a greater variety of destinations, including western Europe.

For those studying the contemporary world, migration and globalisation might seem inextricably linked. The growth of a more integrated international society is widely recognised to be the product of the sharp rise in geographic mobility that occurred in the late twentieth and early twenty-first centuries. As more and more people have been able to move more and more quickly, so societies and politics have been re-shaped around the globe. By contrast, the historical relationship between empire, migration and globalisation is less well understood. The social science literature on globalisation still tends to focus on the period after the Second World War, while scholars in the humanities have only recently delineated earlier episodes or eras of globalisation: 'archaic', 'pre-modern' and 'modern'.[4]

To explore the origins or 'ancestry' of modern globalisation requires us to reintegrate what have lately become increasingly separated historical specialisms, and to take more seriously branches of historical enquiry – especially economic history – that seem to have fallen out of favour in recent years.[5] It also requires a greater dialogue between historical study and the social sciences.[6] Hence, our study of the cultural and economic history of the later-nineteenth and early-twentieth-century 'British World' – those regions of empire and elsewhere (most notably the United States) where people from Britain settled

---

[4]   The most chronologically wide-ranging overview is provided by A. G. Hopkins (ed.), *Globalization in World History* (London: Pimlico, 2002). For further theoretical reflections, see G. Eley, 'Historicizing the Global, Politicizing Capital: Giving the Present a Name', *HWJ* 63 (2007), 154–88. For a key study of the international economy in the pre-First World War era, albeit weighted towards the western world, see K. O'Rourke and J. G. Williamson, *Globalization and History: The Evolution of a Nineteenth-Century Atlantic Economy* (Cambridge, MA: Harvard University Press, 1999). For a sophisticated, global history of the 'long' nineteenth century, which pays greater attention to the extra-European world, see C. A. Bayly, *The Birth of the Modern World, 1780–1914: Global Connections and Comparisons* (Oxford: Oxford University Press, 2004).

[5]   *Ibid.*

[6]   A. G. Hopkins, 'Introduction: Interactions between the Universal and the Local', in Hopkins (ed.), *Global History: Interactions between the Universal and the Local* (Basingstoke: Palgrave Macmillan, 2006), p. 4. For a good example of this revival, see the Global Economic History Network (including its 'imperialism and colonialism' theme) led by the London School of Economics: www.lse.ac.uk/collections/economic_History/GEHN.

in substantial numbers – will combine economic and sociological approaches from the social sciences with cultural approaches from the humanities. More specifically, in exploring the material foundations of this British World, we draw on economic theory and econometric techniques to analyse trade, investment and remittance flows; on social network theory, emerging from political science and sociology, to analyse how notions of trust impacted upon the way economic knowledge was created, disseminated and consumed; and on histories of identity, race and culture, to analyse how an expansive, yet racially restricted sense of Britishness shaped patterns of economic, as much as religious and political, behaviour.

It will be apparent that our perspective on the relationship between empire and globalisation eschews both the unbridled enthusiasm of some proponents of globalisation, and the abject pessimism of some of its detractors. Instead, we offer a view of economic life that highlights the importance of co-ethnic networks in expanding the scope of migration, finance and trade. Distinct structures of economic opportunity developed around the diaspora of migrants that left Britain in search of greater opportunity, real or imagined, in the wider world. Yet, if the trans-national networks fashioned by British migrants expanded the possibilities for economic growth, they could equally work to limit and distort it. The powerful and pervasive appeal of ethnic identification made trade and investment with racial or other 'outsiders' less appealing, and thus skewed these economic activities (further) towards those communities perceived to be ethnically 'British'.

The Introduction to the book opens up the question of how, in a period when putatively 'impersonal' market forces had taken hold, ethnicity and culture could still influence economic behaviour. We also explore the notion of an 'imperial economy' and discuss the various forms that it could assume. Here we identify the 'British World' economy of the nineteenth and early twentieth centuries as a system whose make-up was as much cultural as it was political, and whose ability to function depended upon only the most limited guidance from the British state.

Chapter 1 provides the crucial historiographical context for our enquiry, focusing in particular upon spatial conceptions of empire and the new imperial history's use of the network metaphor to conceptualise the sets of connections that developed not only between metropole and colony, but increasingly between the colonies themselves. Here we also explore conceptions of 'Britishness' – as they developed both at home and overseas – and the extent to which these conceptions underpinned the economic integration of the British World. Across the empire's settler societies, there were non-white and indigenous elite groups who were attracted to the vision of moral and material progress promised by British imperialism. Yet, over the period in question, we show how it became more and more apparent that Victorian notions of free wage labour, secure property rights, equality before the law and a non-racial franchise were not, in fact, open to all. On racial, ethnic and religious grounds, there were those who were wholly or partly excluded from this greater British community, and its economic possibilities were always circumscribed therefore.

In Chapter 2 we turn to the literature on 'social capital', and what it reveals about the impact of trans-national networks upon global economic behaviour. Here we argue that the networks forged by migrants created economic value, with specific benefits flowing from the trust and reciprocity they built; people were therefore prepared to 'invest' in these networks, and this social investment was, in itself, an important determinant of economic activity. Locating these networks at the heart of the British World economy, we then explore their role in improving the quality and quantity of information flows, and in fostering co-operative, collaborative and remunerative forms of economic exchange.

Chapters 3, 4 and 5 consider in turn three key spheres of economic activity: migration, trade and investment. After surveying the main flows of migration, within and beyond the empire, Chapter 3 seeks to show that what drew people to the colonies was not just the forces of industrialisation and demography – important as they were – but the sense of trust and hope that 'over there' was recognisably similar to 'over here', and, indeed, that the two were somehow comparable and there to be compared. In particular, we highlight how a variety of social networks oiled the wheels of imperial migration and shaped migrants' responses to the world around them, drawing particular attention to a hitherto neglected yet fundamental aspect of the migrant's experience – the sending of monies (or 'remittances') home. Newly discovered data from the Post Office Archives have enabled us to reconstruct remittance patterns across the English-speaking world, and to assess the impact and importance of these monetary flows. Chapter 3 also considers how British migrant networks co-existed, yet also came into conflict with, other ethnically based migrant networks, especially those forged by Chinese and Indian contract labourers, and by the merchants and middlemen who recruited and resettled them. In South Africa, Australia and Canada the presence of these 'foreign' workers increasingly

disturbed a sense of British community, which in turn provoked powerful outbursts of exclusionary (Anglo-Saxon) racial thinking.

Chapter 4 explores the nature of colonial markets and cultures of
consumption. We introduce comparative data drawn from Britain and
her colonies' official trade statistics to shed new light on the proportion of income spent on British products by colonial, American and
Argentine consumers. These data raise the question of whether, and to
what degree, British producers in the colonies enjoyed 'non-market' or
'imperial' advantages, either overtly in terms of official policy or indirectly and informally through family, professional and other networks.
We argue that, to the extent that such non-market advantages mattered,
it was the commercial opportunities afforded by personal contacts and
communication rather than the consequences of official policy that
counted the most. We show how the empire acted as the midwife for a
variety of trans-national networks that helped to reduce the risks and
costs of long-distance trade.

Chapter 5 concerns itself with Britain's other great export of the
pre-First World War era: its capital. Drawing upon an array of newspapers and contemporary publications, as well as on bank and insurance company archives and personal records, the chapter investigates
the basis upon which British investors made their decisions about how
and where to invest overseas. The enquiry highlights how British World
networks provided prospective investors with rich information flows
from the dominions, which in turn affected the geographical distribution of British investments. However, as both the variety of outlets and
intensity of competition for British capital increased towards the end of
the nineteenth century, so these informational asymmetries gradually
diminished, with the result that capital moved further than labour or
commodity markets towards full globalisation before 1914.

The Conclusion draws together preceding arguments about the type
of globalisation that arose from the growth of this British World economy, and then considers the implications of our key findings for how we
think about globalisation today. Part of the problem facing any scholar
trying to pin down the relationship between 'empire' and 'globalisation' is that the latter presents itself as something of a shifting target.
To be sure, there is a measure of consensus around globalisation's fundamental features – which include 'interconnectedness', 'interdependence' and the 'compression of time and space'. Beyond this, however,
there have been vigorous debates about the geographical reach of globalisation, about its impact across different economic sectors and about
the (unequal) distribution of benefits arising from it. Concepts such as

'semi-globalisation', 'regionalised globalisation' and 'de-globalisation' have emerged from these debates. Proponents of these concepts are more mindful of the limits of the globalising forces at work in today's international economy, and they question the still widely held view that globalisation is somehow inevitable and irreversible. There seems little doubt that the current crisis in the world's financial markets will fortify their resolve.

It is worth reminding ourselves just how much the extent of this crisis has taken the vast majority of politicians and economists by surprise. We seem to be sailing into an economic storm of unknown ferocity and uncertain duration. The near-collapse of the global banking system at the start of the twenty-first century has required government intervention on a scale that few global or financial theorists would have countenanced even a few years ago. Liquidity has dried up, securitisation markets have all but closed, derivatives are discredited and 'light-touch' regulatory polices are under the spotlight. Talk is rife of a creeping mercantilism in capital markets, an incipient protectionism in trade and (even) tighter restrictions on immigration – what we might more colloquially call 'me-first-ism' in all matters economic. Though the international financial system will no doubt rebound, there will be much less triumphal talk of globalisation for the foreseeable future.

Does the historical record shed any light on these contemporary events? Can a greater awareness and better understanding of previous episodes of globalisation inform the way governments try to manage (and to mitigate) its adverse consequences today? The 'lessons' of the past rarely present themselves in easily applicable ways. History does, however, reveal the limits of the first wave of modern globalisation, shaped as it was by the forces of migration and empire, which came crashing down on the rocks of the First World War. It also reveals that many of the trans-national networks upon which this globalisation was built then quickly turned in on themselves at the moment of diplomatic, economic and military crisis, providing a vehicle by which racial, ethnic and class tensions could be parleyed into protectionism, nationalism and xenophobia – with baleful domestic and international consequences. Avoiding such an outcome is a challenge we face once again. We need policy that discourages the tendency to retreat inwards. Yet we must not delude ourselves. The causes of the crisis are deep and will not be easily rectified. Action to promote and protect open and inclusive networks in order to maintain and, where possible, to expand the free flow of capital, labour and goods will not of itself prevent a 'backlash' against globalisation as it is experienced today. But if such action can help to spread and diversify the number of people who continue willingly to participate in the world economy, because they recognise the benefits of doing so,[7] the depth of any future backlash – and, more importantly, the pain and lost potential it brings in its wake – may well be diminished.

[7] For the (perceived) threat to cultural identity and economic prosperity posed by a more tightly integrated world economy, see for example V. Cable, *The World's New Fissures: Identities in Crisis* (London: Demos, 1994), pp. 21–2.

Acknowledgements

All books are works of collaboration. However, in our case this is true twice over. Not only have we worked together over several years to synthesise economic and culturalist approaches to the study of empire – along the way, we have benefited from the advice and guidance of colleagues working across the humanities and social sciences. Saul Dubow and Dane Kennedy read the whole manuscript in draft; we are indebted to them both for their thoughtful observations upon the project. David Omissi gave generously of his time towards the end of the project to help us draw our conclusions together; we are especially grateful to him therefore.

The exchange of emails with Tony Hopkins highlighted the importance of historical perspectives upon globalisation, and alerted us to how a better understanding of globalising forces in the past might in turn shed light upon their operation in the present. Meanwhile, Peter Buckley drew our attention to new work in the field of international business theory on globalisation, in particular its regionalised character. Alan Lester and Simon Potter guided us through the growing literature upon imperial networks, and helped us to sharpen and refine our ideas upon the subject. Antoinette Burton and Andrew Thompson wrote a joint piece on geographical conceptions of empire that fed into the chapter on the historiography of the British World. Kent Fedorowich, Marjory Harper and Eric Richards shared their ideas upon overseas migration, and took an interest in our study of migrant remittances, while Simon Hall supplied references to key texts on migration to the United States. Mike Collins and Mae Baker guided us through the literatures on insurance and banking, sharing the fruits of their own recent research, as well as commenting upon the chapter on investment. Max Corden and Sisira Jayasuriya provided us with many valuable insights from trade theory.

Our South African case studies draw on the knowledge of Greg Cuthbertson and Vivian Bickford-Smith. Moreover, it was thanks to Greg that we were able to present an early version of our thesis as a

plenary lecture at the South African Historical Association's Jubilee
Conference at the University of Pretoria in June 2006. At that conference we were also fortunate to be able to listen to Robert Ross's
presentation on the global history of clothing, and then to correspond
with him on the importation of clothing into South Africa. Meanwhile,
Elizabeth Elbourne provided helpful references on indigenous clothing
in West and South Africa.

Margaret Maynard's work on Australian clothing and fashion was
of tremendous help when writing about the material culture of empire,
and we are very grateful to her for corresponding with us on this subject. Richard Broome guided us through the complexities of Aboriginal
dress and culture, kindly supplying copies of key primary texts, and
discussing his own important researches.

Further help came from long-standing colleagues who have sup-
ported us over many years: Peter Cain, John Darwin, David Eastwood,
John Gooch, Richard Grayson, Brian Harrison, Roberto Raimondo,
Graeme Snooks and Richard Whiting.

Both of us received fellowships and grants that were vital to the
completion of this study. Special thanks to the Institute of Advanced
Study at La Trobe University for Andrew Thompson's Distinguished
Professorial Fellowship in 2006, and to Richard Broome, Barry Carr,
Anthony Hammerton, Jon Jenkin, William Murray, Alexander Tyrrell
and Robert Young for their hospitality and kindness. We are also grateful to Carl Bridge at the Menzies Centre for Australian Studies at King's
College London, for Gary Magee and Andrew Thompson's Australian
Bicentennial Fellowships in 2005 and 2006 respectively. Gary Magee
also benefited from visiting fellowships at the University of Oxford – at
the Department of Economics and Greyfriars Hall – in 2005, and at
the Leeds Humanities Research Institute, University of Leeds, in 2006.
We were fortunate to be assisted by several librarians and archivists
who gave generously of their time: Jane Saunders at the Brotherton
Library at the University of Leeds; Mary-Lynn Suttie at the Library
of the University of South Africa, Pretoria; Edwin Green at the HSBC
Group Archives in Canada Square, London; and the staff at the Post
Office Archives, then located at Farringdon Road, London.

While writing this book, one of us became Dean, the other Head
of School – combining these roles with research would not have been
possible without the tremendous support we had from Jan Franklin
in Leeds and Colleen Harte in Melbourne, who both worked wonders
with our diaries to protect time for writing and for overseas travel. We
are also indebted to Meaghan Kowalsky for helping us to chase down

references, for editing the footnotes, and for producing the bibliography. Further thanks go to Michael Watson at Cambridge University Press for contracting the book, for all his encouragement along the way and for suggesting the subtitle.

Separating work and home life is never easy for academics, and special thanks are due to Sarah Lenton for appreciating this, and for providing Andrew with companionship throughout the project.

Abbreviations

Abbreviations used in the text

AEG	Allgemeine Elektrizitäts-Gesellschaft
ALU	Agricultural Labourers' Union
ASE	Amalgamated Society of Engineers
BNZ	Bank of New Zealand
BWEA	British Women's Emigration Association
CCCE	Congress of Chambers of Commerce of the Empire
CPR	Canadian Pacific Railway
EIO	Emigrants' Information Office
FMCES	Female Middle Class Emigration Society
IMM	*Investor's Monthly Manual*
LJSB	London Joint Stock Bank
OECD	Organisation for Economic Co-operation and Development
P&O	Peninsular and Oriental Steamship Company

Abbreviations used in the footnotes

AHR	*American Historical Review*
EcHR	*Economic History Review*
HJ	*Historical Journal*
HMSO	Her Majesty's Stationery Office
HWJ	*History Workshop Journal*
JBH	*Journal of British History*
JBS	*Journal of British Studies*
JICH	*Journal of Imperial and Commonwealth History*
JSAS	*Journal of South African Studies*
OECD	Organisation for Economic Co-operation and Development
SAHJ	*South Africa Historical Journal*
TRHS	*Transactions of the Royal Historical Society*

Introduction

At the start of the third millennium, the times are very much a-changing; or at least there are many who would wish us to believe that this is so. 'Globalisation' is the word that has been coined to capture this sense of living in an age of transformation – one in which little can be taken for granted and no-one quite knows what the future might bring.[1] 'Globalisation' trips off the tongues of journalists and politicians in a way it manifestly did not before, while university libraries now struggle to make space for the swathe of new studies of our globalised world and how it came to be so.[2] Few disciplines in academia have been left untouched by globalisation's claims, or have remained immune to its conceptual allure. Readily translatable into French, Spanish, German and other European languages, 'globalisation' is perhaps the pre-eminent way of conceptualising contemporary change.[3] A growing number of sceptics question its novelty, feel frustrated by its lack of specificity and are critical of its Eurocentricity.[4] 'A messy idea for an anxious world' is the verdict of one recent commentator upon the concept.[5] Yet there are many more champions of globalisation. Indeed, like the discourse of 'evolutionism' in the nineteenth century, globalisation has been

---

[1] For the recent history of the concept, see N. Bisley, *Rethinking Globalization* (Basingstoke: Palgrave Macmillan, 2007), pp. 1–31.

[2] For the currency or purchase of the concept, see A. Giddens' 1999 Reith Lectures, published as *Runaway World: How Globalisation Is Reshaping Our Lives* (New York: Routledge, 2002), pp. xi, 7; and Z. Bauman, *Globalization: The Human Consequences* (Cambridge: Cambridge University Press, 1998), pp. 1–2. For its impact upon academe, see C. Hay and D. Marsh, 'Introduction: Demystifying Globalization', in Hay and Marsh (eds.), *Demystifying Globalization* (Basingstoke: Palgrave Macmillan, 1999), p. 1.

[3] It has also been likened to a prism through which major debates about the human condition – capitalism, modernity, inequality, ecology, gender, identity etc. – are now refracted; see J. Nederveen Pieterse, *Globalization and Culture: Global Mélange* (Oxford: Oxford University Press, 2003), pp. 1, 7.

[4] For a powerful critique, see F. Cooper, *Colonialism in Question: Theory, Knowledge, History* (Berkeley: University of California Press, 2005), pp. 91–112.

[5] J. Garvie, 'Globalisation and Its Cures', *Times Literary Supplement*, 18 February 2008.

readily appropriated for a variety of (often competing) causes. Talk of 'globality',[6] 'global society', 'global governance', 'global economy', 'global justice', 'global warming', the 'global war against terror' and a 'new global order' is, for the moment, here to stay.

Globalisation is about the interconnectedness of different parts of the world.[7] It is best understood as a process, or a set of processes, that compress time and space, and accelerate the 'interdependence' of societies and states.[8] It tends to be assumed that globalisation is deepening, not least because of recent and rapid advances in communications, which have transformed the speed, and often substantially lowered the cost, of human travel, correspondence and conversation.[9] However, while

[6] Some commentators distinguish 'globality' from 'globalisation'; others leave the relationship between the two undefined. For the former, see U. Beck, *What Is Globalization?* (Cambridge: Cambridge University Press, 2000), which suggests that 'globality', which is supposedly irreversible, means that 'we have been living for a long time in a world society, in the sense that the notion of closed spaces has become illusory', whereas globalisation denotes 'the processes through which sovereign national states are criss-crossed and undermined by trans-national actors with varying prospects of power, orientations, identities and networks', pp. 10–11.

[7] There are diverse perspectives on the more specific meanings of the concept: see, *inter alia*, Nederveen Pieterse, *Globalization and Culture*, pp. 1–18; and Bisley, *Rethinking Globalization*, pp. 17–31. For agreement upon globalisation's 'fundamentals' or 'core features', see Roland Robertson, *Globalisation: Social Theory and Global Culture* (London: Sage, 1992), p. 8, who refers to the concept as 'the compression of the world and the intensification of consciousness of the world as a whole'; and Barrie Axford, *The Global System: Economics, Politics and Culture* (Oxford: Polity, 1995), p. 27: 'The core of the idea is that the world is undergoing a process of ever-intensifying interconnectedness and interdependence, so that it is becoming less relevant to speak of separate national economies, or separate national jurisdictions founded upon principles like to sovereignty of the territorial nation-state.'

[8] The different nuances of the concept are explored in more detail in the chapters that follow. Fred Halliday unpacks this particular definition further to argue for three aspects of globalisation: 'a marked reduction in the barriers between societies and states, an increasing homogeneity of societies and states and an increase in the volume of interactions between societies'; see *The World at 2000: Perils and Promises* (Basingstoke: Palgrave Macmillan, 2001), p. 61. See also D. Held and A. McGrew, 'The Great Globalization Debate: An Introduction', in Held and McGrew (eds.), *The Global Transformations Reader: An Introduction to the Globalization Debate* (Cambridge: Cambridge University Press, 2000), p. 3, who identify 'distance', 'time-space compression', 'accelerating interdependence', 'shrinking world' and 'integration' as key elements of definitions of the term. Some, yet by no means all, commentators further emphasise that globalisation's intensification of mutual dependence necessarily undermines the sovereignty of nation states; see, for example, Beck, *What is Globalization?*, p. 8.

[9] See W. H. McNeill, 'Globalization: Long Term Process or New Era in Human Affairs?', *New Global Studies* 2:1 (2008), 1–9. McNeill defines globalisation as 'the way recent changes in transport and communication have tied mankind in all parts of the earth together more closely than ever before', though he is mindful of the impact of steam transport and electrical communication on the 'global pace of change' in the past, pp. 1, 4.

cutting-edge technology, such as today's electronic and news media, can provide the means for greater integration, there is a growing recognition that globalisation is as much about people as machines, and that its roots extend back in time.[10] Thus the progress of globalisation has recently been traced through distinct phases, the latest of which may be more inclusive than its predecessors yet which is by no means wholly distinct from them.

Historians of migration have played an important role in delineating earlier 'eras' or 'episodes' of globalisation.[11] The large-scale movement of people across state borders during the nineteenth century is widely regarded as a key feature of the making of the 'modern' world.[12]

---

[10] For the view that globalisation has long been a fact of life, see Cooper, *Colonialism in Question*, pp. 94–7, 100–4; and Halliday, *The World at 2000*, p. 62. For the argument that the era of (modern) globalisation is characterised by 'a sense of living in the midst of unprecedented change' – a sense that has 'dominated social and political sensibilities, and that can be traced back to the early nineteenth century' – see A. McKeown, 'Periodizing Globalization', *HWJ* 63 (2007), 218–30 (quotations are taken from p. 219).

[11] See, for example, M. Kearney, 'The Local and the Global: The Anthropology of Globalization and Transnationalism', *Annual Review of Anthropology* 24 (1995), 547–65 (p. 549); and Nederveen Pieterse, *Globalization and Culture*, pp. 4, 32. For the way in which experiences of globalisation have been shaped by mass migration, the modern media and their joint effect on the 'social imagination', see A. Appadurai, *Modernity at Large: Cultural Dimensions of Globalization* (Minneapolis: University of Minnesota Press, 1996); M. P. Smith and L. E. Guarnizo (eds.), *Transnationalism from Below* (New Brunswick, NJ: Transaction Publishers, 1998); and S. Vertovec (ed.), *Migration, Diasporas and Transnationalism* (Cheltenham: Edward Elgar, 1999). Trans-national migration, in the form of the slave trade, is understood to have been a defining feature of Africa's 'encounter with the "modern world"', and one with 'lasting global implications', not least in terms of how Africans would be 'located in the emerging global order'; see M. Vaughan, 'Africa and the Birth of the Modern World', *TRHS* (2006), 143–62 (pp. 155–8). For the view that contemporary international migrations arise from the accelerating process of global integration, and that more countries are currently and simultaneously being affected by migratory movements, see S. Castles and M. Miller (eds.), *The Age of Migration: International Population Movements in the Modern World*, 2nd edn (Guilford Press, 1998), pp. 4, 8. Alejandro Portes also recognises the importance of migration to globalisation, again coupled mainly to twentieth-century changes in technology (airplanes, telephones, fax machines and electronic mail); see A. Portes, 'Globalization from Below: The Rise of Transnational Communities', in W. P. Smith and R. P. Korczenwicz (eds.), *Latin America in the World Economy* (Westport: Greenwood Publishing Group, 1996), pp. 151–68.

[12] For a persuasive periodisation of globalisation, which has been influential in framing the debate, see A. G. Hopkins (ed.), *Globalization in World History* (London: Pimlico, 2002), and *Global History: Interactions between the Universal and the Local* (Basingstoke: Palgrave Macmillan, 2006), especially Hopkins' 'Introduction', pp. 1–38. See also G. Eley, 'Historicizing the Global, Politicizing Capital: Giving the Present a Name', *HWJ* 63 (2007), 154–88. For the 'prehistory' of globalisation, and how earlier periods both empowered and challenged the 'nineteenth century international system', see C. A. Bayly, *The Birth of the Modern World, 1780–1914: Global Connections and Comparisons* (Oxford: Oxford University Press, 2004), pp. 41–4.

Waves of emigration, or 'diasporas' – ethnic groups in dispersal – not only helped to mesh large portions of the world together materially, spiritually and intellectually, but left in their wake new, more trans-national ways of thinking.[13] The great transatlantic migrations, as well as migrations of contract or indentured labourers from and across Africa and Asia, were central to this first major phase of modern globalisation in the half-century prior to the First World War. These migratory flows, it is claimed, profoundly altered 'the economic, cultural and political geography' of the world.[14] Their scale, timing and direction – whether coerced, semi-voluntary or free – were intimately tied up with territorial expansion and the consequent dispossession of indigenous peoples.

Within Europe, the British peoples were prolific migrants.[15] From the mid nineteenth century they comprised a major part of a great global

---

[13] The word 'diaspora' derives from the Greek: *dia*, 'through'; and *speirein*, 'to scatter'. Hence the word embodies the notion of a 'home' or 'centre' from where dispersal occurs, as well as the idea of settling down and putting one's roots elsewhere. See A. Brah, *Cartographies of Diaspora: Contesting Identities* (London: Routledge, 1997), pp. 181–2. Several commentators allow for the formation of European diasporas through conquest and colonisation. For the classic text, see R. Cohen, *Global Diasporas: An Introduction* (London: Routledge, 1997). 'Victim diasporas' (e.g. the Jews, Armenians and Africans) were involuntary movements of people, driven or deported from their homes; as such, they loom large in the popular imagination. But the concept of a 'diaspora' can be used more broadly to encompass peoples who imagine themselves as part of a nation while residing outside their homeland. Scattered to many corners of the globe, diasporic migrants nonetheless retain their language and other elements of their culture, at least for a few generations. They also tend to be involved economically with the society they have left behind. For an important study of a 'voluntary' diaspora, couched in these broader terms, see D. R. Gabaccia, *Italy's Many Diasporas* (London: UCL Press, 2000). Her defin-ition, based around the idea of a trans-national ethnic community, and a grow-ing sense of group consciousness arising from migration, has also been applied to today's Indian diaspora: see B. Parekh, G. Singh and S. Vertovec (eds.), *Culture and Economy in the Indian Diaspora* (London: Routledge, 2003). For the suggestion that a sense of 'Greater Britishness' or 'imperial Anglo-Saxonism' might usefully be conceived as a form of 'diasporic transnationalism', see R. C. Young, *The Idea of English Ethnicity* (Oxford: Blackwell, 2007), pp. 226, 231: 'So it was that during the course of the nineteenth century, Englishness was translated from the national identity of the English living in England into a diasporic identity beyond any geo-graphical boundaries which included all the English who had now emigrated all over the globe' (quotation from p. 231).

[14] McKeown, 'Periodizing Globalization', pp. 226–7; J. Darwin, *After Tamerlane: The Global History of Empire* (London: Allen Lane, 2007), p. 251.

[15] The notion of a British 'diaspora' has received much less consideration than that of its Jewish, Italian, Indian or Chinese counterparts: for an early use of the term, see H. Tinker, 'The British Diaspora', in Tinker (ed.), *The Diaspora of the British*, Collected Seminar Papers of the Institute of Commonwealth Studies (London: Institute of Commonwealth Studies, 1982), pp. 1–9. For a definition of 'diaspora' that encom-passes migrants from Europe, see Gabaccia's 'a way of life that connects family, work and consciousness in more than one territory': *Italy's Many Diasporas*, p. 11.

movement of population.[16] Ethnically, racially and culturally defined, this outflow of human capital from Britain saw millions of individuals leave their homes voluntarily in search of greater opportunity, real or imagined, in the wider world.[17] Their complex, multi-layered set of migrations encompassed the 'settler' colonies, the United States, and a host of smaller 'expatriate' communities in the empire's dependent territories and regions of so-called 'informal' colonial rule.

Crucially, emigration from Britain underpinned a new division of labour in the international economy, one effect of which was to 'put a different order of strain' on native peoples everywhere,[18] another to make 'transnationalism' – living in and identifying with more than one country or place – a normal way of life for many British people in the half-century before 1914.[19] Shared conceptions of 'Britishness' gave rise

[16] For key works, covering the period up to 1914, see D. Baines, *Migration in a Mature Economy: Emigration and Internal Migration in England and Wales, 1861–1900* (Cambridge: Cambridge University Press, 1985); M. Harper, *Adventurers and Exiles: The Great Scottish Exodus* (London: Profile Books, 2004); H. L. Malchow, *Population Pressures: Emigration and Government in the Late Nineteenth Century* (London: Sposs, 1979); and B. Thomas, *Migration and Atlantic Growth: A Study of Great Britain and the Atlantic Economy* (Cambridge: Cambridge University Press, 1954). Further references are provided in Chapter 3. For the latest publications, see R. Bickers (ed.), *Settlers and Expatriates: Britons over the Seas* (Oxford: Oxford University Press, 2010); M. Harper and S. Constantine, *Migrants and Settlers* (Oxford: Oxford University Press, 2010); K. Fedorowich, 'The British Empire on the Move, 1760–1914', in S. Stockwell (ed.), *The British Empire: Themes and Perspectives* (Oxford: Oxford University Press, 2007); and, especially, E. Richards, *Britannia's Children: Emigration from England, Scotland, Wales and Ireland since 1600* (London: Continuum International Publishing Group, 2004).

[17] 'Ethnicity', 'race' and 'culture' are, of course, all overlapping and imprecise concepts, open to differing interpretations. For further consideration of 'race' and racial attitudes across the 'British World', see Chapter 1 ('Reconfiguring empire'), as well as the discussions of indentured and contract labour (Chapter 3) and cultures of consumption among indigenous peoples (Chapter 4). For a working definition of 'culture', see below, p. 13 and n. 36. 'Ethnicity' figures prominently in social science, as well as public policy discourses. A useful introduction to the concept is provided by Steve Fenton: *Ethnicity* (Cambridge: Polity, 2004), which refers to ethnic groups as 'descent and culture communities' (p. 13). As Fenton is at pains to point out, this definition is only a starting point: ethnicity, like race, is not a fixed category but rather is socially constructed: 'People or peoples do not just possess cultures or share ancestry; they elaborate these into the idea of a community founded upon these attributes' (pp. 3–4). For a skilful exposition of the view that ethnic (and cultural) identity is as much 'a matter of becoming' as a matter of 'being', see S. Hall, 'Cultural Identity and Diaspora', in J. Rutherford (ed.), *Identity: Community, Culture, Difference* (London: Lawrence and Wishart, 1998), pp. 222–37, esp. pp. 222–8. For the argument that 'English ethnicity was effectively globalized' during the nineteenth century, and 'moved out from the centre to absorb the remotest colonial peripheries', see Young, *The Idea of English Ethnicity*, pp. xi–xii, 1–2, 196–230, 231–27 (quotation from p. 225).

[18] Bayly, *The Birth of the Modern World*, p. 439.

[19] Or, more precisely, the co-existence of intense social, economic and political ties across national boundaries; for this definition see S. Vertovec, 'Transnationalism and Identity', *Journal of Ethnic and Migration Studies* 27 (2001), 573–82.

to the notion of a 'British World',[20] a world whose foundations were cultural as much as political, personal as well as official, and changeable rather than fixed. While those who belonged to this 'British World' might have struggled to trace its outlines on a map, it was a concept that nonetheless meant something important to them. Migrants to Britain's settler colonies remained 'British', or at least partly so; and being 'British' had material implications, not only shaping consumer tastes and preferences, but impacting more broadly on the very nature and orientation of economic activity and behaviour. The so-far unexplored history of this British World economy is the subject of this book.

There is, however, a problem. Why, in the economic sphere, would rational, self-interested individuals prefer to interact with particular cultural or ethnic groups? In pre-modern times, when reliable market institutions were weak or did not exist, economic actors had little option but to rely on personal connections – the risks of dealing with strangers were high, whereas those whom you knew were felt more likely to be trustworthy. Co-ethnic and co-religious networks, therefore, offered a relatively secure way of expanding the scope of economic activity. Such solutions, however, were supposedly no more than second best, and by the nineteenth century, when the workings of impersonal markets had become ensconced, there remained potentially much less need for such devices. Economic behaviour could surely now become culturally neutral. After all, to those engaged in trade, it was ultimately the exchange itself that mattered, not the identity of those with whom they did business. Nineteenth-century consumers would thus buy from the cheapest seller, sellers would supply the buyer who was prepared to pay the most or to pay the most promptly, migrants would go to societies where their skills would be best rewarded, and capital would flow to projects that promised the highest or most secure return. In short, key economic decisions could (and should) have been made on the basis of profit-maximisation and the rational calculation of material well-being. If we follow this logic, then little room is left for non-economic considerations. Yet, as this book demonstrates, there is overwhelming evidence that the influence of such non-economic considerations did not disappear, but remained active and strong in the British World of the later nineteenth and early twentieth centuries. A distinct 'British World economy' existed: how was this possible?

The answer to this question lies in the uneven process of globalisation. Barriers to integration frequently impede economic interaction by

---

[20] For an introduction to the literature, see C. Bridge and K. Fedorowich, *The British World: Culture, Diaspora and Identity* (London: Taylor and Francis, 2003).

obstructing or diverting certain types of economic behaviour. There are three conceptually distinct if, in practice, inter-related, types of barrier.

The first type is cultural, ethnic or religious. Differing tastes, values, expectations and beliefs, in the past as now, tend to complicate cross-societal economic activity. A trader wishing to sell English meat products in the Middle East, for example, will have little success if he or she does not appreciate the distinctiveness of Middle Eastern tastes or understand Islamic law about appropriate foodstuffs and the manner of slaughter. Attempts to sell non-halal meat would inevitably prove fruitless. The scope for such economically disadvantageous misunderstanding is typically reduced when the people involved share similar cultural backgrounds.

The second type of barrier is informational.[21] The flow and differing availability of information in different contexts can block, retard or even re-orientate the focus of integration. Markets need information to work efficiently. One can make optimal economic choices only if one has adequate, accurate and relevant knowledge of all the available options. Thus, while our British meat trader may have the potential to adapt his or her products profitably to Middle Eastern demands, he or she may be simply unaware of the market opportunities that pertain there. In other words, there is no-one to tell him or her that a rewarding market exists in the Middle East. Instead, the trader continues to supply the British and western Europe markets exclusively, even though greater profits could, in theory, have been made by catering for the Middle Eastern customer. Moreover, even within Europe, information can skew the direction of the trader's exports in ways that appear economically 'irrational'. If our British trader were more familiar with and, hence, better informed about, say, French markets than Italian, he or she would tend, *ceteris paribus*, to export more to the former than the latter – again irrespective of the real relative profitability of either. In a world of less than perfect information (the real world), the uneven creation, dissemination and distribution of knowledge will inevitably influence the extent and direction of economic activity.[22]

---

[21] For two key studies of the influence of information and communication flows on economic (and political) life, see D. R. Headrick, *When Information Came of Age: Technologies of Knowledge in the Age of Reason and Revolution, 1700–1850* (Oxford: Oxford University Press, 2000); and H. A. Innis, *Empire & Communications* (Victoria, BC: University of British Columbia, 1986).

[22] For the social organisation of knowledge, and its implications for debates about globalisation, see Hay and Marsh, 'Introduction', pp. 12–13.

The third type of barrier to market integration is political. Export prohibitions, tariffs and the whole panoply of other devices are designed to protect trade. Our British meat trader may be aware of and able to supply Middle Eastern demand, but be prevented from doing so by an embargo on such trade imposed by a British parliament concerned about local food supplies, or by a Middle Eastern tariff designed to protect local butchers. Either way, domestic and commercial policies and regulations can place limits on the expansion of all types of economic activity. While such barriers exist, markets are not free to develop to the fullest extent.

The growth of cross-cultural economic activity therefore depends upon the ongoing mitigation of these barriers. The state can assist this process by removing obstructions to the movement of people, goods and capital across societies, by providing physical and legal protection to those who seize the opportunities, and by creating an infrastructure that enables information and 'social capital' to flow more freely across borders.[23]

In the pages that follow we explain how the migration of the British peoples during the 'long' nineteenth century was integral to the birth of a British World economy. The spread of 'neo-British' communities reduced all three of the above barriers – cultural, informational and political – thereby facilitating trade, investment and further rounds of migration between the United Kingdom and British settler societies overseas.[24] Yet, at the same time, information flows engendered by such a culturally and ethnically led expansion of economic activity tended to make comparable activity with racial or other 'outsiders' relatively less appealing. These flows skewed trade, investment and migration patterns, for a time at least, further towards those perceived as being 'British'. Of course, the economic effects of being 'British' were never absolute. Despite the best efforts of empire loyalists and 'constructive imperialists', British colonies continued to consume and attract people, products and monies from elsewhere, and barriers to integration were

---

[23] For a definition of 'social capital', see Chapter 2, pp. 46–51 below.
[24] For the term 'neo-Britons', see J. Belich, 'The Rise of the Angloworld: Settlement in North America and Australasia, 1784–1918', in P. Buckner and D. Francis (eds.), *Rediscovering the British World* (Calgary: University of Calgary Press, 2005), pp. 39–58. Critics object to the term on the grounds that it can be taken to imply the erasure of pre-colonial, distinctively non-British societies and the recreation of their landscapes as replica Britons. This was certainly not Belich's intention. However, the empire's settler societies (and, to a degree, the United States) did face certain common challenges as a result of having imported a good deal of their population, ideology, cultural baggage and lifestyle. On this point, see A. S. Thompson, 'The Languages of Loyalism in Southern Africa, *c.* 1870–1939', *English Historical Review* 118 (2003), 617–50 (pp. 617–18).

never completely eradicated, but continued to exist (to different degrees, and hence with differing outcomes) across locations. That said, places that had well-established British communities were better known and more welcoming, and could provide greater support and protection to the British emigrant, investor and merchant, so that cultural, informational and political barriers tended to be accordingly less problematic.[25] The incompleteness of the process of integration helps to explain why nineteenth-century reality (like any other reality) varied from the hypothetical world of the perfectly neutral market, and why there remained space for a distinctively British World economy not only to survive, but to flourish. Incomplete integration also explains how an economic system ostensibly based on free trade could have and retain an 'imperial' (or more accurately 'British') component to it.

Yet what we identify in this book is a very different type of 'imperial' economic system from that usually depicted. The British imperial economy is often cast in one of two starkly contrasting moulds: it is conceived either as a largely fictitious entity or as a very real one based on hegemonic power relations. The former position typically derives from the observation that, while Britain's internal and external economic policies were guided by the principle of laissez-faire, there could be little scope – beyond the provision of basic infrastructure, education, and law and order – for government involvement in the economy.[26] According to this view, the course of economic development and integration was driven by self-interested individuals operating within free markets in a manner that paralleled the neo-classical trade theories of modern economics. Moreover, within this tradition, the focus of much historical writing about nineteenth-century global economic development is not the wider British Empire but more the so-called 'Atlantic world'.[27] For

[25] For the 'unprecedented globalisation of information' in the British Empire of the later nineteenth century, see C. A. Bayly, 'Informing Empire and Nation: Publicity, Propaganda and the Press 1880–1920', in H. Morgan (ed.), *Information, Media and Power through the Ages* (Dublin: University College Dublin Press, 2001), pp. 179–98, although this 'global information order' could be used as much by fledgling nationalist movements to challenge colonial power, as it could by agents of British rule to shore it up.

[26] To some, these principles of small government and liberal institutions were in fact the greatest (and most beneficial) of Britain's legacies to its empire. See N. Ferguson, *Empire: The Rise and Demise of the British World Order and the Lessons for Global Power* (London: Basic Books, 2002), pp. xxi–xxiii.

[27] This is the definition provided by K. O'Rourke and J. Williamson in *Globalization and History: The Evolution of a Nineteenth Century Atlantic Economy* (Cambridge, MA: Harvard University Press, 1999), p. 6. Effectively they mean today's OECD countries. Even were their definition to be reworded as 'countries that first experienced *the impact of* industrialisation' it would still be contentious.

example, according to Kevin O'Rourke and Jeffrey Williamson, it was this Atlantic region that industrialised first and experienced the 'first great globalisation boom'. By implication, the British empire – formal or informal – was largely irrelevant to the unprecedented integration of capital and commodity markets, and to the consequent convergence of real wages and per capita gross domestic product (GDP) witnessed by this group of countries during the later nineteenth and early twentieth centuries.[28] Certainly, in such accounts, the British empire rarely rates a mention.[29]

Meanwhile, to many others, the view that imperial factors played no major role in the evolution of either global commodity or financial markets in the nineteenth century would seem, at the very least, contentious. There is, after all, a long tradition of political thought dating back at least to Hobson and Lenin that not only acknowledges the role of empire, but places it at the heart of late-nineteenth-century economic development.[30] Such approaches are typically based around ideas of dependency, exploitation and coercion.[31] Their assumptions about supposedly unequal power relations between the metropolis and periphery lead them to highlight how the trajectories of extra-European economies were subject to, and shaped by, the requirements of an industrialised Britain.[32] Moreover, they usually present Britain's 'imperial economy' either as part of some 'grand design', concocted in Whitehall and implemented at the highest reaches of government, or as an inherent expression of an emerging global (and exploitative) capitalist system.

These two approaches, however, have one thing in common: they both attempt to understand the prevailing economic system in terms of broader policy frameworks, social aggregates and political economy. While there is no doubt that they can shed light on those things upon which they choose to focus, neither truly provides a complete or entirely accurate description of what the British World economy was

---

[28] *Ibid.*

[29] For a further example of a major work where the empire barely figures, see L. E. Davis and R. E. Gallman, *Evolving Financial Markets and International Capital Flows: Britain, the Americas, and Australia, 1865–1914* (Cambridge: Cambridge University Press, 2001).

[30] J. A. Hobson, *Imperialism: A Study*, 3rd rev. edn (London: Allen and Unwin, 1902); V. I. Lenin, *Imperialism: The Highest Stage of Capitalism. A Popular Outline by V. I. Lenin* (London: Pluto Press, 1917).

[31] These approaches have developed out of the work of A. G. Frank and I. Wallerstein. For an overview of their work and for more recent iterations, see B. N. Ghosh, *Dependency Theory Revisited* (Aldershot: Ashgate, 2001).

[32] See, for example, J. Osterhammel, *Colonialism: A Theoretical Overview* (Princeton: Markus Wiener Publishers, 1997), pp. 72–3.

or how it really functioned. By portraying individuals in stylised and highly abstracted ways as profit-maximisers, or as members of certain classes, each theory fails to address the mechanisms that such individuals utilised or the behaviours they adopted to achieve their goals within the system. Hence, while these approaches can provide answers to broader questions such as why protectionism was adopted in certain places and times, and why the international division of labour emerged in the manner in which it did, they are less helpful in explaining how British exporters found their markets, how British investors acquired information about overseas investment opportunities, and how potential emigrants chose their destinations. These latter questions are, crucially, about actual economic behaviour rather than theories of political economy. Providing answers to these 'real world' questions requires us to place the 'economics' back into the analysis of the 'imperial' or British World system.

In discussing the economic relationships arising from empire, one therefore needs to bear in mind that no single set of characteristics, taken together, in itself constitutes an 'imperial' economy. Rather, Britain's economic relationships with its settler colonies could (and did) assume a variety of forms. The key to understanding this variety is the realisation that enduring economic systems do not arise entirely by accident. Their creation, evolution and maintenance are contingent upon an array of government and individual actions. Government action and policy provide the formal structural underpinnings of the economic system. These actions and policies are, in turn, shaped by official perceptions of the nature of the desired economy and of the state's role in creating it. Excluding non-market, centrally planned empires (which have little relevance in this context), the state's approach to economic affairs can take three forms: *dirigiste*, *guided*, or *laissez-faire*.

In the first, dirigiste, form, the state becomes the conscious architect of the economic system, a system that is usually explicitly designed to favour economic activity with certain groups (such as those within the empire), often to the exclusion of those outside it. The *guiding* state, on the other hand, may provide the basic infrastructure of the system, yet decide to take a less interventionist role and allow the economy to evolve in response to prevailing conditions. In this context, policy is used to make the system as efficient as possible within current circumstances, and at times to nudge economic activity in certain preferred directions. Thus, whereas a dirigiste state might protect, say, intra-imperial trade simply by prohibiting all extra-imperial imports, a guiding state might prefer to provide incentives to local consumers and producers to 'think imperially' rather than explicitly directing economic activity. Finally, laissez-faire states may typically choose to allow their economies to be shaped by market forces alone and, hence, have no desire at all to orientate themselves economically towards empire.

Yet government policy alone cannot make an economic system. If trade chooses not to follow the flag, even the most earnest of intentions can create little more than the appearance of economic integration. The essence of any economic system reflects the actions of those who utilise it, so that the extent to which private interests – be they individual, organisational or even institutional – support or actively seek closer economic integration will shape the outcome. Self-interest may, of course, support closer imperial economic bonds,[33] while political belief also has a role to play. Cultural affinity, understanding and prejudice are likely to be even more powerful drivers of private attitudes: for example, a feeling of a genuine sense of attachment towards the 'imperial' or 'British' project, or of kinship with fellow Britons across the globe. An economic orientation towards the empire may, moreover, have been more likely when the existing stock of knowledge was moulded by the empire itself. All decisions have to be made on the basis of the available information. If one of the consequences, whether intended or unintended, of Britain's imperial relations was that its producers, consumers and investors were blessed by a rich flow of information about commercial and financial opportunities in the colonies, and comparatively ignorant about those outside the empire, it is easy to see how even the most hard-headed economic rationalist might choose to buy, sell or invest in the empire. Like cultural attachment, this informational bias in favour of empire varied in intensity across contexts.

The ways in which private and state perceptions of, and information about, the economy interact with each other thus shape the nature of any economic system. When the effects of such interactions are allowed for, it becomes clear that a variety of different economic forms are possible. These forms range from, at one end of the spectrum, free trade – where individuals regard markets within the British imperial world no differently from any other, and the government consciously provides just the basic infrastructure necessary for market activity to occur – to, at the other end, a strong culturally orientated customs union – one in which both individuals and government are strongly committed to the idea of actively shaping economic relations in purely 'imperial' terms. Of course, other possible forms lie somewhere between these two

---

[33] Indeed, if the return on the activity is high enough, even the most dispassionate businessman can willingly subscribe to closer economic bonds within the empire; declarations of imperial piety are always easily made when they come at no cost.

positions, and the British World economy analysed in this book is to be found in this intermediate space. As we shall see, the British World was an economic form that typically had as strong a cultural dimension as a political one, and one that saw the British state play at most a limited 'guiding' role.[34] As subsequent chapters also demonstrate, the lack of strong political direction certainly did not impede its ability to survive, develop and expand.

The interplay between the cultural and economic dynamics of globalisation today is a subject of growing interest.[35] In exploring the relationship between empire and globalisation in the past we, too, seek to integrate these two dimensions. Until recently, the humanities appeared to have turned away from 'economy' and towards 'culture'.[36] Imperial historiographies, in particular, seem of late to have bifurcated into 'new' imperial histories that lay particular claim to the social and cultural terrain, and older histories that focus on the political, military and economic.[37] Yet to think of the empire as a series of interlocking networks or webs, which impacted as much on metropolitan as on colonial life,

---

[34] There was, of course, room for significant variation between different parts of the British World, since at certain times and in certain places the effects of cultural and political influence could significantly differ.

[35] See, for example, Hay and Marsh, 'Introduction', pp. 12–13.

[36] Scholars tend to be much less comfortable around the word 'culture' than 'economy'. Like 'class', there is no generally accepted definition of the term 'culture'. P. Burke, for instance, refers to it as 'a concept with an embarrassing variety of definitions' (see *History and Social Theory* (Cambridge: Cambridge University Press, 1992), p. 118), and R. Williams as 'one of the two or three most complicated words in the English language' (see *Keywords: A Vocabulary of Culture and Society* (Oxford: Oxford University Press, 1976), p. 76). That said, many definitions have at their core the idea of 'culture' as the embodiment of a group's experiences, which refers to patterns of thinking, feeling and acting that are shared by groups of people (large or small) who live in the same social environment, while recognising that these patterns are learned, not inherited. See, for example, Brah, *Cartographies of Diaspora*, pp. 18–21; G. Hofstede, *Cultures and Organisations: Software of the Mind* (London: McGraw-Hill Professional, 1991), pp. 4–5; and E. L. Jones, *Cultures Merging: A Historical and Economic Critique of Culture* (Princeton: Yale University Press, 2006), p. ix. A potential problem with such broad-based definitions is that it is not entirely clear where 'culture' stops and where 'society', the 'social' or 'social institutions' begin. (The difficulty of isolating 'culture' as a variable is, of course, one reason why economists fight shy of it in their explanations.) In view of the fact that the study of migration is central to our enquiry, we see little profit in trying completely to separate 'culture' and 'society'. Rather we understand 'culture' in terms of patterns of beliefs, values and expectations, or 'norms' that, if widely shared and strongly felt, can influence and be influenced by the social and economic conditions, attitudes and behaviours of individuals and groups.

[37] For a notable exception, see P. J. Cain and A. G. Hopkins, *British Imperialism, 1688–2000* (Harlow: Longman, 2001), which, in elaborating the notion of 'gentlemanly capitalism', deftly weaves together social and economic histories.

requires us to place economy and culture in the same analytic frame.[38] Although imperial power has long been recognised as crucial to the mobilisation and distribution of material resources, there is a growing consciousness of how economics, like any other form of human activity, is culturally influenced. We therefore need a merging of cultural and economic histories – a recognition of culture as the matrix in which economic life occurs.[39]

We use the term 'cultural economy' to highlight how cultural factors can influence economic behaviour. Our starting point is the idea that all economies operate within cultural contexts, and that, since the advent of the 'first wave' of modern globalisation, both cultures and economies have been increasingly trans-national by nature. 'Cultural economy', it should be noted, complements rather than supersedes the concept of 'political economy'. The political context, of course, matters: the influence of politics is both direct (in that policy effects economic activity), and indirect (in that political structures and policy frameworks influence the ability of cultures to expand and assert themselves, including within the realm of economic activity). Yet our study also allows culture a measure of economic significance.

We do not see 'culture' simply as the creature of the economy, though nor do we deny that cultural practices may sometimes be subordinated to economic ends or demands. How, then, did cultural features underpin different forms of economic organisation? Some scholars identify a 'work' or 'entrepreneurial' culture, whereby individual companies, or whole immigrant or other groups, exhibit certain characteristics or

[38] There is some frustration among historians of empire regarding the reluctance of specialists in postcolonial studies to take adequate account of the economics of imperialism. For a powerful manifesto for future research, bridging the divide, see A. G. Hopkins, 'Back to the Future: From National History to Imperial History', *Past & Present* 164 (1999), 198–243, esp. p. 199. For the sense of frustration, see N. Ferguson, 'We Must Understand Why Racist Belief Systems Persist', *Guardian*, 12 July 2006, p. 26. Meanwhile, there is now greater, if overdue, recognition from a small but growing number of economists of the importance of culture in understanding economic development and performance. See M. Casson, 'Cultural Determinants of Economic Performance', *Journal of Comparative Economics* (1993), 418–42, and *Enterprise and Competitiveness: A Systems View of International Business* (Oxford: Oxford University Press, 1990), pp. 86–104; D. S. Landes, *The Wealth and Poverty of Nations: Why Some Are So Rich and Some So Poor* (London: W. W. Norton, 1999), pp. 516–18; D. North, *Understanding the Process of Economic Change* (Princeton: Yale University Press, 2005). Sociologists insist that 'economic processes do not operate outside of cultural and ideological conditions'; see S. Hall and B. Gieben (eds.), *Formations of Modernity* (Cambridge: Cambridge University Press, 1992), pp. 13–14. For an acknowledgement from cultural theory that economic matters cannot be ignored, see L. Ray and A. Sayer (eds.), *Culture and Economy after the Cultural Turn* (London: Sage, 1999), esp. pp. 1–21.

[39] J. Gascoigne, 'The Expanding Historiography of British Imperialism', *HJ* 49 (2006), 577–92 (p. 591).

behaviours. Of particular relevance here is the 'moral aspect of culture', and the extent to which networks of trust, arising principally from religious or family ties, can help to lower transaction costs and thereby give firms a competitive advantage.[40] Meanwhile, there is an emerging interest in how far British companies operating overseas exhibited a specifically 'imperial culture', whether in terms of employment and recruitment practices, the organisation of expatriate life, the marketing of their produce, or the backgrounds and personal beliefs of their leaders.[41] While we offer only a limited number of company case studies in this book, we do touch upon some of the above issues when we discuss colonial markets and cultures of consumption.[42]

The literature also pays attention to the type of cultural meanings attached to economic activity,[43] whether in terms of consumption, scientific and technical knowledge, or the context in which such knowledge was created and the means by which it was disseminated.[44] In each case, it is clear that cultural influences were mediated not only through direct prohibitions or encouragements of certain types of behaviour, but through their impact on the nature and flow of information. We share this perspective. By bringing about a larger market for information (vital for settler societies in the early stages of economic growth), migration permitted a wider range of choices, fashioned new types of consumption, and furthered the take-up of new technologies. To this extent, cultural reproduction and economic integration across the British World were mutually reinforcing. Yet it was, above all, personal connections and social networks that embedded economic activity within cultural contexts, and, as a result, many of the trends we observe and the patterns we describe, although trans-national in nature, were nonetheless racially circumscribed – an issue to which we shall later return.

So far we have alluded to, yet have not directly addressed, the spatial imagination of migrants. In particular, we have highlighted the

---

[40] Casson, 'Cultural Determinants of Economic Performance', pp. 419–20, 425–7, and *Enterprise and Competitiveness*, pp. 87–8.

[41] For a spirited exploration of the 'imperial culture' of leading British multinationals, see V. Johnson, 'British Multinationals, Culture and Empire in the Early Twentieth Century', unpublished Ph.D. thesis, University of London (2007).

[42] See our previously published work on empire markets and consumer cultures: G. B. Magee and A. S. Thompson, 'A Soft Touch? British Industry, Empire Markets and the Self-Governing Dominions, *c.* 1870–1914', *EcHR* (2003), 689–717.

[43] For the possibilities of a new history of economic culture, see, for example, M. Finn's study of the cultural meanings attached to personal debt: *The Character of Credit: Personal Debt in English Culture, 1740–1914* (Cambridge: Cambridge University Press, 2003).

[44] For a review of recent work in the field, see M. W. Jackson, 'A Cultural History of Victorian Physical Science and Technology', *HJ* 50 (2007), 253–64.

'networks' of contact and communication forged by migrants, and how they gave rise to a wider consciousness of the British peoples. What is the relation between these 'networks' and the other terms that we have been using: 'globalisation', 'diasporas' and 'trans-nationalism'? How far do they overlap? Some studies of social networks tie them explicitly to the concept of trans-national (rather than truly global) communities – they are understood to have bridged British (and other European) societies at home and overseas, as well as to have provided mutual support for migrants in their newly adopted country.[45] But other studies place financial and communications networks at the heart of economic globalisation,[46] or accord knowledge-based networks a central role in the forging of a global public sphere,[47] or use the concept of 'network power' (defined as a shared norm or convention in language, technology or the law) as a signifier of global co-ordination, eclipsing local standards: a type of 'new imperialism'.[48]

We were drawn to the concept of networks as a way of analysing with greater precision long-distance connections over extended periods of time. We conceive of these networks as the 'software of empire', the most important of which arose from migration. Informal and integrative, migrant networks operated supra-nationally.[49] They were built upon kinship structures, religious institutions, ethnic societies and fraternal organisations. They connected private, unofficial and provincial interests in Britain with their overseas contacts and communities. It was through them that ideas and information were exchanged, trust was negotiated, goods were traded and people travelled. Part of the attraction of such a networked conception is that it helps us to see the empire more clearly for what it really was: an interconnected zone constituted by multiple points of contact and complex circuits of exchange; not just the preserve of an 'official mind' in Whitehall, but, as John

---

[45] Portes, *Globalization from Below*; Kearney, 'The Local and the Global', p. 548.
[46] R. J. Barnett and J. Cavanagh, 'A Globalizing Economy: Some Implications and Consequences', in B. Mazlish and R. Buultjens (eds.), *Conceptualizing Global History* (Boulder, CO: Westview Press, 1993), pp. 153–73 (pp. 155–60); M. Castells, *The Information Age: Economy, Society and Culture*, 3 vols., Vol. I: *The Rise of the Network Society* (Malden: Routledge, 2000), pp. 101–6.
[47] R. Holton, 'The Inclusion of the Non-European World in International Society, 1870s–1920s: Evidence from Global Networks', *Global Networks* 5 (2005), 239–59.
[48] D. S. Grewal, 'Network Power and Globalization', *Ethics and International Affairs* 117 (2003), 89–98.
[49] Nor were they exclusively white: for a study of Punjabi migrant networks, as they operated in an imperial context, see T. Ballantyne, *Between Colonialism and Diaspora: Sikh Cultural Formations in an Imperial World* (Durham, NC: Duke University Press, 2006).

Darwin and Alan Lester have remarked, a field of enterprise for the whole of British society.[50]

This view of the empire as a species of global networking is, however, not free from pitfalls. It has been suggested that Britain's international pre-eminence during the 'long' nineteenth century was built on a complex and overlapping series of social networks, which expanded through railway, telegraph and steamship technology (the 'hardware of empire');[51] that after 1850 such networks became much more diverse and extensive; and that they had a marked impact on the transmission of news, opinion and values within the British imperial world – indeed, that they helped to hold it together.[52] But this still leaves several questions begging. Were all networks of equal significance? How do we set about evaluating those networks radiating in and out of Britain to the colonies, compared to those that meshed the different colonies together? What were the relative strengths of the impulses flowing through these different types of connection? What were the limitations on them? What sort of controls or restrictions were they subject to?

Although these questions are pursued further in the chapters that follow, there are two points worth emphasising here. First, the type of traffic that moved through networks was very much shaped by their location. In terms of *material* flows around the empire, the place that mattered most was undoubtedly Britain. It was, after all, Britain (and frequently London) that was the node through which information, people, capital and commodities often moved. In many cases these movements were relatively simple back-and-forth flows between metropole and each (settler) colony, rather than movements between the colonies themselves. Yet it would be wrong to think of the British world in terms of the spokes of a bicycle wheel; connections were not simply radial, connecting different parts of the so-called 'periphery' with

[50] J. Darwin, 'The Descent of Empire: Post-Colonial Views of Britain's Imperial History', annual guest lecture given to the Leeds Institute of Colonial and Postcolonial Studies, University of Leeds, 4 May 2006; A. Lester, *Imperial Networks: Creating Identities in Nineteenth Century South Africa and Britain* (London: Routledge, 2001).
[51] T. Ballantyne, 'Empire, Knowledge and Culture: From Proto-Globalization to Modern Globalization', in Hopkins (ed.), *Globalization in World History* (London: Pimlico, 2002), pp. 116–140; R. Grove, *Ecology, Climate and Empire: Colonialism and Global Environmental History, 1400–1940* (Cambridge: Cambridge University Press, 1997); C. Bridge and K. Fedorowich, 'Mapping the British World', in Bridge and Fedorowich, *The British World*, pp. 1–15.
[52] R. W. Desmond, *The Information Process: World News Reporting to the Twentieth Century* (Chicago: University of Iowa Press, 1978), p. 289; Bridge and Fedorowich, 'Mapping the British World', p. 6; S. J. Potter, *News and the British World: The Emergence of an Imperial Press System, 1876–1922* (Oxford: Oxford University Press, 2003).

the 'core'.[53] Across our period, there were growing linkages between the colonies, and especially between the settler colonies, arising from skilled labour migration;[54] indentured labour;[55] organised crime and prostitution;[56] women's, humanitarian and religious movements;[57] peripatetic professionals and officials;[58] even scandal and gossip among the ruling class.[59] It is these inter-colonial connections and exchanges that partly account for the attraction of the web metaphor in analysing British World relations.

Second, the different characters of the settler colonies themselves affected the networks we discuss later in this book, including the strength of the impulses travelling along them. Put simply, it mattered that Canada was among the first dominions to develop a strong manufacturing base;[60] that, in southern Africa, power was at first contested, but later increasingly shared, between two white elites;[61] that convict transportation loomed large in the early history of migration to Australia;[62] and that the journey by steamship to America was cheaper, quicker and more comfortable than it was to the rest of the 'Anglo'

---

[53] S. J. Potter, 'Webs, Networks, and Systems: Globalization and the Mass Media in the Nineteenth- and Twentieth-Century British Empire', *JBS* 46 (2007), 621–46.

[54] J. Hyslop, *The Notorious Syndicalist: J. T. Bain, a Scottish Rebel in Colonial South Africa* (Johannesburg: Jacana Media, 2004), and 'The Imperial Working Class Makes Itself "White": White Labourism in Britain, Australia and South Africa before the First World War', *Journal of Historical Sociology* 12 (1999), 398–424.

[55] D. Northrup, *Indentured Labour in the Age of Imperialism, 1834–1922* (Cambridge: Cambridge University Press, 1995).

[56] C. Van Onselen, 'Jewish Marginality in the Atlantic World: Organised Crime in the Era of the Great Migrations, 1880–1914', *SAHJ* 43 (2000), 96–137.

[57] I. Fletcher, L. E. Nym Mayhall and P. Levine (eds.), *Women's Suffrage in the British Empire: Citizenship, Nation and Race* (London: Routledge, 2000); Z. Laidlaw, 'Integrating Metropolitan, Colonial and Imperial History: The Aborigines [*sic*] Select Committee of 1835–1837', in T. Banivanua Mar and J. Evans (eds.), *Writing Colonial Histories: Comparative Perspectives* (Melbourne: RMIT Publishing, 2002), pp. 75–91.

[58] Z. Laidlaw, *Colonial Connections, 1815–45: Patronage, the Information Revolution and Colonial Government* (Basingstoke: Palgrave Macmillan, 2005); A. S. Thompson, *The Empire Strikes Back? The Impact of Imperialism on Britain from the Mid-Nineteenth Century* (Harlow: Pearson Education, 2005), pp. 17–29.

[59] K. McKenzie, *Scandal in the Colonies: Sydney and Cape Town, 1820–1850* (Melbourne: Melbourne University Press, 2004).

[60] See, for example, our discussion of the Empire Chambers of Commerce in Chapter 4, pp. 145–50, in which Toronto and Montreal merchants and businessmen had a leading voice – although manufacturers from Victoria were also prominent.

[61] See, for example, the implications of Anglo-Afrikaner relations, during and after the period of Milnerite reconstruction, for the ability of American and German firms to penetrate the region's markets, in Chapter 4, pp. 141–3.

[62] The heightened emphasis on 'respectability' among middle-class Australian consumers from the mid century makes more sense when set in this context in Chapter 4, pp. 157–8, 161.

world.[63] None of this is to imply that British World networks cannot be talked about as generalised phenomena; but given their intrinsically geographical nature, it is important not to overlook the influence of place and space upon them.[64]

Another question is how far migrant networks were truly *imperial* in the sense of being confined to the colonies and largely absent from the United States. There is a discreet silence on this subject in the literature. When exactly did the United States leave the 'British World' for an 'American World'? By what yardstick should we decide? Is the Anglo-American connection best approached through the realm of geo-politics, diplomacy and military co-operation (which is the basis of much writing on the 'special relationship' of a later period), or is there a case for revisiting Britain's involvement with America, and vice versa, from the perspective of grass-roots society, family histories and various forms of popular culture? In the chapters that follow we caution against focusing too much on the imperial sphere. We seek to show how, in exploring the economic effects of migrant networks, it is helpful to include the United States and, indeed, other extra-imperial sites, such as Latin America. Many of the networks forged by British migrants were not confined to the formal British imperial world. By comparing the effects of networks within and beyond the empire's settler societies we can see more clearly what was distinctive about them in their particular contexts.

The ambivalent relationship between the two great halves of the 'Anglo-World' has, of course, been a central theme in modern world history.[65] What we try to establish in this book is how, from the mid nineteenth century, demographic expansion, allied to improved communications technology, created a consciousness of 'Britain beyond the seas', a consciousness that neither fully embraced, nor wholly excluded, the United States. The sense that America was a part of the British diaspora was real, but it was also ambivalent, open to dispute by contemporaries, and it eroded over time. Protectionism placed limits on the spread and survivability of 'foreign' cultures of consumption, whereas the shifting origins of migratory flows to the United States – whereby migrants from Britain were at first matched in number by those from

---

[63] See, for example, how this underpinned the distinctive return and remittance behaviour of US migrants in Chapter 3, pp. 99, 104–5.

[64] See especially here D. Lambert and A. Lester, 'Introduction: Imperial Spaces, Imperial Subjects', in D. Lambert and A. Lester (eds.), *Colonial Lives across the British Empire: Imperial Careering in the Long Nineteenth Century* (Cambridge: Cambridge University Press, 2006), pp. 3–8.

[65] J. Darwin, 'The British Empire and the "British World"', keynote lecture at *Defining the British World*, 11–14 July 2007.

Germany, and later overshadowed by those migrating from central and eastern Europe – ensured that, by the end of our period, the United States had become the home to many diasporas, more so than any other part of the world.

Finally, any study of imperial networks must address the question of forms of inclusion and exclusion, and how they changed over time. To what extent did networks incorporate elements of non-European or indigenous society? Largely constructed by settler-colonial interests, participation in imperial networks was racially defined. This racial exclusiveness, however, was not universal. Some non-Anglophone groups were able to attach themselves, with varying degrees of success, to imperial networks maintained by Britons. The humanitarian networks forged by the Aborigines Protection Society, and knowledge-based networks such as the African Society and Asiatic Society, would be obvious examples yet by no means the only ones.[66] Freemasonry, for instance, based as it was on claims to universal brotherhood, sometimes championed the rights of colonial subjects to join. 'Indigenous members who were engaged in commercial pursuits or who travelled extensively welcomed access to the global network of lodges and brethren.'[67] That said, even in more inclusive networks, the role for non-white and non-Anglophone groups tended to diminish through the nineteenth century. This, in turn, spurred indigenous peoples to create and maintain counter-networks of their own. Here one might point specifically to the response of Indian merchants to their treatment by the colonial authorities in Natal (see pp. 149–50) and, more generally, to the migrant networks fashioned by Indian and Chinese indentured labourers, described by one scholar as 'a crucial ... response to the economic and cultural pressures of colonialism'.[68]

British migrants' investment in a self-consciously worldwide British community brought with it new economic possibilities and potential. At the same time, participation in the networks upon which such a community was built tended to be racially and ethnically circumscribed. Social scientists usually present networks in progressive and cosmopolitan terms. They do so with some justification. By improving the quantity and quality of information flows around the British world,

---

[66] Holton, 'The Inclusion of the Non-European World', pp. 249–55; Lambert and Lester, 'Introduction', p. 12.

[67] J. L. Harland-Jacobs, *Builders of Empire: Freemasons and British Imperialism, 1717–1927* (Chapel Hill: University of North Carolina Press, 2007), pp. 216–22, 232 (quote from p. 232). Though outright racial prejudice also erected barriers to the admission of coloured and black Masons.

[68] Ballantyne, *Between Colonialism and Diaspora*, p. 31.

by bridging relations between producers and consumers, and by facilitating the adoption of new technologies, imperial networks did indeed contribute powerfully to the growth in trade and to the convergence of income levels that were such marked features of economic globalisation, as experienced by English-speaking societies, from 1850 to 1914.[69] However, we must remember that the co-ethnic networks studied in this book were equally systems of power and domination that incorporated some parts of colonial society and marginalised others. Hierarchies of race and class determined access to the commercial, financial and professional networks spawned by the empire in just the same way as notions of status and gentility shaped patterns of colonial consumption. Only by analysing the material foundations of the British World in these terms can we perceive the cultural and institutional realities implicit in them. Such interplay of culture and economy is characteristic of all marketplaces, and historians are increasingly recognising how markets have been deeply embedded in distinctive traditions and practices that influence both how they are conceived and how they functioned.[70] To understand the British World better we now need to uncover what these traditions and practices actually were.

[69] O'Rourke and Williamson, *Globalization and History*.
[70] M. Bevir and F. Trentmann (eds.), *Markets in Historical Contexts: Ideas and Politics in the Modern World* (Cambridge: Cambridge University Press, 2004).

1 Reconfiguring empire: the British World

Introduction

The twenty-first century belatedly rediscovered empire. The forces of globalisation – with their apparent lack of respect for national borders – have propelled a remarkable revival of interest in our imperial past. Whether perceived as precursors to modern globalisation, or its 'first wave', empires are widely believed to hold the key to understanding globalisation's historical roots.[1] As one leading scholar has aptly remarked, what were empires if not 'transnational organisations ... created to mobilise the resources of the world? Their existence and their unity were made possible by supra-national connections. Their longevity was determined by their ability to extend the reach and maintain the stability of these connections.'[2]

This belief that trans-national impulses and ideas were intrinsic to the operations of empire, and had far-reaching historical consequences,[3] goes a long way to explain why consideration of space and place has loomed so large in the 'new' imperial history.[4] A 'radical re-imagining of space and of human relationships to it' was a concomitant of British expansion overseas.[5] Spatial concepts of empire have, of course, long

[1] For studies that bring together the diverse consequences of globalisation today, and its important historical antecedents, see A. Hoogvelt, *Globalisation and the Postcolonial World: The New Political Economy of Development*, 2nd edn (Basingstoke: Palgrave Macmillan, 2001); and S. Hall, 'The Local and the Global: Globalisation and Ethnicity', in A. McClintock, A. Mufti and E. Shohat (eds.), *Dangerous Liaisons: Gender, Nation and Postcolonial Perspectives* (Minneapolis: University of Minnesota Press, 1997), Chapter 9.
[2] A. G. Hopkins, 'Back to the Future: From National History to Imperial History', *Past & Present* (1999), 198–243 (p. 205).
[3] K. Grant, P. Levine and F. Trentmann (eds.), *Beyond Sovereignty: Britain, Empire and Transnationalism, c. 1880–1950* (Basingstoke: Palgrave Macmillan, 2007), pp. 12, 7.
[4] D. Lambert and A. Lester, 'Introduction: Imperial Spaces, Imperial Subjects', in Lambert and Lester (eds.), *Colonial Lives across the British Empire: Imperial Careering in the Long Nineteenth Century* (Cambridge: Cambridge University Press, 2006), pp. 1–31 (p. 3).
[5] H. Michie and R. Thomas (eds.), *Nineteenth Century Geographies: The Transformation of Space from the Victorian Age to the American Century* (Rutgers: Rutgers University

underpinned writing about Europe's imperial experiences, whether British, French, Dutch, Spanish or Portuguese. Yet it is only relatively recently, after almost half a century of neglect, that the empire's settler societies – those places where indigenous people were dispossessed, and where Europeans came to form a significant part of the population – have begun to be examined more explicitly, and indeed comparatively, by scholars of empire.[6]

In Britain's case, it is apparent that territorial expansion was as much demographic as it was religious, military or bureaucratic.[7] From the mid nineteenth century new forms of technology reconfigured the spaces between metropolitan Britain and the overseas 'British' societies of the empire, which, in an age of steamship, railway and telegraph, interacted in ways unimaginable even fifty years before. Recent studies focus on the movement of people, goods and capital within these regions of the empire, and the transfer of knowledge and experience among them. They move away from the old historiographical binaries of British 'metropole' and colonial 'periphery' to visualise the empire as an interconnected zone constituted by multiple points of contact and complex circuits of exchange. In doing so, they raise several significant questions. How did societies that imported a great deal of their population, cultural baggage, ideology and lifestyle, yet jealously guarded their powers of self-government, 'work out their destinies'? How far did this process involve recognition of their common heritage, as well as 'an informed appreciation' of the efforts of British migrants elsewhere to adapt to their distinctive local settings while maintaining links to their imperial homeland?[8] What, indeed, were the ties – ancestral,

---

Press, 2002), p. 14. For the impact of mass migration from Britain after 1850 on the 'manner in which people viewed the world and their relationship to it', see D. A. Bell, 'Dissolving Distance: Technology, Space and Empire in British Political Thought, 1770–1900', *Journal of Modern History* 77 (2005), 561–2.

[6] For new approaches to the comparative study of settler colonialisms (British, French, German and Japanese), see C. Elkins and S. Pedersen (eds.), *Settler Colonialism in the Twentieth Century* (New York: Routledge, 2005). For a previous study setting different types of settler societies in a comparative framework, see D. Tasiulis and N. Yuval-Davis (eds.), *Unsettling Settler Societies: Articulations of Gender, Race, Ethnicity and Class* (London: Sage, 1995).

[7] 'Blinded by national historiographies and mesmerised by the exotic colonial "other" we have lost contact with what was always the heart of the imperial enterprise, the expansion of Britain and the peopling and building of the trans-oceanic British World.' See C. Bridge and K. Fedorowich, 'Mapping the British World', in Bridge and Fedorowich (eds.), *The British World: Culture, Diaspora and Identity* (London: Taylor and Francis, 2003), pp. 1–15 (p. 11).

[8] For these (and other) questions skilfully posed, see S. Macintyre, 'History Wars and the Imperial Legacy in the Settler Societies', in P. Buckner and D. Francis (eds.), *Rediscovering the British World: Culture and Diaspora* (London: Taylor and Francis, 2003), pp. 381–97 (p. 383).

institutional, linguistic, cultural – that bound this 'British World' together? In the words of an historian of modern South Africa: 'Writing about the British World should do more than tell us about events which happened in that world. It should necessarily involve exploring how such a world was constructed and maintained in its various geographical parts through time ... writing about the British World should involve "history-of-the-British World", not just "history-in-the-British World".'[9]

Living in, thinking about and identifying with more than one country at once became a defining way of life for many inhabitants of this British World in the half-century before 1914. Various types of migration worked to stitch together the British peoples, with the result that political events, economic cycles and cultural fashions reverberated through the literal and imaginative domains of empire with greater frequency and power. Human movement and human memory, moreover, could often work together to reinforce each other. A cultural knowledge of ancestry and lineage could help to make sense of a connection that may have spanned generations, whether through personal items (such as photographs) or through the realm of material culture: goods branded by cities (lawnmowers from Birmingham, toilets from Staffordshire, cutlery from Sheffield and bicycles from Nottingham) were one way of evoking the proximity, even romance, of Britain.[10]

It is, therefore, perhaps not surprising that scholarship on the British World has evinced a marked enthusiasm for all kinds of trans-national history.[11] Temperance reform,[12] women's movements and migration,[13] marriage,[14] child rescue and welfare,[15] popular reading habits,[16] labour

[9] V. Bickford-Smith, 'Revisiting Anglicisation in the Nineteenth-Century Cape Colony', in Bridge and Fedorowich, *The British World*, pp. 82–95 (p. 82).

[10] We are grateful to Saul Dubow for this observation.

[11] For two key works exploring the role of empire in developing trans-national ideas and institutions, see A. Bashford, *Imperial Hygiene: A Critical History of Colonialism, Nationalism and Public Health* (Basingstoke: Palgrave Macmillan, 2004); and Grant, Levine and Trentmann, *Empire and Transnationalism, c. 1880–1950*.

[12] J. Sturgis, 'Temperance Reform in the British World', paper given at the British World Conference, Institute for Commonwealth Studies, London, 1998.

[13] M. Oppenheimer, 'Women's Movements and the Empire, 1880–1920', paper given at the British World Conference, Institute for Commonwealth Studies, London, 1998. See also A. McGrath, *Entangled Frontiers: Marriage and Sex across Colonizing Frontiers in Australia and North America* (New Haven: Yale University Press, forthcoming).

[14] B. Bradbury, 'Rethinking Marriage, Civilization and Nation in Nineteenth-Century White Settler Societies', in Buckner and Francis, *Rediscovering the British World*, pp. 135–57.

[15] S. Swain, 'Centre and Periphery in British Child Rescue Discourse', paper given at the British World Conference, University of Melbourne, July 2004.

[16] I. Hofmeyr, 'Making Bunyan English via Africa', paper given at the British World Conference, Institute for Commonwealth Studies, London, 1998, subsequently

disputes and doctrines,[17] bourgeois consumption,[18] penal police and criminal justice,[19] and the evolution of land rights and forms of settler racial practices[20] – each of these topics has lent itself to fruitful comparative analysis. Part of the attraction of focusing on settler societies as a way of writing trans-national history is that their ideas and institutions stemmed from common roots; they also faced similar problems, especially with respect to their indigenous populations and the political rights and legal status they were to be accorded. The British World concept has thus helped historians to climb out of their national bunkers, making them more aware of what hitherto they may have taken for granted about their own societies, and more mindful of the growing significance of non-national affiliations within them.[21]

Yet as soon as we begin to re-imagine imperial geographies, we are faced with the tricky question of where power spatially resided.[22] For the logic of a 'networked' or 'decentred' approach to studying empires

published as *The Portable Bunyan: A Trans-national History of the Pilgrim's Progress* (Princeton: Yale University Press, 2004); C. Hilliard, 'The Tillotson Syndicate and the Imperial Trade in Fiction', paper given at the British World Conference, University of Auckland, July 2005.

[17] F. Bongiorno, 'Fabian Socialism and British Australia, 1890–1972', in Buckner and Francis, *Rediscovering the British World*, pp. 209–31; and J. Hyslop, 'The British and Australian Leaders of the South African Labour Movement, 1902–1914: A Group Biography', in K. Darian-Smith, P. Grimshaw and S. Macintyre (eds), *Britishness Abroad: Transnational Movements and Imperial Cultures* (Melbourne: Melbourne University Press, 2007), pp. 90–108, and *The Notorious Syndicalist: J. T. Bain, a Scottish Rebel in Colonial South Africa* (Johannesburg: Jacana Media, 2004). See also N. Kirk, *Comrades and Cousins: Globalization, Workers and Labour Movements in Britain, the USA and Australia from the 1880s to 1914* (London: Merlin Press, 2003).

[18] S. Banfield, 'Towards a History of Music in the British Empire: Three Export Studies', in K. Darian-Smith, P. Grimshaw and S. Macintyre (eds.), *Britishness Abroad: Transnational Movements and Imperial Cultures* (Melbourne: Melbourne University Press, 2007), pp. 63–90.

[19] See also B. Godfrey and G. Dunstall (eds.), *Crime and Empire, 1840–1940: Criminal Justice in Local and Global Context* (Uffculme: Willan, 2005).

[20] J. McLaren, A. R. Buck and N. E. Wright (eds.), *Land and Freedom: Law, Property Rights and the British Diaspora* (Aldershot: Ashgate, 2001), and *Despotic Dominion: Property Rights in British Settler Societies* (Vancouver: University of British Columbia Press, 2005); J. Evans, P. Grimshaw, D.Phillips and S. Swain (eds.), *Equal Subjects, Unequal Rights: Indigenous People in British Settler Colonies* (Manchester: Manchester University Press, 2003).

[21] For the potential of cross-national, comparative studies to achieve these and other things, see especially G. M. Frederickson, 'From Exceptionalism to Variability: Recent Developments in Cross-National Comparative History', *Journal of American History* 82 (1995), 587–604 (pp. 587–8, 604); Hopkins, 'Back to the Future', p. 217.

[22] See, for example, C. Daniels and M. V. Kennedy (eds.), *Negotiated Empires: Centers and Peripheries in the Americas, 1500–1820* (New York: Routledge, 2002), which argues for peripheries occupying a more central position in the early modern colonial world, and carrying more power in relation to metropolitan centres than scholars have often allowed.

is that metropole and settler colony acted and reacted upon each other in complex ways, and that sovereignty in the colonies, far from being static or stable, was subject to constant negotiation and renegotiation by a variety of settler and non-settler groups.

Nor was the British World sealed off from the rest of the globe. Far from being exclusively British, many of the networks we study over-lapped and intersected with other types of network, including those embedded in a wider 'Atlantic world', as well as in other western European (the French especially) and extra-European (Ottoman, Chinese and Russian) empires.[23] If we are to understand how consumer, investor and merchant networks functioned in the colonies, they need to be placed in this wider international context. As people, goods, ideas and practices moved between and beyond different sites of colonisa-tion, such movement in and of itself shaped and re-shaped experiences of overseas settlement. This, in turn, helps to explain the analytical purchase of categories like 'space' and 'place': they enable us better to appreciate what was global – and what was not – about Victorian and Edwardian imperialism.

The rest of this chapter explores three key themes that underpin our analysis of the interplay of culture and economy in this book: imperial networks, 'Britishness' and the Anglo-American relationship. The final section relates more recent writing on the British World to previous writing on the imperial economy, especially that on 'settler colonialism' and on the 'dominion' model of export economy.

Imperial networks

In a study of the relationship between empires, networks and dis-courses, the historian of Africa, Frederick Cooper, argues powerfully for the value of the network concept in analysing with greater precision long-distance connections over extended periods of time.[24] Cooper's working definition of a network is a good place to begin:

I am using network in a loose sense, although I am aware that this word is used in a highly formalised way. My interest is in forms of affiliation and

[23] For a striking example of this point, see C. Van Onselen, *The Fox and the Flies: The World of Joseph Silver, Racketeer and Psychopath* (Richmond: University of Virginia Press, 2007), which tells the chilling story of the trafficking of prostitutes, and related criminal activity, from Britain and France to the United States, southern Africa, Argentina and Chile, replete as it is with episodes of seduction, rape, deception, extortion, burglary and murder.

[24] F. Cooper, 'Networks, Moral Discourse and History', in T. Callaghy, R. Kassimir and R. Latham (eds.), *Intervention and Transnationalism in Africa* (Cambridge: Cambridge University Press, 2001), pp. 23–46 (p. 23).

association that are less defined than a 'structure' but more than just a collection of individuals engaging in transactions. Networks are organisations which stress voluntary and reciprocal patterns of exchange ... A network may or may not have ideological contents; it may consist of people with a set of strong commitments, or it may deepen and reconfigure the commitments participants have; it may be built around a set of norms, yet as its interactions work out areas of commonality and disagreement, it may define and redefine a normative framework.[25]

Building on this definition, we show how the networks studied in this book had three key characteristics, each of which betrayed their British origins. First, they were *voluntary* in nature – individuals belonged to them by choice. Voluntary associations, it will be recalled, were a unifying force in British urban society, a defining feature of the Victorian era. Second, these networks bound people together, nurturing as well as reflecting a sense of shared cultural, religious or ideological commitment and purpose among their members. Third, they transcended boundaries – in our case territorial boundaries. Indeed, what is striking about imperial networks is their capacity to transform the transmission of news and opinion across imperial spaces, and to markedly expand people's mental horizons in the process.[26]

Imperial networks ranged from familial and communal forms of association to more formal structures such as humanitarian, administrative, scientific and educational bodies. Reconstructing their influence is vital if we are to appreciate how the British World 'interacted through friendship, acquaintance, travel, business, correspondence, and ... the sharing of news'.[27] It also needs to be emphasised that business and commercial networks cannot be isolated from the other types of network that spanned the British World: economic knowledge moved through a variety of channels, including those along which all sorts of other information passed.

For those who participated in them, networks reinforced a sense of belonging to a worldwide British community. In fact, they have been

[25] *Ibid.*, p. 24.
[26] For how this might work in practice, see Elizabeth Elbourne's study of the influence of trans-national networks, including, for example, newspapers, parliamentary chambers and courtrooms, in informing British policy towards, and shaping ideas and debates about, Aboriginal peoples: *Blood Ground, Colonialism, Missions and the Contest for Christianity in the Cape Colony and Britain, 1799–1853* (Montreal: McGill-Queen's University Press, 2002), and 'Indigenous Peoples and Imperial Networks in the Early Nineteenth Century: The Politics of Knowledge', in Buckner and Francis, *Rediscovering the British World*, pp. 59–85.
[27] S. J. Potter, 'Communication and Integration: The British and Dominions Press and the British World, *c.* 1876–1914', in Bridge and Fedorowich, *The British World*, pp. 190–207 (p. 191). See also Lambert and Lester, 'Introduction', esp. pp. 3–13.

likened to the 'cultural glue' that held the British World together.[28] They created strong personal and community ties that shaped people's daily lives. They helped to make the imperial 'centre' more permeable – from the mid century, people were able to move in and out of it with increasing ease and regularity. And they opened up channels of communication *between* the colonies, as settlers developed a wider range of geographical reference and displayed a growing tendency to think of themselves, and their struggles, in relation to settlers elsewhere.[29]

Migrant networks (discussed in Chapter 3) were powerful vehicles for disseminating British styles of architecture, fashion, fiction, food and music. Rapidly evolving communications meant people could move around the world with greater confidence. Steamships, telegraphs, ocean cables and newspapers took the 'tyranny' out of distance. Migrants began to imagine their social and political spaces in new ways, thereby making their migrations a defining aspect of their identity. Knowledge began to circulate more freely too, not least as a result of the press. It is widely recognised that news agencies such as Reuters were among the world's first trans-national corporations. Yet it was not only Reuters that ushered in a new reciprocity to news distribution. A plethora of papers (national, regional and provincial), in both Britain and the colonies, helped to define the limits for the acceptable integration of Britain and its settler colonies.[30] During the later nineteenth and early twentieth centuries, Britain, Canada, Australia, New Zealand and South Africa were drawn together by what has been called an 'imperial press system'. Newspaper enterprises across these societies yoked together the three main geographical bases for British identity – regional, national and imperial – with the emphasis shifting according to the commercial interests of the paper in question. As a result of voluntary co-operation between commercially driven newspaper enterprises, the flow of information and press communication

[28] Bridge and Fedorowich, 'Mapping the British World', p. 6.
[29] A. Lester, 'British Settler Discourse and the Circuits of Empire', *HWJ* 54:1 (2002), 24–48 (p. 28); Bell, 'Dissolving Distance', pp. 523–62.
[30] See, especially, S. J. Potter, *News and the British World: The Emergence of an Imperial Press System, 1876–1922* (Oxford: Oxford University Press, 2003). For papers presented on the press, see E. Ihd, 'Formulating Britishness: Using a colonial newspaper to establish identity in new South Wales', paper given at the British World Conference, University of Melbourne, July 2004; and D. Cryle, 'Interdependent or Independent? Australia–British Relations at the Melbourne Imperial Press Conference', in K. Darian-Smith, P. Grimshaw, K. Lindsey and S. McIntyre (eds.), *Exploring the British World: Identity-Cultural Production-Institutions* (Melbourne: RMIT Publishing, 2004), pp. 890–907. For an interesting collection of essays on the subject, see J. F. Codell (ed.), *Imperial Co-Histories: National Identities and the British and Colonial Press* (Madison, NJ: Farleigh Dickinson University Press, 2003).

occurred predominantly within an imperial framework up to and indeed beyond 1914.[31]

Professional networks were also influential.[32] The demand for professionally qualified accountants, academics, doctors, engineers, lawyers, nurses, teachers and others grew rapidly from the 1850s, in response to the pace of socio-economic development in the dominions. Professional people began to organise themselves more effectively, with the aim of securing recognition from the state and advancing the interests of their members.[33] Some professional bodies had their headquarters in London and extensive branch networks across the dominions. Others formed more on a national basis but co-operated closely with kindred bodies elsewhere. Professional people, moreover, spearheaded the formation of other types of knowledge-based networks – literary societies, libraries, galleries and museums – that together helped to foster a 'Britannic' civic culture.[34] In the fields of academia, law, medicine and science, for example, middle-class settlers saw themselves as a part of a wider British community, carrying not only their professional ideals and practices overseas, but, more generally, their beliefs about codes of civilised conduct and the proper ordering of society. Nor was this elite networking an exclusively male affair. By the end of the nineteenth century, women's organisations were increasingly prominent in the spheres of migration, nursing, philanthropy, and war relief and commemoration.[35]

[31] Codell, *Imperial Co-Histories*, p. 212.
[32] S. Dubow, 'The Commonwealth of Science: The British Association in South Africa, 1905 and 1929', in S. Dubow (ed.), *Science and Society in Southern Africa*, (Manchester: Manchester University Press, 2000), pp. 66–100; R. Morley, 'Dropping Off in the Rounding: The Origins and Significance of Affiliations between British and New Zealand Accounting Partnerships', in K. Darian-Smith, P. Grimshaw, K. Lindsey and S. Mcintyre (eds.), *Exploring the British World: Identity, Cultural Production, Institutions. Proceedings of British World Conference III* (Melbourne: RMIT Publishing, 2004), pp. 1003–21; D. Zabiello, 'The Role of the Architectural Pattern Book in British Colonial Expansion in the Nineteenth Century', in Darian-Smith *et al.*, *Exploring the British World*, pp. 854–68; and H. Macdonald, ' "Subjects for Dissection": Regulating Anatomy in a British World', paper given at the British World Conference, University of Melbourne, July 2004. See also J.-G. Prevost and J.-P. Beaud, 'A Study in Failure: The 1920 Imperial Statistical Conference', in Darian-Smith *et al.*, *Exploring the British World*, pp. 869–89; and Z. Laidlaw, *Colonial Connections, 1814–45: Patronage, the Information Revolution and Colonial Government* (Basingstoke: Palgrave Macmillan, 2004).
[33] A. S. Thompson, *The Empire Strikes Back? The Impact of Imperialism on Britain from the Mid-Nineteenth Century* (Harlow: Pearson Education, 2005), pp. 17–20.
[34] For the role of professional networks in transmitting knowledge about the empire, and how they could foster within the colonies a wider sense of imperial identity, see especially Saul Dubow, *A Commonwealth of Knowledge: Science, Sensibility and Colonial Identity in South Africa* (Oxford: Oxford University Press, 2006).
[35] L. Chilton, 'A New Class of Women for the Colonies: Female Emigration Societies and the Construction of Empire', *JICH* 31:2 (May 2003), 36–56; K. Pickles, *One*

Chapters 3–5 explore the significance of these networks of contact and communication for patterns of economic behaviour and decision-making. In particular, they draw attention to the role of networks in forging shared cultures of consumption and setting norms of desirable lifestyles across English-speaking societies, and to their role in spreading new technologies and commercial practices across geographically disparate markets. These networks were not all equivalent, however. Some were more transient than others, some more powerful, and some impinged more on people's day-to-day lives. Hence it is necessary to look closely at their content as well as their volume, and to be precise about their effects.

Britishness at home and abroad

The fact that British expansion was as much a demographic as it was a military, administrative or religious phenomenon has profound implications for the study of imperial culture within Britain.[36] We take as our starting point the idea that the empire was of as much concern to those who settled in it as it was to those who administered it, or fought for it, or preached in it. Migration loomed large in the imperial imaginary: it was a force to be reckoned with in nineteenth-century British society. Crucially, it shaped people's views of what kind of empire Britain possessed, and how that empire might be fashioned towards their own particular designs.

Flag, One Throne, One Empire: Canada's Imperial Order Daughters of the Empire and Women's Part in the Making of the British Imperial Past (Manchester: Manchester University Press, 2002); E. van Heyningen and P. Merrett, ' "The Healing Touch": The Guild of Loyal Women of South Africa, 1900–1912', paper given at the British World Conference, University of Cape Town, July 2002; J. Carey, 'Recreating British Womanhood: Ethel Osborne and Melbourne Society in the Early Twentieth Century', in Darian-Smith *et al.*, *Exploring the British World*, pp. 21–39; B. Theron, 'Challenging Gender Conventions: Some English-Speaking Women in South Africa during the Anglo-Boer War', paper given at the British World Conference, University of Melbourne, July 2004; and K. Pickles, 'Female Imperialism in the British World', paper given at The British World Conference, Universitiy of Auckland, July 2005. See also J. Bush, *Edwardian Ladies and Imperial Power* (London: Continuum International Publishing Group, 2000).

[36] The questions of what the settler empire meant to people living in the British Isles, and of how it relates to Britain's 'domestic' history, have generated a great deal of debate. For key protagonists, see C. Hall, *Civilising Subjects: Metropole and Colony in the English Imagination, 1830–67* (Cambridge: Cambridge University Press, 2002); B. Porter, *The Absent-Minded Imperialists: Empire, Society and Culture in Britain* (Oxford: Oxford University Press, 2004); and Thompson, *The Empire Strikes Back?*. See also S. Ward's review essay, 'Echoes of Empire', *HWJ* 62 (2006), 264–78, esp. pp. 268–71.

In remaking 'British' society and culture overseas, colonists were not passive recipients of empire.[37] Rather, they developed and defined 'Britishness' in their own distinctive ways. Indeed, British migrants not only reaffirmed, they often sought to improve upon the communities they left behind. Many of the more positive aspects of 'Britishness' – responsible government, the secret ballot, universal manhood suffrage, free state education – were beamed back to Britain from its settler colonies. What propelled these exchanges? The markedly enhanced mobility of migrants from the mid century, including their increased rates of return to Britain (see p. 64), was one factor. There was also the greater facility with which migrants could stay in touch with and remain involved with family and community 'back home' through correspondence and remittances (see pp. 97–105), while knowledge circulated more freely through a growing body of networks that linked the British in Britain with the British overseas and carried information and ideas of all kinds between them (see pp. 78–97).

While many colonists were aware of a 'living and enduring connection to their European beginnings', the nationalism they espoused was based upon notions of co-operation, partnership and mutuality – notions intended to replace older forms of domination and control.[38] Thus Keith Hancock (1898–1988), the first Australian elected to an All Souls Fellowship, and one of the foremost imperial historians of the inter-war era, insisted that it was 'not impossible for Australians, nourished by a glorious literature and haunted by old memories, to be in love with two soils.'[39] Hancock's constitutional-based histories of Anglo-Dominion

[37] A resurgence of migration history over the last decade or so has laid the foundations for a thorough reappraisal of the British 'diaspora'. Key works include E. Richards, *Britannia's Children: Emigration from England, Scotland, Wales and Ireland since 1600* (London: Continuum International Publishing Group, 2004), and his paper at the British World Conference, University of Melbourne, July 2004: 'The British Diaspora: In Wide Angle'; M. Harper, *Adventurers and Exiles: The Great Scottish Exodus* (London: Profile Books, 2004); M. Harper and S. Constantine, *Migrants and Settlers* (Oxford: Oxford University Press, 2010); and P. Payton, *The Cornish Overseas* (Fowey: Alexander Associates, 1999). For an analysis of the 'diaspora' concept, see H. Tinker (ed.), *The Diaspora of the British*, Collected Seminar Papers of the Institute of Commonwealth Studies (London: Institute of Commonwealth Studies, 1982); and S. Constantine, 'British Emigration to the Empire-Commonwealth since 1880: From Overseas Settlement to Diaspora?', in Bridge and Fedorowich, *The British World*, pp. 16–35. Some historians prefer the term 'dispersal' as Britain's was overwhelmingly a voluntary movement of population, especially from the mid nineteenth century.
[38] See especially here J. Eddy and D. Schreuder, 'Introduction: Colonies into "New Nations"', in Eddy and Schreuder (eds.), *The Rise of Colonial Nationalism* (Sydney: Allen and Unwin, 1988), pp. 1–15 (quote from p. 6).
[39] W. K. Hancock, *Australia* (London: Benn, 1930), p. 68.

relations set out to show how a wider pan-British identity could be reconciled with separate statehood. Firmly of the view that dominion nationalism did not preclude a sense of belonging to a wider British community, he argued that 'national loyalties, so far from being disruptive of the Empire, were the stuff out of which it must be re-created'.[40]

The idea that 'national' and 'imperial' sentiment in the dominions could be mutually reinforcing is a running theme of twentieth-century imperial historiography. As early as 1969, Carl Berger's pioneering study of Canadian political thought presented the conflict between imperial and anti-imperial positions in Canada in terms of divergent conceptions of the colony's history and place in the world. More specifically, Berger argued that while Canadian imperialists could embrace the empire 'as the vehicle in which Canada would attain national status', Canadian anti-imperialists were inclined to see all schemes for co-operation as 'reactionary and anti-national'.[41] More recently, John Darwin has revisited the Anglo-Dominion connection in order to posit a 'composite Britannic culture', or British 'race' sentiment, which was continuously reinforced by new migrants, and by a British-centred system of global communications transmitting news, ideas and values. Such was the purchase of this Britannic culture, Darwin argues, that as late as the 1950s it retained its capacity to reconcile national autonomy and imperial identity in the 'old dominions'.[42] Similarly, in a re-examination of the relationship between Dominion status and decolonisation, Tony Hopkins speaks of a 'core concept of Britishness' that continued, beyond the Second World War, to 'give unity and vitality to a Greater Britain overseas', and that only began to shrivel in the 1960s as the proportion of non-British immigrants increased and indigenous peoples began to assert more forcefully their equal rights with other citizens.[43] Elsewhere Hopkins usefully contrasts the British diaspora of the 'long' nineteenth century with some of today's migrant diasporas. As he shrewdly remarks, 'imperial power promoted a form of cosmopolitanism that strengthened its own

[40] W. K. Hancock, *Survey of British Commonwealth Affairs*, 3 vols., Vol. I: *Problems of Nationality, 1918–1936* (Oxford: Oxford University Press, 1937), pp. 26–41. The quotation, originally from Richard Jebb's *Studies in Colonial Nationalism* (1905) is taken from p. 41 of Hancock's book.

[41] C. Berger, *Imperialism and Nationalism, 1884–1914: A Conflict in Canadian Thought* (Toronto: University of Toronto Press, 1969).

[42] J. Darwin, 'A Third British Empire? The Dominion Idea in Imperial Politics', in W. R. Louis and J. Brown (eds.), *The Oxford History of the British Empire*, 5 vols., Vol. IV: *The Twentieth Century* (Oxford: Oxford University Press, 1999), pp. 64–87.

[43] A. G. Hopkins, 'Rethinking Decolonisation', *Past & Present* 200 (2008), 211–47 (pp. 215, 218–9, 228–32).

sense of national identity, whereas the global forces that impinge on today's world have challenged and often weakened national institutions and identities'.[44]

We now need to look in more detail at how a sense of British identity was reinforced and reconfigured by the settlement of large numbers of overseas migrants in a wider British World.[45] It was the New Zealand-born historian, and pioneer of the 'new' British history, J. G. A. Pocock, who first called for British history to be written in terms of the 'intercultural' story of 'conflict and crossbreeding between societies differently based'.[46] This 'new' British history conceived of 'Britishness' as a multi-ethnic identity forged across the British Isles.[47] It inspired historians of empire to cast their gaze beyond the British Isles to explore how 'Britishness' could be a powerful motivating ideology capable, within racially defined limits, of joining people together across the settler world.

---

[44] Hopkins, Back to the Future', pp. 242–3.

[45] There is also the separate, yet related, question of how English identities were affected by empire; see R. J. C. Young, *The Idea of English Ethnicity* (Oxford: Blackwell, 2007), which argues that 'Englishness was created for the diaspora – an ethnic identity designed for those who were precisely not English, but rather of English descent – the peoples of the English diaspora moving around the world: Americans, Canadians, Australians, New Zealanders, even, at a pinch, the English working-class' (quotation from p. 1).

[46] J. G. A. Pocock, 'British History: A Plea for a New Subject', *Journal of Modern History* 47 (1975), 604–5. See also his essays, 'The Limits and Divisions of British History: In Search of the Unknown Subject', *AHR* 87 (1982), 311–36, and, more recently, 'Conclusion: Contingency, Identity, Sovereignty', in A. Grant and K. J. Stringer (eds.), *Uniting the Kingdom? The Making of British History* (London: Routledge, 1995), pp. 292–302. Pocock delivered a plenary address at the Auckland British World Conference (14 July 2005), 'British History and the British World'. His conception of British history beyond the British Isles goes back to the seventeenth and eighteenth centuries, and rests on the idea of an Atlantic 'archipelago' or 'empire' – British history, therefore, includes the reasons why American history ceased to be 'British'. It was Britain's entry into Europe, and, in particular, its disruption of the identity of New Zealanders (*pakeha*), that prompted him to consider the dominion dimensions of Britishness. On this point, see J. G. A. Pocock, 'History and Sovereignty: The Historiographic Response to Europeanisation in Two British cultures', *JBS* 31 (1992), 358–89.

[47] N. Davies, *The Isles: A History* (Oxford: Oxford University Press, 1999); H. Kearney, *The British Isles: A History of Four Nations* (Cambridge: Cambridge University Press, 1989); K. Robbins, *Nineteenth Century Britain: Integration and Diversity* (Oxford: Oxford University Press, 1988), and *Great Britain: Identities, Institutions and the Idea of Britishness* (Harlow: Longmans, 1998); and R. Samuel (ed.), *Patriotism: The Making and Unmaking of a British National Identity*, 3 vols. (London: Routledge, 1989). Fuelled by present-day uncertainties as to what it means to be British, the volume of publication on this subject shows no sign of letting up. See, for example, the substantial collection of essays on the relationship between the question of history and British identity by H. Brocklehurst and R. Phillips (eds.), *History, Nationhood and the Question of Britain* (Basingstoke: Palgrave Macmillan, 2003).

If the British World was an 'imaginary' as well as 'geo-political' construct, held together not merely by political and military ties, but by a
shared sense of identity,[48] what precisely did being 'British' entail? A
plurality of identities and their interconnectedness were part and parcel
of the nineteenth-century British World. Shared traditions and values
served for many as markers of their British identity, with loyalty to the
Crown chief among these. Through royal tours, ceremonies and celebrations, the monarchy served to promote a sense of cultural identification
with Britain, and acted as a powerful agent of political assimilation.[49]
The call of King (or Queen) and empire was most conspicuous during the Boer War and two world wars, when the British peoples rallied
together and visibly demonstrated their unity. To what extent this unity
was real or illusory is a moot point.[50] It has been argued that these
conflicts polarised opinion in dominion societies, exacerbating existing
social and political divisions within them, and even sowing the seeds
of the British World's eventual unravelling.[51] Others, however, insist
that the intensification of dominion national consciousness resulting
from the world wars did not undermine their relationship with Britain.
Colonial public schools promoted and celebrated the war-time service

[48] J. Darwin, 'The Descent of Empire: Postcolonial Views of Britain's Imperial History',
annual guest lecture given to the Leeds Institute of Colonial and Postcolonial Studies,
University of Leeds, 4 May 2006.

[49] D. Smith and P. Buckner, 'The Canadianized Monarchy: The Invention of
Tradition? Royal Tours to Canada of 1860 and 1901', paper given at the British
World Conference, Institute of Commonwealth Studies, London, 1988; P. Buckner,
'Casting Daylight upon Magic: Deconstructing the Royal Tour of 1901 to Canada',
JICH (2003), 158–89; B. Wellings, 'Crown and Country: Britishness and Australian
Nationalism since 1788', paper given at the British World Conference, University
of Melbourne, July 2004; and S. Worthy, 'Royal Tours, Dominion Identity, and
Imperial Competition, 1900–1930', paper given at the British World Conference,
University of Auckland, 2005. See also D. Lowry, 'The Crown, Empire Loyalism and
the Assimilation of Non-British White Subjects in the British World: An Argument
against "Ethnic Determinism"', in Buckner and Francis (eds.), *Rediscovering the
British World*, pp. 158–89.

[50] For a spirited effort to unravel the complex effects of the wars on the Anglo-
Dominion relationship, in particular their role in both creating and frustrating
the impetus towards a Greater Britain, see J. Grey, 'War and the British World in
the Twentieth Century', in Buckner and Francis, *Rediscovering the British World*,
pp. 233–50.

[51] The first two claims are more easily staked than the third. For the complex effects of
the world wars on dominion self-consciousness, see Bridge and Fedorowich, 'Mapping
the British World', p. 7; S. Constantine, 'Britain and Empire', in S. Constantine,
M. Kirby and M. Rose (eds.), *The First World War in British History* (London: Edward
Arnold, 1995), pp. 268–70; and R. Holland, 'The British Empire and the Great
War, 1914–1918', in Louis and Brown, *Oxford History of The British Empire*, Vol. IV,
pp. 125–33.

of their 'old boys'.[52] The nationalist sentiment of dominion officers was inextricably linked to pro-empire traditions.[53] The reading matter of dominion soldiers was pro-British and frequently jingoistic.[54] At the end of both world wars, there was also considerable emphasis in the dominions on their British heritage and values in the commemorative ceremonies and memorials.[55]

A continuing sense of attachment to Britain was likewise fostered through cultural practices and the use of language. The importation of British games and entertainments, the suppression of indigenous ones, and the ideological values that went with this process, combined as one means by which personal memories of Britain were preserved.[56] So, too, was the material culture of settlers. Early generations of migrants surrounded themselves with furniture, pictures, books and other such items that reminded them of 'home'. In fact, the very language of 'home' was a popular trope in settler discourse.[57] English-speakers in South Africa referring to Britain as 'home' were roundly condemned by Afrikaners

[52] J. Lambert, '"Munition Factories ... Turning Out a Constant Supply of Living Material": White South African Elite Boys' Schools and the First World War', *SAHJ* 51 (2004), 67–86.

[53] P. H. Brennan, 'The Other Battle: Imperialist versus Nationalist Sympathies within the Officer Corps of the Canadian Expeditionary Force, 1914–19', in Buckner and Francis, *Rediscovering the British World*, pp. 251–65.

[54] A. Laugesen, 'Australian Soldiers and the World of Print during the Great War', in M. Hammond and S. Towheed (eds.), *Publishing the First World War* (Basingstoke: Palgrave Macmillan, 2007), pp. 93–110.

[55] J. Lack and B. Zino, 'A New Imperialism? The Imperial War Graves Commission and the Great War', paper given at the British World Conference, Melbourne, July 2004.

[56] We are grateful to Vivian Bickford-Smith for his advice on this point. See also B. Stoddart, 'Sticky Wickets: Cricket, Culture and Imperialism, 1880–1960', paper given at the British World Conference, Institute for Commonwealth Studies, London, 1998; A. Grundlingh, '"Gone to the Dogs". The Cultural Politics of Gambling: Rise and Fall of British Greyhound Racing on the Witwatersrand, 1932–49', paper presented at the British World Conference, University of Cape Town, July 2002; T. Collins, '"We Are Just as British as You Are": Masculinity and Working-Class Imperial Loyalty in Rugby Football', paper given at the British World Conference, University of Melbourne, July 2004; J. Kallinikios, '"An Orgy of Britishness": Soccer in Melbourne in the 1950s', paper given at the British World Conference, University of Melbourne, July 2004; and T. Collins, 'Rugby and the Making of Imperial Manhoods', paper given at the British World Conference, University of Auckland, July 2005.

[57] For the example of Australia, see J. Hughes (ed.), *Australian Words and Their Origins* (Oxford: Oxford University Press, 1989), p. 259; K. S. Inglis, 'Going Home: Australians in England, 1870–1900', in D. Fitzpatrick, *Home Or Away? Immigrants in Colonial Australia* (Canberra: Australian National University, 1992), pp. 105–30; E. Richards, 'Return Migration and Migrant Strategies in Colonial Australia', in Fitzpatrick, *Home or Away?*, pp. 64–104; and A. Woollacott, '"All This Is the Empire, I Told Myself": Australian Women's Voyages "Home" and the Articulation of Colonial Whiteness', *AHR* 102 (1997), 1003–29 (pp. 1003–4).

who took the utterance of this word as evidence of their implied disloyalty to the country.[58] The use of such language was complex, however.
'Home' was invoked to refer to both 'England' and 'Britain', almost
interchangeably, while settlers sometimes spoke of 'home' in the sense
that it existed wherever people of English stock had chosen to settle.[59]
The etymology of the word, and the variety of meanings ascribed to
it, merit further investigation. What is not in doubt is that the English
language denoted a shared history and culture for white settlers,[60] and
that, for many non-white subjects, an ability to speak it provided a gate-
way to 'respectability' and 'civilisation'.[61]

The picture of what it meant to be British is further complicated by the
fact of a moving racial and religious frontier. The appeal of the Crown as
a source of justice, and of popular constitutionalist rhetoric as a source
of equal rights, ensured that, rather than being a singular doctrine,
Britishness had the potential to integrate a wide variety of settler and
non-settler groups. The pro-imperial identity of groups that lay beyond
the core of the 'diaspora' has been referred to as 'adopted'[62] or 'subal-
tern'[63] Britishness, the idea being that those settlers who were not directly
of British descent could still identify with British symbols and espouse
British values, partly to carve out a niche in colonial society, and partly
as a way of framing their aspirations to self-government. The pro-British
sympathies of Cape Afrikaners,[64] French Canadians,[65] and elite Scottish
and Irish Catholics[66] have all been presented in these terms. In each case

[58] J. Lambert, '"An Unknown People": Writing a Biography of White English-Speaking
      South Africans', unpublished article, p. 14. Copy kindly supplied by the author.
[59] G. R. Searle, *A New England? Peace and War, 1886–1918* (Oxford: Oxford University
      Press, 2004), p. 42.
[60] M. Davie, *Anglo-Australian Attitudes* (London: Secker and Warburg, 2000), p. 7.
[61] Bickford-Smith, 'Revisiting Anglicisation in the Cape Colony', p. 85.
[62] P. Buckner and C. Bridge, 'Reinventing the British World', *The Round Table* 368
      (2003), 77–88 (p. 81); Lowry, 'The Crown, Empire Loyalism and the Assimilation of
      Non-White British Subjects', pp. 99, 102, 113–16.
[63] R. Ross, 'The Battle for Britain in the Cape Colony, 1830–60', paper given at the
      British World Conference, University of Cape Town, July 2002.
[64] M. Tamarkin, *Cecil Rhodes and the Cape Afrikaners: The Imperial Colossus and the
      Colonial Parish Pump* (London: Routledge, 1996).
[65] M. Sarra-Bournet, 'For the Empire ... at Last: French Canadians in the Boer War',
      paper given at the British World Conference, University of Cape Town, July 2002.
[66] J. Ridden, 'Liberal Worlds: Empire, Identity and Citizenship in the Nineteenth
      Century', paper given at the British World Conference, University of Melbourne, July
      2004, and 'Britishness as an Imperial and Diasporic Identity: Irish Elite Perspectives,
      c. 1820–70s', in P. Gray (ed.), *Victoria's Ireland? Irishness and Britishness, 1837–1901*
      (Dublin: Four Courts Press, 2004), pp. 88–105 (pp. 94, 104–5); and M. Murray,
      'Prayers, Ploughs and Pastures: Moidart Emigrants in the Western District of
      Victoria', paper given at the British World Conference, University of Melbourne, July
      2004.

a 'liberal' and 'loose-fitting' form of British identity is understood to have helped these groups to maintain their cultural identity and have conferred upon them a measure of political power.

Yet what of those non-white and indigenous groups seeking to negotiate for themselves a place in the British World? If Britishness was a contested identity, nowhere was this more so than in respect of the coloured communities of the settler empire.[67] Demanding the rights of colonial citizenship, a variety of indigenous groups – Australian Aborigines,[68] Maori,[69] Cape Coloureds[70] and Natal Indians[71] – affirmed their belief in Victorian notions of free wage labour, secure property rights, equality before the law and a non-racial franchise. Some appealed directly to the Crown for help in their dealings with labour- and land-hungry settlers, in the hope of securing greater political representation. For the most part, however, they were turned away empty-handed, learning through bitter experience that their imperial loyalty was a one-way street. The language of 'betrayal' was never far from the lips of the British World's indigenous peoples, therefore, particularly among those who protested their imperial loyalty.[72]

[67] For Britishness as disputed racial territory, see D. Lorimer, 'From Victorian Values to White Virtues: Assimilation and Exclusion in British Racial Discourse, *c.* 1870–1914', in Buckner and Francis, *Rediscovering the British World*, pp. 109–34.

[68] R. Broome, *Aboriginal Australians: Black Response to White Dominance, 1788–1980* (London: Allen and Unwin, 1983), p. 166, and *Aboriginal Victorians: A History since 1800* (Crows Nest, NSW: Allen and Unwin, 2005). See also C. Morgan, 'Creating Transatlantic Worlds? Aboriginal Peoples in Britain, 1830s–1870s', paper given at the British World Conference, Auckland, July 2005.

[69] M. Treagus, 'Spectacles of Empire: Maori Tours of England in 1863 and 1911', paper given at the British World Conference, University of Melbourne, July 2004. See also A. Ballara, *Iwi: The Dynamics of Maori Tribal Organisation from c. 1769 to c. 1945* (Wellington: Victoria University Press, 1998), p. 308; L. Cox, *Kotahitanga: The Search for Maori Political Unity* (Oxford: Oxford University Press, 1993), pp. 57–8, and P. Te H. Jones, *King Potatau: An Account of the Life of Potatau Te Wherowhero, the First Maori King* (Wellington: Polynesian Society of New Zealand, 1960), p. 160.

[70] M. Adhikari, 'Ambiguity, Assimilationism and Anglophilism in South Africa's Coloured Community: The Case of Piet Uithalder's Satirical Writings, 1909–22', *SAHJ* 47 (2002), 115–31, and ' "Give us the Benefit of Our British Blood": Changing Perceptions of Coloured Identity in South Africa', paper given at the British World Conference, University of Auckland, July 2005. See also P. Limb, 'The Ambiguities of British Empire Loyalism and Identities in the Politics and Journalism of Early ANC Leaders', paper given at the British World Conference, Cape Town, 2002.

[71] G. Vahed, 'Race, Class and Loyalty to Empire: Durban's Indians during the First World War', paper given to the British World Conference, University of Cape Town, July 2002.

[72] A. S. Thompson, 'The Languages of Loyalism in Southern Africa, *c.* 1870–1939', *English Historical Review* 118 (2003), 617–50 (pp. 638–9, 648–50). For the ambiguities of African 'loyalty', see J. Starfield, 'A Dance with the Empire: Modiri Molema's Glasgow Years, 1914–21', *JSAS* 27 (2001), 479–503.

Across the empire's settler societies, therefore, Britishness was a concept capable of a range of notions of identity. To be sure, we must be careful not to impute to these British identities a strength that they did not in fact possess. Even English-speaking settlers who proclaimed their Britishness often meant different things by it. Neither should we take such proclamations at face value. English-speakers were not always 'celebrating a fully formed sense of community'; more likely they were 'advocating the strengthening of an identity that they believed could, if properly cultivated, provide the basis for a pan-imperial unity'.[73] Conversely, although skin colour was never in theory a bar to British citizenship, in practice it often proved to be so, and, by the end of the nineteenth century, those non-white groups who sought the protection and privileges provided by that citizenship increasingly found that Britishness was racially defined.

A 'British' or an 'Anglo-' World?

How far did the British World cast its geographical shadow?[74] As an Anglophone cultural community did it embrace the United States? The boundaries of the British World remain decidedly ambiguous – and thus open to interpretation.[75] Opinion is divided on the question of when or even whether the United States was lost to the British World. Some see the British World as synonymous with the self-governing dominions. The antipathy towards America that existed in parts of British society, and the isolationist and anti-colonial attitudes of the United States, reinforce their view.[76] Others, however, speak of an 'Anglo-World', comparing the experiences of the frontier societies of America (and Argentina) to those of Canada, Australia, New Zealand and South Africa.[77] They draw attention to how 'improving' ideologies of

---

[73] Potter, *News and the British World*, p. 5.

[74] For some perceptive remarks on this issue, see Bridge and Fedorowich, 'Mapping the British World', p. 10.

[75] Buckner and Francis, 'Introduction' to *Rediscovering the British World*, pp. 9–20 (p. 13).

[76] For the ways in which British and American attitudes over such fundamental questions of public policy as race could differ significantly over time, see J. Dickenson, '"Nice Company for Christian Men!" Adela Pankhurst Walsh and the British Empire', in Darian-Smith *et al.*, *Exploring the British World*, pp. 40–59; D. Goodman, 'Anglophilia and Racial Nationalism in the Debate about US Entry into World War Two', in Darian-Smith *et al.*, *Exploring the British World*, pp. 107–25; and D. Torrance, 'Race and the Rhodes Scholarship in America and South Africa', paper given at the British World Conference, University of Melbourne, July 2004.

[77] See especially J. Belich, 'The Rise of the Angloworld: Settlement in North America and Australasia, 1784–1918', in Buckner and Francis, *Rediscovering the British World*, pp. 39–58. We are grateful to Professor Belich for supplying us with a copy of his paper prior to publication.

migration, constructed around the rural ideal of the independent yeoman farmer, or its urban counterpart, that of the free British (skilled) labourer, circulated around an English-speaking world, to which the United States very much belonged.[78] In a similar vein, studies of the Welsh 'disapora' have shown how settlers fashioned their cultural identity through American journals and newspapers – the print-media of Welsh migrants were particularly powerful in the United States.[79] The similarity in British-imperial and American-republican racial discourses has also been noted. A study of the Anglo-American settler world argues forcefully that the idea of a 'white man's country', and the exclusionary and discriminatory practices it fostered, were a transnational phenomenon: new ways of thinking about racial identification in these societies did not emerge simply in parallel but were 'dynamically inter-connected'.[80]

Britain's demographic, commercial and financial ties to the United States are interwoven with our study of the British World economy. In the realms of migration (Chapter 3) and investment (Chapter 5) we are struck by the similarities in Anglo-Dominion and Anglo-American relations, while in the realm of trade (Chapter 4) we draw greater lines of differentiation. Of course, this is an over-simplification. Different patterns of migration within and beyond the empire led to different types of migrant experience (see, for example, the analysis of migrant remittance behaviour in Chapter 3). Conversely, notwithstanding the intensifying commercial competition between Britain and America during the late nineteenth century, intermarriage and consumption habits extending across an 'Anglo-' (not just a 'British') World acted as a counter-weight to the feeling that what had previously been regarded as a friendly offshoot of Britain was now to be viewed with a measure of jealousy and suspicion. One's perspective on Anglo-Americanism changes according to one's vantage point, therefore.[81] A narrow focus on high society and politics runs the risk of elevating security and trade as the defining

---

[78] Belich, 'The Rise of the Angloworld'; Hyslop, 'The British and Australian Leaders of the South African Labour Movement'; and R. Waterhouse, 'The Yeoman Ideal and the Australian Experience', in Darian-Smith *et al.*, *Exploring the British World*, pp. 440–59. See also R. D. Grant, *Representations of British Emigration, Colonisation and Settlement: Imagining Empire, 1800–1860* (Basingstoke: Palgrave Macmillan, 2005), pp. 37–8, 41, 44.

[79] A. Jones and B. Jones, 'The Welsh World and the British Empire, *c.* 1851–1939: An Exploration', *JICH* 31:2 (2003), 57–81.

[80] M. Lake and H. Reynolds, *Drawing the Global Colour Line: White Men's Countries and the International Challenge of Racial Equality* (Cambridge: Cambridge University Press, 2008), pp. 1–12 (quote from p. 5).

[81] For the latest, synoptic study, see K. Burk, *Old World, New World: The Story of Britain and America* (London: Little Brown Book Company Ltd, 2007).

issues in this close if fractious relationship. Such a perspective gives little sense of the cultural depth to their interactions. The 'underbelly' of Anglo-American relations – the bonds of language, literature and kinship that underpinned this transatlantic exchange – merit more attention.

The British World economy

While explored as a political, cultural and ideological concept, the British World's economic foundations have not received as much attention.[82] This neglect should not surprise us. With the increased prominence of cultural studies, the economic dimensions of imperial history have, more generally, suffered from want of attention in recent years.[83] However, before we turn to the relationship between migration, trade and finance, and the informal ties of culture, networking and association discussed above, it is worth recalling the commentary upon Anglo-Dominion relations provided by an older literature on the global development of settler capitalism and dominion export economies.

Among the main consequences of the expansion of British power in the generations before the First World War was the creation of a group of settler societies with distinct economic characteristics.[84] These hitherto sparsely populated regions occupied a privileged position in the first 'global' economy constructed by British free traders during the nineteenth century.[85] With an abundance of fertile land, but a lack of capital and labour, they had an almost magnetic attraction for British investors and emigrants. Integration into the international economy was a sine qua non for their rapid development. By drawing in large numbers of immigrants and large amounts of capital, by building

---

[82] As always, there are notable exceptions to the rule: see, especially, the analysis of Anglo-Dominion financial relations in P. J. Cain and A. G. Hopkins, *British Imperialism, 1688–2000* (Harlow: Longman, 2001), pp. 205–42.

[83] The role of finance and services in underpinning Britain's continuing connection to the neo-Britains is a major exception here; see Cain and Hopkins, *British Imperialism*, esp. pp. 205–9, 241; and Hopkins, 'Back to the Future', pp. 206, 218, 232–3.

[84] The importance of external economic relationships in explaining the distinctive evolution of settler societies was first recognised by 'staples theory', albeit that its advocates tended to focus on particular societies rather than look at them comparatively; see especially the work of Harold Innis, *On Canada: Essays in Canadian Economic History* (Toronto: University of Toronto Press, 1956), pp. 200–10, 273–89; and D. Drache (ed.), *Staples, Markets and Cultural Change: Selected Essays* (Montreal: McGill-Queen's University Press, 1995). For the staples theory revisited, see C. B. Schevdin, 'Staples and Regions of Pax Britannica', *EcHR* 43 (1990), 533–59.

[85] See, for example, C. K. Harley, 'The World Food Economy and Pre-World War I Argentina', in S. N. Broadberry and N. F. R. Crafts (eds.), *Britain in the International Economy* (Cambridge: Cambridge University Press, 1992), pp. 244–68 (pp. 244–6).

modern transport infrastructures and by exporting a narrow range of 'staple' commodities (mainly foods and raw materials), they were able to achieve impressive levels of growth and high per capita incomes. They tend to be referred to as 'regions of recent settlement', 'temperate colonies' or 'white' dominions. Australia, Canada, New Zealand and Argentina are usually taken to be the centrepieces in comparative studies of their economies, although South Africa and Uruguay are sometimes also included.

The pioneer of this comparative study of dominion economies is Donald Denoon.[86] His analysis of six settler societies (Australia, New Zealand, South Africa, Argentina, Chile and Uruguay), while allowing for differing responses to world economic conditions, nonetheless firmly places them in their own distinct category of development.[87] Settler capitalists, separated from Europe by large distances and yet self-consciously 'European' in their attitudes and aspirations, pursued export-led growth to considerable material advantage. They were, of course, dependent on Britain for both capital and markets. Denoon, however, sees this relationship as a state of 'unforced dependence' that was perfectly compatible with 'wide autonomy', even if it dissipated the energies of some groups who might otherwise have driven these societies towards greater self-reliance.[88]

Our study of the British World economy likewise sees significant strands of commonality among the dominions, even if our explanation of that commonality differs in certain respects from that outlined above. It is important, for example, to recognise how some parts of the British World were more than just primary producing export economies, and

[86] D. Denoon, 'Understanding Settler Societies', *Historical Studies* 18 (1979), 511–27, and *Settler Capitalism: The Dynamics of Dependent Development in the Southern Hemisphere* (Oxford: Oxford University Press, 1983).

[87] P. Ehrensaft and W. Armstrong also draw attention to the 'privileged cultural, social and political linkage' of settler societies to British imperialism, which they see as a defining characteristic of their economic development. Their study focuses on Canada, Australia and New Zealand (within the empire), and Argentina and Uruguay as 'honorary dominions' (outside it), highlighting how their colonial ruling groups were intent upon constructing labour markets from large-scale 'free' wage labour from Europe rather than from indigenous or indentured workers. See P. Ehrensaft and W. Armstrong, 'The Formation of Dominion Capitalism: Economic Truncation and Class Structure', in A. Moscovitch and G. Drover (eds.), *Inequality: Essays on the Political Economy of Social Welfare* (Toronto: University of Toronto Press, 1981), pp. 95–105.

[88] See also R. Kubicek, who argues that 'peripheral autonomy' rather than 'peripheral dependence' best captures the situation of Australia, Canada and South Africa by 1911: 'Economic Power at the Periphery: Canada, Australia and South Africa, 1850–1914', in R. E. Dummett (ed.), *Gentlemanly Capitalism and British Imperialism: The New Debate* (London: Longman, 1999), pp. 113–26 (pp. 124–6).

how the scale of manufacturing and service industry, by the later nineteenth century, was greater in provinces like Victoria and Ontario than is sometimes assumed. By this time, the cities of Melbourne and Toronto were richly diversified economies, much more than mere processing depots for the export of primary products. By world standards, of course, their manufacturing sectors were modest. Yet as early as the 1860s and 1870s, they were already showing some signs of rapid development that would follow, giving work to tens of thousands of artisans and labourers, and producing goods worth millions of dollars every year.[89] Their manufacturers, moreover, were becoming much better organised, and exerting increased pressure on public policy, especially with regard to tariffs (See Chapter 4).

Our geographic frame of reference also differs from previous comparative studies of dominion economies. We pay closer attention to the United States as a recipient of British migrants and capital, and a link in the chain of 'Anglo-bourgeois' consumption.[90] Furthermore, while recognising that South Africa's integration into the world economy was different from that of Britain's other dominions, and that its export-led growth was more mineral-based, we give it similar weight in our analysis to Canada, Australia and New Zealand. This is partly because contemporary conceptions of the British World did so, partly because (like the other dominions) it collaborated with Britain from a position of strength, partly because imperial networks developed there on a similar basis to those in the dominions, and partly because of the 'non-market' advantages enjoyed by British exporters there (see Chapter 4).[91]

Conversely, while referring to Latin America (principally Argentina) as a point of comparison, we draw stronger distinctions between this region and other parts of the British World. Differences in political tradition and the origins of immigrant populations are significant here,[92] as

[89] M. Bliss, *Northern Enterprise: Five Centuries of Canadian Business* (Toronto: University of Toronto Press, 1987), pp. 243–4.

[90] The presentation of data on migrant remittances (Chapter 3) and overseas capital investment (Chapter 5) explains in more detail why we feel the inclusion of America to be necessary in any study of the economy of the British World. Also of relevance here are the late Charles Feinstein's observations on export economies, and, in particular, the strong similarities he sees in small-scale, intensive homestead farming across the regions of the United States, Canada, Australia and New Zealand, and the type of growth this was able to sustain: *An Economic History of South Africa: Conquest, Discrimination and Development* (Cambridge: Cambridge University Press, 2005), pp. 91–2.

[91] The case for South Africa's inclusion is well made by Kubicek's 'Economic Power at the Periphery', pp. 113–26.

[92] So much is recognised by scholars who have placed Argentina, Canada and Australia in the same analytic frame; see, for example, D. C. M. Platt and G. di Tella, 'Introduction', in Platt and di Tella (eds.), *Argentina, Australia and Canada: Studies in Comparative Development, 1870–1965* (London: Macmillan, 1985), pp. 1–19 (pp. 2, 17).

is the very nature of the migration that took place. Take, for instance, the Italians who moved to Argentina. They did so as temporary or seasonal migrants, leasing pampas land on short-term contracts, or selling their labour during harvest. This diminished the risk and avoided the burden of fixed investments, while allowing them to accumulate considerable amounts of capital to remit home.[93] Compare this with migrants to the Canadian prairies from eastern Canada, the USA and the British Isles, who made land ownership their main goal. They moved with an eye to setting up permanent enterprises, and their preference was for self-employment rather than for selling their labour.[94] While the explanation for their behaviour rests partly in prevailing property relations (common-property commutation favoured large owners in Argentina, and smallholders in Canada), settler ideology also came into play. As noted above, within the British World of the later nineteenth and early twentieth centuries a 'secular utopianism' entered into the emigrant creed; it was premised on the myth (or promise) of the yeoman freehold, and vigorously propagated by a plethora of emigrant literature.[95] Hence the very nature of migration cautions against situating Latin America firmly within the British World. We return to this point in Chapter 4 when we examine the operation of migrant networks.

Another difference between our study and previous ones of dominion economies is that we are less concerned by class analysis, and more by the social science literature on networks. The ideas and information that flowed through imperial networks had a major impact on the economic development of the British World. Thus an examination of these networks – how they were formed, who belonged to them, and what they achieved – offers a way of reintegrating economic and cultural history, and, more specifically, of exploring the influence of culture and ethnicity upon economic behaviour.[96] Imperial power, to be sure, has long

---

[93] For example, we know that between 1889 and 1990, and 1913 and 1914, Italian migrants in Argentina remitted 7,386,869 lira or, at 1913 exchange rates, around £288,367 back home; W. Dean, *Remittances of Italian Immigrants from Brazil, Argentina, Uruguay and the USA* (New York: New York University Press, 1974), p. 3.

[94] J. Adelman, *Frontier Development: Land, Labour and Capital on the Wheatlands of Argentina and Canada, 1890–1914* (Oxford: Oxford University Press, 1994), pp. 1–5, 260–3. See also Platt and di Tella, 'Introduction', p. 5; and Schevdin, 'Staples and Regions', pp. 537–8.

[95] Belich, 'The Rise of the Angloworld'.

[96] Hopkins, 'Back to the Future', p. 199; D. S. Landes, *The Wealth and Poverty of Nations: Why Some Are So Rich and Some So Poor* (London: W. W. Norton, 1999), pp. 516–18. The links between culture and economy have been fruitfully explored in relation to physical science and technology; see, for example, M. W. Jackson, 'A Cultural History of Victorian Physical Science and Technology', *HJ* (2007), 253–64; and B. Marsden and C. Smith (eds.), *Engineering Empires: A Cultural History of Technology in Nineteenth-Century Britain* (Basingstoke: Palgrave Macmillan, 2005).

been recognised as crucial to the mobilisation and distribution of material resources. Yet equally economic behaviour, like any other form of human activity, was influenced by cultural attitudes and beliefs. By merging cultural and economic histories we hope to anchor more securely some of the more 'free-floating forms of cultural history' in imperial structures, so that culture is not artificially separated from material conditions.[97] We emphasise how culture served to enhance economic integration, and how economic activity, in turn, served to enhance a sense of cultural connectedness. We also show how 'culture', in the context of the networks upon which this study focuses, was to a large extent bounded by ethnicity. As dizzying as they often were, therefore, the economic possibilities of the British World were also racially circumscribed.

The next chapter draws upon new research from the social sciences to explore further the nature, origins and consequences of these transnational networks.

[97] J. Gascoigne, 'The Expanding Historiography of British Imperialism', *HJ* 49 (2006), 577–92 (p. 591).

2 Networks and the British World

Introduction

The idea that social connections matter, and can be thought of in networked terms, should startle few scholars. Dubbed a 'metaphor for our times',[1] networks are currently given a prominent role in historical and contemporary social analysis, as well as in debates about globalisation.[2] Yet the term 'network' tends to be employed rather casually. The technological and social aspects of networks are not always sufficiently differentiated, while networks seemingly encompass an ever-wider range of human activities and forms of interaction. At worst, the network concept serves as little more than a shorthand for human behaviour deemed too collective to be determined by pure individual choice, yet too diffuse and personal to be taken up by formal state or market institutions. There is clearly a danger here. If networks can be taken to mean almost any kind of informal set of interpersonal connections, the term is likely to be too imprecise to have much purchase. As one commentator warns, 'if everything is a network then nothing is'.[3]

---

[1] R. Robertson and J. A. Scholte, *Encyclopedia of Globalization*, 4 vols. (New York, 2007), Vol. III, p. 868.

[2] For important historical studies of the network concept see T. Ballantyne, 'Empire, Knowledge and Culture: From Proto-Globalization to Modern Globalization', in A. G. Hopkins (ed.), *Globalization in World History* (London: Pimlico, 2002), pp. 115–40; F. Cooper, 'Networks, Moral Discourse and History', in T. Callaghy, R. Kassimir and R. Latham (eds.), *Intervention and Transnationalism in Africa* (Cambridge: Cambridge University Press, 2001), pp. 23–46; R. Holton, 'The Inclusion of the Non-European World in International Society, 1870s–1920s: Evidence from Global Networks', *Global Networks* 5 (2005), 29–59, esp. pp. 246–55; A. Lester, *Imperial Networks: Creating Identities in Nineteenth Century South Africa and Britain* (London: Routledge, 2001); and the introduction of D. Lambert and A. Lester (eds.), *Colonial Lives across the British Empire* (Cambridge: Cambridge University Press, 2006).

[3] G. F. Thompson, 'Is All the World a Complex Network?', *Economy and Society* 33 (2004), pp. 411–24 (quotation from p. 413). See also Holton, 'The Inclusion of the Non-European World', p. 247 and 'Network Discourses: Proliferation, Critique and Synthesis', *Global Networks* 5 (2005), 209–15.

Hence great care is required in assessing the importance of networks as agents of historical change. In the following chapters we explore how a variety of social networks created links between individuals and groups, and how these links in turn facilitated the movement of commodities, money, information and people across national or, more accurately, colonial borders. That said, it must be emphasised at the outset that causative relationships between two phenomena cannot be inferred from spatial and temporal co-existence alone. The fact that people join networks at a time when the economy is growing rapidly does not in itself prove that the two events are related. They may be, but before such a claim can be substantiated an analytic framework linking networks to material culture and economic behaviour needs to be elaborated and tested against the evidence.

The current chapter presents such a framework. We contend that much can be learned about the British World by perceiving it as a species of global networking, that is, as a system that was sustained and animated as much by personal connections as official policy. But how did such an atomistic, unco-ordinated and trans-national system function, and to what effect? In taking up this question we turn to recent research in the social sciences. Two concepts of particular relevance are explored: 'social capital' and 'network dynamics'. The significance of these ideas for our understanding of the British World economy is then spelt out, and the resulting framework subsequently applied to the British World of the later nineteenth and early twentieth centuries with respect to migration (in Chapter 3), material culture and trade (Chapter 4), and overseas investment (Chapter 5).

Social capital

Recent work in the social sciences shows how investment in community can bring the potential of economic reward. Realising that potential, of course, is not automatic: it depends upon the existence of social capital: that is, on the prior accumulation of an appropriate set of social knowledge, skills and relationships. Although first coined by the economist Glenn Loury to capture the intangible resources utilised by families and communities to advance the social development of their children, the concept of 'social capital' proved attractive to sociologists, who were quick to recognise that its significance extended beyond an understanding of the rearing of the young.[4] Its leap to the centre stage of

---

[4] G. C. Loury, 'A Dynamic Theory of Racial Income Differences', in P. A. Wallace and A. M. LaMond (eds.), *Women, Minorities, and Employment Discrimination* (Lexington:

both empirical and theoretical research in the social sciences followed closely in the wake of Robert Putnam's seminal study of the positive relationship between civic engagement and economic performance in Italy and the United States.[5] Putnam, a political scientist, has perhaps done more than anyone else to popularise the term. He defines social capital as those 'features of social organization, such as trust, norms, and networks that can improve the efficiency of society by facilitating coordinated actions'.[6]

This idea – that wide-ranging individual and societal benefits can flow from normal social interaction – has lately become all the rage in public policy circles. Put simply, social engagement is said to matter, and investing time in the community pays off not only in personal satisfaction, but in terms of economic rewards.[7] Practically, therefore, social capital can be understood as a concept that attempts to capture the value of community-based methods of problem-solving. As such, it arises from and satisfies the normal human need to belong, and consists of many of those things that make life bearable.[8] As one public policy analyst explains, at its essence social capital is a highly personal concept:

Whether you are seeking support in hard times, looking for a night on the town with friends, or searching for a new job opportunity, who you know matters. Moreover what is true for individuals is also true for communities: those with a stronger stock of social capital are able to negotiate the various challenges they may face more effectively.[9]

In recent years the literature exploring the different dimensions (and benefits) of social capital has blossomed.[10] For example, we now know

University of Michigan Press, 1977), pp. 153–186; P. Bourdieu, 'The Forms of Social Capital', in J. G. Richardson (ed.), *Handbook of Theory and Research for the Sociology of Education* (New York: Greenwood Press, 1986), pp. 241–58.

[5] R. D. Putnam and R. Leonardi, *Making Democracy Work: Civic Traditions in Modern Italy* (Princeton: Princeton University Press, 1994); R. Putnam, *Bowling Alone: The Collapse and Revival of American Community* (New York: Simon and Schuster, 2000).

[6] Putnam and Leonardi, *Making Democracy Work*, p. 167.

[7] More formally, social capital can be defined as 'the sum of the resources, actual or virtual, that accrue to an individual or a group by virtue of possessing a durable network of more or less institutionalized relationships of mutual acquaintance and recognition'. See P. Bourdieu and L. Wacquant, *An Invitation to Reflexive Sociology* (Chicago: University of Chicago Press, 1992), p. 119.

[8] R. F. Baumeister, 'The Need to Belong: Desire for Interpersonal Attachments as a Fundamental Human Motivation', *Psychological Bulletin* 117 (1995), 497–529.

[9] R. Judge, 'Social Capital: Building a Foundation for Research and Policy Development', *Policy Research Initiative* 6 (2003), 3. Accessed at http://policyresearch.gc.ca/page.asp?pagenm=v6n3_art_03 on 10 May 2004.

[10] A good survey of the literature can be found in M. Woolcock, 'Social Capital and Economic Development: Toward a Synthesis and Policy Framework', *Theory and Society* 27 (1998), 151–208.

that past accumulation of social capital has *inter alia* enhanced economic growth rates;[11] promoted the development of high-schooling in the American Midwest;[12] ameliorated the effects of individual-specific economic shocks in South Africa;[13] provided protection to local economies from the onslaught of globalisation;[14] fostered good governance;[15] and predicted mortality rates in Chicago neighbourhoods,[16] and levels of educational attainment in Toronto (and elsewhere).[17] While some maintain that social capital might also hinder aspects of economic development,[18] most of the literature has found its effects on balance to be salutary.[19]

What, then, is the mechanism by which the potential of social capital is realised? Since community involvement is typically a matter of individuals acting, independently or collectively, within highly personalised contexts, researchers believe that social capital is in practice most commonly accessed through participation in, and engagement with, informal associations and networks.[20] As we will see in Chapters 3 to 5, individuals were able to tap into an amazing variety of such networks in the nineteenth-century British World – networks characterised by

---

[11] S. Knack and P. Keefer, 'Does Social Capital Have an Economic Payoff? A Cross-Country Investigation', *Quarterly Journal of Economics* 112 (1997), 1251–88.

[12] C. Goldin and L. Katz, 'Human Capital and Social Capital: The Rise of Secondary Schooling in America, 1910–1940', *Journal of Interdisciplinary History* 29 (1999), 683–723.

[13] M. Carter and J. Maluccio, 'Social Capital and Coping with Economic Shock: An Analysis of Stunting of South African Children', *World Development* 31 (2003), 1147–63.

[14] J. Helliwell, *Globalization and Well-Being* (Vancouver: University of British Columbia Press, 2002).

[15] S. Bowles and H. Gintis, 'Social Capital and Community Governance', *Economic Journal* 112 (2002), 419–36.

[16] K. Lochner, I. Kawachi, R. Brennan and S. Buka, 'Social Capital and Neighborhood Mortality Rates in Chicago', *Social Science and Medicine* 56 (2003), 1797–805.

[17] J. Hagan, R. MacMillan and B. Wheaton, 'New Kid in Town: Social Capital and the Life Course Effects of Family Migration on Children', *American Sociological Review* 61 (1996), 368–85; C. R. Leana and F. K. Pil, 'Social Capital and Organizational Performance: Evidence from Urban Public Schools', *Organization Science* 17 (2006), 352–66.

[18] A. Portes, 'Social Capital: Its Origins and Application in Modern Sociology', *Annual Review of Sociology* 24 (1998), 1–24 (pp. 15–18); A. Portes and P. Landolt, 'The Downside of Social Capital', *American Prospect* 26 (1996), 1–24 (pp. 1–5); D. Stolle and T. R. Rochon, 'Are All Associations Alike?', *American Behavioral Scientist* 42 (1998), 47–65; and K. Annen, 'Inclusive and Exclusive Social Capital in the Small-Firm Sector in Developing Countries', *Journal of Institutional and Theoretical Economics* 157 (2001), 319–30.

[19] S. N. Durlauf and M. Fafchamps, 'Social Capital', National Bureau of Economic Research Working Paper 10485 (2004), p. 11.

[20] *Ibid.*, p. 5.

voluntary, reciprocal patterns of communication and exchange, and yielding various types of social and economic advantage.

Social capital itself can take a variety of forms. Some researchers distinguish between bonding, bridging and linking capital, where *bonding* social capital is that which holds homogeneous groups together (i.e. the connections that exist between, for example, members of the same ethnic or religious associations); *bridging* social capital that which brings heterogeneous groups together horizontally (i.e. the connections that exist between, for example, members of different ethnic communities); and *linking* social capital that which acts to unite heterogeneous groups vertically (i.e. the connections that, for example, bring people of different strata of wealth and status together).[21]

While each of these categories is analytically distinct, it is important to note that, as we shall see later, each type of social capital in fact co-exists, interacts with and feeds off the others. Thus, the information that a middle-class Anglican professional person might acquire from an aristocratic acquaintance (via *linking* social capital) may be shared with members of his or her church (via *bonding* social capital), some of whom then may in turn pass it on to business friends in the Quaker community (via *bridging* social capital). One of the outcomes of this process of networking is that a Quaker, unknown to our Anglican professional, has benefited from that professional's personal connections with the aristocracy. Thus part of the 'magic' of social capital is that its fruits are often enjoyed more widely than one might expect. Expressed more formally, an important characteristic of social capital is that the social rate of return on investment in it tends to exceed the private rate.

One area of ambiguity in social capital theory is whether the concept itself is describing an attribute of the individual or of society. Researchers who subscribe to the latter view typically emphasise the roles of rules, values, laws and organisations in promoting social cohesion. They maintain that it is structures that overcome problems of collective action and unleash social efficiency.[22] Such an approach, however, has difficulty in disentangling the effects of social capital from other social features like institutional form and culture. Indeed, it tends to merge all of these factors together into a single analytical mass: something

---

[21] J. Frank, 'Making Social Capital Work for Public Policy', *Policy Research Initiative* 6 (2003), 2–3. Accessed at http://policyresearch.gc.ca/page.asp?pagenm=v6n3_art_02 on 10 May 2004.

[22] See for example Putnam and Leonardi, *Making Democracy Work*, p. 167; J. S. Coleman, *The Foundations of Social Theory* (Cambridge, MA: Harvard University Press, 1990); and F. Fukuyama, *Trust: The Social Virtues and the Creation of Prosperity* (New York: Penguin, 1995).

that complicates matters for those seeking to isolate the contribution of social capital alone.

By contrast, others prefer to stress the role of individuals in seeking to optimise the benefits they derive from social interaction. From the individual's perspective, social interaction and networking are said to pay off because they deter the opportunism of others and, in the absence of reliable market institutions, provide a mechanism through which some economic activity can safely take place. Gaining access to financially rewarding networks is thus imperative for individual advancement. If the private incentives are strong enough, even the most selfish of individuals will invest in social interaction. In a nutshell, the key to this approach is the belief that social capital is possessed and exploited by individuals, not society. As Edward Glaeser, David Laibson and Bruce Sacerdote have pointed out, it is 'a person's social characteristics – including social skills, charisma, and the size of his Rolodex – which enable him to reap market and non-market returns from interactions with others. As such, individual social capital might be seen as the social component of human capital.'[23] Moreover, an individual's ability to enjoy the benefits of social capital is understood at all times to remain contingent on maintaining a good public image; when that is lost, so is everything else. This threat of exclusion and lost earning potential provides powerful and credible checks against short-term opportunistic behaviour. Naked self-interest in social contexts where there is memory is simply self-defeating.[24]

Yet, how can such an individualistic approach be reconciled with the societal dimension of the concept? The answer lies in the duality of social ties that are at the same time both a resource accessible to individuals and, when aggregated, the stuff out of which community is built. By examining the nature of social ties, the individual and societal effects of social capital can both be brought into focus in a consistent manner.[25] Unsurprisingly, then, most recent literature has come to view social capital as primarily a network-based phenomenon. Pierre Bourdieu expressed the prevailing opinion neatly: 'the volume of social capital possessed by a given agent depends on the size of the network connections he can effectively mobilize and on the volume of the capital

---

[23] E. L. Glaeser, D. Laibson and B. Sacerdote, 'The Economic Approach to Social Capital', National Bureau of Economic Research Working Paper 7728 (2000), p. 4.

[24] For good examples of this approach to social capital see Glaeser, Laibson and Sacerdote, 'Economic Approach', pp. 2–4, 29; and K. Annen, 'Social Capital, Inclusive Networks, and Economic Performance', *Journal of Economic Behavior and Organization* 50 (2001), 449–63.

[25] F. van Dijk, *Social Ties and Economic Preference* (London: Springer, 1997), p. 182.

(economic, cultural or symbolic) possessed in his own right by each of those to whom he is connected'.[26] To understand social capital, one needs to know about networks.

Network dynamics

If social capital is created and realised through networks, what factors influence the efficiency of this relationship? It is evident that the existence of social interaction in itself is insufficient to guarantee beneficial results: some networks just prove more fruitful than others. What, then, is the source of these differences?

The social science literature provides us with some guidance. It shows how the benefits derived from networks depend upon the opportunities that individuals have to turn their personal relationships to pecuniary gain. There is no hard and fast rule here, though. The 'value' extractable from network relationships varies considerably across time and contexts. Questions of network size, composition and nature matter. Information technology, attitudes to outsiders and the sophistication of the economic system in which the network operate all affect the ultimate payoff from social engagement as well. Nor are such factors always mutually reinforcing; indeed, some may be contradictory. In seeking to construct the 'perfect' network, one needs to realise that arrangements and structures that are optimal in one context need not necessarily be so in others. There are, moreover, implicit trade-offs to be made. As Kurt Annen has explained:

> There is a trade-off between self-enforcement and the magnitude of gains from trade that depends on the inclusiveness of the network, the complexity of the exchange setting in which the network operates (complexity constraint), and the network's capacity to communicate information about members' identity (communication constraint). In a developing economy with increasing complexity, social capital is valuable if networks are able to soften the communication constraint without reducing inclusiveness.[27]

This situation exists because as inclusiveness (the relative willingness of the network to welcome new members, irrespective of their background) grows, the range of contacts and potentially productive outcomes that the

---

[26] Bourdieu, 'Forms of Social Capital', p. 249. More recently N. Lin, *Social Capital* (Cambridge: Cambridge University Press, 2001), pp. 24–5 likewise concluded that social capital is 'resources embedded in social networks and accessed and used by actors for actions'. On this point, also see Durlauf and Fafchamps, 'Social Capital', p. 61; and P. Dasgupta, 'Social Capital and Economic Performance: Analytics', Faculty of Economics Working Paper, University of Cambridge (2002).

[27] Annen, 'Social Capital', p. 449.

network provides broadens. But this is true only if the information cours-
ing through the networks about business opportunities *and* the character
of fellow members remains reliable. A key characteristic of trans-national
social networks is their capacity to generate information quickly and accurately, and to deploy it effectively.[28] However, both increasing membership
and the growing complexity of economic exchange place considerable
strain on the ability of networks to communicate. If this communication
constraint is not steadily eased with the regular introduction of new technologies or more information-efficient forms of organisation, ever-greater
inclusiveness only serves to further complicate and confuse information
flows within the network and to reduce the net gains of membership.
Likewise, in societies where the levels of economic and technological
development are low and communication proves problematic, restricting
entry to one's network to a small band of individuals whom you know
makes economic sense.[29]

These considerations aside, the literature emphasises the relative superiority of more inclusive networks. The difficulty is that inclusive networks are hard to construct. In fact, once established, networks can
become increasingly exclusive, as existing members begin to fear their present advantages being denuded by newcomers. For those on the inside
of the network, the simplest response to these pressures is to slam the
door closed. Such exclusion can certainly be effective in holding onto
the privileges of those fortunate enough to be 'club' members. Viewed
from the perspective of society, however, it is a counter-productive move,
which blocks off new opportunities for economic activity, accentuates
income inequalities, and dampens incentive for the development of more
formal, secular institutions of exchange.[30] Thus, over the longer term,
experience indicates that successful networks survive by expanding membership and cleverly utilising new technologies to overcome communication barriers, initially within their own regions and countries, but later
internationally.

Central to almost all analysis of networks is the integral role played
by trust. For co-operative exchanges to endure, network members need
to be confident that they are acting upon reliable information. Here one
needs to be able to trust not only the people with whom one is directly

---

[28] M. E. Keck and K. Sikkink, *Activists beyond Borders: Advocacy Networks in International
Politics* (Ithaca, NY: Cornell University Press, 1998), p. 10.
[29] Annen, 'Social Capital', pp. 460–3.
[30] A. Grief, 'Cultural Beliefs and the Organization of Society: A Historical and
Theoretical Reflection on Collectivist and Individualist Societies', *Journal of Political
Economy* 102 (1994), 912–50; Durlauf and Fafchamps, 'Social Capital', p. 15; and
Glaeser, Laibson and Sacredote, 'Economic Approach', p. 14.

dealing but also those elsewhere in the network who, although unknown, are likewise crucial links in the information chain. Peter Mathias notes that this interdependence of individuals within a network necessitates the cultivation of strong notions of obligation and reciprocity between members, irrespective of their actual personal closeness.

> If businessman A had bonds of trust and mutual confidence with business-man B, then A could recommend a third party C, in whom he placed his own personal confidence, to B – with B having an obligation through his friendship with A to oblige C, provided that this was within the limits of prudence and reasonableness (in his view). A, for his part, would not wish to put his friend-ship with B under strain by seeking an 'unreasonable' favour on behalf of C. C then had the obligation of dealing honourably with B or risking his friendship with A, who had intermediated on his behalf. Networks of mutual trust and obligation were built up on such personal recommendations to mutual advan-tage. Of course, the chain of personal trust might be broken if obligations were not fulfilled, and this could then ramify through the network as the reverse dynamic took hold.[31]

This need to instil trust and a mutual sense of obligation among net-work members explains why many of the more successful networks are based around individuals sharing similar origins, culture, background or outlook on life. It is well known that individuals imbued with a sense of group identity tend to act with greater community spirit and less opportunism, and are more prone to altruism.[32] Such identity-induced behaviour is particularly common in co-ethnic groupings. Thus, according to the statistical evidence, bravery was most prevalent among those Union soldiers in the American Civil war who happened to serve in companies comprising recruits with the same ethnic and occupa-tional identity.[33]

These types of 'close' networks tend to be particularly effective in promoting trust and co-operation, for two reasons. First, since net-work participants share similar backgrounds, values and expectations, social distance and misunderstanding between individuals in the net-work tends to be reduced. Insiders, after all, have more information

[31] P. Mathias, 'Risk, Credit and Kinship in Early Modern Enterprise', in J. J. McCusker and K. Morgan (eds.), *The Early Modern Atlantic Economy* (Cambridge: Cambridge University Press, 2000), pp. 15–36 (p. 31). For a more theoretical treatment of the complementarities and 'social multiplier' effect of networking, see Glaeser, Laibson and Sacredote, 'Economic Approach', p. 11.

[32] G. A. Akerlof and R. E. Kranton, 'Economics and Identity', *Quarterly Journal of Economics* 115 (2000), 715–73; C. Fershtman and U. Gneezy, 'Discrimination in a Segmented Society: An Experimental Approach', *Quarterly Journal of Economics* 116 (2001), 351–77.

[33] D. Costa and M. Kahn, 'Cowards and Heroes: Group Loyalty in the American Civil War', *Quarterly Journal of Economics* 118 (2003), 519–48.

(explicit and implicit) about other members' behaviour and history than outsiders.[34]

Second, established communities and groups, whether ethnic, religious or otherwise, have their own well-defined value systems, behavioural expectations, hierarchies and, crucially, methods of dealing with those who break group conventions and customs. The prospect of community disapproval and punishment or even ostracism provides a very powerful incentive against anti-social and opportunistic behaviour. What makes the threat of communal retribution all the more credible is the fact that in all societies there exists a considerable proportion of the population (called 'strong reciprocators' in the literature) who feel that it is their duty to hold transgressors to account whatever the personal costs.[35] These community-imposed checks on individual behaviour are significant because they present co-ethnic and co-religious networks in particular with powerful, ready-made enforcement mechanisms.[36] There is little need for these networks independently to design and enforce rules of conduct themselves. The possibility that misdeeds may lead to punishment by one's own community (both inside and outside the network) automatically induces many to moderate their behaviour within the network.

An additional factor, which enhances network efficiency, is the presence of individuals in the network whose role is to ensure that information circulates as freely and widely as possible. Such individuals are in many ways the true architects of social capital. There is no specific background or training that singles people out for this role. They can be politicians, bureaucrats, entrepreneurs, professionals, spiritual teachers or just highly motivated individuals. Yet, whatever their origins, their work, if embedded within a conducive institutional environment, can be pivotal in making networks work well. Crucial to the functioning of medieval fairs of Champagne, for example, were the private judges that operated under the Law Merchant. According to Paul Milgrom, Douglass North and Barry Weingast, one of the duties of these judges was 'to transmit just enough information to the right person in the right circumstances to enable the reputation mechanism to function

[34] Glaeser, Laibson and Sacredote, 'Economic Approach', p. 13; Bowles and Gintis, 'Community Governance', p. 423.

[35] Bowles and Gintis, 'Community Governance', p. 425.

[36] A. Cohen, *Customs and Politics in Urban Africa: A Study of Hausa Migrants in Yoruba Towns* (Berkeley: University of California Press, 1969); A. Grief, 'Reputation and Coalitions in Medieval Trade: Evidence on the Maghribi Traders', *Journal of Economic History* 49 (1989), pp. 857–82; A. Grief, 'Contract Enforceability and Economic Institutions in Early Trade: The Maghribi Traders' Coalition', *American Economic Review* 83 (1993), 525–48.

effectively for enforcement'.[37] As we will see in subsequent chapters, such individuals played similarly prominent roles in a variety of nineteenth-century British World networks.[38] While these network 'leaders', 'architects' or 'agents' could appear in any type of network, given the pre-existence of community leaders and hierarchies and notions of responsibility, co-ethnic, co-national and co-religious networks started out with distinct advantages in this regard.[39]

Are networks then simply creations of particular regions and communities – organisations that lose their vitality when taken from their places of origin? How does the movement of peoples across boundaries and borders, for example, influence their effectiveness? Turning to the literature, one finds that the relationship between migration and effective networking is rather nebulous. Since social capital is community-specific, emigration is generally regarded as deleterious to its formation. Leaving one's home, after all, breaks ties and connections. The costs borne by the emigrant are both financial and psychic.[40] As Alfred Marshall noted back in 1890 when discussing the failure of labour markets to respond as rapidly as other markets to price signals, the destruction of 'old associations ... will often turn the scale against a proposal to seek better wages in a new place'.[41] By extension, emigrants who do opt to make that break face significant challenges in their new homes. The social capital and networks they need for survival have to be reconstructed *de novo*. Thus, migration and national borders have the potential to fragment networks and limit their inclusiveness.

Such a pessimistic assessment derives from an assumption that the emigration of each individual is, in effect, an isolated event. The historical reality, of course, is different. One person's emigration is typically part of a much larger movement of people from one location to another. Emigrants rarely select their departure date or destination randomly; rather they closely follow the paths beaten by others before them. As we

---

[37] P. R. Milgrom, D. C. North and B. R. Weingast, 'The Role of Institutions in the Revival of Trade: The Law Merchant, Private Judges, and the Champagne Fairs', *Economics and Politics* 2 (1990), 1–23 (p. 3).

[38] See for example Edward Jenkins, W. T. R. Preston, Alexander Begg, Archer Baker and Christopher Holloway in Chapter 3; Joseph Nathan, W. H. Ritchie, William Westgarth, A. W. Wright (and, more generally, the Crown Agents) in Chapter 4; and the Fourth Earl of Grey, Robert Nivison and Edgar Vincent in Chapter 5.

[39] Durlauf and Fafchamps, 'Social Capital', p. 23.

[40] L. A. Sjaastad, 'The Costs and Returns of Human Migration', *Journal of Political Economy* 70 (1962), 80–93; B. P. McCall and J. J. McCall, 'A Sequential Study of Migration and Job Search', *Journal of Labor Economics* 5 (1987), 452–76; Putnam, *Bowling Alone*; van Dijk, *Social Ties*, pp. 182–3; B. Routledge and J. von Amsburg, 'Social Capital and Growth', *Journal of Monetary Economics* 50 (2003), 167–94.

[41] A. Marshall, *Principles of Economics* (New York: Macmillan, 1948), p. 567.

will see in Chapter 3, this was especially true for the British emigrants of the nineteenth and early twentieth centuries, who disproportionately migrated to the settler societies of North America and Australasia. The choice confronting these emigrants, therefore, was not as stark as between staying in Britain and enjoying the fruits of their social connections, or migrating to the social vacuum of the New World. The prior migration of family, friends, fellow believers and acquaintances meant that many emigrants could look forward to a warm welcome and that it was easier for them to integrate into their new surroundings. This fact in itself could act as a strong lure to relocate. Moreover, over the course of the century, as information technology increased the ability of individuals in different parts of the world to keep in touch, the potential for Old and New World networks to intertwine steadily grew. Thus, rather than signalling the end of old associations, emigration often provided the means by which those associations could expand and diversify trans-nationally.

Such an outcome was not unique to the world of nineteenth-century migration. Social scientists point to the positive interplay between contemporary emigration and social capital formation.[42] Some even argue that the trans-national social networks moulded by emigrants tend to be more tightly bonded than national or regional ones: a consequence, it is claimed, of the desire of emigrants to stick together and to use all the resources at their disposal to overcome the uncertainty of their situation. In their new setting, new arrivals are often more reliant and intent on accessing and accumulating social capital, both of the old and new vintage, than they had hitherto been 'back home'.[43] As we will see, these findings certainly appear to resonate with the experiences of British emigrants from the mid nineteenth century to the First World War.

Networks and the British World economy

So far we have provided an overview of recent research on social capital and networks, in order to identify the key features of network dynamics.

---

[42] D. Massey, L. P. Goldring and J. Durand, 'Continuities in Transnational Migration: An Analysis of 19 Mexican Communities', *American Journal of Sociology* 99 (1994), 1492–533; A. Palloni, D. S. Massey, M. Ceballos, K. Espinosa and M. Spittel, 'Social Capital and International Migration: A Test Using Information on Family Networks', *American Journal of Sociology* 106 (2001), 1262–98.

[43] A. Portes, 'Globalization from Below: The Rise of Transnational Communities', in W. P. Smith and R. P. Korczenwicz (eds.), *Latin America in the World Economy* (Westport: Greenwood Publishing Group, 1996), pp. 151–68.

Networks, we have learned, are built upon trust, reciprocity and moral obligation. They work better when they are inclusive by nature, allow information to flow more freely, comprise people who share a common sense of identity, and when personal or institutional leadership is provided. We have also discovered that national barriers, while posing problems, need not place limits on the trans-national expansion of networks.

This book draws upon this research to place networks at the heart of the British World economy. We argue that networks had a profound effect on how economic knowledge was created, disseminated and consumed across the British World, and that they provided the basis for co-operative, collaborative and, crucially, remunerative forms of economic exchange. Yet to benefit from these connections, one needed access to them. Given the basis of most of the networks in question, many of which were formed as a result of migration, the extent to which one could achieve access to them was, in some respects, a proxy of 'Britishness'. In other words, these networks frequently combined material support with more symbolic attractions, including a continuing sense of cultural identity in new circumstances.[44] They involved a commitment to a certain set of beliefs and values, as well as a shared desire for pecuniary gain.

There are several implications of this conceptualisation of 'imperial networks'. First, an excessively top-down approach to studying them will fail to take account of the significance of much network activity 'from below'. The majority of networks discussed in Chapters 3 to 5 belonged to civic society rather than the realm of officialdom, though there are significant exceptions here.[45]

Second, although non-Anglophone groups did participate in some of the networks maintained by Britons, their role tended to diminish over time, as what it meant to be 'British' became increasingly racially circumscribed. Put simply, material power relations exposed the limits of these imperial networks to provide a counter-weight to the ethnic divisions, discrimination and dispossession associated with settler colonialism. There were, of course, exceptions, such as humanitarian networks like that of the Aborigines' Protection Society; while, by the end of the nineteenth century, indigenous subjects were increasingly

---

[44] On the different properties of 'global' networks, see Robertson and Scholte, *Encyclopedia of Globalization*, pp. 867–72.

[45] For semi-official and official networks, see the Colonial Land and Emigration Commission, the Emigrants' Information Office, the Dominion Emigration Agents, the Crown Agents, the Patent Agents, and the Congress of the Chambers of Commerce of the Empire.

able to create and maintain counter-networks of their own,[46] often preferring to make claims for inclusion rather than fostering outright colonial resistance.[47] Nonetheless, few of the networks discussed in Chapters 3–5 offered much scope for African or Asian peoples to join and exploit them.

Third, while varied in nature and composition, imperial networks engendered a sense of interdependence. They bridged the 'Old' world and the 'New', creating strong and enduring linkages between Britain and its colonies – linkages that shaped people's daily lives. They did this partly by fostering shared habits of consumption and norms of desirable lifestyles, especially among the more affluent middle classes; partly by building knowledge systems that enhanced the diffusion of economic ideas and information across colonial spaces, thereby integrating the different parts of the British World; and partly by encouraging entrepreneurship and the spread of new technologies, commercial ideas and practices across geographically disparate markets.

Thus our approach to networks emphasises the importance of social familiarity, even in the efficient, impersonal markets of the later nineteenth and early twentieth centuries. Such a finding runs against the grain of much of the historical literature that tends to view networks as a crucial stage of organisation *on the way* to the development of modern, well-functioning states and markets. In such pre-modern contexts, the only thing you could trust was what you knew. By bringing people together, networks thus played a vital, albeit transient, role in extending the range of trade and financial opportunities. As a form of organisation, though, networks were ultimately destined to yield to the superior efficiency of the modern state.[48] Mathias even posits this as a 'general law', whereby 'the weaker the institutional context, from a wide variety of sources of risk and uncertainty, then the higher the premium to be

---

[46] V. Bickford-Smith, 'The Betrayal of Creole Elites, 1880–1920', in P. D. Morgan and S. Hawkins (eds.), *Black Experience and the Empire* (Oxford: Oxford University Press, 2004), pp. 194–227; A. S. Thompson, 'The Languages of Loyalism in Southern Africa, *c.* 1870–1939', *English Historical Review* 118 (2003), 617–50.

[47] Holton, 'The Inclusion of the Non-European World'.

[48] For this strand of the literature, see D. North, *Institutions, Institutional Change, and Economic Performance* (Cambridge: Cambridge University Press, 1990); J. Scott, *Social Network Analysis: A Handbook* (London: Sage, 1991); M. Casson and M. B. Rose (eds.), *Institutions and the Evolution of Modern Business* (London: Taylor and Francis, 1993); R. E. Kranton, 'Reciprocal Exchange: A Self-Sustaining System', *American Economic Review* 86 (1996), 830–51; R. Kali, 'Endogenous Business Networks', *Journal of Law, Economics, and Organization* 15 (1999), 615–36; Grief, 'Contract Enforceability'; P. D. Curtin, *Cross-Cultural Trade in World History* (Cambridge: Cambridge University Press, 1984); and K. Arrow, 'Gifts and Exchanges', *Philosophy and Public Affairs* 1 (1972), 343–62.

placed on dealings with known individuals, personal trust and kinship nexus'.[49]

Stressing the importance of later-Victorian and Edwardian networks also runs counter to another strand of the literature, which sees trans-national networks as a uniquely *contemporary*, grass-roots response to the pressures of modern globalisation. Far from being a relic of the past, business networks are alive, well and all around us. Furthermore, their importance is tipped to strengthen in the twenty-first century as information technology improves and international migration and capital flows continue to grow in importance.[50] Some even deny that nineteenth-century immigrants were able to forge such trans-national ties: according to Portes, for example, 'communications and transportation technologies were such as to make it prohibitive for the turn-of-the-century immigrants to make a living out of bridging the cultural gap between countries of origin and destination or lead simultaneous lives in both'.[51] As Chapters 3 to 5 demonstrate, such a conclusion is misplaced and underestimates both the extent and variety of types of trans-nationalism at work within the Anglo- and British worlds at that time.

Surveying the literature, therefore, leaves one with a rather strange and confusing impression: networking is seen as a phenomenon that was and is widely practised in the contemporary and pre-modern eras, but somehow not in the modern period.[52] By contrast, our position is to emphasise continuity. For us, the forging of networks represents a type of social and economic behaviour that is timeless: it is an innovation of neither the nineteenth nor the twenty-first centuries. Nor do we regard networks and community-based activities simply as second-best substitutes for well-functioning state and market institutions, or as foils against the increasingly global reach of big business. Rather, we contend here that networks survive now – as they did in the past – precisely because they work alongside more formal institutions in order

---

[49] Mathias, 'Risk, Credit and Kinship', p. 17.

[50] J. E. Rauch, 'Business and Social Networks in International Trade', *Journal of Economic Literature* 39 (2001), 1177–203 (p. 1200); D. Encaoua and A. Jacquemin, 'Organizational Efficiency and Monopoly Power: The Case of French Industrial Groups', *European Economic Review* 19 (1982), 25–51; Annen, 'Social Capital'.

[51] Portes, 'Globalization from Below', p. 17.

[52] The same pattern is apparent in imperial historiography. Historians of Britain's eighteenth-century empire readily acknowledge the importance of networks in the expansion of British Atlantic trade at this time. The discussion of economic and trade networks, however, is much more limited with respect to the nineteenth-century empire. It is not clear why. For an excellent survey of imperial networks in the eighteenth century, see N. Glaisyer, 'Networking: Trade and Exchange in the Eighteenth Century British Empire', *HJ* 47 (2004), 451–76.

to facilitate the spread of markets. Networks are not just mechanisms designed to cope with the intense risk of developing markets (as most of the historical literature emphasises) – though that function is not denied – but continue to provide benefits long after that risk has been mitigated by formal institutions (effective courts and commercial laws) and the emergence of market-based solutions (such as insurance companies). We believe that there are synergies between well-constructed networks and solid institutions. While governments can provide a framework and a conducive environment within which networks operate, they do not have the wealth of grass-roots information about individual behaviour, capabilities and needs to make their policies work without community support. Networks thus enable government and community to work better hand-in-hand. Hence neighbourhood watch schemes are effective against crime if, and only if, they are backed up by police support; community-based health clinics are more likely to succeed when reinforced by an appropriate public hospital system.[53]

In a similar tone, this book asserts that, in so far as imperial networks functioned efficiently and effectively, they did in no small measure because their security and safety were assured by the formal military power of the colonial state. We must not sanitise these networks. Britain's armed forces underwrote the webs of migration, trade and investment studied in the next three chapters, and thereby ensured that a high degree of confidence could be placed in them. Indeed, the networks we study were nourished and sustained by the empire. Its legal and political systems provided rule of law, enforcement of contract and common standards that enhanced the transfer of goods and capital. Official attitudes, if not actual policy, at times privileged the interest of British World networks over non-British. Meanwhile, the movement of civil servants, military personnel, religious officers and professionals across the British World further acted to broaden the range of connections made.

This book also shows how these networks created economic value and promoted common identity across the British World. Hence the interplay between the economy, on the one hand, and Britishness, on the other, is central to our analysis. One effect of the networks we study was to build a sense of belonging to a trans-national community of British peoples. This sense of identity, in turn, motivated migrants to act in favour of the community. Such an alignment of interests came about partly because of shared tastes and outlooks, partly because of a moral obligation to help and support other members of the same community.

---

[53] Bowles and Gintis, 'Community Governance', pp. 423–31.

Most importantly, the networks of the British World shaped knowledge flows in powerful ways. The availability and supply of information are crucial in understanding how and why decisions are made. Decision-makers can act only on the basis of what they know (or think they know). The dataset with which they work is thus vital.[54] One of the most distinctive features of these networks was that they channelled (intentionally and unintentionally) rich information flows about 'British' products, demands, tastes, laws, conventions and peoples back and forth between the UK, its settler colonies and the rest of the British diaspora. Various mechanisms ensured this torrent of information: *inter alia* official reports; personal contacts; and the workings of imperial organisations; as well as acquired knowledge of existing trade, transportation and communication links. This, though, was a very specific brand of 'in-house' knowledge. The same informational flows were not shared, or not shared to the same extent, with other parts of the world; nor did those parts at this time supply the British with the same density of information. Consequently, British decision-makers operated not with complete information, but with a stock of knowledge that was heavily weighted in favour of the opportunities that existed within the British World. Moreover, as technological advances in this era tended to manifest themselves first within and along British trade routes, this 'informational asymmetry' intensified over time. In subsequent chapters, we show how this asymmetry played itself out in various guises: in the choice of migrant destination, in the patterns of colonial consumption and in the preferences of British investors.

Conclusion

By focusing on the relationship between 'culture' and 'economy', we offer a new perspective on the British World during the 'first wave' of modern globalisation. We take as our starting point the flows of information and knowledge that accumulated within a range of wide-reaching imperial networks, and the effects of these networks upon the British people's perceptions of the empire and their relationship to it.[55] In recent years, scholars of globalisation have become interested in the impact of 'dissolving distance' upon people's sense of space. What is argued here is that co-ethnic networks, which became markedly more diverse and extensive during the half-century or so before 1914, helped

---

[54] P. Milgrom and J. Roberts, *Economics, Organization and Management* (Upper Saddle River, NJ: Prentis Hall, 1992), p. 26.
[55] D. A. Bell, 'Dissolving Distance: Technology, Space and Empire in British Political Thought, 1770–1900', *Journal of Modern History* 77 (2005), 523–62.

to foster a sense of belonging to a pan-British community based on shared values, trust and reciprocity. This sense of belonging in turn eased the flow of people, commodities and capital between Britain and its settler colonies, and led to major changes in the way economic knowledge was created, disseminated and consumed.

We believe our analysis of imperial networks sheds light on the origins of modern globalisation. The later nineteenth and early twentieth centuries were a period when globalisation gathered considerable momentum – demographic, technological and financial; they were also the time when the British empire expanded most vigorously.[56] In a new and provocative study, Niall Ferguson has coined the neologism 'Anglobalization' to describe how the empire imposed free markets, the rule of law, investor protection and relatively incorrupt government on its colonies. According to Ferguson, Britain's major imperial achievement was to have benevolently spread 'economic liberalism' to 'roughly a quarter of the world'.[57] This thesis has some merit. As we contend, by integrating labour, commodity and capital markets, and by dramatically improving the quality and quantity of information circulating around Britain and its settler colonies, the empire *did* contribute to the convergence of income levels that was such a marked feature of the capitalist economies of the English-speaking world during the period 1850 to 1914.

However, contra Ferguson, 'imperial globalisation', as presented in this book, was far from being truly global in its reach. Rather it was focused on particular ethnic groups and exhibited a strong bias towards the empire's Anglophone societies. Nowhere was this more so than in places like southern Africa where the networks displayed marked ethnic and social prejudice. These powerful exclusionary tendencies not only skewed the distribution of the economic gains that came from the British World, they ensured that the globalising forces of the pre-First World War era were circumscribed by geography and culture. The significance of these 'intermediate historical spaces' for an understanding of the ancestry of present-day globalisation is argued forcefully by a recent study of the interconnectedness of the peoples of the Indian Ocean rim during the heyday of the British Raj.[58] 'Just as waves in one

---

[56] K. O'Rourke and J. G. Williamson, *Globalization and History: The Evolution of a Nineteenth-Century Atlantic Economy* (Cambridge, MA: Harvard University Press, 1999).

[57] N. Ferguson, *Empire: How Britain Made the Modern World* (London: Allen Lane, 2003), pp. xxiii–xxv.

[58] S. Bose, *A Hundred Horizons: The Indian Ocean in the Age of Global Empire* (Cambridge, MA: Harvard University Press, 2006).

ocean produce fluctuations in sea levels in others, the human history of the Indian Ocean is strung together at a higher level of intensity in the interregional area while contributing to and being affected by structures, processes, and events of global significance.'[59] Interestingly, this (historical) interpretation of globalisation also seems to resonate with recent scholarship from international business theory, which is increasingly moving away from the idea of today's world economy as one in which distinct national economies are subsumed and rearticulated into the system by international processes and transactions.[60] Instead international business theory now lays greater emphasis on the reality of 'regionalised integration'.[61] Likewise, this book emphasises the regionalised nature of the so-called 'first wave' of modern globalisation that centred on the settler states of the empire. Understood in this way, the British World did indeed help to diminish the divisions between a diverse group of 'national' economies, yet it manifestly lacked the capacity to create a 'borderless world'.

[59] *Ibid.*, p. 3.
[60] R. Hirst and G. Thompson, *Globalisation in Question: The International Economy and the Possibilities of Governance* (Cambridge: Cambridge University Press, 1996), p. 8.
[61] For the importance of regional trading blocs within an integrating global economy, see especially P. Buckley and P. N. Ghauri (eds.), *The Internationalisation of the Firm* (London: International Thomson Business Press, 1999), and 'Globalisation, Economic Geography and the Strategy of Multinational Enterprises', *Journal of International Business Studies* 35 (2004), 81–98. For the view of regional trading blocs as an 'optimistic response to the new challenges of globalized markets' as well as a 'defensive strategy' in the face of the challenges and threats of globalisation, see B. Axford, *The Global System: Economics, Politics and Culture* (Oxford: Polity, 1995), pp. 121–2. It is also worth remembering here that the Asian 'emerging economies', sometimes held up as exemplars of globalisation, in fact grew their economies behind tariff barriers and protected infant industries from international competition.

3   Overseas migration

Introduction

Migration was deeply woven into the fabric of British life.[1] This was partly a function of numbers: the sheer – and unprecedented – scale of those who left the British Isles. More than that, it points to the fact that many people leaving the 'old' country were emphatically not cutting loose. A variety of networks helped migrants not only to move overseas and adapt to their new environments, but, crucially, to stay in touch and involved with the society they had left behind.[2] Migrants, indeed, showed considerable determination and skill in forging and sustaining links to friends and family 'back home'.

Return migration and modern technology contributed to this developing sense of a relationship between British people 'at home' and British peoples overseas. It is estimated that, from 1860 to 1914, as many as 40 per cent of all English emigrants came back to Britain – some two million returnees, each with first-hand knowledge of the colonies or the United States.[3] Some returned for good, others temporarily – to marry someone from their former village, to attend the funerals of loved ones, or simply to see family and old friends. Meanwhile, by taking advantage of the transatlantic telegraph, and fast and reliable postal and remittance services, migrants were able, as never before, to keep abreast of what was happening in the United Kingdom, and to sustain family ties there.[4]

---

[1] See for example R. Floud, *The People and the British Economy, 1830–1914* (Oxford: Oxford University Press, 1997), p. 54; and K. T. Hoppen, *The Mid-Victorian Generation, 1846–86* (Oxford: Oxford University Press, 1998), pp. 522–5, 547, 560, 564, 569, 573.

[2] On the importance of networks to migrant diasporas, see L. E. Guarnizo and M. P. Smith, 'The Locations of Transnationalism', in Guarnizo and Smith (eds.), *Transnationalism from Below* (New Brunswick: Transaction Publishers, 1998), pp. 3–34.

[3] E. Richards, *Britannia's Children: Emigration from England, Scotland, Wales and Ireland since 1600* (London: Continuum International Publishing Group, 2004), p. 169; M. Harper (ed.), *Emigrant Homecomings: The Return Movement of Emigrants, 1600–2000* (Manchester: Manchester University Press, 2005).

[4] For an early recognition of the significance of migration for British society in the nineteenth century, see G. M. Trevelyan, who argued that the ingrained insularity of the

The information that filtered through personal and familial networks was crucial to a migrant's choice of destination. Later in this chapter we assess the relative trustworthiness of the various types of network and information flows into which a prospective migrant could tap. We then go on to look at their impact on the migration process – the first such survey of its kind. This is followed by an examination of a vital if neglected dimension of the migrant experience – remittances, or the sending of monies home. Through newly discovered Post Office archive data we consider how and why migrants chose to remit a part of their incomes to friends and family back in Britain, and the social and economic consequences of their doing so.

Migrants were key players in Britain's exploitation of global resources. The exodus of people from Britain during the 'long' nineteenth century opened up ethnically and culturally influenced flows of trade to house, clothe and feed migrants, and of investment to create the necessary infrastructure to transport them and their goods. Migration further facilitated new forms of technology transfer and new patterns of patenting. In this way, greatly increased levels of economic activity resulted from the process of migration itself. Thus the main body of the chapter focuses on what motivated migrants to leave the United Kingdom for the 'New' world, and how they contributed to the economic life of the colonies after they had settled there.

It is, however, important to understand that the global migrations of the long nineteenth century that caused such a significant shift in the distribution of the world's population were not only European. The 'free' British migrants who left the United Kingdom for other parts of the world built networks to support themselves that often overlapped, and indeed interfered, with other ethnically based migrant networks, especially those arising from the great flows of Asian labour – Indian and Chinese.[5] This exodus of people from Asia to work in British colonies in the Caribbean, South East Asia, South Africa and the Pacific is perhaps less well-known than its European counterpart.[6] Yet the presence of these 'foreigners', or ethnic outsiders, was just as important to the

---

English was broken down during Victoria's reign as the Imperial Penny Post (1898) kept people at home in touch with family and friends who had 'gone to the Colonies', and emigrants periodically visited the UK with money in their pockets and 'tales of new lands of equality and self-help': *English Social History: A Survey of Six Centuries. Chaucer to Queen Victoria* (London: Longmans, Green and Co., 1944), pp. 582–3.

[5] For the significance of Asian and African migrations as part of modern world history, see especially A. McKeown, 'Global Migration, 1846–1940', *Journal of World History* 15 (2004), 155–89.

[6] For its significance, see C. A. Bayly, *The Birth of the Modern World, 1780–1914: Global Connections and Comparisons* (Oxford: Oxford University Press, 2004), pp. 133–4.

expanding global political economy, whether they laboured on colonial plantations, in the mines or on the railways. Recruited as contract labour, or on credit ticket systems, in circumstances that ranged from near-slavery to free migration, these Indian and Chinese migrants travelled mostly alone, with the intention of earning enough money to support their families back home.[7] One recent study aptly describes them as the 'global working class of the British empire'.[8] Yet their presence in the workplace tended to disturb a sense of British community, and this in turn provoked powerful outbursts of exclusionary racial thinking, resulting in discriminatory treatment in the labour market, anti-immigration campaigns from burgeoning labour movements, and various forms of state immigration restriction and exclusion that were adopted across the settler–colonial world from the later nineteenth century.[9]

By exploring migrant networks – both the European networks embraced by the colonies, and, more briefly, the non-European networks that were not – this chapter provides the foundation for the two that follow, which investigate the nature of trade and investment within the British World.

The flows of migrants from Britain: an overview

In 1776 Adam Smith observed that 'man is of all sorts of luggage the most difficult to be transported'.[10] Smith was referring to the difficulties rural labourers were experiencing in travelling around the United Kingdom. He could hardly have predicted that, less than a century later, these very same labourers would be pouring forth to the New World in

[7] D. Northrup, *Indentured Labour in the Age of Imperialism, 1834–1922* (Cambridge: Cambridge University Press, 1995).

[8] M. Lake and H. Reynolds, *Drawing the Global Colour Line: White Men's Countries and the International Challenge of Racial Equality* (Cambridge: Cambridge University Press, 2008), p. 23.

[9] L. Barrow, 'White Solidarity in 1914', in R. Samuel (ed.), *Patriotism: The Making and Unmaking of British National Identity*, 3 vols., Vol. I: *History and Politics* (London: Routledge, 1989), pp. 275–87; D. Avery, *Reluctant Host: Canada's Response to Immigrant Workers, 1896–1994* (Toronto: McLelland and Stewart, 1995); N. Kirk, *Comrades and Cousins: Globalization, Workers and Labour Movements in Britain, the USA and Australia from the 1880s to 1914* (London: Merlin Press, 2003), pp. 59–148; J. Martends, 'A Transnational History of Immigration Restriction: Natal, 1896–7', *JICH* 34 (2006), 323–44; P. O'Connor, 'Keeping New Zealand White, 1908–20', *New Zealand Journal of History* 2 (1968), 41–65; C. Price, *The Great White Walls Are Built: Restrictive Immigration to North America and Australasia, 1836–1888* (Canberra: Australian National University Press, 1974); A. T. Yarwood, *Asian Migration to Australia: The Background to Exclusion* (Melbourne: Melbourne University Press, 1964).

[10] A. Smith, *The Wealth of Nations* [1776], ed., with an Introduction and notes, A. Skinner, Books 1–3 (Harmondsworth: Penguin, 1974); Books 4–5 (New York: Penguin, 1999), Book 1, Chapter 8, p. 79.

search of a better life. Between the mid nineteenth century and the end of the First World War a staggering number of people migrated from the British Isles – 13.4 million in total.[11] Moreover, whereas most of the three-quarters-of-a-million people who had left the British Isles for America and the Caribbean from 1630 to 1820 were indentured labourers, those who subsequently migrated did so mainly of their own volition.

A catalyst for this unprecedented movement of population was the Victorian revolution in transport and communications. The 1860s saw a rapid shift from sail to steam on transatlantic services, with specialised passenger ships making their first appearance. Subsequent improvements in steamship technology – the compound engine, for example – made journeys cheaper, quicker and more comfortable.[12] Meanwhile the building of railways simplified transport to points of departure and from ports of arrival to places of settlement.[13] As a result of these developments, many more people contemplated relocating overseas. As one commentator remarks, 'no other nation had ever been able to move its people about the world with such confidence'.[14]

Where did they go? There was a bewildering choice of destinations for the nineteenth-century would-be migrant. British people tested the possibilities of settlement across America, Canada, Australia, New Zealand and South Africa, while smaller enclaves of officials, traders and missionaries sought to establish themselves in the plantations of the West Indies and Ceylon; the treaty ports of South America, China and West Africa; the highlands of East Africa; and the length and breadth of the Indian subcontinent.

The colonies were not, it must be emphasised, the only or even the main destination. Indeed, across Europe people tended to migrate away from the empires of their own country. Migrants from Italy, Austria, Germany and Spain either eschewed their colonies altogether, or moved in much larger numbers elsewhere.[15] For British migrants, America was

---

[11] Of these migrants, 9.5 million came from England, Scotland and Wales, and 3.9 million from Ireland. Figures have been automatically rounded to the nearest thousand and are taken from B. R. Mitchell, *British Historical Statistics* (Cambridge: Cambridge University Press, 1988), pp. 81, 85. The Irish figure does not include Irish emigration to England or Scotland.

[12] R. Kubicek, 'British Expansion, Empire and Technological Change', in A. Porter (ed.), *The Oxford History of the British Empire*, 5 vols, Vol. III: *The Nineteenth Century* (Oxford: Oxford University Press, 1999), pp. 247–70 (p. 251).

[13] See K. O'Rourke and J. G. Williamson, *Globalization and History: The Evolution of a Nineteenth-Century Atlantic Economy* (Cambridge, MA: Harvard University Press, 1999), pp. 35, 55 on the significance of falling international transport costs.

[14] Richards, *Britannia's Children*, p. 177.

[15] P. Manning, *Migration in World History* (New York: Routledge, 2005), p. 153.

the chief magnet.[16] The Irish, who sustained the highest rates of emigration, preferred the United States to the colonies; America's Irish-born population exceeded its English-born from 1850.[17] What was manifestly true of the Irish was likewise true, if not to the same degree, of emigrants from England, Scotland and Wales (see Table 3.1). Until the end of the century more than two-thirds of people leaving the British Isles chose the United States as their destination. Emigration to America gathered pace during the 1830s and 1840s, and markedly increased during the first great emigration 'boom' of the 1850s. By 1862, the radical politician John Bright could confidently declare America the 'home of the working man'. During the preceding fifteen years, Bright observed, over two million British workers had migrated there, the equivalent to 'eight Birminghams being transplanted from this country and set down in the United States'.[18]

Emigration to America and Britain's settler colonies fluctuated over time (see Figure 3.1). Not until the early part of the twentieth century did the settler colonies become the main destination for emigrants from Britain, although when the move towards the empire did occur it was as sudden as it was striking.[19] From 1900–12, 2.5 million people left Britain, 58 per cent of them for the colonies. In 1913, a bumper year for emigration, this figure increased to 80 per cent. Interestingly, there was no corresponding swing in the direction of Irish migration, which went to the United States in much the same proportions as before, albeit that after the turn of the century it was increasingly Great Britain rather than Ireland that was the major source of migration from the United Kingdom.[20]

Canada was the chief recipient of the extraordinary surge of emigration prior to the First World War. The dominion experienced six of the ten largest annual immigration levels ever recorded between 1903 and 1913, and, in 1905, for the first time since the 1830s, more people left Britain for Canada than for the United States. Eight years later, Canada was taking many more migrants from Britain (142,622) than was the

---

[16] A fact emphasised by all leading historians of migration. But for a recent recognition and exploration of the significance of America as a destination for British migrations, see especially Richards, *Britannia's Children*, p. 119: 'the single most important fact of the British diaspora was its orientation to the American Republic'.

[17] Of 7.7 million Irish who migrated from 1815 to 1910, 62 per cent headed for the US, compared with 19 per cent to Britain, 14 per cent to Canada, 5 per cent to Australasia and less than 1 per cent to South Africa.

[18] Quoted in Richards, *Britannia's Children*, p. 154.

[19] See here M. A. Jones, 'The Background to Emigration from Great Britain', in D. Fleming and B. Bailyn (eds.), *Dislocation and Emigration: The Social Background of American Immigration* (Cambridge, MA: Harvard University Press, 1974), pp. 33–4, from which the figures below are taken.

[20] *Ibid.*

Table 3.1. *Outward movement of people from the British Isles, by destination, 1853–1920 (in 1,000s).*

	USA	Canada	Australasia	South Africa	Other	Total
1853–60	230.8	58.7	273.1	12.7	—	575.3
1861–70	441.8	90.2	184.4	12.1	24.9	753.4
1871–80	637.9	152.2	241.5	46.7	58.0	1,136.3
1881–90	1,087.4	257.4	317.3	76.1	86.0	1,824.2
1891–1900	718.7	176.4	116.2	160.0	110.6	1,281.9
1901–10	837.5	793.2	218.9	269.8	213.8	2,333.2
1911–20	379.3	822.0	352.6	94.1	180.8	1,828.8
1853–1920	**4,333.4**	**2,350.1**	**1,704.0**	**671.5**	**674.1**	**9,733.1**

Note: Canada includes Newfoundland. Before 1912 these figures, recorded by the Colonial Land and Emigration Commission, and then the Board of Trade, were for outward-bound passengers, chiefly travelling steerage, rather than emigrants as such. Not until 1912 were migrants travelling to the USA, Canada, Australia and New Zealand counted separately in the statistics. See N. H. Carrier and J. R. Jeffrey, *External Migration: A Study of the Available Statistics 1815–1950* (London: HMSO, 1953), p. 96.

Source: P. Cain, 'Economics and Empire', in A. Porter (ed.), *The Oxford History of the British Empire*, 5 vols., Vol. III: *The Nineteenth Century* (Oxford: Oxford University Press, 1999), pp. 31–52 (p. 47).

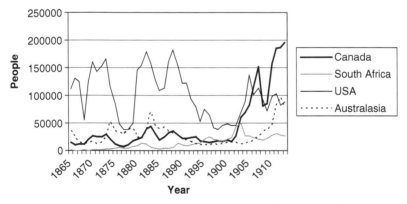

Figure 3.1 Outward movement of people from the British Isles, 1865–1913. Canada includes Newfoundland. See notes to Table 3.1.

United States (107,530). Opportunities in America were diminishing for British labour: unskilled workers faced severe competition from southern and eastern Europe, while the demand for skilled work was increasingly met domestically. Meanwhile western Canada was experiencing rapid growth. The total population of the prairies almost tripled between the census years 1901 and 1911 from 598,169 people to 1,720,601 people.[21] In 1913, the year of greatest immigration, there were over 400,000 new arrivals, including 138,121 people from Britain.[22] Most impressive of all was the expansion of Canada's urban population, which occurred on the back of five main centres: Winnipeg, Calgary, Edmonton, Regina and Saskatoon. Sharing the so-called 'booster spirit',[23] these cities controlled commercial activity in their domains, and paved the way for the huge increases in wheat exports from the Canadian West to Britain before 1914.[24]

It is urban growth that explains much of Canada's new-found popularity with British migrants: the prospect of employment in the towns and cities rather than on the land motivated them to move.[25] In the winter of 1905–6 the radical critic of empire, J. A. Hobson, travelled across the dominion and penned his study, *Canada To-Day*. Hobson marvelled at the colony's amazing growth rate; Winnipeg alone had developed from a little country town of 13,000 inhabitants into a city of nearly 100,000 in only a quarter-of-a-century. Hobson observed how many of the immigrants pouring into Canada passed through Winnipeg, as did a growing proportion of England's daily bread. The city, he concluded, was playing an ever more visible role in 'English common life'.[26]

Canada was indeed becoming much more prominent in the British imagination. During the 1870s and 1880s it had attracted little attention from the 'mother country', whereas by the turn of the century it was enjoying a good deal of coverage in the British press, and was the centre of key political debates, not least those over fiscal policy and tariff reform.[27]

---

[21] J. A. Lower, *Western Canada: An Outline History* (Vancouver: University of British Columbia Press, 1983), p. 171.

[22] Of these 95,107 were English, 9,706 Irish, 30,735 Scottish and 1,699 Welsh.

[23] Namely, a belief in the desirability of growth and the necessity of material success; see, for example, A. F. J. Artibise, 'Boosterism and the Development of the Prairie Cities, 1871–1913', in R. D. Francis and H. Palmer (eds.), *The Prairie West: Historical Readings* (Edmonton: Pica Pica Press, 1985), pp. 408–35 (quotation from p. 411).

[24] P. Voisey, 'The Urbanization of the Canadian Prairies, 1871–1916', *Histoire sociale/Social History* 8 (1975), 77–101.

[25] Although recruitment, and much published correspondence, continued to highlight opportunities on the land, and tried to divert people from the towns and cities.

[26] J. A. Hobson, *Canada To-Day* (London: T. Fisher Unwin, 1906), pp. 13–19 (quotation from p. 19). Hobson travelled to Canada to make a special enquiry into the issue of tariff reform, with particular reference to Canada's relations with Britain on the one hand, and the United States on the other. A large part of his book was first published in the form of letters to the *Daily Chronicle* newspaper.

[27] A. R. Dilley, 'Gentlemanly Capitalism and the Dominions: London Finance, Australia and Canada', unpublished D.Phil thesis, University of Oxford (2006); S. J. Potter, *News*

What of Britain's other colonies? Up until the mid century Australia had struggled to escape its image as a 'convict colony'; many emigrant ballads of the time recounted the misery of those forced to leave England, while an Australian convict ship, docked near Tower Bridge, provided a vivid reminder of the horrors of transportation.[28] The gold discoveries of the 1850s and 1860s put Australia on the voluntary emigrant's map,[29] as did the availability of assisted passages, the appointment of recruiting agents (especially for Victoria and New South Wales) and Queensland's grants of land.[30] Keen to compete in the market for emigrants, the governments of the Australian colonies and New Zealand began a recruitment drive. By the 1870s significant financial inducements were being offered, and the level of promotional activity had outstripped that of both Canada and the United States. Yet Australia and New Zealand continued to suffer from the cost and length of the journey there. Migrant horizons did not markedly widen until the opening of the Suez Canal, and the advent of bigger steam-propelled ships. These two developments shortened journey times considerably, which in turn helped the Pacific dominions to attract larger numbers of settlers. The 1880s saw a notable expansion of immigration into New Zealand as nearly 150,000 people entered the colony from Britain during this decade – gold again being the catalyst.[31]

Migration to South Africa, by comparison, was modest. Although the railway boom and mineral discoveries of the 1870s and 1880s – diamonds at Kimberley, gold on the Witwatersrand – helped establish the Cape and Transvaal as destinations for British (and Australian) skilled workers, much of this migration was temporary and confined to urban

---

and the British World: The Emergence of an Imperial Press System, 1876–1922 (Oxford: Oxford University Press, 2003), pp. 106–31.

[28] A. S. Thompson, *The Empire Strikes Back? The Impact of Imperialism on Britain from the Mid-Nineteenth Century* (Cambridge: Cambridge University Press, 2005), pp. 56–7.

[29] From 1853 to 1860, 28 per cent of British emigrants went to Australia, as opposed to only 9 per cent to Canada; from 1861 to 1870 the gap began to narrow. For migratory patterns to the colonies in the mid century, see K. Fedorowich, 'The British Empire on the Move, 1760 to 1914', in S. Stockwell (ed.), *The British Empire: Themes and Perspectives* (Oxford: Blackwells, 2008), pp. 82–6.

[30] Richards, *Britannia's Children*, pp. 126–7, 153, 194; J. Jupp, *The English in Australia* (Cambridge: Cambridge University Press, 2004), pp. 28–9. In 1855, for example, 50,000 migrants left Liverpool for the United States, 40,000 for Australia and only 15,000 for Canada; see D. V. Glass and P. A. M. Taylor, *Population and Emigration* (Dublin: Irish University Press, 1976), pp. 61, 70. At various times in the second half of the nineteenth century, agents were appointed for all of the Australian colonies and for the provinces of New Zealand.

[31] Though many of these migrants then left during the so-called 'exodus' of the late 1880s and early 1890s. See T. Simpson, *The Immigrants: The Great Migration from Britain to New Zealand, 1830–1890* (Auckland: Godwit, 1997), pp. 183–7.

centres. The assisted settlement schemes promoted by Alfred Milner as South African High Commissioner (1897–1905), which aimed at re-establishing British supremacy in rural areas, proved a damp squib; of the 400,000 British and 30,000 colonial troops who served in South Africa from 1899 to 1902, fewer than 2,000 joined these schemes. Natal fared worse, receiving only a small number of British settlers. The assisted settlement schemes promoted by its government during the 1870s, which promised English and Scottish small farmers an idyllic existence in southern Africa, soon ran into difficulty when it was realised that the reality of immigrant life was much harsher. Many of those who settled in the colony felt angry and cheated. Moreover, as Natal's economy moved to sugar production, it became clear that cheap coloured rather than relatively expensive white labour was required. From the 1860s to 1911, 152,932 Indian workers entered the colony; by 1920 its Indian population outnumbered Europeans.[32] Throughout the period in question, therefore, there is a sense in which all of the settler colonies were competing with each other, as well as with the United States, for migrants from the United Kingdom. We will return to this point later when looking at the impact of social networks on a migrant's choice of destination.

An empire effect?

British immigrants enjoyed a remarkable freedom of entry to the colonies, which sought only to exclude the sick, political dissidents and individuals likely to become a public charge.[33] At the same time Britain and its settler colonies never formed a self-contained region of labour mobility, and large numbers of people moved beyond imperial boundaries, in particular to and from the United States. This raises the question, therefore, of whether the British government, or the colonial authorities, or migrants themselves favoured the empire, and, if so, how?

For its part, the British government stuck resolutely to a policy of non-intervention, with two notable exceptions. The first was the Colonial Land and Emigration Commission (CLEC). Between 1840 and 1869 the CLEC assisted over 340,000 labourers and domestics to migrate,

---

[32] D. Northrup, 'Migration from Africa, Asia, and the South Pacific', in A. Porter (ed.), *The Oxford History of the British Empire*, 5 vols., Vol. III: *The Nineteenth Century* (Oxford: Oxford University Press, 1999), pp. 88–91, 96; Richards, *Britannia's Children*, p. 128.

[33] S. Constantine, 'Migrants and Settlers', in J. M. Brown and W. R. Louis (eds.), *The Oxford History of the British Empire*, 5 vols., Vol. IV: *The Twentieth Century* (Oxford: Oxford University Press, 1999), pp. 163–88 (p. 172).

mainly to Australasia. The money for their relocation – almost £5 million – came from colonial land sales.[34] The second was the Emigrants' Information Office (EIO), set up within the Colonial Office in 1886. The EIO worked on a shoestring budget, offering advice to prospective migrants but refusing to be drawn into a more active role. Its reluctance stemmed from the belief that state assistance would undercut the work already being carried out by the voluntary emigration sector, from a fear of appearing to favour one colony at the expense of another, and from an aversion to (further) subsidising the internal development of the colonies.[35] There was, in short, no 'emigration policy' adopted by the British government, other than to allow the free flow of migrants to their choice of destination, and, from the 1870s, to leave the now largely independent colonies to manage their own immigration policies and programmes.

Although fewer than 10 per cent of all migrants from Britain received state support, as many as a quarter of those who went to the empire may have been the beneficiaries of a subsidised passage or land grant.[36] Colonial authorities gave priority to recruiting kith and kin from the British Isles because they believed that such people would assimilate more easily, that they would strengthen their social fabric and that they possessed the skills necessary to succeed in their labour markets.[37] Thus although migration was, in general, self-initiated, this was more true of the United States than it was of the dominions, where the actions of government agencies helped to direct migratory flows.

As previously noted, from the 1880s there was also a proliferation of immigration restriction and exclusion legislation, of which the 'Natal Acts' (1896–7) and Australia's 1901 Act are the best known. In addition there were the Cape's Immigration Restriction Act of 1902, and the various discriminatory measures taken by British Columbia from 1898 to 1908.[38] This obsession to define outsiders, and to 'rank-order' migrants of other ethnicities, focused on, yet was by no means confined to, African and Asian peoples from other parts of the empire. South Africa, Canada and Australia also looked upon Jewish and Catholic immigration with

---

[34] Richards, *Britannia's Children*, pp. 137–8, 147, 182.
[35] For a fuller discussion, see A. S. Thompson, *Imperial Britain: The Empire in British Politics, c. 1880–1932* (Harlow: Pearson Education, 2000), pp. 139–40, 150.
[36] Richards, *Britannia's Children*, pp. 138, 153.
[37] See for example D. Owram, *Promise of Eden: The Canadian Expansionist Movement and the Idea of the West, 1856–1900* (Toronto: University of Toronto Press, 1980), pp. 129, 137, 143.
[38] In addition to the works already cited see R. A. Huttenback, 'No Strangers within the Gates: Attitudes and Policies towards the Non-White Residents of the British Empire of Settlement', *JICH* I (1972), 271–302.

considerable concern, including those immigrants from southern and eastern Europe.[39]

Migrants from Britain tended to have confidence in the schemes promoted by colonial government agencies, all the more so when their attractions were reinforced by an encouraging letter home from a friend or relative who had already taken advantage of them. Australian subsidies for free migrants (predominantly rural labourers) began in the 1830s with the bounty permits offered by New South Wales and South Australia.[40] So spendthrift was New South Wales that London terminated its bounty payments in 1841, while during the first four years of South Australia's colonisation programme (1836–40) assisted male migrants are said to have been sent out at such a rate that 'one was arriving for every sixty acres sold'.[41] Similar schemes were subsequently adopted by other Australian colonies, although they were wound down during the 1870s and 1880s. After this, only Queensland and Western Australia continued to offer such support.[42] Queensland's programmes assisted more than 150,000 people to migrate by the end of the century, as the colony 'recruited disproportionately against the spontaneous flows across the Atlantic'.[43] After the passage of the Immigration and Public Works Act of 1870, the year the last British troops departed, New Zealand initiated an energetic recruitment drive that lasted for two decades. Free passage was given to single women, and a nomination system allowed New Zealand residents to bring out their relatives and friends. The scheme was revived from 1906 to 1914 when almost a half of migrants to the colony travelled on assisted passages.[44] There were 113,432 recorded nominated and assisted passages to New Zealand: 57,464 from England, 29,880

---

[39] See for example D. R. Gabaccia, *Italy's Many Diasporas* (London: UCL Press, 2000), pp. 78–9, 180–1; and C. Van Onselen, *The Fox and the Flies: The World of Joseph Silver, Racketeer and Psychopath* (Richmond: University of Virginia Press, 2007), pp. 182, 192.

[40] F. J. A. Broeze, 'Private Enterprise and the Peopling of Australia, 1831–50', *EcHR* 35 (1982), 235–53 (pp. 235–7, 245); J. M. McDonald and E. Richards, 'The Great Emigration of 1841: Recruitment for New South Wales in British Emigration Fields', *Population Studies* 51 (1997), 337–55 (p. 338–9).

[41] P. A. Howell, *South Australia and Federation* (Kent Town, OH: Wakefield Press, 2002), p. 38.

[42] It is estimated that, of the 1.6 million free migrants who had arrived in Australia by the end of the century, 750,000 had received state assistance; E. Richards, 'How Did Poor People Emigrate from the British Isles to Australia in the Nineteenth Century?', *JBS* 32:2 (1993), 250–79 (pp. 253–5); D. Denoon and P. Mein-Smith, *A History of Australia, New Zealand and the Pacific* (Oxford: Oxford University Press, 2000), pp. 87–9, 159, 165–6.

[43] Richards, *Britannia's Children*, pp. 194–5.

[44] W. D. Borrie, *Immigration to New Zealand 1854–1938* (Canberra: Australian National University Press, 1991), esp. pp. 190–3; J. Morris, 'The Assisted Immigrants in New Zealand, 1871–79: A Statistical Study', unpublished M.A. thesis, University of Auckland (1973).

from Ireland and 19,624 from Scotland, whereas only 7,596 people were brought out from the European continent on government schemes, less than 7 per cent of the total.

What motivated migrants? This is a key issue, yet one that continues to elude full explanation. Most migrants did not explain their reasons for leaving the United Kingdom. Improving one's standard of living was clearly a major motivation. Average real wages (namely, wages adjusted to indicate purchasing power) were lower in Britain than in Australia, Canada or the United States, especially for skilled workers.[45] Does this mean that individual self-interest rather than British traditions or the growth of imperial sentiment weighed most heavily on a migrant's choice of destination?[46] In 1889, an official in charge of the EIO appeared to confirm this view when he told a parliamentary select committee on colonisation that 'the labouring classes do not have any very strong feeling about remaining under the British flag; they go to the country where they think they can do best, or where they may have friends'.[47] Yet attributing emigrant behaviour to the pursuit of pure pecuniary gain alone is problematic. If the emigrant's choice of destination was essentially driven by relative wages, we need to ask how it was that he or she came to know that wages in one location were more attractive than another. Rational choice, after all, is necessarily constrained by the information available, and for the nineteenth-century British emigrant such information tended to be incomplete and selectively generated.

A variety of social networks, many of them deeply personal, proved to be the most important source of information for the would-be migrant. These networks were not 'unbiased', often favouring – intentionally, or simply through the relative weight and detail of information they could provide – certain destinations over others. While their existence did not, of course, prevent prospective emigrants from engaging in self-interested calculation, it does indicate that there was considerable scope for culture, ethnicity and religious belief to influence the shape of a migrant's deliberations.

Thus recent research makes it clear that, for many emigrants, the decision about where to migrate involved more than merely comparing real wage rates. The vision of 'building Britain's greatness o'er the foam' could be a powerful motivating ideology. Planting regional and national identities

---

[45] O'Rourke and Williamson, *Globalization and History*, pp. 22–3.

[46] A. G. Green, M. Mackinnon and C. Minns, 'Dominion or Republic? Migrants to North America from the United Kingdom, 1870–1910', *EcHR* 55 (2002), 666–96; Jones, 'The Background to Emigration', p. 75.

[47] *Report from the Select Committee on Colonisation*, Sessional Papers, Vol. X (1889), Qns 1938–9, 1944–6.

in an empire 'over which many of these migrants often claimed proprietary rights' mitigated the sense of dislocation consequent upon long-distance population movements.[48] Moreover, even with respect to the economic determinants of migration, quality of life was often as much an issue as the wages on offer: climate, diet, owner-occupation of housing, infant mortality and life expectancy all influenced decision-making.[49] The type of society that awaited migrants mattered too. The settler colonies appealed to people seeking greater equality and improved self-esteem. 'The social freedoms that accompanied colonization' proved particularly attractive to the 'more enterprising and adventurous elements of Victorian society'.[50] Take the case of South Australia. The colony went through a period of tremendous expansion and improvement during the 1870s and 1880s, on the back of the wheat-growing industry.[51] Compared to the UK, good food was cheaper, and the intake of protein, iron, fibre and other beneficial minerals higher; children were taller and healthier; workers' housing was superior, and their prospects of home ownership far greater. New arrivals remarked approvingly on the absence of servility, and of privilege arising from birth. In 1856 South Australians were the first of the Australian colonies to adopt manhood suffrage and the secret ballot for their lower house of parliament,[52] elected on a three-yearly basis. In 1873, they were the first of the Australian colonies to give legal recognition to trade unions.[53]

Other scholars go further to claim that many British migrants were captivated by a spell of 'settler utopianism': the promise of yeoman freeholds, dignified labour, and the opportunity to own one's 'home and horse' in new lands free from the deference and servility of the old country yet still attached to it by cords of sentiment and kin.[54] This ideology of

---

[48] M. Harper, 'British Migration and the Peopling of the Empire', in Porter (ed.), *The Oxford History of the British Empire*, pp. 75–88 (p. 86).

[49] See especially A. Offer, *The First World War: An Agrarian Interpretation* (Oxford: Oxford University Press, 1989), pp. 132–4, 315, and 'The British Empire, 1870–1914: A Waste of Money?', *EcHR* 46 (1993), 215–38.

[50] E. Richards, 'Immigrant Lives', in Richards (ed.), *The Flinders History of South Australia: Social History* (Netley, SA: Wakefield Press, 1986), pp. 143–70 (pp. 148–9).

[51] R. M. Gibbs, *A History of South Australia: From Colonial Days to the Present* (Blackwood: Peacock Publications, 1984), pp. 77ff.

[52] The South Australia Act (1856) provided for a bi-cameral parliament with full legislative authority, subject to some acts requiring royal assent. The parliament's elected legislative council was based on a property suffrage, while its assembly was elected on a broad male franchise, with every male over twenty-one years old entitled to vote after six months' registration. The South Australians were not the only part of the empire to adopt a wider suffrage than Britain at this juncture: the Cape franchise, adopted in 1852, was remarkably inclusive by the standards of the day.

[53] Howell, *South Australia*, pp. 78–9.

[54] J. Belich, 'The Rise of the Angloworld: Settlement in North America and Australasia, 1784–1918', in P. Buckner and D. Francis (eds.), *Rediscovering the British World* (Calgary: University of Calary Press, 2003), pp. 39–58.

settler utopianism, it is suggested, stretched beyond the British World to embrace the United States in general, and the American West in particular. Not all would agree. Back in Britain, it should be recalled, there were growing complaints that emigrants to the United States were responsible for sapping the country's stamina and strength.[55] Thus in 1907, when parliament considered whether public money should be used to promote the advantages of the United States as a field of emigration, Lord Curzon gave short shrift to the idea. People who decided to try their luck there, he warned, would soon be swallowed up 'in the whirlpool of American cosmopolitanism', or 'converted into foreigners and aliens'.[56] Hence if settler utopianism did motivate British migrants, it remains unclear as to whether it was an ideology focused on the colonies, or one that embraced the United States.

Ultimately, as a leading historian of migration reminds us, 'we cannot know what actually passed through the minds of potential emigrants'.[57] Individual choice and personal impulses played a large role, but so too did communal factors. Emigration literature is full of references to enthusiastic 'outbreaks', 'fevers' and 'manias', suggesting that families and neighbourhoods could be swept up by a sense of collective urgency to migrate or by a conviction that migration was their only solution to prevailing distress.[58] It is difficult, therefore, on the basis of the above evidence, to establish a manifest 'empire effect'. Given the amount of lobbying and propaganda on behalf of empire migration, especially from the 1880s onwards, this may seem surprising. 'The disparity between dismissive views of the relationship between emigration and empire and portrayals of British migrants' umbilical attachment to their flag is one of the many paradoxes in the complex mosaic of migration.'[59] One way of addressing this difficulty, and of distinguishing between aspects of migration common across the English-speaking world and those specific to the colonies, is to look more closely at migrant networks and their influence on social mobility.

---

[55] Thompson, *Imperial Britain*, pp. 35–6, 135–6. Concern that the USA was sapping Britain's stamina and strength can also be identified in earlier periods: in the run-up to the War of Independence, it was a key factor behind the prohibition on emigration that operated for the duration of the war, and the complaint intermittently recurred in the press and in some emigrant correspondence during the nineteenth century. We are grateful to Marjory Harper for drawing this to our attention.

[56] Quoted in R. H. Heindel, *The American Impact on Great Britain, 1898–1914: A Study of the United States in World History* (New York: Octagon Books, first published 1940, reprinted 1968), p. 45.

[57] D. Baines, *Emigration from Europe, 1815–1930* (Cambridge: Cambridge University Press, 1995), p. 9.

[58] We are grateful to Eric Richards for drawing these references to our attention, and for discussing the issue of migrant motivation with us.

[59] Harper, 'British Migration', p. 75.

Networks and information flows

A variety of social networks oiled the wheels of long-distance migration, and shaped migrants' responses to the world around them.[60] In theory it was possible for a person to prosper without these networks; in practice, they performed two key functions for many migrants.[61] The quality and availability of information, disseminated through a range of networks examined below, influenced both the direction and timing of migration, especially from the 1840s and 1850s as literacy rates in Britain increased.[62] This knowledge enabled the would-be migrant to compare the advantages to be gained by moving to one place rather than another. Migrant networks, moreover, had a social value. They provided companionship, mutual support and emotional comfort in an unfamiliar environment, and thereby helped to counter feelings of loneliness and dislocation. They might even serve to introduce a migrant to a future marital partner.

When these networks were weak or absent, migratory flows were less likely to establish themselves. By the end of the nineteenth century there was significant migration from Europe to Latin America. Yet only a tiny number of British people settled in that continent, despite the considerable amounts of British capital invested there and the fact that several Latin American governments had set up immigration agencies in the UK.[63]

Take the case of Brazil. Its government provided 'extravagant inducements' to recruit rural labourers from Warwickshire and Gloucestershire in the early 1870s. It met with little success, however. Many of those who

---

[60] For a useful discussion of the meaning and significance of 'social networks' in the process of migration, see E. Delaney and D. M. MacRaild, 'Irish Migration, Networks and Ethnic Identities since 1750: An Introduction', *Immigrants and Minorities* 23 (2005), 127–35.

[61] 'Knowing how to get to a certain destination and being aware of the circumstances that might be faced on arrival had an important role to play in channelling emigrants to certain parts of the world.' See P. Hudson, 'English Emigration to New Zealand, 1839–50: Information Diffusion and Marketing a New World', *EcHR* 54 (2001), 680–98 (p. 682).

[62] See especially here the work of D. Baines, *Migration in a Mature Economy: Emigration and Internal Migration in England and Wales, 1861–1900* (Cambridge: Cambridge University Press, 1985), *Emigration from Europe 1815–1930* (Basingstoke: Palgrave Macmillan, 1991), and 'Population, Migration and Regional Development, 1870–1939', in R. Floud and D. N. McCloskey (eds.), *The Economic History of Britain since 1700*, 3 vols., Vol II: *1860–1939* (Cambridge: Cambridge University Press, 1994), pp. 25–55, esp. pp. 47–50.

[63] Interestingly, some of these agents reported that objections were raised to their work from British officials who wished to see migrants go to the colonies, and who warned of the dangers of migrating to certain Latin American states: see A. Graham-Yooll, *The Forgotten Colony: A History of the English-Speaking Communities in Argentina* (London: Hutchinson, 1981), pp. 179–80. For the activities of these agencies, see D. S. Castro, *The Development of Argentine Immigration Policy, 1852–1914* (San Francisco: Mellen Research University Press, 1991), pp. 155–68.

left Britain for Brazil died shortly after arrival; others moved on to the US or returned home. In the words of one scholar, this episode amply demonstrated 'how favourable conditions were within the anglophile world for the average British emigrant – once they ventured outside the pale their difficulties multiplied'.[64]

Most of the British migrants who did go to Latin America lacked the necessary 'social capital' – the trust, reciprocity and solidarity manifested in kinship groups, co-ethnic organisations and other network types – to make their move a permanent success. Here it is instructive to consider the experiences of the skilled Cornish labourers in the gold and copper mining regions of Brazil, Mexico, Cuba and Chile.[65] Their relocation was encouraged by the fact that many of Latin America's mining companies were set up with British capital; the Cornish directors of these companies liked to employ Cornish mine managers. These managers then looked to the Cornish mines for technical expertise and skilled labour. Cornish workers were recruited on fixed contracts, for an annual specified wage, which covered the cost of their passage out and back, and provided lodgings and healthcare. However, the personal ties upon which these recruiting networks were based were never sufficiently strong to sustain migration over the longer term, as evidenced by the alacrity with which the Cornish moved on to other more attractive destinations within the English-speaking world – at first Australia in the 1850s and 1860s, and later South Africa in the 1880s – where wages were higher and to which the cost of transport had fallen.

Argentina, meanwhile, took 12 per cent of Europe's migrants, and ranked second as a recipient only to the United States.[66] Almost half of these migrants came from Italy, while a third came from Spain. Although Argentina is sometimes spoken of as a region of Britain's 'informal empire', Britons emigrating there to make a new life amounted to approximately 1 per cent of the 6 million people who arrived between 1857 and 1915, a community of less than 30,000.[67] They were a highly selective group, comprising merchants, doctors, engineers, mechanics and other specialised trades. By the end of the nineteenth century they had already begun to train a local cadre of professionals and technicians to take their place.[68]

[64] Richards, *Britannia's Children*, pp. 189–90.
[65] This paragraph draws on S. P. Schwartz, 'Migration Networks and the Transnationalization of Social Capital: Cornish Migration to Latin America', *Cornish Studies* 13 (2005), 256–87. See also A. C. Todd, *The Search for Silver: Cornish Miners in Mexico* (Padstow: Lodenek Press, 1977), esp. pp. 32–43.
[66] J. C. Moya, *Cousins and Strangers: Spanish Immigrants in Buenos Aires, 1850–1930* (Berkeley: University of California Press, 1998), p. 46.
[67] Graham-Yooll, *The Forgotten Colony*, p. 184.
[68] See for example J. Pla, *The British in Paraguay, 1850–1870* (Richmond: University of Virginia Press, 1976), pp. 7–9, 183.

Rural communities of British settlers in Argentina or, for that matter, elsewhere in Latin America, were few and far between. One of the better known is that of Patagonia, which David Lloyd George once famously described as a 'little Wales across the sea'.[69] A few hundred Welsh emigrants first settled in the Lower Chubut Valley in the mid 1860s. They were hoping to establish a stronghold of Welsh nationhood – a place where they could protect their language, religion and customs.[70] Argentine politicians differed on the desirability of a foreign settlement in Patagonia. Some members of Congress vocally opposed it, claiming that 'wherever British colonists managed to establish themselves, the British government would eventually yield to an irresistible urge to claim their territory as inalienably British'. But the Ministry of the Interior wanted to establish Argentina's suzerainty over Patagonia – disputed with Chile – and saw organised settlement as the only effective method of doing so.[71]

The Welsh population of Patagonia swelled to a few thousand through further migration and natural increase. Yet the history of the colony was one of struggle from its inception, and only periodic grants from the Argentine government, and the tenacity of the settlers, kept it going. By the early 1900s, floods, depressed markets and the call-up of young men to serve in the Argentine army had precipitated the departure of 300 of their number. Apart from worsening economic prospects, what rankled with the Welsh settlers was their dislike of living under an alien flag: the territory's first Argentine governor was inaugurated in 1884, and an 1896 law required state schooling to be in Spanish. The growth of the non-Welsh population in the valley, and the decision of the Buenos Aires government to sanction a scheme of Italian colonisation, intensified these concerns. In 1901, William Lewis, a farmer and keen imperialist, set up an Emigration Committee, which lobbied the British government and the dominion authorities to re-establish the Welsh colony somewhere else under the British flag.[72] Although many of the settlers returned to Wales, a small number moved on from Patagonia to Canada (in 1902)

[69] Graham-Yooll, *The Forgotten Colony*, Chapter 12. For the lesser-known Scottish Highland presence in Patagonia, see G. Mackenzie, *Why Patagonia?* (Stornoway: Stornoway Gazette, 1996).

[70] See G. Williams, *The Desert and the Dream: A Study of Welsh Colonisation in Chubut, 1865–1915* (Cardiff: University of Wales Press, 1975), pp. 96–9, 184–8, and, more contextually, *The Welsh in Patagonia: The State and the Ethnic Community* (Cardiff: University of Wales Press, 1991).

[71] G. D. Owen, *Crisis in Chubut: A Chapter in the History of the Welsh Colony in Patagonia* (Swansea: C. Davies, 1977), pp. 7–9.

[72] *Ibid.*, pp. 57–8.

and later to Australia (between 1910 and 1915), enticed by promises of more or better farming land.[73]

British settlers in Latin America could not rely on the dense web of associations that supported their counterparts in the British World. A range of social networks impacted upon migrant behaviour across the settler empire, and a broad conceptual framework can be used to compare them (see Figure 3.2). Underpinning this framework is the assumption that the emigrant's choice of destination was in good part shaped by both the quantity and quality of information at his or her disposal. It is, after all, improbable that anyone would have chosen to relocate to a completely unknown setting. Nor was a person likely to regard information received from all sources with the same credulity: the testimony of some individuals was trusted and valued more than others. Figure 3.2 attempts to relate this notion of relative trustworthiness to the various types of networks into which a prospective migrant could tap.

At the core of this framework sits the migrant and his or her family, indicating that relevant and reliable information most often came from those whom they knew best and with whom they had established personal relationships. Other types of network information mattered, but these were typically valued according to their relative closeness to the migrant's own first-hand experiences. Figure 3.2 depicts this diagrammatically in terms of proximity to the core; the further away the source of information from the personal and familial, the less its sway over the migrant. Thus, radiating out in concentric circles from the family, we see the personal advice and recommendation of friends, followed by the next most common and effective form of encouragement and support for the emigrant – bands of fellowship offered by people from the same neighbourhood, locality or region. Other sources of information were normally less central to the decision-making process, unless, of course, emigrants could not rely on personal contacts or wider community networks in their chosen destination. Emigration agents, charities, pressure groups, trade unions, shipping and railway companies, private landlords, and others could supplement the private flow of information between friends and relatives, and publicise the resources and opportunities of particular locations. A tide of advice and guidance poured forth from these sources. These 'agents of persuasion', however, were generally regarded as less trustworthy because they were seen for what they were – interested parties trying to sell something.[74]

[73] M. Langfield and P. Roberts, *Welsh Patagonians: The Australian Connection* (Darlinghurst: Crossing Press, 2005).
[74] M. Harper, *Adventurers and Exiles: The Great Scottish Exodus* (London: Profile Books, 2004), p. 111.

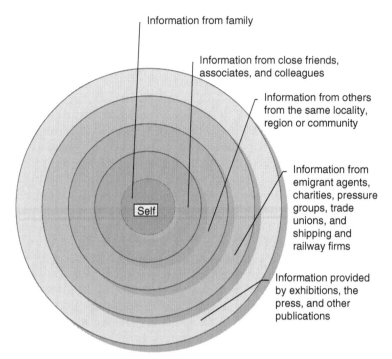

Information from family

Information from close friends, associates, and colleagues

Information from others from the same locality, region or community

Information from emigrant agents, charities, pressure groups, trade unions, and shipping and railway firms

Information provided by exhibitions, the press, and other publications

Self

Figure 3.2 Migrant networks and information in the British World.

Beyond this migration-specific information, there was a variety of peripheral contextual information that was of potential interest to the would-be migrant. Such information could be gleaned from exhibitions, literature and the press, the latter in particular exhibiting an imperial bias during our period.[75] As for the networks that carried such information, it is clear that some of them functioned in a similar fashion across an English-speaking world, especially those based on family ties. But what we know about other migrant networks – in particular settler societies, emigration agents and charities – suggests that they were more active or firmly rooted in the British imperial world than they were in a wider 'Anglosphere'. In some cases they even explicitly favoured the empire over other destinations.

Family networks

Migration was a life-changing event, cushioned by the family – the lynchpin of a migrant's choice of, and adjustment to, his or her new

---

[75] D. Read, *The Power of News: The History of Reuters, 1849–1989* (Oxford: Oxford University Press, 1992); Potter, *News and the British World.*

environment.[76] First of all, the family carved out channels of emigration 'because families and friends were in close contact even when separated by wide oceans, [and] immigrants seldom left their homelands without knowing exactly where they wanted to go and how to get there'.[77] The information provided by relatives and friends was current and candid, and served as a useful corrective to the publicity drives and advertisement campaigns of the railway and steamship companies and colonial governments.[78] Such information often arrived in the form of a personal letter home that contained details of employment prospects and wages. Indeed, precisely because the information contained in such letters was considered superior, it was not uncommon for them to be circulated around neighbourhoods and communities.

In view of the cost of postage, letter-writing was quite restricted in the mid nineteenth century, when unstamped letters were sometimes sent home with a pre-arranged device scrawled on them to denote good news, thereby saving relations the expense of redeeming the mail.[79] By the 1860s, however, letter-writing was on the increase. The volume of correspondence between Britain and Australia grew by 7 per cent during this decade and, by the mid 1870s, the Postmaster General could report that the public now attached more importance to the speed than the cost of postage to the colonies. Thus, by the late 1880s, well before the introduction of the Imperial Penny Post,[80] the sending of letters and parcels was regular and widespread. This was partly a result of the formation in July 1875 of the Postal Union, a single postal territory embracing the great majority of the world's correspondents. Several British colonies subsequently joined the Union, although Post Office archives do not give a clear indication of the amount of mail being exchanged between Britain and various parts of the empire until the early 1900s. The volume of correspondence grew most rapidly between Britain and Canada, a finding consistent with the view that it was letters from family and friends that did the most to facilitate secondary migration. Table 3.2 offers snapshots of the situation in 1904 and 1909.

Moreover, as we shall see, the significance of family correspondence went well beyond the provision of information. Remittances – at first

---

[76] Manning, *Migration in World History*, pp. 121, 124.

[77] J. E. Bodnar, *The Transplanted: A History of Immigrants in Urban America* (Bloomington: Indiana University Press, 1985), p. 57.

[78] See for example P. Hudson and D. Mills, 'English Emigration, Kinship and the Recruitment Process: Migration from Melbourn in Cambridgeshire to Melbourne in Australia in the Mid-Nineteenth Century', *Rural History* 10 (1999), 71–4.

[79] H. Robinson, *The British Post Office: A History* (Princeton: Greenwood Press, 1948), p. 394.

[80] R. M. Pike, 'National Interest and Imperial Yearnings: Empire Communication and Canada's Role in Establishing the Imperial Penny Post', *JICH* 26 (1998), 22–48.

Table 3.2. *Mail exchanged by the United Kingdom with the colonies, 1904 and 1909 (measured in 1,000 lb).*

	Despatched in 1904 to	Received in 1904 from	Despatched in 1909 to	Received in 1909 from
India	2,983	582	3,675	818
South Africa	3,764	860	2,513	601
Egypt	390	77	618	139
West Indies	508	87	549	83
Canada	1,367	668	5,022	1,362
Australia	1,753	629	2,080	841
New Zealand	771	328	1,103	462

Notes: The figures for Egypt for 1909 also include post to and from Morocco. The West Indies includes foreign as well as British territories. Canada includes Newfoundland. New Zealand includes Fiji.

Source: 51st and 56th Reports of the Postmaster General on the Post Office (1905 and 1910), Appendix B, Post Office Archives, Freeling House, Phoenix Place, London.

enclosed as cash in letters, later more commonly sent in the form of money or postal orders – paid for the fares of relatives left behind to join family members who had already migrated.

As well as helping to pay for and direct the flow of migrants to particular locations, family-based networks supported the process of resettlement.[81] Among the first challenges faced by migrants was that of finding suitable housing and employment. Kinship groups could be of great help here. By pooling experience, knowledge and capital they gave a new migrant a much wider range of connections and contacts than would otherwise have been the case. Thus kith and kin ties not only played a role in financing and planning emigration, they contributed to the survival and upward social mobility of migrants after their arrival.

Above all, it was the reliability of family networks that put them at the centre stage of migration. For those who did not enjoy kinship support, substitute or surrogate forms of family network were often the next best

[81] See for example the recent work that has appeared on migration to New Zealand, including: T. Brooking, 'Weaving the Tartan into the Flax: Networks, Identities, and Scottish Migration to Nineteenth-Century Otago, New Zealand', in A. McCarthy (ed.), *A Global Clan: Scottish Migrant Networks and Identities since the Eighteenth Century* (London: I. B. Tauris, 2006), pp. 183–201; L. Fraser, 'Irish Migration to the West Coast, 1864–1900', *New Zealand Journal of History* 34 (2000), 317–40; A. McCarthy, *Irish Migrants in New Zealand, 1840–1937: 'The Desired Haven'* (Woodbridge: Boydell Press, 2005), and 'Personal Letters and the Organisation of Irish Migration to and from New Zealand, 1848–1925', *Irish Historical Studies* 33 (2003), 297–319.

thing.[82] In Canada, for example, boarding houses, immigrant hostels and lodges are said to have prospered precisely because they offered residents 'a familiar, often familial, environment'.[83] So much can be seen from the protection these institutions gave to many vulnerable single female migrants, who were met at railway stations, 'mothered' by matrons and helped to find employment in domestic service. It is also apparent from the way boarding houses, hostels and lodges portrayed themselves as 'homes away from home', spatially segregated, and attractive to recently arrived migrants by virtue of their English character, and their familiar food, accents, conversation and values.

Settler societies

Settler societies proliferated during the second half of the nineteenth century, offering 'a recognisable form through which a social network could be created'.[84] Part of their attraction was that they sought to maintain some form of attachment, however loose, vague or sentimental, to the 'mother country'.[85] They also practised a form of ethnic exclusivity, smoothing an immigrant's path with introductions to people of the same religion or from the same region. Thus, in an era before state welfare, these societies gave their members a competitive advantage in employment markets, took on roles of mutual aid, offered companionship and fellowship, and sponsored a whole range of cultural activities, particularly in the sphere of education.[86] Instances are also recorded of their members returning to their 'home' communities to recruit more migrants.[87]

Settler societies also fused a sense of provincial sentiment with national belonging. Many English and Scottish emigrants took particular pride in their place of origin within the British Isles. Aberdeen, Cambrian,

---

[82] A. R. McCormack, 'Networks among British Immigrants', in H. Tinker (ed.), *The Diaspora of the British*, Collected Seminar Papers 31, Institute of Commonwealth Studies, University of London (1982), pp. 62–4.

[83] A. R. McCormack, 'Cloth Caps and Jobs: The Ethnicity of English Immigrants', in J. M. Bumsted (ed.), *Interpreting Canada's Past*, 2 vols., Vol. II: *After Confederation* (Toronto: University of Toronto Press, 1986), p. 182.

[84] See, for example, R. Sweetman, 'Towards a History of Orangeism in New Zealand', in B. Patterson (ed.), *Ulster–New Zealand Migration and Cultural Transfers* (Dublin: Four Courts Press, 2006), pp. 154–64 (quote from p. 159).

[85] B. Jones, 'Welsh–Australian Organizations and the Promotion of British and Welsh Identities in the 1930s and 1940s', paper given at the British World Conference, University of Melbourne, July 2004.

[86] *Ibid.*, p. 175.

[87] See for example the chief of the Scottish Caledonian Society, Inverness-shire-born Hugh Fraser's visit to the Highlands in 1882–3, in E. Richards, 'Scottish Voices and Networks on Colonial Australia', in A. McCarthy (ed.), *A Global Clan* (London: B. Tauris, 2006), pp. 150–83 (p. 164).

Cornish, Cumberland, Devonian, Glasgow, and Lancashire and Yorkshire Associations, in addition to the better-known Sons of England, Caledonian and St Andrew's Societies, and the Orange Order, all flourished in the colonies. They were cultural rather than political, a forum for settlers from the same city or county to meet and mix. They evinced a highly regionalised sense of what it meant to be English, Scottish, Irish or British.

Although research into settler societies is still in its infancy, it is clear that they played an important, if somewhat neglected, role in the rapid assimilation of many British migrants into colonial society. For example, their proliferation among the English-speaking communities of the Cape, Natal and Transvaal was a striking feature of the social history of South Africa in the later nineteenth century. Settler societies helped new arrivals to find work. They made social introductions. They dispensed charitable aid to those who had fallen on hard times. They assisted the victims of wars, and commemorated the sacrifices made by colonial troops during imperial campaigns.[88] Caledonian societies were probably the most successful. The Scots were a large and strong community in South Africa, retaining a distinctive sense of their cultural identity well into the twentieth century, albeit positioning their Scottishness firmly within a wider British context.[89] Yet settler societies were also popular among the English – especially the Cornish. They met regularly to remember the 'old folks' at home and to preserve local customs and traditions, which became harder to keep alive over time as a result of intermarriage and assimilation.

Canadian settler organisations similarly promoted friendly relations between migrants who hailed from the same town, city or region. They did so by organising recreational activities, such as music, dance and sport; by providing material support (insurance, medical and other benefits); and by helping the newly arrived to find work – for example, through the patronage of other members who had supervisory responsibilities. The origins of Scottish settler societies in Canada stretch back to the early nineteenth century: a party of Lewis emigrants were supposedly saved

[88] A. S. Thompson, 'The Languages of Loyalism in Southern Africa, c. 1870–1939', *English Historical Review* 118 (2003), 617–50 (pp. 629–30); J. Lambert, ' "Preserving Britishness": English-Speaking South Africa's Patriotic, Cultural and Charitable Associations', paper given to the Jubilee Conference of the South African Historical Association, University of Pretoria, July 2006.

[89] J. Hyslop, 'Cape Town Highlanders, Transvaal Scottish: Military "Scottishness" and Social Power in Nineteenth and Twentieth Century South Africa', *South African Historical Journal* 47 (2002), 96–114; J. MacKenzie with N. R. Dalziel, *The Scots in South Africa: Ethnicity, Identity, Gender and Race, 1772–1914* (Manchester: Manchester University Press, 2007).

from starvation in 1841 when a donation from Montreal's St Andrew's Society enabled them to reach their final destination.[90] Throughout the rest of the century such societies trumpeted Scottish ethnicity, preserved Scottish symbols and gave members the opportunity to celebrate their national origins through a range of social functions.[91] Meanwhile, the Sons of England – an English cultural society that, in the words of a Cumberland woman from Winnipeg, aimed 'to keep the British tradition going' – had about 40,000 Canadian members by 1913.[92]

The Orange Lodge Order – the fraternity at the heart of Ulster Unionism – was likewise well established in the dominion, where it functioned as a 'community-building frontier organisation'.[93] Its birthplace was in Ontario among loyalist settlers who were determined to maintain their religious convictions and defend British institutions, and who 'shared a belief in future greatness and progress achieved as an integral part of the British Empire'.[94] There were possibly as many as 100,000 Ontarian Orangemen by the end of the nineteenth century.[95] For Irish Protestants in the province Orangeism was a way of life. Its branches (or lodges) were 'an avenue of association', serving to extend 'a colonial frame of mind' among settlers who were becoming increasingly aware of the growing threat from the world's great republic to the south, and from Catholic, French-speaking Quebec to the east.[96] Thus, by the early 1900s, the Order was a social and political force to be reckoned with.[97]

In 1867, the Orange Order was renamed the 'Imperial Grand Orange Order of the World'. This new title neatly captures the way in which the

---

[90] Harper, *Adventurers and Exiles*, p. 357.

[91] J. M. Bumsted, 'Scottishness and Britishness in Canada, 1790–1914', in M. Harper and M. E. Vance (eds.), *Myth, Migration and the Making of Memory: Scotia and Nova Scotia, c. 1700–1990* (Edinburgh: John Donald, 1999), p. 99; Harper, *Adventurers and Exiles*, p. 359.

[92] Richards, *Britannia's Children*, p. 230.

[93] R. M. Sibbett, *Orangeism in Ireland and throughout the Empire, 1688–1938* (Belfast: Henderson and Co., 1914), 2 vols., Vol. II, pp. 522, 541.

[94] C. J. Houston and W. J. Smyth, 'Transferred Loyalties: Orangeism in the United States and Ontario', *American Review of Canadian Studies* 14 (1984), 193–211 (quotation from p. 197), and *The Orange Order in Nineteenth Century Ontario: A Study of Institutional Cultural Transfer* (Toronto: University of Toronto Press, 1977); D. Fitzpatrick, 'The Orange Order', paper given to *Ireland and Empire* workshop, University of Leeds, March 2006.

[95] The total membership is uncertain but was certainly well into the tens of thousands in Ontario. See here H. Senior, *Orangeism: The Canadian Phase* (Toronto: McGraw-Hill Ryerson, 1972), pp. 47, 59.

[96] A. Bielenberg, 'Irish Emigration to the British Empire', in Bielenberg (ed.), *The Irish Diaspora* (Harlow: Longman, 2000), pp. 251–72 (p. 228).

[97] There were more Orange lodges in Canada than there were in Ireland – some 2,000 in total – and many of its members held major public offices.

empire was built into the terminology of Orangeism, but in a way that did not exclude the United States. With regard to the law, language and other facets of culture, America remained a part, if an ambiguous one, of the British diaspora. That said, the Order was weaker in the United States, where, by the later nineteenth century, there were approximately only 10,000 members belonging to some 350 lodges (6 per cent of the world's total), largely confined to the north-east and areas adjacent to the Canadian border. Unsurprisingly, the American republic did not warm to an organisation devoted to the maintenance of British constitutional and cultural forms. Orangemen living there had to downplay their monarchist tradition and imperial sympathies, and to look instead to other 'nativist' groups – such as the American Protestant Association – to defend their religious interests.[98]

English migrants to America, meanwhile, did not tend to regard themselves as a separate group. In *The American Commonwealth* (1888), James Bryce, the Liberal statesman and later British Ambassador to Washington (1907–13), went so far as to suggest that the English lost their identity almost immediately on arrival in the United States, where they were 'absorbed into the general mass of native citizens'.[99] Recent scholarship supports Bryce's claim. It shows how the American-English evinced much less concern than their Welsh or Scottish counterparts for 'old-country culture',[100] and were thus less likely to form ethnic communities or to produce ethnic publications.[101] Moreover, in so far as they did exist, English immigrant institutions were less elaborate than those of the Scots, Welsh or Irish: the English in America did not sense their culture was under threat and so felt less of a need to preserve it.[102] They were joining a society that was, in some measure, already familiar to them by

[98] Houston and Smyth, 'Transferred Loyalties', pp. 194, 200, 206.
[99] J. Bryce, *The American Commonwealth*, 2 vols. (London: Macmillan, 1888), Vol. II, pp. 360–1.
[100] R. T. Berthoff, *British Immigrants in Industrial America* (New Haven: Harvard University Press, 1953) p. 176.
[101] W. E. Van Vugt, *Britain to America: Mid-Nineteenth Century Immigrants to the United States* (Urbana: University of Illinois Press, 1999), p. 4.
[102] A. Murdoch, *British Emigration, 1603–1914* (Basingstoke: Palgrave Macmillan, 2004), p. 117; O. Handlin, *Boston's Immigrants: A Study in Acculturation* (Cambridge, MA: Harvard University Press, 1959), p. 161; B. Perkins, *The Great Rapprochement: England and the United States, 1895–1914* (New York: Atheneum, 1968), p. 143. There were, of course, exceptions. In the late nineteenth century, the Sons of Malta, the Sons of St George and the Albion Society were active in bringing Englishmen together in the American West, but such organisations appear to have been less prevalent among the English than among other nationalities. See C. C. Spence, *British Investments and the American Mining Frontier, 1860–1901* (Ithaca, NY: Cornell University Press, 1958), p. 13.

virtue of previous flows of English migrants from the early seventeenth century.[103]

Emigration agents, railways, and shipping companies

Representing the interests of colonial governments, and railway and shipping companies, professional agents were active across the British Isles throughout the nineteenth century. Their influence, especially with regard to choice of destination, could be crucial.[104] Initially newspaper editors, emigrants or first-generation colonials, later war veterans or career civil servants, their task was to go into local communities, to extol the advantages of migration and to promote the virtues of particular places. To do this, they travelled widely in their districts, distributing pamphlets, delivering lectures, organising agricultural displays and, most important of all, corresponding with and interviewing potential migrants – personal contact and persuasion, as well as the individual testimony of successful migrants, were key to successful recruiting.

As early as the 1840s, the New Zealand Company had a team of a hundred local recruiting agents informing people about its colonisation project. These agents made extensive use of the local press and met potential migrants in the area for which they were responsible. They raised New Zealand's profile, and supplied potential migrants with information regarding soil conditions, the climate and food prices.[105]

A decade or so later, the Canadian government began to promote immigration. It opened an emigration office in Liverpool and stationed itinerant agents across the United Kingdom. From 1874 these agents were supervised by a Chief Emigration Agent, Edward Jenkins, and from 1880 by Canada's newly appointed High Commissioner, Sir Alexander Galt. Both Galt and his successor, Sir Charles Tupper, were 'greatly concerned with the promotion of emigration and devoted much of their time to this matter'.[106] From 1899, Canadian emigration work was placed in the hands of a special Emigration Commissioner, W. T. R. Preston. He

---

[103] Van Vugt, *Britain to America*, pp. 156–7.
[104] On the work of emigration agents, see especially M. Harper, *Emigration from North-East Scotland*, 2 vols., Vol. II: *Beyond the Broad Atlantic* (Aberdeen: Aberdeen University Press, 1988), pp. 16–18, 21–3, and *Emigration from Scotland between the Wars* (Manchester: Manchester University Press, 1988), pp. 53–66; Hudson, 'English Emigration to New Zealand'; Hudson and Mills, 'English Emigration, Kinship and the Recruitment Process', pp. 66ff; and H. Gordon Skilling, *Canadian Representation Abroad: From Agency to Embassy* (Toronto: University of Toronto Press, 1945), pp. 1, 16.
[105] Hudson, 'English Emigration to New Zealand', pp. 684–5, 688, 690–1.
[106] Gordon Skilling, *Canadian Representation Abroad*, p. 8.

was responsible for the work of agents in Britain and on the European continent,[107] and his role was primarily one of promotion. Agents were carefully chosen for their local contacts and knowledge. As well as distributing huge supplies of advertising material, they were expected to make direct contact with prospective migrants by giving illustrated lectures and by attending agricultural markets and fairs. Their aim was to create a mood favourable to Canada among the British public, and to advertise its advantages over other destinations.

The reports these Canadian agents sent back to Ottawa were often pessimistic in tone. They highlighted the depth of poverty among rural labourers, and the higher levels of assistance provided by the Australasian colonies. Nonetheless, it is agent activity that partly accounts for the remarkable interest in Canada shown by British emigrants during the quarter-century before the First World War. From 1896 to 1906, the Canadian government and trans-continental railway companies spent 4 million dollars publicising the opportunities for settlement on the western prairies, while the Minister of the Interior, the youthful and energetic Clifford Sifton (1896–1905), completely overhauled the publicity and immigration programmes of his department, and brought Canada's representatives in Britain under the closer direction of Ottawa.[108]

Sifton's preference was for farmers and farm labourers – this was why he also made a determined effort to recruit immigrants from the American West.[109] His successor, Frank Oliver (1905–1911), although similarly committed to populating 'the last, best West', took a different approach. He gave precedence to ethnic and cultural origins over occupation, and cared little whether British migrants came from the towns or the countryside.[110] Whatever their origin, Oliver felt that migrants from the 'mother country' were 'ready-made' citizens for Canada who would reinforce its British heritage. Under his tutelage, new immigration offices were opened in Exeter, York and Aberdeen, and bonuses were paid to shipping and government agents for each labourer recruited from Britain and placed in Ontario or Quebec.

Like the Canadian government, the Canadian Pacific Railway (CPR) – the largest private landowner in western Canada – undertook immigration work. The rapid development of the prairies was essential to the

[107] Harper, 'British Migration', p. 84.
[108] M. F. Timlin, 'Canada's Immigration Policy, 1896–1910', *The Canadian Journal of Economics and Political Science* 26 (1960), 517–20.
[109] F. Hawkins, *Critical Years in Immigration: Canada and Australia Compared* (Kingston: McGill-Queen's University Press, 1989), pp. 5–6.
[110] V. Knowles, *Strangers at Our Gates: Canadian Immigration and Immigration Policy, 1540–1997* (Toronto: Dundurn Press, 1997), pp. 79–88.

expansion of the company's passenger and freight traffic, and the CPR
lost no time in launching a vigorous campaign to encourage migration
from Britain.[111] Its first agent was the Quebec-born businessman and
journalist, Alexander Begg (1839–97), who spent four years (1883–7)
extolling the attractions of rural life in Canada through a mixture of press
releases, advertisements, pamphlets and posters. After only six months,
Begg could report that over one million pieces of literature had been
distributed in Britain. He was particularly keen on publishing settler tes-
timonies in an effort to counteract misleading representations of Canada
in the British press. The main innovation of his successor, Archer Baker,
was a 'Travelling Exhibition Van', which is known to have notched up
visits to 500 places in the year 1893, when it was inspected by well over a
million people.[112] From 1903, the CPR introduced its own steamer service direct to Canada in the hope of stemming the loss of those people
who, having landed in US ports, then succumbed to the country's lure.

The 'easy dominance of the flow to the United States' meant that the
settler colonies made greater use of agents' services to divert migrants
to their shores.[113] These agents, it must be remembered, were trying to
recruit migrants from a relatively fixed pool. It was not unknown for
them to embellish information, even if they were not quite as culpable
in this regard as the railway and shipping companies, which had a not
entirely undeserved reputation for peddling false impressions and making fraudulent promises.[114] Some recruiting campaigns actually provoked
rebuttals in the local press, either from emigrants who had taken the
journey only to be disappointed by what awaited them on their arrival,
or by other local figures (such as religious ministers) who took it upon
themselves to go and see whether conditions in the colonies were all they
were cracked up to be.

In the case of the railways, however, the United States did use emigration agents extensively.[115] By the mid nineteenth century American

---

[111] H. A. Innis, *A History of the Canadian Pacific Railway* (Toronto: David and Charles, 1971), pp. 205–6, 223–6, 292; W. K. Lamb, *History of the Canadian Pacific Railway* (New York: Macmillan, 1977), pp. 218, 251–4.

[112] J. B. Hedges, *Building the Canadian West: The Land and Colonization Policies of the Canadian Pacific Railway* (New York: Read Books, 1939), pp. 94–104.

[113] *Ibid.*, pp. 152–3.

[114] For an insightful discussion of the 'emigration business', and the role of agents within it, see B. Jones, *'Raising the Wind': Emigrating from Wales in the Late Nineteenth and Early Twentieth Centuries*, annual public lecture, Cardiff Centre for Welsh American Studies, Cardiff University, 2003 (Cardiff: Cardiff Centre for Welsh American Studies, 2004), pp. 15–20. Accessed at www.cardiff.ac.uk/welsh/resources/RaisingTheWind.pdf on 7 September 2009.

[115] It is even claimed that some of the most 'seductive' emigration propaganda came from this source. See, for example, Richards, *Britannia's Children*, pp. 184–5.

railroad companies were 'the single most important factor' in the colonisation of the region west of the Mississippi.[116] Prairies had to be rapidly converted into homesteads if the railways were to generate enough passenger and freight traffic to make a profit. To provide a return on their capital, railroads thus vigorously pursued settlers. They had land of their own to sell, close to new and projected rail tracks and granted to them by government. But they also worked consistently for the colonisation of government lands. Their objective was to promote settlement of all types.

As we shall see in Chapter 5, British investors had large sums of capital tied up in the American railways. In the case of the Illinois Central Railroad, they went so far as to appoint their own investigators to assess the potential of the company's lands. The investigators were no less than the manufacturer and radical MP, Richard Cobden (1804–65), and the agricultural authority, James Caird (1816–92).[117] In 1857, Cobden published a letter endorsing the possibilities for land settlement offered by the Illinois Central. This was not entirely disinterested. Cobden had been declared bankrupt in the mid 1840s, and a sizeable portion of the £80,000 raised by well-wishers on his behalf had been invested in the railway. Meanwhile, in 1858, Caird went out to the United States to survey the company's lands. He traversed the entire line several times, interviewing farmers, traders and leading politicians along the way. His letters to the press contributed to the Illinois Central's sophisticated advertising campaign in England, as did his booklet, *Prairie Farming in America* (1859), of which thousands of copies were distributed. The booklet reminded British farmers that America was now only a fortnight's journey away, and claimed that the Illinois lands were superior to any other in the West: cheap, fertile, available on easy credit, and with a plentiful supply of nearby labour.

Where the Illinois Central led, other railroad companies soon followed. The Northern Pacific Railroad, chartered in 1864, had 'vast areas to sell in Minnesota and further west' – 190,000 km^2 in all.[118] It set up a subsidiary land company that, in turn, organised a Bureau of Immigration seeking to attract settlers to the sparsely populated and undeveloped region it served. Between 1871 and 1873 the Bureau issued a newspaper in Britain, *Land and Emigration*, and from its Liverpool agency it also sent out hundreds of thousands of posters, handbills and cards to its local agents. Two specifically English settlements were established in

[116] J. B. Hedges, 'The Colonization Work of the Northern Pacific Railroad', *The Mississippi Valley Historical Review* 13 (1926), 311–42 (p. 311).

[117] P. W. Gates, *The Illinois Central Railroad and Its Colonisation Work* (Cambridge, MA: Harvard University Press, 1934), pp. 214–17.

[118] Hedges, 'The Colonization Work', pp. 314–42.

Minnesota at this time – the Yeovil Colony (a religious and temperance group), and the Furness Colony. By 1883 the company could draw on the services of some 831 'active local agents' stationed across the British Isles, compared to its 124 'general agents' in other parts of Europe. An advertisement placed in a west of England newspaper neatly summed up the Pacific's message: 'For the amount of a single year's rental in Great Britain, a British tenant farmer may obtain in Minnesota the freehold of a large and productive farm.'[119]

Yet we must not get carried away. The results of all this railroad advertising were hardly equal to the effort involved. On the contrary: the majority of British farmers and agricultural labourers appear to have made their own way across the Atlantic. The number who settled in Minnesota, Kansas, Missouri or elsewhere as a direct result of railroad propaganda was never large, and none of the farming communities that owed their existence to these colonisation schemes grew beyond a few hundred people.[120] Moreover, by the 1890s there was little railroad land left at prices that European immigrants could afford, and remaining homesteads were mostly in places unattractive to them.[121] Increasingly, transatlantic shipping lines took the railroads' place in promoting colonisation. Much of their extensive advertising was little more than the announcement of sailings and fares, as many newspapers came to incorporate regular columns of this type of information. To be sure, the shipping lines did employ local booking agents and passage brokers, who had the task of selling tickets to migrants, and who, having other occupations, often worked part-time.[122] In 1890, the five biggest shipping lines had approximately 3,600 such people working on commission for them in the British Isles.[123] However, interested in their own rewards, and with limited personal knowledge of the places they promoted, booking agents and passage brokers were not perhaps the best people to proffer advice to migrants, a point later emphasised by the Dominions Royal Commission (1912–17).

Charities

By the late nineteenth century, migrants received help from sixty or more charities. Some of these organisations catered for special categories of

---

[119] P. M. Taylor, *The Distant Magnet: European Emigration to the USA* (New York: Harper and Row, 1971), pp. 78–9.
[120] Jones, 'The Background to Emigration', p. 63.
[121] *Ibid.*, p. 79.
[122] Passage brokers date back to the 1820s, when firms began charting vessels for transporting migrants, and employed (often unscrupulous) agents to drum up business. The competition between them probably kept fares lower than they would otherwise have been.
[123] *Ibid.*, p. 80.

people; others embraced migration as a solution to the problems of the urban poor as a whole. The Salvation Army led the way. In pursuit of its goal of rehabilitating the 'submerged tenth' of the British population it became the largest single emigration agency in the British empire. The Salvation Army selected colonists, supervised their relocation and secured them work. By the early twentieth century it had helped tens of thousands of working-class men and women to make their way to the colonies, the majority to Canada.[124] Barnardo's was another charity involved in migration work. Along with the Salvation Army and a clutch of other philanthropic emigration agencies, Barnardo's became noticeably more imperial in its operation from the 1870s onwards.[125] This shift in policy was partly the product of imperial idealism. Edwardian philanthropists increasingly spoke of children as the 'bricks' from which the 'edifice' of empire was to be built. Thus from 1882 Barnardo's began sending juveniles to the colonies in large numbers. By 1914 over 30,000 children had left Britain under the auspices of the society to work as urban apprentices or as servants in rural homes: 28,689 to Canada and 2,342 to Australia.[126] Barnardo's schemes were not without controversy, for a significant number of these children were effectively abducted from their parents, leaving without their consent or even their knowledge.

By the early 1900s British charities were playing a bigger part in organising overseas migration than ever before. The majority operated on a more modest scale than the Salvation Army or Barnardo's. For example, from 1901 to 1911 the Self-Help Emigration Society assisted 5,317 migrants, the Church Emigration Society 4,327, and the Charity Organisation Society 17,631. Virtually all of them prioritised migration to the colonies over that to the United States. In 1910, they clubbed together under the umbrella of the Royal Colonial Institute to lobby for state support for empire migration, without which they argued that larger schemes of resettlement were unlikely to emerge.[127]

Single women were a particular focus for the philanthropy of promoters of empire migration.[128] During the 1860s a network of women's societies, working in conjunction with the colonial authorities, set about improving the management of female migration. Their aim was to ensure

---

[124] Thompson, *The Empire Strikes Back?*, p. 157.
[125] Thompson, *Imperial Britain*, pp. 147–50. For precursors to Barnardo's, see the emigration work of the social reformers Maria Rye and Annie MacPherson in the 1860s and 1870s, under which a total of approximately 17,000 children emigrated to Canada; I. Pinchbeck, *Children in English Society*, 2 vols., Vol. II: *From the Eighteenth Century to the Children Act of 1848* (London: Routledge and Kegan Paul, 1973), pp. 562–75.
[126] Harper, 'British Emigration', p. 82.
[127] Thompson, *Imperial Britain*, pp. 46–9, 139–40.
[128] See especially L. Chilton, *Emigrating Women: British Female Migration to Canada and Australia, 1830s–1930* (Toronto: University of Toronto Press, 2007).

a 'healthy' gender balance in the colonies. They took it upon themselves
to find suitable female migrants, to supervise their voyages, to arrange
for their reception and protection on arrival, and to assist with funding
through subsidies and repayable loans. Their major achievement was to
make emigration a more respectable and less dangerous experience than
it had been earlier in the century.[129]

Women's emigration societies tapped into the demand for colonial
female labour. With the lure of assisted passages, they recruited significant numbers of women to their schemes. A leading organisation was the
Female Middle Class Emigration Society (FMCES). It was formed in
1861–2 to find occupations for educated middle-class women, mainly as
governesses. Two offshoots of the FMCES were the Colonial Intelligence
League and the South African Colonisation Society, both of which also
catered for middle-class women. In 1884, the British Women's Emigration
Association (BWEA) was formed. The BWEA's interests included the
recruiting and transfer of domestic servants. Rooted in Christian philanthropy and imperial patriotism, it and other kindred bodies assisted
approximately 20,000 women to migrate to the colonies between 1884
and 1914.[130] Of course, many British women still preferred the United
States, yet female emigration societies helped to secure for the colonies
a larger share than would otherwise have been so.[131] Moreover, many of
the women whom they helped to move to the colonies continued to participate in, and take advantage of, these networks after arrival:

> Membership within an empire-wide community of women emigrators and emi-
> grants, who were linked by their ties to Britain and by their shared assumptions
> concerning the benefits bestowed upon colonial societies by the immigration of
> virtuous British women, provided emigrants with a framework within which
> to situate their own experiences and attitudes towards migration and settle-
> ment. For some women this sense of community was immensely helpful. It
> provided them with a clear sense of identity and purpose – not as outcasts from
> their homeland, not as foreigners to their new locales, but as participants in a
> mass movement of like-circumstanced British female emigrants.[132]

More practically, female migrants provided useful information regarding
local conditions to charities back in Britain, took care of the reception of
new migrants, and served as friends to those who had recently settled in
their neighbourhoods and communities.[133]

---

[129] A. J. Hammerton, *Emigrant Gentlewomen: Genteel Poverty and Female Emigration, 1830–
1914* (London: Croom Helm, 1979), pp. 148–86.
[130] Thompson, *Imperial Britain*, p. 142.
[131] Van Vugt, *Britain to America*, p. 129.
[132] Chilton, *Emigrating Women*, p. 261.
[133] For a Canadian organisation acting as host to female migrants, and feeding back into
debate about migration in Britain, see K. Pickles' study of the Imperial Order of the

Trade unions

Trade unions were lukewarm to emigration, yet there were exceptions to this rule. During the 1840s several unions in Britain began to develop colonial connections by setting up emigration funds, which were sometimes seen as an alternative to tramp relief and as an outlet for surplus labour. Thus many of the skilled craftsmen who emigrated from Britain to New Zealand in the mid century had their journey subsidised by a trade union in their home country.[134] The London Typographical Society went a step further. It regularly corresponded with typographical associations in Australia to assess the state of the trade there and to report back to its members on opportunities for employment.[135] Some of the emigration agents employed by the colonies in the second half of the nineteenth century also had trade union backgrounds. They (and their unions) played an important role in the steep rise in the number of assisted emigrants to New Zealand during the 1870s.

One of these agents was Christopher Holloway of the Agricultural Labourers' Union (ALU). The New Zealand authorities paid Holloway to travel throughout the colony in 1874 so that he could interview migrants and send favourable accounts of their experiences to the ALU's journal. After his return to Britain in 1875 Holloway then took a post as a peripatetic recruiter, 'a position he filled most effectively for the next five years'.[136] Indeed, it was the ALU that probably did the most of all unions to promote emigration during the last decades of the nineteenth century. Yet it lacked the resources to do this under its own steam, and was heavily reliant on the assistance provided by colonial governments to sponsor the emigration of its members. From 1872 to 1881 it is estimated that 40,000 to 50,000 agricultural labourers and their families may have taken advantage of this assistance.[137]

From the early 1900s several major trade unions moved to establish overseas branches, the best known of which was the Amalgamated Society of Engineers (ASE). In 1907, the ASE had 101,837 home members, 5,209 colonial members and 3,038 American members.[138] Many of its 'globe-hopping' members moved frequently between the mines, plantations, and railway and port construction projects across the British

---

Daughters of the Empire: *Female Imperialism and National Identity: The Imperial Order of the Daughters of Empire* (Manchester: Manchester University Press, 2002).

[134] Simpson, *The Immigrants*, p. 143.

[135] Thompson, *The Empire Strikes Back?*, p. 69.

[136] Simpson, *The Immigrants*, pp. 179–80.

[137] P. Horn, 'Agricultural Trade Unions and Emigration, 1872–1881', *HJ* 15 (1972), 87–102.

[138] Thompson, *The Empire Strikes Back?*, p. 70. For the ASE's fluctuating Australian membership, see Kirk, *Comrades and Cousins*, p. 96.

World.[139] The CPR used the ASE's branch network to attract skilled labour from Britain – as many as 30 per cent of the artisans in certain CPR divisions were recruited this way. Significantly, the ASE was strongest in Montreal where British immigrants dominated the CPR's workshops. Union members who rose to supervisory positions frequently discriminated in favour of the ASE when hiring, and the company appeared happy to accept this custom as an effective means of sourcing skilled workers.[140]

Migrant remittances

Reconstructing the day-to-day world of the nineteenth century emigrant is not easy. To do so, most historians have turned to individual testimony.[141] 'The personal letter sent throughout interlinked national postal systems was the most widespread instrument of migrant communication through the nineteenth and most of the twentieth century.'[142] Such letters relate the origins, expectations, successes and failures of migrants. But little private correspondence of this kind survives, and what there is comes mainly from the more literate parts of the migrant population. Meanwhile published letters were frequently subject to editorial improvement.[143] It is hard to know how representative these sources actually are.

There is, however, another key dimension of the migrant's experience, closely entwined with their family structures – remittances. These were the one-off and regular payments made by migrants to support people 'back home'. An emerging body of literature on today's remittance activity draws attention to the scale of these monetary flows and their role in alleviating poverty in recipient countries.[144] By comparison, remittance

---

[139] Kirk, *Comrades and Cousins*, pp. 2–3.

[140] McCormack, 'Networks among British Immigrants', pp. 66–7.

[141] For a selection of the key works, see C. Erickson, *Invisible Immigrants: The Adaptation of English and Scottish Immigrants in Nineteenth Century America* (London: London School of Economics, 1972); D. Fitzpatrick, *Oceans of Consolation: Personal Accounts of Irish Migration to Australia* (Ithaca, NY: Cornell University Press, 1994); McCarthy, *Irish Migrants in New Zealand*; K. Miller, *Emigrants and Exiles: Ireland and the Irish Exodus to North America* (Oxford: Oxford University Press, 1985); and P. O'Farrell, *Letters from Irish Australia* (Kensington, NSW: New South Wales University Press, 1984).

[142] B. S. Elliott, D. A. Gerber and S. M. Sinke, 'Introduction', in Elliott, Gerber and Sinke (eds.), *Letters across Borders: The Epistolary Practices of International Migrants* (Basingstoke: Palgrave Macmillan, 2006), pp. 1–29 (p. 2).

[143] For a critical evaluation of letters as a source, see E. Richards, 'Voices of British and Irish Migrants in Nineteenth Century Australia', in C. G. Pooley and I. D. Whyte (eds.), *Migrants, Emigrants and Immigrants: A Social History of Migration* (New York: Routledge, 1991), pp. 19–41.

[144] See for example *BME Remittance Survey: Research Report*, prepared for the Department of International Development by ICM, 27 July 2006.

practices have received much less attention from historians, mainly because it was not clear until recently what type of source material could be used to reconstruct them.

Newly discovered data in the Post Office Archives offers unparalleled insights into how much money was sent home by British migrants, and allows us to explore their variety of motives for doing so. It gets us 'up close' to the nature of a migrant's attachment to, and involvement with, the society he or she left behind. It also sheds light on how far remittance behaviour differed between those who left Britain for the colonies and those who left for the United States.

A lack of data notwithstanding, remitting monies home has long been recognised as an accepted part of the emigrant experience, a constant reminder that physical separation from families had not dissolved a migrant's emotional ties and financial responsibilities towards them. Two factors in particular are known to have motivated the majority of remitters: a sense of obligation to fund the next round of emigration (via one-off payments and pre-paid tickets to finance the voyages of other family members), coupled with a desire to provide more regular material support to friends and relatives left behind.[145]

If the payment of remittances was common throughout the nineteenth century, it was not until the 1870s that their total volume began to rise rapidly, a product of the growing wealth and numbers of emigrants and the increasing ease with which they could transfer funds internationally.[146] In the early part of the century migrants had to rely on established methods of communication or on personal contacts to send money home. 'Pocket' and 'envelope' transfers were the usual means of doing so. Migrants carried money on a trip back home, or entrusted a friend or relative to do so, or they sent it through the post in cash. All types of people were in the habit of remitting. There is even record of illiterate prostitutes using scribes to send money back home to the 'old country'.[147] The fact that

---

[145] Baines, *Migration in a Mature Economy*, p. 17; Erickson, *Invisible Immigrants*, pp. 38, 238, 242; P. O'Farrell, *The Irish in Australia: 1788 to Present* (Sydney: University of Notre Dame Press, 2000), pp. 69, 86; Murdoch, *British Emigration*, pp. 111, 118; A. Schrier, *Ireland and the American Emigration: 1850–1900* (Minneapolis: University of Minnesota Press, 1958), pp. 16–17, 103; D. C. North, 'The United States Balance of Payments, 1790–1860', in National Bureau of Economic Research, *Trends in the American Economy in the Nineteenth Century: Studies in Income and Wealth* (Princeton: Yale University Press, 1960), p. 616; Richards, *Britannia's Children*, pp. 142, 144, 145, 164–5, 167; Taylor, *The Distant Magnet*, pp. 101–4.

[146] For a fuller account of migrant remittances in the English-speaking world, see G. B. Magee and A. S. Thompson, 'Lines of Credit, Debts of Obligation: Migrant Remittances to Britain, *c.* 1875–1913', *EcHR* 59 (2006), 539–77, and 'The Global and the Local: Explaining Migrant Remittance Flows in the English-Speaking World, 1880–1914', *Journal of Economic History* 66 (2006), 177–202.

[147] Van Onselen, *The Fox and the Flies*, p. 200.

these transfers were largely invisible to official eyes explains why virtually no record of their magnitude exists. By the mid nineteenth century,
shipping firms, exchange and press agencies, and immigrant groups were
also acting as intermediaries, while banks and financial houses offered
remittance services to their customers, albeit only for those wishing to
transfer large sums of money.

For the typical migrant, though, the real breakthrough came later with
the money and postal order systems operated by the British and colonial
post offices, which allowed for small amounts of cash to be sent through
the mail. By 1873, a reliable international money order service was in full
swing between the United Kingdom and the majority of its colonies, as
well as with a number of other foreign countries, including the United
States. From its inception the system proved very popular and brought
large volumes of funds from overseas migrants to the UK. Postal orders,
introduced domestically in 1881, were extended throughout the empire
with the creation of the Imperial Postal Order Service in 1904. They
experienced a high annual growth rate in the decade up to the First
World War, though they were not exchanged with foreign countries.

From 1873 to 1913 somewhere between £200 million and £270 million was remitted to and from the United Kingdom (see Table 3.3).
When allowance is made for outward monetary flows, the net gain to the
UK was around £130 million to £200 million, equivalent to 3.4 per cent
of British exports or 0.79 per cent of gross domestic product (GDP) in
1913. The USA, Canada, Australia, New Zealand and South Africa were
the most important source of remittances. It is worth noting here that
the colonies were the main beneficiaries of remittances *from* the UK;
Australia, Canada and South Africa took 56, 42 and 17 per cent respectively of the value of the remittances they had sent to the UK: the USA
only 12 per cent.

It is clear from Table 3.3 that America, by some margin, remitted the
most money to the UK. Other than in the late 1890s, remittances from
America grew on average at a steady 7 to 8 per cent each year. By contrast, remittances from the empire grew at about 5 per cent per annum
until 1900, after which their rate of growth increased to over 12 per cent,
an acceleration that allowed the empire as a whole to overtake America
as the main source of remittances prior to the First World War.

Within the empire different patterns of remittance emerge. As one
might expect, it was the neo-Britains, or self-governing dominions, that
contributed most of the money received back home. Australia, until the
late 1880s, was the leading remittance source. With the onset of its major
depression at the end of that decade, however, real remittance flows con-
tracted sharply. They recovered again only during the years immediately

Table 3.3. *Total real remittances to the United Kingdom, 1875–1913 (1913 £millions).*

	Gross (Estimate 1)	Net (Estimate 1)	Gross (Estimate 2)	Net (Estimate 2)
Australia	8.6	3.8	11.1	6.1
Canada	14.6	8.5	18.9	12.6
New Zealand	4.0	2.6	5.2	3.7
South Africa	15.5	12.9	20.2	17.4
India	7.0	2.2	9.2	4.0
Empire	64.8	43.1	84.3	61.2
USA	86.1	75.5	117.9	106.7
Total	**199.4**	**132.6**	**268.5**	**197.8**

Note: Before 1895, South African figures are calculated from data on South and West Africa and the Cape Colony. Canada includes Newfoundland. Two estimates are provided, based on different assumptions. Estimate 1 is the more 'conservative' method.

Source: Magee and Thompson, 'Lines of Credit'.

before the First World War, when there was a renewed surge in its remittance activity, consistent with the rapid increase in empire migration at this time. New Zealand and Canada experienced a similar pre-war explosion of remittances, with the value of transfers from New Zealand more than doubling, and that from Canada quadrupling, between 1900 and 1913. In the latter part of the nineteenth century, the real remittances of both of these colonies had exhibited a much slower growth, punctuated at times by periods of actual decline, such as in the late 1880s and early 1890s in New Zealand, and in the late 1890s in Canada. In contrast, remittances from South Africa grew rapidly throughout the nineteenth century, reaching a peak during the Boer War, when thousands of British servicemen remitted pay back to their families.

Typical remitters in 1910–13 sent significantly more funds back to the UK than did their counterparts in 1875–9 (see Figure 3.3). Within the empire, South Africans and New Zealanders were typically the most generous remitters. In fact, until the second half of the 1890s they matched, if not exceeded, Americans in the sums of monies they were willing to send. The other striking feature of Figure 3.3 is the scale and almost continuous growth of remittances received from the average American remitter. Starting from a situation of parity in 1875–9, the average Briton residing in the United States was, by 1914, remitting more than three times as much as his or her compatriots in the

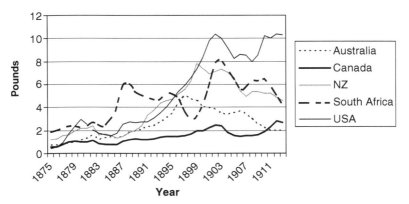

Figure 3.3 Real remittances to the UK per remitter, 1875–1913 (1913 £millions). Estimate 1 of remittances has been used. Canada includes Newfoundland.

settler societies of the empire.[148] Even in those parts of the British World where individuals were most keen to remit back to Britain – New Zealand and South Africa – the amounts each remitter transferred were the equivalent to no more than half of the corresponding American figure at this time.

The proportion of the average remitter's income sent to Britain can be read as a measure of his or her financial 'connectedness' to friends and family back home. The data in Figure 3.4 put the generosity of Canadian remitters in a more favourable light. They suggest that in the 1870s Canadians were a society that, on a personal level, was comparatively well connected to Britain. The data further confirm the high and growing level of involvement of migrants to America with their families in Britain. In the mid 1870s migrants in America and the settler colonies remitted roughly similar proportions of their income. Thereafter, a divide opens up. By 1910–13, the average American remitter was choosing to send a proportion of income back to the UK around four times greater than his or her counterpart in the neo-Britains – in other words, roughly one in every six to seven dollars earned compared to one in every twenty-five.

[148] What explains the size of the average US remittance? It is worth remembering (a) that the nature of the US labour market, and the cheapness and ease of getting to the US, made it attractive to early returners who brought back capital to buy assets in the UK; and (b) that migrants often exceeded average savings rates in Britain, as many left the country on their own, yet determined either to bring their families out later or to return themselves: contemporary remittance behaviour underlines this point.

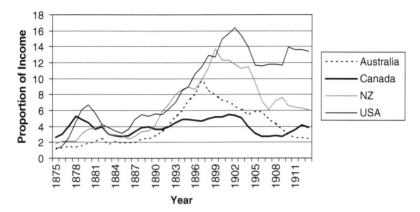

Figure 3.4 Proportion of average remitter's income sent as remittances to the UK, 1875–1913. South Africa has not been included in this figure since GDP data prior to 1913 are not available. Estimate 1 of remittances has been used. Canada includes Newfoundland.

The Cornish in South Africa were among the most prolific remitters.[149] From the 1880s Cornwall provided a highly mobile and skilled workforce that made a major contribution to the gold-mining industry around Johannesburg – they formed about a quarter of the white mining workforce by the beginning of the twentieth century, some 10,000 miners in all.[150] Though some were permanent settlers who took their loved ones with them, most went alone. The families whom they left behind would anxiously await the arrival of a regular remittance in the South African

---

[149] Our reason for selecting Cornwall to illustrate the importance of remittances for local communities is simple: there is a rich historiography on the Cornish diaspora, much of which has been published under the aegis of the Institute of Cornish Studies at the University of Exeter. See especially here P. Payton, *The Cornish Overseas* (Fowey: Alexander Associates, 1999). That said, the social and economic impacts of remittance transfers can also be explored for other regions in the UK. Here the reader's attention is directed towards Marjory Harper's seminal studies of Scottish emigration, helpfully summarised in her recent *Adventurers and Exiles*, which, *inter alia*, highlights the function of remittances in chain migration, the close relationship between remittances and migrant correspondence, the different patterns of remittance behaviour between farmers and artisans, and the hardship caused by a breakdown in the transmission of earnings to dependants at home; see pp. 93, 111, 188, 27, 306. Meanwhile, C. Erickson (ed.), *Emigration from Europe, 1815–1914: Select Documents* (London: A. and C. Black, 1976), pp. 139, 231–2; and Richards, *Britannia's Children*, pp. 144, 166–8, lay emphasis on the importance of remittances in providing the pre-paid tickets that brought the friends and relatives of migrant labourers and artisans to the USA.

[150] R. Dawe, *Cornish Pioneers in South Africa: 'Gold and Diamonds, Copper and Blood'* (St Austell: Cornish Hillside Publications, 1998), pp. xv, 123.

mail.[151] According to contemporary estimates, in the mid 1890s in Redruth alone a weekly sum of approximately £1,000 was received, while by the early 1900s it was thought that every mail was bringing £20,000 to £30,000 for 'the wives and families and the old folks at home'.[152] Many Cornish families were reliant on the money that came from the Transvaal goldmines. Hence when the South African mail arrived, people would flock into the towns from the surrounding villages to collect their money, and business in local shops would boom.[153] Conversely, when the 'home pay' did not arrive, the county's Board of Guardians were left to pick up the pieces – though they themselves were helped by the charitable work of several Cornish Associations on the Rand, organisations that also played a key role in raising relief funds for the widows and orphans of miners killed in accidents or by lung disease. Other beneficiaries of South African remittances included Cornish schools, places of worship and community projects. In this way, Cornish miners were able to strengthen and reaffirm ties to their former communities. Moreover, this inflow of remittances need not necessarily be viewed pessimistically in terms of 'propping up' an ailing Cornish economy. Rather, it has been argued that remittances played a more constructive role by 'lessening constraints upon production and investment' in several areas of Cornwall.[154] Whether viewed negatively or positively, however, it is clear that the constant flow of remittances from South Africa provided a lifeline for Cornwall until at least the First World War.

A closer analysis of why migrants remitted monies home lends weight to the view that family networks were the lynchpin of the migration process. Above everything else, sending money home to relatives was an expression of obligation to them, and of gratitude for their help in establishing the migrant in more economically rewarding circumstances. Although separated from their family by great distances, migrants continued to feel responsible for the wives, children, parents and other dependent relatives they had left behind. They conceived of their move as a strategy to maximise the income and material well-being not just of themselves but of the family as a whole. Driven by this implicit contract, remittances could be sent almost irrespective of income. Thus it is underlying notions of duty

[151] S. P. Schwartz and R. Parker, *Tin Mines and Miners of Lanner: The Heart of Cornish Tin* (London: Halsgrove Press, 2001), pp. 157–8.
[152] C. Lewis Hind, *Days in Cornwall* (London: Methuen, 1907), p. 352, quoted in Payton, *The Cornish Overseas*, p. 347.
[153] Payton, *The Cornish Overseas*, p. 245.
[154] S. P. Schwartz, 'Cornish Migration Studies: An Epistemological and Paradigmatic Critique', in P. Payton (ed.), *Cornish Studies* 10 (2002), 136–65 (quotation from p. 151).

and kinship that mainly account for these monetary flows – by sending monies home migrants were able to protect the integrity of the family unit, to support and strengthen kinship networks, and to mesh together family and household economies both in the newly adopted country and their place of birth. Indeed, remittances were perhaps the most tangible manifestation of the benefits that migration could bring, and of the tenacity of 'Old'-world social ties.

In several respects, the remittance behaviour of American and empire-bound migrants was strikingly similar. Our data suggest that many migrants to the United States, just like those who left for the colonies, continued to be deeply connected to British society for some time after their arrival. Averaged across our period, remittances per migrant were considerably higher for those people who went to the United States; and this disparity, if anything, grew over time. To be sure, the high levels of monies sent back to Britain by American migrants partly reflect the better economic opportunities and high real wage levels there. Yet, equally, they reflect the strength of kith-and-kin ties – a mutually sustaining and beneficial Anglo-American relationship at 'grass-root' level.

Nonetheless, the distinctive nature of emigration from the United Kingdom to the United States, when compared to other parts of the British World, did lead to real differences in remittance behaviour. Lower transport costs to America facilitated short-term, seasonal labour migration, so that a significant number of skilled workers who migrated across the Atlantic had no fixed intention of staying,[155] and 'even among those who did remain, the possibility of returning to Britain constituted an active alternative choice for some time'.[156] American consuls, for example, remarked on the fact that many British migrants were intent on remaining only for a few years, their objective being to return with enough money to live in comparative comfort in the UK.[157] Such migrants – or 'birds of passage', as they were called – were rarely accompanied by their dependants, and tended to have relatively high rates of saving out of their earned income. Their aim was to build up a nest egg in America with a view to setting up in business or acquiring land on their return, or providing for their retirement in the UK. English bricklayers in New York, Welsh

---

[155] Whereas it is argued that return migration from Australia was much less likely because the 'real and psychic distances between Europe and Australia were much greater than those between Europe and America', and many Australian migrants were 'modest folk' (e.g. domestic servants and agricultural labourers) who were unlikely to have prospered so quickly that they could afford a double passage; see E. Richards, 'Running Home from Australia: Intercontinental Mobility and Migrant Expectations in the Nineteenth Century', in Harper, *Emigrant Homecomings*, pp. 77–104.

[156] Erickson, *Invisible Immigrants*, p. 236.

[157] Magee and Thompson, 'The Global and the Local', p. 192.

colliers in Pennsylvania, Aberdeen granite masons in New England and Sheffield steel workers in Pittsburgh all fit this pattern.[158] They either remitted money in anticipation of their return, or returned home with their savings. For such US-based remitters, earning capacity was paramount; funding future rounds of migration, or accumulating assets in America, were matters of lesser importance.

The most striking feature of the remittance story of the 'long' nineteenth century is the skill and tenacity with which British migrants forged long-distance social ties. The sending of monies home – both the sheer scale of the flows *and* the variety of purposes to which they were put – is testimony to how previous generations of migrants were able to construct complex webs or networks of association stretching all the way from their place of settlement to their place of origin. By so doing, migrants maintained a multiplicity of involvements in their home and host societies, on an ongoing and regular basis. The role of the latest round of technological innovations in promoting trans-nationalism can easily be exaggerated, therefore. While airplanes, fax machines, mobile phones and electronic mail have, in the late-twentieth and early-twenty-first centuries, greatly facilitated contact between people of the same background, they should not be seen as the sine qua non of trans-national communities.[159] What we need to appreciate is that many British migrants before the First World War were effectively living in two places simultaneously – resident overseas yet displaying a psychological and practical commitment to their 'homeland'. For these people, whether they left for the colonies, or for the United States, their departure was not so much a case of 'cut and run', as of run, remit and eventually (perhaps) return.

Britishness

The whole process of migration provides many more possibilities for identity. For the British it had three main implications. First, they began to generalise about themselves in relation to others, and to express ethnic, racial and religious solidarities in new ways.[160] A strong sense of cultural

---

[158] Bodnar, *The Transplanted*, pp. 60–1; W. D. Jones, *Wales in America: Scranton and the Welsh, 1860–1920* (Cardiff: University of Wales Press, 1993), pp. xx, 11, 16, 178–88, 195–201; M. Harper, 'Transient Tradesmen: Aberdeen Emigrants and the Development of the American Granite Industry', *Northern Scotland* 9 (1989), 53–74 (pp. 56–7); Murdoch, *British Emigration*, pp. 111, 118; S. Thuernstorm (ed.), *Harvard Encyclopaedia of American Ethnic Groups* (Cambridge, MA: Harvard University Press, 1980), pp. 326, 330.

[159] A. Portes, 'Globalization from Below: the Rise of Transnational Communities', in W. P. Smith and R. P. Korczenwicz (eds.), *Latin America in the World Economy* (Westport: Greenwood Publishing Group, 1996), pp. 151–68.

[160] Manning, *Migration in World History*, pp. 138–9, 154.

superiority developed among them,[161] as they increasingly defined themselves not just in terms of who they were but who they were not.[162] This negative and oppositional sense of British identity was sharpened by settlers' contact with indigenous peoples and by the arrival of migrants from other places – the impact of the latter upon labour markets is considered briefly below. Suffice it to say here that the mass migration of the British peoples during the 'long' nineteenth century provoked fierce struggles with the original inhabitants of colonised lands,[163] as well as settler resistance to other types of non-European migration, expressed most explicitly by the 'White' Australia policy that effectively barred the vast majority of Asians from entering the dominion on a permanent basis, and whose discriminatory effects were experienced by immigrants for decades to come.[164]

Second, the family was a foundational form of migrant identity from which other forms of group identity, including national identity, grew. More than anything else, the 'bridge' or 'chain' that linked the 'New' world to the 'Old' was the family. It was frequently in response to overtures from relatives that migrants decided to relocate overseas, while their adaptation to a new and unfamiliar environment was eased by structures of 'kith and kin'. This meant that 'Britishness' was not only a geographically expansive concept but a highly personalised one. It reflected, in a very practical sense, the desire of migrants to continue to be involved in a society that they might have left behind but had certainly not abandoned.

Third, from the mid nineteenth century, the nation state, whether imagined as a piece of territory or a framework of administration, could no longer serve as the sole repository of a British identity.[165] The transnational networks of exchange and participation examined earlier in this

---

[161] Bayly, *The Birth of the Modern World*, pp. 432–50; M. J. Daunton and R. Halpern (eds.), *Empire and Others: British Encounters with Indigenous Peoples, 1600–1850* (Philadelphia: University of Pennsylvania Press, 1998); L. Russell (ed.), *Colonial Frontiers: Indigenous–European Encounters in Settler Societies* (Manchester: Manchester University Press, 2001).

[162] L. Colley, 'Britishness and Otherness: An Argument', *JBS* 31 (1992), 309–29; C. Hall, *Civilising Subjects: Metropole and Colony in the English Imagination, 1830–67* (Cambidge: Cambridge University Press, 2002); J. K. Walton, 'Britishness', in C. Wrigley (ed.), *A Companion to Early Twentieth Century Britain* (Oxford: Oxford University Press, 2003), pp. 518, 522.

[163] For a penetrating account of the impact of European settlement on indigenous peoples, and the dynamics of black–white interaction that result, see R. Broome, *Aboriginal Victorians: A History since 1800* (Crows Nest, NSW: Allen and Unwin, 2005). For an insightful study of how racial knowledge and the idea of a 'white man's nation' circulated across an Anglo-American settler world, see Lake and Reynolds, *Drawing the Global Colour Line*.

[164] J. Jupp, *From White Australia to Woomera: The Story of Australian Immigration* (Cambridge: Cambridge University Press, 2002).

[165] For the diasporic identities resulting from migration, and their implications for the nation state, see Guarnizo and Smith, 'The Locations of Transnationalism', pp. 3–34.

chapter were grounded upon a perception that emigrants from Britain shared a common identity based on their place of origin and the cultural and linguistic traits associated with it.[166] The new technologies of the Victorian era – railways, steamships, overland and undersea cables, remittance and postal services – all worked to expand a migrant's geographical horizons and to encourage him or her to adopt a wider frame of reference.

These new structures of settler consciousness did not escape contemporary comment. Inspired by the vision of a 'racial community of Britons',[167] Sir Charles Dilke (1843–1911), James Anthony Froude (1818–94) and Sir John Seeley (1834–95) all spoke poignantly about the social consequences of demographic expansion, and how it had engendered a sense of the British peoples as a trans-oceanic community, tied together by a shared sense of purpose and a collective memory. Seeley's *The Expansion of England* (1883) put migration at the heart of British national identity: 'our Empire is not an Empire at all in the ordinary sense of the word. It does not consist of a congeries of nations held together by force, but in the main one nation, as much as if it were no Empire but an ordinary state'.[168]

Migrants were proud of their heritage.[169] Yet this did not mean they were content simply to keep alive 'old' sentiments, institutions and

For the British case specifically, see D. Marquand, 'How United is the Modern United Kingdom?', in A. Grant and K. J. Stringer (eds.), *Uniting the Kingdom?: The Making of British History* (London: Routledge, 1995), pp. 277–92 (pp. 286–8), and 'The Twilight of the British State? Henry Dubb versus Sceptred Awe', in S. J. D. Green and R. C. Whiting (eds.), *The Boundaries of the State in Modern Britain* (Cambridge: Cambridge University Press, 1996), pp. 57–69.

[166] For the relationship between these two concepts, see S. Vertovec, 'Transnationalism and Identity', *Journal of Ethnic and Migration Studies* 27 (2001), 573–82.

[167] See for example R. Coll's observation that 'The crown colonies were administered by the imperial state but not considered a part of that state, except ceremonially. The "white" dominions were self-governing and considered close, close enough to be admitted to the counsels of state.' R. Coll, *Identity of England* (Oxford: Oxford University Press, 2002), p. 93.

[168] J. R. Seeley, *The Expansion of England*, ed. and introduced J. Gross (Chicago: Cosimo, 1971), p. 44.

[169] There is a growing body of literature on how migrants evaluated their struggles and successes in the light of what they knew about their brethren in other settler societies. On science, see S. Dubow, 'The Commonwealth of Science: The British Association in South Africa, 1905–29', in Dubow (ed.), *Science and Society in Southern Africa* (Manchester: Manchester University Press, 2000), pp. 66–100. On skilled labour, see J. Hyslop, *The Notorious Syndicalist: J. T. Bain, a Scottish Rebel in Colonial South Africa* (Johannesburg: Jacana Media, 2004), and 'The Imperial Working Class Makes Itself "White": White Labourism in Britain, Australia and South Africa before the First World War', *Journal of Historical Sociology* (1999), 398–424. On administrators, see Z. Laidlaw, *Colonial Connections, 1815–45: Patronage, the Information Revolution and Colonial Government* (Basingstoke: Palgrave Macmillan, 2005). On missionaries and

values.[170] Rather, they 'insisted that they had the freedom to improve upon the parent culture in lands of "new" beginnings'. Within carefully prescribed racial boundaries, therefore, migrant conceptions of what it meant to be 'British' tended to place merit and virtue before class and status. Responsible government, the secret ballot, women's suffrage, 'secular, compulsory and free' schooling – all these were established in the colonies well before they were in the United Kingdom.[171] As we have seen, the settler colonies not only experimented with these ideas about how best to order society: they exported them back to Britain.[172]

Possibly the most complex of the dimensions to the diasporic identity of the British peoples, however, is that arising from the Anglo-American connection. Prominent personalities of the age – Winston Churchill, Sir Charles Dilke, Cecil Rhodes, Lord Rosebery and W. T. Stead – conceived of 'Greater Britain' as a wider English-speaking rather than a narrowly imperial union of peoples.[173] But not all politicians and businessmen were so receptive to ideas of an Anglo-Saxon brotherhood. What had once been a loyal and friendly offshoot of Britain was increasingly viewed with a measure of jealousy and suspicion.[174]

How large, then, did an 'Anglo-Saxon' mentality loom in the imaginations of the British peoples before the First World War? What implications did it have for the construction of 'British' identities? Legal, religious, literary and marriage ties have all been invoked to explain why the United States and Britain 'drifted together' after 1850, as have the influence of American inventions, the growth of travel between the two countries and the long-term presence of several wealthy American families in London.[175] The evidence presented in this chapter strongly suggests

humanitarians, see E. Elbourne, *Blood Ground: Colonialism, Missions and the Contest for Christianity in the Cape Colony and Britain, 1799–1853* (Montreal: McGill-Queen's University Press, 2002); and A. Lester, *Imperial Networks: Creating Identities in Nineteenth Century South Africa and Britain* (London: Routledge, 2001). On professional migrants more broadly, see Thompson, *The Empire Strikes Back?*, pp. 17–29.

[170] Owram, *Promise of Eden*, p. 144.

[171] C. Bridge and K. Fedorowich, 'Mapping the British World', in Bridge and Fedorowich (eds.), *The British World: Culture, Diaspora and Identity* (London: Taylor and Francis, 2003), pp. 1–15 (p. 6).

[172] *Ibid.*, pp. 6–7. See also M. Taylor, 'The 1848 Revolutions and the British Empire', *Past & Present* 166 (2000), 146–80 (pp. 178–9); C. Hall, 'Rethinking Imperial Histories: The Reform Act of 1867', *New Left Review* 208 (1994), 3–29 (pp. 9, 14–15, 29), and *Civilising Subjects*, pp. 12, 21, 424–5; and Thompson, *The Empire Strikes Back?*, pp. 144–6.

[173] Although each interpreted Anglo-Saxonism differently: see Heindel, *The American Impact on Great Britain*, pp. 126–9. See, for example, the examination of Charles Dilke's 'Anglo-Saxonism', and his views of Anglo-American relations, in R. C. Young, *The Idea of English Ethnicity* (Oxford: Blackwell, 2007), pp. 196–207.

[174] Thompson, *Imperial Britain*, p. 36.

[175] See here Bayly, *The Birth of the Modern World*, pp. 432–50; Perkins, *The Great Rapprochement*, pp. 149–53; and G. R. Searle, *A New England? Peace and War, 1886–1918*

that, from the 1850s through to the First World War, migration worked to forge a stronger consciousness of America in British society than is sometimes appreciated. There was, in fact, an 'astonishing increase in popular knowledge of the United States' throughout the British Isles, resulting from emigrant guidebooks and publicity material, and a flood of novels and newspapers describing American geography, economic life, institutions and, above all, pioneer life in the West.[176] For example, as newspapers in Wales carried ever-greater volumes of news and information from America, several Welsh settlements there became 'household names' in areas of high out-migration.[177]

This is not to deny that the experience of British migrants to America was different from that of those to the colonies. Indeed, there are several reasons why this was so. Partly it was because of what happened to the English who went to America. They 'felt stronger pressure than other immigrants to prove their patriotism', so much so that it was by no means uncommon for those who 'spoke fondly of their place of birth' to be 'confronted with accusations of disloyalty'.[178] There are even stories of farmers in the Old Northwest painting great American flags on their barns at the time of the Civil War (1861–5) so as to leave no doubt of loyalty to their adopted country. Others went further and lined up for military service on the side of the Union. For many, the Civil War itself intensified the process of Americanisation, making them more than ever 'invisible immigrants'.

Americans, therefore, tended to be suspicious of English immigrants, especially when they did not readily agree on the superiority of the United States' system of (republican) government. To some extent, these attitudes softened later in the nineteenth century, as more Americans began to recognise their historic and cultural ties to Britain, and to regard the Anglo-Saxon inheritance as a joint possession of both countries.[179] That

---

(Oxford: Oxford University Press, 2004), pp. 26–8. For the significance of Anglo-American technological exchanges, see Graeme Gooday's study of the early domestication of electricity: *Domesticating Electricity: Technology, Uncertainty and Gender, 1880–1914* (London: Pickering and Chatto, 2008). For an earlier recognition of the importance of literature and travel in forging an Anglo-American culture, see Heindel, *The American Impact on Great Britain*, pp. 43ff, 299ff.

[176] M. A. Jones, *American Immigration* (Chicago: University of Chicago Press, 1992), p. 84; Murdoch, *British Emigration*, p. 136; J. Rose, *The Intellectual Life of the British Working Classes* (New Haven: Yale University Press, 2002), pp. 350–62.

[177] B. Jones, '*Raising the Wind*', pp. 36–40.

[178] Van Vugt, *Britain to America*, pp. 145–8, from which all of the following quotes are sourced.

[179] H. M. Jones, *The Age of Energy: Varieties of American Experience, 1865–1915* (New York: Viking Press, 1971), p. 265; W. E. Van Vugt, *British Buckeyes: The English, Scots, and Welsh in Ohio, 1700–1900* (Kent, OH: Kent State University Press, 2006), pp. 56–8.

said, hostilities to Britain were from time to time reignited by diplomatic rivalries, such as those stemming from the intervention of the Cleveland administration in a boundary dispute between Britain and Venezuela between 1895 and 1896,[180] as well as by economic rivalries in overseas markets and a dispute over a proposed trade reciprocity treaty between the USA and Canada in 1910–11.[181]

More than anything else, however, it was the rapidly changing complexion of America's migrant population that explains why it is so hard to pin down its position in the British World. By the end of the nineteenth century, immigrants to the United States were arriving from many more places than immigrants to Britain's settler colonies.[182] In 1860, people born in the United Kingdom and Germany made up no less than 80 per cent of America's foreign-born population. (The significance of German immigrants should not be underestimated here. A German–American Alliance, formed in 1901, had a membership of over 2 million by 1914.)[183] Forty years later, the English, Scots and Welsh together accounted for just 14 per cent of America's foreign-born population, compared to 30 per cent for the Germans, still the largest single foreign-born group. The Irish accounted for a further 11 per cent.

By this time, the rate of natural population increase was decelerating in the west of Europe while increasing in the south and east, as the latter rapidly established itself as the main source of immigration to the United States.[184] Natives of Russia, Austria-Hungary and Italy, which in 1860 had made up only 1.2 per cent of America's foreign-born population, were now no less than 37.5 per cent of the total.[185] The arrival of immigrants with unfamiliar languages and cultures was one of the reasons why Britons and Americans became more aware of what they had in common.[186] A comparison with Canada is instructive. The complexion of Canada's prairie population likewise began to diversify during the early twentieth century. Yet Britain continued to be the main source of immigration to western Canada all the way up to 1914, accounting for a half of the population of Manitoba and British Columbia, and a third

---

[180] A. Orde, *The Eclipse of Great Britain: The United States and British Imperial Decline, 1895–1956* (Basingstoke: Palgrave Macmillan, 1996), pp. 10–11.

[181] W. E. Davies, *Patriotism on Parade: The Story of Veterans' and Hereditary Organisations in America* (Cambridge, MA: Harvard University Press, 1955), pp. 310–16; Thompson, *Imperial Britain*, pp. 96–7.

[182] W. T. K. Nugent, *Crossings: The Great Transatlantic Migrations, 1870–1914* (Bloomington: University of Indiana Press, 1992), pp. 150–1.

[183] Perkins, *The Great Rapprochement*, p. 141.

[184] W. Arthur Lewis, *Growth and Fluctuations, 1870–1913* (London: G. Allen and Unwin, 1978), p. 181.

[185] Figures from Jones, *American Immigration*, p. 178.

[186] Van Vugt, *British Buckeyes*, p. 61.

of that of Saskatchewan and Alberta.[187] It was the gradual dilution of America's demographic connection to Britain that diminished the sense that 'it was still the product of the diaspora'. By the end of our period 'it had become home to many different diasporas, most notably those of Italy and Eastern Europe'.[188]

Conclusions

If the phenomenon of globalisation is about 'the closer integration of the countries and peoples of the world',[189] then flows of migrants across national borders have long been integral to it. The great migration of the 'long' nineteenth century was the most intensive period of migration in human history. It saw an unparalleled 100 million people move around the world – perhaps as many as one in every ten people may have been affected by this experience.[190] A quarter of these migrants were European, and the United Kingdom was the largest source of migrants within Europe, exporting on average around 2 million people per decade from the 1870s to the 1920s.

One effect of this mass movement of peoples was an impressive convergence in living standards across Britain, the United States, Canada and Australasia – a key measure of economic integration according to a leading historical study of globalisation.[191] Yet for globalisation to be useful as a concept it needs to take account not only of the physical 'conquest of distance' but of the resulting 'intensification of consciousness of the world as a whole'.[192] In his exploration of the cultural dimensions of globalisation, Arjun Appadurai makes precisely this point. He argues that mass migration has transformed the way 'the imagination works as a social force' in today's world.[193] For Appadurai and other cultural theorists this development has largely been a recent one – the conjunction of modern forms of migration and electronic forms of communication. This is questionable. Mass migration from Britain after 1850 had a profound impact on the 'manner in which people viewed the world

[187] J. Barman, *The West beyond the West: A History of British Columbia* (Toronto: University of Toronto Press, 1996), p. 382.
[188] Richards, *Britannia's Children*, p. 209.
[189] J. E. Stiglitz, *Globalization and Its Discontents* (London: W. W. Norton, 2002), p. 9.
[190] Manning, *Migration in World History*, p. 149; A. MacGillivray, *A Brief History of Globalization: The Untold Story of Our Incredible Shrinking Planet* (London: Carroll and Graf, 2006), pp. 151–2.
[191] O'Rourke and Williamson, *Globalization and History*, pp. 1–28.
[192] R. Robertson, *Globalization: Social Theory and Global Culture* (London: Sage, 1992), p. 8.
[193] A. Appadurai, *Modernity at Large: Cultural Dimensions of Globalization* (Minneapolis: University of Minneapolis, 1996), p. 6.

and their relationship to it'.[194] The technological developments of these years did not simply 'open up dizzying possibilities of enhanced global mobility'.[195] They also affected how migrants – and the families they left behind – imagined their social and political spaces, thereby making their migrations a defining aspect of their identity. Improvements in communications and transport technology – in their time no less powerful than those we are witnessing at present – brought the British peoples 'at home' and overseas into more frequent and intimate contact with each other. One consequence of this was that many of those who left Britain saw themselves as belonging, to varying degrees, to a 'commonwealth of nations', the nucleus of which was the Anglo-Dominion relationship, but which radiated outwards towards other English-speaking societies, including the United States.

Of course, mass migration was not exclusively European. A considerable international flow of indentured or contract labour was generated by British (and French) colonialism, and there were domestic flows of indigenous labour within colonial regions.[196] For the most part, however, these two streams of migration, voluntary and coerced, did not mix. 'Differences in economic circumstances, geography, and imperial polices were responsible for directing most European immigrants to other temperate destinations, while African, Asian and Pacific Islanders went largely to tropical ones.'[197] Yet there were regions where these two migratory streams did mix, and here the power of imperial networks to discriminate against coloured peoples, and to exclude them from 'the privileges of responsibility and skill', was markedly apparent.[198] This power consisted not only of the formal power of the colonial state, but the informal power conferred by belonging to a pan-British community, membership of which, while open to negotiation,[199] was profoundly skewed along ethnic and racial lines.

[194] Bell, 'Dissolving Distance: Technology, Space and Empire in British Political Thought, 1770–1900', *Journal of Modern History* 77 (2005), 561–2.

[195] Constantine, 'Migrants and Settlers', p. 163.

[196] Northrup, *Indentured Labour in the Age of Imperialism*, and 'Migration from Africa, Asia, and the South Pacific', pp. 88–100; O. W. Parnaby, *Britain and the Labor Trade in the South West Pacific* (Durham, NC: Duke University Press, 1964); S. Marks and P. Richardson (eds.), *International Labour Migration: Historical Perspectives* (London: Maurice Temple Smith for the Institute of Commonwealth Studies, 1984); H. L. Wesseling, *The European Colonial Empires, 1815–1919* (Harlow: Pearson–Longman, 2004), pp. 18–19.

[197] Northrup, 'Migration from Africa, Asia, and the South Pacific', p. 96.

[198] Offer, *The First World War*, p. 168.

[199] As J. Ridden argues, 'Debates about identity were concerned with pragmatic benefits and power relations, as well as issues of emotional and cultural attachment.' For Irish Catholics, see J. Ridden, 'Britishness as an Imperial and Diasporic Identity: Irish Elite Perspectives, *c.* 1820–70s', in P. Gray (ed.), *Victoria's Ireland? Irishness and Britishness, 1837–1901* (Dublin: Four Courts Press, 2004), pp. 88–105 (quotation from p. 89).

The railways were one of the major sites of conflict between British, Asian and African migrant workers. Take the case of South Africa. Well before the mineral revolution's escalating demands for wage labour, racial discrimination was a firm feature of economic networks there. During the 1870s, the building of the Cape railways saw large numbers of white workers arrive from Britain via an emigration service that was supported by Cape funds, employed a full-time agent and staff in London, and exploited contacts in the labour market in the west of England.[200] In this way, the Cape railways were able to draw in British workers, who eventually comprised a third of the total workforce. They were employed as skilled artisans, and as semi- and unskilled navvies tackling rock-cutting and other heavy work. The need for speed and economy in railway construction partly explains the Cape government's willingness to pay a higher price for white labour. But there were also powerful pressures from colonists to keep the wage rises of black workers within bounds, and to swell the 'civilised sector' of the population by further settlement from Britain.

The construction of the CPR – one of the great feats of nineteenth-century railway building – was also a source of racial tension. This time the conflict was between the white workers who were laid off on the CPR's completion, yet decided to remain in Canada, and the so-called Chinese 'coolies', migrants mostly from the poorer rural districts of south-east China. The Chinese workers were brought out on the initiative of a young American entrepreneur and federal government contractor, Andrew Onderdonk. Tasked with building the most difficult mountain section of the line, running from the Rockies to the Pacific, Onderdonk relied heavily on the Chinese. He knew of their capabilities through having managed major public works in San Francisco on which they had previously been employed. In the early 1880s approximately 15,000 Chinese men entered British Columbia, many of them travelling in organised groups and residing in railroad camps supervised by a contracting agent.[201]

A significant number of these Chinese contract labourers lost their lives to injury and disease.[202] Those who survived discovered that they

---

For anglicised Afrikaners, see M. Tamarkin, *Cecil Rhodes and the Cape Afrikaners: The Imperial Colossus and the Colonial Parish Pump* (London: Routledge, 1996).

[200] A. J. Purkis, 'The Politics, Capital and Labour of Railway Building in the Cape Colony, 1870–1885', unpublished D.Phil. thesis, University of Oxford (1978), pp. 330–90, 441–56. See also A. S. Thompson, 'The Power and Privileges of Association: Co-Ethnic Networks and the Economic Life of the British Imperial World', *SAHJ* 56 (2006), 43–59 (p. 56).

[201] M. Bliss, *Northern Enterprise: Five Centuries of Canadian Business* (Toronto: University of Toronto Press, 1987), pp. 216, 219.

[202] Knowles, *Strangers at Our Gates*, p. 50.

were not to be repatriated after their contracts expired, earlier promises notwithstanding.[203] Despite having little choice but to stay in Canada, they were accused by British Columbia's infant labour movement of taking jobs away from Europeans and of threatening their rates of pay. In fact, Chinese immigrants in Canada were mostly employed casually in work no-one else wanted to do, such as logging, farming or salmon canning, or domestic service or laundry, although there were direct clashes with white workers in the sugar mills and the coalmines. Their presence in Canada resulted in the formation of anti-Chinese societies to curb workplace competition, as well as the introduction of company regulations and restrictive legislation that forbade the use of Chinese labour.[204] Subsequently, such measures were extended to ban the Chinese from government employment, to subject them to special taxes, to deny them certain forms of legal protection and to prevent male residents from acquiring wives overseas. There were also riots in Vancouver in 1887 and 1907 aimed at intimidating the Chinese from competing with white workers.

British migrants, by contrast, enjoyed privileged access to the networks via which they moved, and proved adept at exploiting these networks for their own gain.[205] Indeed, as recent research shows, the dynamic international labour market that was such a marked feature of the nineteenth-century English-speaking (or Anglophone) world, and of the integration of its commodity and financial markets, was animated by a shared sense of proletarian Britishness.[206] A doctrine of 'white labourism' or racial socialism was widely espoused. It manifested itself particularly powerfully during the controversy over Chinese indentured labour in South Africa, when skilled workers from England, Wales, Scotland and Ireland who had migrated to Transvaal challenged the presence of 'ethnic outsiders' in the workplace who threatened to undercut their wages. But the doctrine is evident more broadly in the remittance capital flows examined above, and the networks that underpinned them. Remittances might

---

[203] Barman, *The West beyond the West*, pp. 133–48; Lower, *Western Canada*, pp. 147–8.

[204] For the discrimination they faced, see, especially, P. S. Li, *The Chinese in Canada* (Toronto: Canadian Historical Association, 1988), pp. 11–31; P. Ward, *White Canada Forever: Popular Attitudes and Public Policy toward Orientals in British Columbia* (Montreal: McGill-Queen's University Press, 1978), p. 1048; E. Wickberg (ed.), *From China to Canada: A History of Chinese Communities in Canada* (Toronto: McClelland and Stewart, 1982), pp. 21–7.

[205] M. Boyd, 'Family and Personal Networks in International Migration: Recent Developments and New Agendas', *International Migration Review* 23 (1989), 638–70.

[206] Hyslop, 'The Imperial Working Class Makes Itself "White"'. See also Kirk, *Comrades and Cousins*, pp. 14, 158–9, 203ff, who draws distinctions between the attitudes of

even be likened to a form of imperial-wide social insurance – part of a bigger push to shore up a separate racial status, including job security, better pay and higher standards of welfare, for *British* citizens.

In several spheres, these migrant networks exercised an important influence upon economic behaviour. The case of the law is instructive.[207] With the exceptions of Quebec and South Africa, a common-law culture spread throughout the British World and remained largely peculiar to it.[208] Commercial law (property, contract and tort) was wedded to English solutions. This was not a result of jurists in Canada, Australia and New Zealand deferring to the 'mother country'; nor was it because of the threat of appeal to the Privy Council. Rather, colonial jurists saw 'the Law of Westminster' as supreme. Here it is important to appreciate that, for much of our period, the settler colonies had relatively few jurists who were born and trained in their own land – the first Australian-born jurist was not appointed in New South Wales until 1881. The majority of jurists were professional emigrants, who regarded themselves 'as proud bearers of Britain's common-law tradition'. Unlike their American counterparts – and in this respect the USA *did* differ from Britain's settler colonies – they were not empowered to make new common law for themselves. To be sure, they tended to ignore English precedent when it stood in the way of their own perceptions of social justice. Yet locally fashioned law was offset by a body of English precedent contained in legal reports and treatises, which, it should be noted, were much more widely available in the colonies than were the reports of American judicial authorities.

As well as taking their legal culture with them, migrants carried their material culture too. They had to be clothed, housed and fed, and this presented opportunities for British manufacturers, the nature and significance of which are explored in the next chapter. In their rapid creation

socialists in Britain and those in the settler colonies, the former asserting the supremacy of class over race and racism, the latter race over class. For an exploration of the racial attitudes of British workers through the prism of the Chinese indentured labour controversy in the early twentieth century, see Thompson, *The Empire Strikes Back?*, pp. 69–72.

[207] The rest of this paragraph draws on P. Karsten's path-breaking study: *Between Law and Custom: 'High' and 'Low' Legal Cultures in the Lands of the British Diaspora. The United States, Canada, Australia and New Zealand, 1600–1900* (Cambridge: Cambridge University Press, 2002), esp. pp. 7–9, 498–519. All quotations are from this source. On the spread of (capitalist) concepts of property, see also A. R. Buck, J. McLaren and N. E. Wright (eds.), *Land and Freedom: Law, Property Rights and the British Diaspora* (Aldershot: Ashgate, 2001).

[208] In Quebec, there was an explicitly civil (French) law jurisdiction by the end of the nineteenth century. In South Africa, there were substantial elements of Roman–Dutch law. India, by contrast, drew heavily upon Hindu and Muslim systems of law, as well as that of England.

of new infrastructure – especially transport infrastructure – migrants, moreover, needed capital and credit. British investors, both institutional and private, supplied much of this money. Their information-determined preference for colonial stocks and shares was an important feature of financial markets in the second half of the nineteenth century, and is explored in Chapter 5.

4   Markets and consumer cultures

Introduction

This chapter explores a key feature of late-nineteenth and early-twentieth-century globalisation, namely the emergence of the empire's settler societies as the fastest-growing export market for the British 'metropole'.[1] Not only did these colonies consume comparatively high levels of British exports, the share of income they devoted to British goods also deepened relative to other parts of the developed and developing world over time. The latter is an intriguing fact with implications for how we perceive the evolution of colonial consumer behaviour prior to the First World War. Most importantly, it suggests a quickening of economic relationships within the British World at this time: a more precise and intensive drawing together of the interests and needs of Britain and its settler colonies. Migrant consumers, it seems, were becoming more, not less, wedded to the British product, as other competing uses for their income, such as the consumption of local or foreign (non-British) goods and services, became available to them. Why, then, did British products fare so well in these markets, and why did colonial consumers, by that time free to buy from anyone in the international marketplace, spend such a large share of their income on them?

We argue that a good part of the answer lies in the rich and layered interconnections that characterised the British World – the ethnic and cultural ties that bound settlers emotionally, financially and spiritually to 'home'. Thus, at root, the dominions' ability to absorb high volumes of British imports from the mid century had its origins in British

---

[1] Detailed studies of the character of British colonial trade date back at least as far as John Stuart Mill. According to Mill, British colonial trade was so 'British' that it was not really external trade at all, but domestic. Mill's focus, however, was on the mid nineteenth century and the colonial dependencies – territories not at liberty to set their own fiscal or monetary policy, and which functioned as specialised producers for a wider economy, the financial and commercial centre of which was very much in the United Kingdom. For a useful discussion of Mill's views, see I. Greaves, 'The Character of British Colonial Trade', *Journal of Political Economy* 62 (1954), 1–11.

emigration. It was emigration that conditioned consumption habits within the colonies such that their tastes, expectations and values were readily familiar, communicable and comprehensible to manufacturers back in Britain; and it was emigration that enabled a rapid establishment of trust between commercial partners in the colonies and Britain, thereby facilitating long-distance trade.

The British 'diaspora' was hardly unique in this regard. Trade often develops more readily between peoples sharing a common identity, whether that identity be ethnic, religious or political.[2] Exploiting such ties was a perfectly rational response to the challenges of the market economy, rather than a form of economic escapism. Ethnic groups, in particular, are known to have developed distinct structures of economic opportunity.[3] The dense set of associations found within such groups promoted forms of co-operative behaviour that were distinctly (and materially) advantageous to group members.[4] Instead of relying on impersonal contractual bonds, which, when available, may often be unreliable, merchants and manufacturers from the same ethnic background have frequently looked to effective 'trust networks' to provide fast and accurate information about business conditions, to co-ordinate multiple far-flung transactions, and to secure good behaviour from distant, difficult-to-monitor clients. Consumption, meanwhile, is recognised to have been profoundly influenced by the 'cultural baggage' that settlers carried.[5] Settlers attached specific meaning and value to the goods that they purchased. These goods, and the lifestyle that went with them, were thus very much part of the global cultural flows set in train by mass migration.

Applying these insights to the study of the British World economy allows us to move away from the rather hackneyed view of colonial markets as passive 'bolt-holes' or 'safe havens' from the competitive forces of an international economy. By improving the quality and quantity of information flows, by bridging relations between producers and consumers, and by facilitating the adoption of new technologies, imperial networks contributed powerfully to the growth in trade and the convergence of

---

[2] See for example A. Grief, 'Contract Enforceability and Economic Institutions in Early Trade: The Maghribi Traders' Coalition', *American Economic Review* 83 (1993), 525–48; T. Menkhoff and S. Gerke (eds.), *Chinese Entrepreneurship and Asian Business Networks* (London: Taylor and Francis, 2002); and G. T. Haley, C. T. Tan and V. C. V. Haley (eds.), *New Asian Emperors: The Overseas Chinese, Their Strategies and Competitive Advantages* (London: Butterworth Heinemann, 1998).

[3] A. Portes and M. Zhou, 'Gaining the Upper Hand: Economic Mobility among Immigrant and Domestic Minorities', *Ethnic and Racial Studies* 15 (1992), 491–522.

[4] J. S. Coleman, 'Social Capital in the Creation of Human Capital', *American Journal of Sociology* 94 (1988), 95–120.

[5] See especially L. Young, *Middle Class Culture in the Nineteenth Century: America, Australia and Britain* (Basingstoke: Palgrave Macmillan, 2003).

income levels that were such marked features of English-speaking societies from 1850 to 1914.[6] Moreover, they did so without sealing off Britain or its settler colonies from the wider international economy. The co-ethnic webs of trade explored in this chapter were, however, also systems of power and domination that incorporated some parts of colonial society and not others. Hierarchies of race and class determined access to the business and professional networks spawned by the empire, just as notions of status, gentility and gender shaped patterns of colonial consumption. Such interplay of culture and economy is, of course, characteristic of all marketplaces, and historians are increasingly recognising how deeply embedded markets are in distinctive traditions and practices that influence how they are conceived and how they function.[7] In the case of British World markets, much work remains to be done to uncover what these traditions and practices actually were.

We begin with Britain's trade statistics, introducing new comparative data on the proportion of income spent on British products by colonial, American and Argentine consumers. This data reveals how 'non-market' advantages can help to explain why such large volumes of British products were typically absorbed by the settler colonies, while making it clear that much of the *increase in the proportion* of British exports going to these markets was the result of their mounting affluence, and not simply of their (growing) fondness for the wares of British producers. With the quantitative groundwork laid, the chapter then moves on to explore the more qualitative underpinnings of the British exporter's engagement with the settler colonies. What were the main sources of the advantages that Britain enjoyed there? The analysis is conducted under three headings: commercial policy and structures, international trade networks, and cultures of consumption. In each case it is shown how it was the social and institutional consequences of demographic expansion that struck most decisively at the roots of economic activity within the British World, albeit in ways more subtle and complex than has often been appreciated.

Exports and empire

An important aspect of Britain's trade history of the later nineteenth and early twentieth centuries is the rise of Britain's settler colonies as a major outlet for its exports. Table 4.1 neatly illustrates this 'imperial

---

[6] K. O'Rourke and J. G. Williamson, *Globalization and History: The Evolution of a Nineteenth-Century Atlantic Economy* (Cambridge, MA: Harvard University Press, 1999).

[7] M. Bevir and F. Trentmann (eds.), *Markets in Historical Contexts: Ideas and Politics in the Modern World* (Cambridge: Cambridge University Press, 2004).

Table 4.1. *British exports by regions, 1871–1913 (quinquennial average percentages).*

	1871–5	1881–5	1896–1900	1909–13
British settlement colonies	12.0	16.2	16.7	17.5
British India	8.9	12.9	11.8	11.9
Rest of the empire	5.9	5.9	5.6	5.6
Developed countries	47.2	39.4	39.3	35.9
Rest of the world	26.0	25.6	26.6	29.1

Source: P. J. Cain and A. G. Hopkins, *British Imperialism, 1688–2000* (London: Pearson Education, 2001), pp. 153, 432.

drift'. Between 1871 and 1913, the proportion of all British exports going to the empire rose from 26.8 per cent to 35 per cent, a rise in stark contrast to the shrinking share taken by the developed countries of industrial Europe and the United States. Not all parts of the empire, however, shared equally in this growth. In fact, the leading recipients of the increased flow of British exports to the empire were the settler colonies – Australia, New Zealand, Canada and South Africa.

Why did these particular markets prove so accessible to the British manufacturer? Attempts to answer this question go back to the end of the nineteenth century, when the trend first became apparent.[8] Since then a wide variety of factors have been adduced, the most common of which are shared language, currencies, tastes, institutions and expectations; the use of preferential tariffs; their governments' practice of buying British first where possible; dependence on British investment for continued development; and the density of their transport and communication links with Britain.[9] Taken separately or together, such considerations are thought to

[8] For a contemporary view, see A. W. Flux, 'The Flag and Trade: A Summary Review of the Trade of the Chief Colonial Empires', *Journal of the Royal Statistical Society* 62:3 (1899–46), 489–533, esp. pp. 522–33; for subsequent scholarly assessments see P. J. Cain, 'The Economic Philosophy of Constructive Imperialism', in C. Navari (ed.), *British Politics and the Spirit of the Age: Political Concepts in Action* (Keele: Keele University Press, 1996), pp. 41–65; F. Coetzee, *For Party or Country: Nationalism and the Dilemmas of Popular Conservatism in Edwardian England* (Oxford: Oxford University Press, 1990), pp. 42–8, 61–70, 85–98, 117–25; A. L. Frieberg, *The Weary Titan: Britain and the Experience of Relative Decline, 1895–1905* (Princeton: Princeton University Press, 1988), pp. 24–79; E. H. H. Green, 'The Political Economy of Empire, 1880–1914', in A. Porter (ed.), *The Oxford History of the British Empire*, 5 vols., Vol. III: *The Nineteenth Century* (Oxford: Oxford University Press, 1999), pp. 346–70; and A. S. Thompson, *Imperial Britain: The Empire in British Politics, c. 1880–1932* (Harlow: Pearson Education, 2000), pp. 85–9, 104–9.

[9] D. K. Fieldhouse, 'The Metropolitan Economics of Empire', in J. M. Brown and W. R. Louis (eds.), *The Oxford History of the British Empire*, 5 vols., Vol. IV: *The Twentieth*

have afforded British exporters unique advantages in the markets of both Britain's formal and informal empire.

While many contemporaries clearly saw these advantages as a godsend that, if properly built upon, could secure the future for British industry in troubled times,[10] later commentators have been more inclined to regard them as temptations that in the long run promised – and indeed delivered – ruination.[11] Yet how reasonable is it to draw such a strong and

Century (Oxford: Oxford University Press, 1999), pp. 88–113; D. K. Fieldhouse, 'For Richer, for Poorer?', in P. J. Marshall (ed.), *Cambridge Illustrated History of the British Empire* (Cambridge: Cambridge University Press, 1996), pp. 110–12; F. Capie, 'Britain and Empire Trade in the Second Half of the Nineteenth Century', in D. Alexander and R. Ommer (eds.), *Volumes not Values: Canadian Sailing Ships and World Trades* (Memorial University Newfoundland: Maritime History Group, 1979), pp. 3–29; F. Crouzet, 'Trade and Empire: The British Experience from the Establishment of Free Trade until the First World War', in B. M. Ratcliffe (ed.), *Great Britain and Her World, 1750–1914: Essays in Honour of W. O. Henderson* (Manchester: Manchester University Press, 1975), pp. 209–35; F. L. McDougall, *Sheltered Markets: A Study of the Value of the Empire Trade* (London: J. Murray, 1925); D. C. M. Platt, 'Trade Competition in the Regions of Recent Settlement', in D. C. M. Platt with A. J. H. Latham and R. Michie (eds.), *Decline and Recovery in Britain's Overseas Trade, 1873–1914* (London: Macmillan, 1993), pp. 91–138; and S. B. Saul, *Studies in British Overseas Trade, 1870–1914* (Liverpool: Liverpool University Press, 1960).

[10] A. J. Sargent, *British Industries and Empire Markets* (London: HMSO, 1930); F. L. McDougall, *The Growing Dependence of British Industry upon Empire Markets* (London: HMSO, 1929).

[11] As Feinstein noted, 'those who foresaw a grim prospect of increasing foreign competition and declining sales, looked for a solution in the expansion of Britain's exports to the empire'; C. H. Feinstein, 'The End of Empire and the Golden Age', in P. Clarke and C. Trebilcock (eds.), *Understanding Decline: Perceptions and Realities of British Economic Performance* (Cambridge: Cambridge University Press, 1997), p. 218. To many, however, it was to prove no more than a short-term fix, because, by isolating itself from the vivifying effects of competition, dependence on the 'soft' markets of the empire 'dulled the senses of many exporters' and ensured the continued decline of British industry. For similar statements and sentiments, see E. J. Hobsbawm, *Industry and Empire* (London: Pantheon Books, 1969), pp. 191–2; W. A. Lewis, *Growth and Fluctuations, 1870–1913* (London: Allen and Unwin, 1978), p. 121; Saul, *British Overseas Trade*, p. 229 (from which the 'dulled the senses' quotation comes); C. P. Kindleberger, 'Foreign Trade and Economic Growth: Lessons from Britain and France, 1850–1913', *EcHR* 14:2 (1961), 295–300; F. Crouzet, *The Victorian Economy* (London: Routledge, 1992), p. 357; C. Barnett, *The Lost Victory: British Dreams, British Realities, 1945–1950* (London: Macmillan, 1995), p. 12; and G. Owen, *From Empire to Europe: The Decline and Revival of British Industry since the Second World War* (London: HarperCollins, 1999), pp. 185–7. For researchers who have cast doubt on the assumption that Empire markets were necessarily 'soft', see S. Pollard, *Britain's Prime and Britain's Decline: The British Economy, 1870–1914* (London: E. Arnold, 1989), pp. xii, 37, 268; B. W. E. Alford, *Britain in the World Economy since 1880* (London: Longman, 1996), pp. 53–4; C. R. Schenk, *Britain and the Sterling Area: From Devaluation to Convertibility in the 1950s* (London: Routledge, 1994), p. 81; S. J. Nicholas, 'The Overseas Marketing Performance of British Industry, 1870–1914', *EcHR* 37:4 (1984), 489–506 (p. 491); S. J. Nicholas, 'Locational Choice, Performance and the Growth of British Multinational Firms', *Business History* 31:3 (1989), 122–41; B. R. Tomlinson, *The Economy of Modern India, 1860–1970* (Cambridge: Cambridge University Press, 1993), pp. 99–100; and A. S. Thompson and G. Magee, 'A Soft Touch? British Industry, Empire Markets, and the Self-Governing Dominions, *c.* 1870–1914', *EcHR* 56 (2003), 689–717.

damning conclusion of British economic performance from the type of data presented in Table 3.1?[12] A closer examination of the problems of using movements in the share of British exports to a particular location as a gauge of Britain's non-market advantages there is instructive.

The first thing to note is that shifts in the dominions' share of British exports across time tell us relatively little about the nature or extent of the advantages enjoyed there by British manufacturers. Such data cannot distinguish between the different factors that may cause the proportion of a nation's exports to a particular market to vary. In addition to what we might call 'imperial advantages', growth in an exporter's reliance on and penetration of a colonial market may have resulted from a variety of other considerations including greater price competitiveness, income growth, population expansion, better after-sales service and advertising. Given the various factors at play, it would be misleading to take the movements of export or import shares in the British World as a sure sign that Britain's demographic connection to these societies had in itself (positive) repercussions for British trade.

A further difficulty with using export shares to assess the extent of the commercial advantages enjoyed by Britain in the settler colonies is that such an approach looks at these markets, whether as a group or independently, in isolation. Yet 'imperial advantage' was relative rather than absolute. What determined the attractiveness of dominion markets was not just their pro-British tastes, institutions and policies, but the fact that these attributes were not shared to the same extent in other markets. Consequently, the advantages that British exporters enjoyed, say, in New Zealand, were influenced by the nature of Britain's relations not just with New Zealand itself but with consumers, producers and governments in other potential markets, both inside and outside the British World. If governments in these other markets had decided to impose hefty tariffs on British exports, then, *ceteris paribus*, the New Zealand market would have become more open than before to British manufacturers, even though nothing had actually changed in New Zealand. In a world of growing international trade, the benefits of imperial advantage cannot therefore be determined in isolation.

Fortunately, there is an alternative way of examining the nature of British markets in the colonies and elsewhere that addresses these problems. This method considers the habits of typical consumers in those

---

[12] For other cases, where raw exports shares are used, see for example S. B. Saul, 'The Export Economy, 1970–1914', *Yorkshire Bulletin of Economic and Social Research* 17:1 (1965), 5–18 (pp. 5–6); Nicholas, 'Overseas Marketing', p. 491; Schenk, *Sterling Area*, p. 81; and Capie, 'Empire Trade', p. 11.

Table 4.2. *Index of Britain's revealed advantage in selected countries, 1870–1913 (quinquennial average).*

Period	Australia	NZ	Canada	South Africa	Argentina	USA
1870–4	2.78	3.48	2.17		1.85	0.51
1875–9	3.43	4.20	2.12			0.31
1880–4	3.66	3.82	2.13			0.41
1885–9	3.87	3.80	2.20			0.47
1890–4	3.27	3.74	1.90		2.74	0.47
1895–9	3.95	4.24	1.70			0.39
1900–4	3.93	5.14	2.04		1.66	0.35
1905–9	3.16	4.59	1.90		2.13	0.32
1910–13	3.43	4.57	2.07	6.09	1.85	0.30

Notes: Before 1900 the Argentine figure is based on 1870 and 1890 data alone. Similarly, the South African figure for 1910–13 is based on data from 1913 only. The gaps in the South African and Argentine data that this causes arise because there are no continuous GDP series for those countries for the period between 1870 and 1913.

Source: G. B. Magee, 'The Importance of Being British? Imperial Factors and the Growth of British Imports, 1870–1960', *Journal of Interdisciplinary History* 37 (2007), 341–51 (p. 352).

locations, asking specifically whether those consumers purchased disproportionately large volumes of British wares. It is a germane question, for if 'imperial advantages' mattered at all, they must have done so because they actively induced, conditioned or perhaps compelled colonial consumers to spend more of their income on British products than they otherwise would have. Such an approach has the merit of targeting more precisely the commercial benefits of colonial markets than does the mere movement of export shares.

Table 4.2 examines whether this was indeed the case in some of the British manufacturers' most important export markets during the late Victorian and Edwardian era. It reports the share of each of these markets' income devoted to the purchase of British goods *relative* to the proportion spent on average in western European markets (Germany, France, Belgium and the Netherlands) where the British are perceived to have had no special advantage. The resulting figure is called the 'index of revealed advantage'. One could also express this index in per capita terms as the proportion of the average individual's income that was spent on British exports in one market relative to the proportion expended in the 'neutral' markets of western Europe. Either way, the index of revealed advantage – by introducing comparability of consumption and by focusing on the importance of British products in the consumer's overall expenditure – captures the effects of advantage exhibited in any market more precisely than measures based purely on export shares. Moreover, it enables the scale of non-market advantages to be gauged and compared across place and time. The further the index rises above 1, the greater the advantage for British products in the market; at 1 that market's consumption would be identical to the western European.[13]

Turning to Table 4.2 itself, we can see that, right up to the First World War, British producers did enjoy a commercial 'advantage' in the dominions – an advantage that translated itself into a demand for their products, and that was felt most strongly in New Zealand, South Africa and Australia.[14] The advantage grew deeper over time in New Zealand and South Africa, and to a lesser extent in Australia. In 1870, for example, New Zealanders on average allocated about 10 per cent of their income to the purchase of British products (around three-and-a-half times more than a western European consumer did), rising to just over 13 per cent (or just over four-and-a-half times more than a European) by 1913. Canada was also favourably disposed to British exporters in this period, albeit less so than the other dominions. Its rate of consumption remained fairly stable throughout at a level approximately comparable to Argentina's; that is, both Canadians and Argentines on average spent about twice the western European proportion of income on British exports. By contrast, continuous and intensifying struggle for the US consumer's dollar, especially from the 1890s, epitomises the experience of British producers attempting to export to America. Table 3.2 indicates that US consumers on average devoted to British exports between a third and a half of the proportion of income that western Europeans did. Thus, despite its demographic links to Britain and common language and traditions, America remained a comparatively tough market for the British to penetrate. In this regard, Britain was no different from other European exporters wishing to establish a market in the protectionist United States.

Taken together, the figures in Table 4.2 suggest that international markets prior to the First World War were not completely 'neutral'. They

---

[13] Therefore, an index reading of 2.0 literally means that that market's consumers spend twice as much of their income on British exports as a weighted average of western European consumers. By contrast, a reading of less than 1 denotes that consumers in that market use relatively less of their income on British goods than those in western Europe. Such a market might be described as relatively disadvantageous for British exporters. Given space limitations, no attempt is made here to discuss the background to the index of revealed advantage. Readers are referred to G. B. Magee, 'The Importance of Being British? Imperial Factors and the Growth of British Imports, 1870–1960', *Journal of Interdisciplinary History* 37 (2007), 341–51, where a full discussion of the meaning and construction of the index, and the logic underpinning it, is given.

[14] See for example Platt, 'Trade Competition', pp. 110–17.

confirm the view of contemporaries and some later scholars that dominion markets did indeed devote a disproportionately large portion of their
incomes to British imports, and indicate a role for non-market factors in
Britain's nineteenth- and twentieth-century trade history.

Such a finding needs to be interpreted with care, however. That pro-
British advantages existed, does not in itself, for instance, prove the common allegation that dominion markets were 'soft' or 'featherbedded'.
Indeed, as work elsewhere has demonstrated, despite these advantages,
British World markets still proved challenging for many British exporters. By any reasonable criteria, they were certainly no easy escape from
competition.[15]

To understand the nature of dominion markets, it is necessary to grasp
that British manufacturers' turn towards them during the late Victorian
and Edwardian era was strongly governed by the rapidly rising wealth
of these societies.[16] Here there is a crucial distinction between levels of
consumption and what caused those levels to change over time. Level
and change are separate phenomena, a distinction not always appreciated in the literature on Britain's colonial trade. A simple analogy may
help make the point. Imagine that your neighbour likes to eat out at her
local Chinese restaurant. Last year, she spent $250 there, but this year
her accountant observes that she has spent $500. If the accountant there-
fore concludes that your neighbour's love of eating at the local Chinese
has obviously grown in the last twelve months, he would have in essence
assumed that her expenditure patterns have been driven entirely by
changed preferences. Yet, before we can accept such a view, we must rule
out other possible explanations. Has your neighbour's income increased?
Or has the restaurant dropped its prices? If we investigate further and
find that your neighbour's income has doubled over the last year, while
prices at the restaurant have remained unchanged, then it is reasonable
to conclude that her preference for eating out has probably not altered
at all, since she would be actually spending the same proportion of her
income at the Chinese. In other words, while our neighbour's liking for
Chinese food certainly induced her to frequent the restaurant in the first
place, in this instance it did not cause her to spend more of her money
there.

The moral of this story is that, like the accountant above, we must be
wary of committing the fallacy of *post hoc, ergo propter hoc* when examining commercial activity in the British World. What promoted the high

---

[15] Thompson and Magee, 'A Soft Touch?'.
[16] Recent econometric analysis of colonial demand for British products, for example,
provides clear quantitative evidence of the influence of income growth. See Magee,
'Importance of Being British?', pp. 355–67.

levels of consumption of British goods in the past was not necessarily what caused any subsequent increase in demand for British goods in the future. Mindful of this caution, the following sections of the chapter seek to identify some of the main reasons why consumption *levels* of British products remained so relatively high in the settler colonies throughout the late Victorian and Edwardian era.

Official policy

Operated for reasons of power, empires, it is often said, were integrated by force. Yet how did ministers and officials try to mesh together markets in the British World? How far, for example, did they seek to obtain special commercial benefits from the settler colonies? State intervention in the field of discriminatory export duties – or 'preferential tariffs', to use the jargon of the time – generated a great deal of political controversy in the early twentieth century.[17] Businessmen were drawn into these debates,[18] and their attitudes are discussed in greater detail below (see 'Chambers of Commerce', below, pp. 145–50). Yet despite vigorous campaigning on the part of Joseph Chamberlain and the 'constructive imperialists', Britain clung tenaciously to 'his holiness free trade', as Marx disparagingly termed it. For many later Victorian and Edwardian politicians the commitment to free trade was indeed held with all the passion and emotion of a religious belief. The alternative, protection, threatened not only tariffs, and higher prices for consumers, but greater government interference more generally.[19] There were also differing views as to the commercial potential of the English-speaking parts of the empire, and a widespread apprehension as to whether they could ever be economically self-contained.

Britain received a series of tariff preferences in dominion markets from the 1890s, all granted on the latter's initiative, even though it did not finally reciprocate until 1919.[20] Cecil Rhodes led the way in 1896, inserting a clause in the charter of the British South Africa Company. Tariffs on

[17] The classic account remains A. Sykes, *Tariff Reform in British Politics, 1903–13* (Oxford: Oxford University Press, 1979). For more recent contributions to the debate see Cain, 'Economic Philosophy'; E. H. H. Green, *The Crisis of Conservatism: The Politics, Economics and Ideology of the Conservative Party, 1880–1914* (London: Routledge, 1995); and A. S. Thompson, 'Tariff Reform: An Imperial Strategy, 1903–13', *HJ* (1997), 1033–54.
[18] A. Marrison, *British Business and Protection, 1903–32* (Oxford: Oxford University Press, 1996).
[19] Thompson, *Imperial Britain*, p. 104.
[20] Fieldhouse, 'Metropolitan Economics', p. 90. The details below come from Thompson, *Imperial Britain*, pp. 90–6 and L. Trainor, *British Imperialism and Australian Nationalism: Manipulation, Conflict and Compromise in the Late Nineteenth Century* (Cambridge: Cambridge University Press, 1994), pp. 109–18.

British goods entering Rhodesia were not to exceed the level of the Cape Colony tariff prevailing at the time of the Charter. This (latent) preference eventually came into effect in 1906, albeit that Britain's exchange of goods with Rhodesia was too small for it to matter. A more significant step was taken in 1903 when a customs union conference, comprising all of the South African colonies, adopted a general tariff that treated British imports differentially. A further step was then taken in 1906 when a new agreement lowered duties for English exporters while generally raising them on foreign products. This was but one of several tactics used at the time to block further American economic penetration of the South African market. Here political power was certainly made to count – and this episode is discussed below (see pp. 141–2). Subsequently, in 1910, when the Union adopted the Transvaal's protectionist tariff rather than the Cape's revenue-producing tariff, the economic geography of the region began to change. Henceforth British manufacturers had to take local manufacture much more seriously if they were to preserve their market share.

Meanwhile in Canada J. A. Macdonald's Conservative government responded to pressure from local manufacturers, and the spectre of rising unemployment, by introducing in 1879 a 'National Policy' of protective tariffs to secure the home market – competition from American imports was particularly acute at this time.[21] Over the next decade the number of manufacturing establishments, and the capital invested in them, grew. Subsequently, in 1897, Wilfred Laurier's Liberal government adopted a general tariff, maintaining a high level of protection, yet providing for 'moderate but promising preferences on imports from sister countries of the empire'.[22] Rates were reduced on goods for countries that reduced their charges on Canadian exports. The rates on some British imports were lowered by almost a third, which in turn stimulated British export performance to Canada during the early twentieth century.

The New Zealand parliament carried a preferential trade bill in 1903, granting preferences to Britain and providing for similar reciprocal arrangements with Australia and Canada. In 1906 this principle of preference was further extended: the duty on certain British exports dropped by nearly 1 per cent, while the duty on foreign goods increased and preference was extended to a wider range of British goods.

Before 1901 each Australian state devised its own tariff regime. Victoria was staunchly protectionist, while New South Wales adopted

[21] M. Bliss, *Northern Enterprise: Five Centuries of Canadian Business* (Toronto: University of Toronto Press, 1987), pp. 227, 247–9, 300.
[22] *Ibid.*, p. 301.

tariffs for revenue raising purposes. Federation saw the removal of customs houses along state borders. In 1907, a new Australian tariff bill was piloted through the Commonwealth parliament by Alfred Deakin, Joseph Chamberlain's most dependable colonial ally. It gave preference to British goods by increasing the duties on foreign goods, and by increasing the number of goods on an 'empire free list'. By 1909, two-thirds of British imports paid duty, 'but at a rate that on average allowed them to be priced about 5 per cent lower than the competition'.[23]

As Table 3.2 shows, none of the tariff or other forms of preference afforded to British products before 1914 had a marked effect on colonial consumption patterns.[24] There were exceptions, some of which date back to developments earlier in the century. A clause of the 1842 Copyright Act aimed to protect the imperial trade in books by forbidding colonial reprinting of texts copyrighted in Britain. Though difficult to police, it helped British publishers gain access to colonial markets, and a high proportion of the revenues of nineteenth-century London booksellers came from supplying books, magazines and other types of print to British expatriates and settlers. The 'colonial edition' – books published in series that contained mainly new British novels, and sold cheaply as the only likely solution to the problem of pirated publications – was the main device used to try to control the English language market.[25] Colonial editions were commonplace by the early 1900s, with seventeen London publishers issuing them. They were intended to 'share the fruits of British civilisation with Britons abroad', with many titles 'glorifying British virtues and British military success overseas'.[26] Macmillan was the leading publisher of these editions, launching its successful 'Colonial Library' in 1896 and 'Empire Library' in 1913. Australasian and South African booksellers thrived on their sales; Australia was the largest market for British book exports, with rapid growth from 1870 to 1884 and from 1893 to 1914.[27]

The 'economic hegemony' of London publishers could no longer be taken for granted by the end of our period, however, as a result of the arrival of the publishing house advance of the 'old Dominions'.[28] In other

[23] D. Meredith and B. Dyster, *Australia in the Global Economy: Continuity and Change* (Cambridge: Cambridge University Press, 2000), p. 51.
[24] On this point, see also Saul, *British Overseas Trade*, p. 217.
[25] G. Johanson, *A Study of Colonial Editions in Australia, 1843–1972* (Wellington: Monash University Press, 2000).
[26] *Ibid.*, p. 15.
[27] Geographical proximity allowed US publishers to corner the Canadian and West Indian markets, but it was only during the two world wars that they were able to move temporarily into other colonial markets.
[28] Meredith and Dyster, *Australia in the Global Economy*, pp. 370–1.

spheres of consumption the competition was still fiercer. Australia and Canada actually saw the overall level of advantage for British goods fall slightly, rather than rise, during the early twentieth century. The benefits of the preferences, moreover, were often illusory. Duties could be raised on foreign manufactures rather than lowered on British ones. Meanwhile, much dominion protection focused on items locally produced, and thus not directly in competition with British exports anyway.[29]

The only real deviation from this rule of non-interference in international trade were the formal agreements reached by private companies (not governments) in relation to the chemicals and tobacco industries. The chemicals agreement divided the world into 'spheres of influence', with the dominions categorised as 'natural' British markets.[30] It was mainly concerned with alkalis and explosives; not until the 1920s were dyestuffs and fertilisers included. Similarly, American and British tobacco firms agreed to confine themselves to their respective national markets, while transferring all foreign investment and export trade to a British-registered joint venture called British American Tobacco – BAT rapidly became the leading cigarette manufacturer in Australia, Canada and South Africa.[31] The tendency towards cartelisation in these two industries helped to prevent American and German firms from monopolising British World markets, but they were atypical.

The support given by the British government to the development of imperial transport and communications was of greater significance. State-conferred commercial advantages in this sphere are hard to quantify, including as they did the various forms of subsidy offered to private shipping companies by governments (British and colonial), and military expenditure on the Royal Navy, which, *inter alia*, played a vital role in keeping shipping lanes open to imperial (and international) trade. Nonetheless, oceanic transport was a vital dimension in strategic thinking about the empire,[32] and shipping lines clearly had economic as well

---

[29] F. V. Meyer, *Britain's Colonies in World Trade* (Oxford: Oxford University Press, 1948), pp. 90–112; Saul, *British Overseas Trade*, p. 217.

[30] W. J. Reader, *Imperial Chemical Industries: A History*, 2 vols., Vol. I: *The Forerunners, 1870–1926* (Oxford: Oxford University Press, 1970), p. 60.

[31] H. Cox, *The Global Cigarette: Origins and Evolution of British American Tobacco, 1880–1945* (Oxford: Oxford University Press, 2000), pp. 4–6.

[32] J. N. F. M. à Campo, 'Engines of Empire: The Role of Shipping Companies in British and Dutch Empire Building', in G. Jackson and D. M. Williams (eds.), *Shipping, Technology and Imperialism* (Aldershot: Ashgate, 1996), pp. 63–96; R. Kubicek, 'The Proliferation and Diffusion of Steamship Technology and the Beginnings of "New Imperialism"', in D. Killingray, M. Lincoln and N. Rigby (eds.), *Maritime Empires: British Imperial Maritime Trade in the Nineteenth Century* (Woodbridge: Boydell Press, 2004), pp. 100–10 (pp. 63–96); J. F. Munro, *Maritime Enterprise and Empire: Sir William Mackinnon and His Business Network, 1823–93* (Woodbridge: Boydell Press, 2003), pp. 87, 504.

as military and political benefits. This, therefore, was a field of policy in which government and private enterprise were inextricably and beneficially linked. Mindful of the need for regular communications between Britain and its colonies, politicians were reluctant to rely on the vagaries of the free market. This created a context in which private shipowners and shipping companies, conscious of their strategic significance, could lobby effectively for government subsidies and support.

There was, of course, nothing new about government taking an interest in the regulation of shipping. Until 1849 the Navigation Acts had confined all trade to and from the colonies to British or colonial ships, with predominantly British and colonial crews.[33] But in the wake of their repeal, other countries did not throw their ports open to British shipping in the way that had been hoped, and foreign vessels became a familiar presence in trades from which they had been formerly excluded. Competition in shipping grew, especially from America and the Baltic seafaring nations. Aided by heavy investment in steamship technology, Britain managed to claw back some of the ground it lost to these competitors during the 1870s and 1880s. Yet after the 1890s, Britain's position was further eroded, both in terms of the tonnage using her ports and her share of the world's steam tonnage. The exception was shipping services to British possessions: these actually grew before the First World War.[34] In the case of New Zealand, for example, the proportion of shipping movements attributed to British-owned ships increased from 87 per cent in 1890 to 97 per cent in 1910.[35]

Several British shipping companies developed close imperial connections – Donald Currie's Union-Castle Line, Sir Alfred Jones' Elder Demspter & Co., and the Peninsular and Oriental Steamship Company (P&O). Each became adept at portraying itself as a national enterprise carrying on a public service. P&O's steamers have even been referred to as the 'flagships of imperialism'.[36] The network of lines created by the company fanned out to all parts of the empire east of Suez. In peace-time,

---

[33] S. Palmer, *Politics, Shipping and the Repeal of the Navigation Laws* (Manchester: Manchester University Press, 1990). See also S. L. Engerman, 'Mercantilism and Overseas Trade, 1700–1800', in R. Floud and D. N. McCloskey (eds.), *The Economic History of Britain since 1700*, 3 vols., Vol. I: *1700–1860* (Cambridge: Cambridge University Press, 1994), pp. 198–9.

[34] P. J. Cain and A. G. Hopkins, *British Imperialism, 1688–2000* (Harlow: Longman, 2001), p. 159.

[35] J. Mcaloon, 'Scots in the Colonial Economy', in T. Brooking and J. Coleman (eds.), *The Heather and the Fern: Scottish Migration and New Zealand Settlement* (Dunedin: Otago University Press, 2003), pp. 97–8.

[36] F. Harcourt, 'The P&O Company: Flagships of Imperialism', in S. Palmer and G. Williams (eds.), *Charted and Uncharted Waters: Proceedings of a Conference on the Study of British Maritime History* (London: National Maritime Museum, 1981), pp. 6–28.

life in the colonies was made more palatable by the regular delivery of
P&O mails, and by the prospect for emigrants and officials of more frequent journeys home. In war-time, the Admiralty turned to P&O for
troop transports, for hospital ships and for the movement of supplies.
Imperial mail contracting was also important to the development of several steamship companies. Postal subventions were obtained from British
and colonial governments. They 'provided shipowners with the basis for
maintaining a comparatively rapid and regular service, essential to the
stimulation of a dependable flow of commercial traffic which in its turn
brought income'.[37] These contracts in turn brought in other official business for stores, troops and emigrants.

A further way in which the shipping companies restricted competition from foreign rivals in the sphere of colonial trade was by the system
of 'rings' or 'conferences' that controlled rates and allocated business
between national lines.[38] The conference system was introduced to,
among other places, Australia in 1884 and South Africa in 1886. A policy of 'deferred rebates' was offered to merchants who agreed to use its
services exclusively – in South Africa this was 5 per cent of the freight
paid.[39] The conference system ensured that British lines had the right to
carry all merchandise bound for the colonies from continental ports.

Why were British and dominion politicians prepared to tolerate such
collusive arrangements between companies to pool capacity, and to fix
freight rates and the number of sailings? The establishment of steamship
services between Britain and its colonies provided the maritime foundation for the growth of overseas trade. By placing shipping companies
on a more profitable basis, the conference system encouraged investment in services that might otherwise have remained irregular and inad-
equate. The conference system was not without its critics, however. By
1906 there were serious complaints against the working of the South
African shipping 'ring', in particular. A Royal Commission reported in
1909 that the conference system was necessary and its practices justified.
Three years later, the South African government finally moved to end the
rebate system, albeit that the conference continued to exist; merchants
agreed to carry on shipping their goods by conference lines and the lines
in turn charged uniform rates previously agreed.[40]

[37] A. N. Porter, *Victorian Shipping, Business and Imperial Policy: Donald Currie, the Castle Line and Southern Africa* (Woodbridge: Royal Historical Society, 1986), p. 273.
[38] P. N. Davies, 'Shipping and Imperialism: The Case of British West Africa', in G. Jackson and D. M. Williams (eds.), *Shipping, Technology and Imperialism* (Aldershot: Scolar Press, 1996), pp. 46–63 (pp. 54–60).
[39] A. W. Kircaldy, *British Shipping: Its History, Organisation and Importance* (London: Kegal Paul, Trench, Trübner and Co., 1919), pp. 184–5.
[40] *Ibid.*, p. 198.

A more direct source of advantage to British exporters to dominion markets came from the Crown Agents for the colonies. Like the Colonial Land and Emigration Commission (see Chapter 3), the Crown Agents were an ancillary administrative agency.[41] Part of their function was to provide advice on financial legislation to the Colonial Office and the Treasury. They also helped the dominions (and Crown Colonies) to raise loans in the City (see Chapter 5). But their remit extended to commercial affairs, and they regularly executed major construction projects for the colonies. With responsibility for drawing up and supervising contracts for these projects, they purchased, inspected and shipped all the materials required. The settler colonies subsequently withdrew their patronage and established agencies of their own in London, so by 1880 the operations of the Crown Agents were mainly restricted to the dependent empire, although they continued to act for the Cape Colony, Natal, New Zealand, Western Australia, the Orange River Colony and the Transvaal on certain financial matters into the early twentieth century.

A major aspect of the public works supervised by the Crown Agents was the building of railways. In 1868 Queensland (a separate colony from 1859) decided to obtain its railway materials through the Crown Agents, and by the mid 1870s the Cape and Natal were doing likewise. The sheer volume of this work led to successive increases in the size of the Crown Agents' Office and in their procurement activities.[42] Here they enjoyed wide powers of discretion. They provided all of the materials and equipment necessary for the construction and maintenance of railways, obtaining supplies through their own list of approved firms. On receiving an order, the Crown Agents contacted one of these firms or solicited bids from several of them. Supplies ranged from engines, trucks and carriages to rails, bridges and workshop machinery, to lighting, cement and coal. The Agents looked either to firms already used extensively by English and Scottish railway engineers, or to firms that had a proven track record of working for colonial governments. This practice undoubtedly worked to the advantage of British manufacturers. Crown Agents also appointed the engineers, inspectors and staff who were involved in preparing designs and specifications, and in supervising the railway's construction and subsequent operation; this again worked to the advantage of British firms.

Not surprisingly, charges of monopoly and accusations of favouritism were levelled at the Agents, especially from the companies that had failed to obtain concessions and contracts. But the policy of preferential

---

[41] L. E. Davis and R. A. Huttenback, *Mammon and the Pursuit of Empire: The Economics of British Imperialism* (Cambridge: Cambridge University Press, 1986), p. 13.

[42] A. W. Abbott, *A Short History of the Crown Agents and Their Office* (London: The Crown Agents, 1959), p. 23.

purchasing was vigorously defended at the time, and has been since.[43] The Agents, it is argued, had a wide range of contacts and experience through their work in building railways throughout the empire, from which the colonies stood to gain. The list of companies they utilised was extensive, and long-term business relationships were developed with them. Firms on the list had a good deal to gain by remaining in the Crown Agents' favour, and there were remarkably few complaints about the quality of materials they supplied. The Agents, moreover, were not a profit-making organisation, and economies of scale made their services cheap. Ultimately, the survival of the Agency depended on colonial satisfaction with the performance of its duties. There were significant strengths to the system, therefore. Hence when the Cape's Agent-General took over from the Crown Agent in 1881, the list of approved firms for railway materials was extended but it continued to consist of British firms of known reliability. Indeed, according to one recent study, 'the benefits provided by the Office of the Crown Agents for the Colonies in the vital areas of purchasing and loan management were too evident' to succumb to 'mere petty carping'.[44]

To summarise: the empire was not an active ingredient in economic policy-making, but neither did the British state eschew any role whatsoever in promoting imperial trade. At the level of basic infrastructure, it clearly encouraged private interests to develop transport and communication networks, and provided the naval and military power to make these networks safer and more secure. British and colonial governments were happy for Crown Agents to purchase primarily or even exclusively from British producers. What they were not prepared to do was consciously shape the empire into an economic system with pre-determined characteristics: this was the logic of a system of preferential tariffs, whether they aimed at a full-blown imperial *Zollverein* (customs union) or merely closer market integration. The dominant policy of free trade did not allow for commercial relations to be shaped purely in imperial terms. However, as we are about to see, free trade did not prevent British producers from exploiting certain 'non-market' advantages in the settler colonies.

Trans-national networks

Long-distance trade is challenging. Transport, information and monitoring costs are all high, and foreign markets tend to be less predictable than

[43] See for example D. Sunderland, *Managing the British Empire: The Crown Agents, 1833–1914* (Woodbridge: Boydell Press, 2004), pp. 18, 21, 60.
[44] Davis and Huttenback, *Mammon and the Pursuit of Empire*, p. 188.

those at home. Scholars of international business even have a name for this – 'psychic distance'.[45] They suggest that the level of uncertainty in a foreign market is influenced by differences in the education, language, customs and legal systems of the 'home' and 'host' country. The less the differences, the smaller the 'psychic distance', and the more likely goods are to flow between markets.

A variety of trading networks helped British merchants and business-men to operate in geographically distant markets.[46] These networks nur-tured a sense of shared purpose among their members, secured good behaviour, and disseminated up-to-date and accurate information about business conditions and individual reputations. Networks of fam-ily and kin, for example, developed effective trust in trade, especially in the eighteenth century when other more formal types of network were not yet established.[47] To be sure, there were drawbacks to the family as a form of trans-national enterprise: the 'pool of talented members was usually small and the capacity to check or punish delinquency was often limited'.[48] Nonetheless, kin-based enterprises could draw strength from the loyalty that existed within the family core, from intermarriage between family members, and from their hierarchical structure and the 'patriarchal' authority exercised by the head of the family.[49]

A good example of a colonial business emerging from an extended fam-ily network is that of the Glaxo Company.[50] Glaxo's origins lie in the mer-chant firm of Joseph Nathan, a Londoner who migrated to the goldfields of Victoria in the 1850s and who subsequently settled in Wellington, New

[45] B. Kogut and H. Singh, 'The Effect of National Culture on the Choice of Entry Mode', *Journal of International Business Studies* 19 (1988), 411–32; Nicholas, 'Locational Choice', pp. 122–41.
[46] For the distinction between formal trading networks and personal or semi-formal trad-ing networks, see S. Sugiyama and L. Grove (eds.), *Commercial Networks in Modern Asia* (Richmond, Surrey: Curzon, 2001), pp. 2–3: once created, the former (often infrastruc-tural) continued to operate regardless of what happened to the individuals or groups that created them. Whereas the latter shared their resources and services only with the individuals or groups that created and/or belonged to them.
[47] N. Zahedieh, 'Economy', in D. Armitage and M. J. Braddick (eds.), *The British Atlantic World, 1500–1800* (Basingstoke: Palgrave Macmillan, 2002), pp. 51–68 (p. 66).
[48] *Ibid.*
[49] G. H. Boyce, *Information, Mediation and Institutional Development: The Rise of Large-Scale Enterprise in British Shipping, 1870–1919* (Manchester: Manchester University Press, 1995); J. Forbes, *Munro, Maritime Enterprise and Empire: Sir William Mackinnon and His Business Network, 1823–93* (Woodbridge: Boydell Press, 2003).
[50] The detail below is drawn from H. Jephcott, *The First Fifty Years: An Account of the Early Life of Joseph Edward Nathan and the First Fifty Years of His Merchandise Business that Eventually Became the Glaxo Group* (Ipswich: n.p., 1969); R. P. T. Davenport-Hines and J. Slinn, *Glaxo: A History to 1962* (Cambridge: Cambridge University Press, 1992), pp. 7, 13–14, 27–8, 30, 37–9, 43–5.

Zealand. He set up a general merchandise business with his brother-in-law, Jacob Joseph, exporting wool and importing goods such as groceries, stationery, patent medicines, drapery and ironmongery. By the end of the 1870s the firm's agencies and stores reached into most parts of New Zealand, while Nathan's economic interests had expanded to include property development, banking and transport. The organisation of the firm was based on the dispersal of Joseph's several sons, some based permanently in Wellington, others in London. New Zealand remained the centre of trading, and the working capital continued to be provided by Joseph, who, from 1894, made London his home.

By the end of the century, Nathan's company was importing a wide range of merchandise from England that it then sold to various farmers' co-operative associations. It also acquired several agencies from British firms, and began exporting frozen butter and cheese to Britain as agents for New Zealand farmers on commission. In the early 1900s the firm made a major commercial breakthrough when it developed dried milk powder for infant food, using the name 'Glaxo', which was registered as a trademark in 1906. One of Joseph's sons was sent to England to develop a market for the product, which was sold to infirmaries, infant welfare clinics and local municipal authorities across the country. Although the business had now developed the formal structure of a company, it was still very much a family affair. Indeed, Glaxo shows how an internationally dispersed family network could continue to provide a cost-efficient method of doing business across imperial spaces well into the twentieth century.[51]

Religious groups likewise provided the basis for successful trading networks. Faith communities such as the Jews or the Quakers developed channels of communication across the British World that provided members with strong support in times of need and sanctioned certain types of behaviour. As with the family, members of a religious group could take a person's word as his bond. Take the Quakers, for example. They owned some of Britain's most famous food and drink enterprises, the fortunes of which were dependent on colonial supplies of raw material or the tastes of colonial consumers: Cadbury's and Fry's (chocolate), Rowntree's (cocoa), Huntley and Palmer (biscuits), and the Sturges (soft drinks) spent much of their time procuring high-quality colonial ingredients or developing lucrative markets among settlers.[52] Interestingly,

---

[51] M. Casson and H. Cox, 'International Business Networks: Theory and History', *Business and Economic History* 22 (1993), 42–53 (pp. 47–8).

[52] C. Delheim, 'The Creation of a Company Culture: Cadburys, 1861–1913', *AHR* 92 (1987), 13–44; R. Fitzgerland, *Rowntree and the Marketing Revolution, 1862–99* (Cambridge: Cambridge University Press, 1995); T. C. Kennedy, *British Quakerism, 1860–1920: The Transformation of a Religious Community* (Oxford: Oxford University Press, 2001);

the enlightened polices these firms pursued towards their workforces in Britain could be extended to workers in the colonies only by taking direct responsibility for production. The Sturges did so successfully in British-controlled Montserrat, although they never hired any of their management staff locally, nor did they consider making and bottling their drinks there. Meanwhile, Cadbury's became embroiled in a controversy over the treatment of plantation workers on the Portuguese islands of San Thome and Principe – plantations that they did not own but from which they bought part of their supply of cocoa beans.

Trust was not, of course, confined to family or faith networks. During the second half of the nineteenth century other types of association – freemasonry is a case in point – spread British influences, practices and traditions overseas.[53] The Masonic brotherhood functioned as 'a kind of global patronage network that helped men to find employment, secure promotion, and cope with hardship'.[54] From the mid century, 'ideas, information, money, and people flowed with increased intensity across the whole Masonic network'.[55] By the late 1880s, there were over 820 lodges to be found across the empire. Merchants, planters and professionals were all widely involved, with respectability a key aspect of membership.[56]

The export not only of masonry, but of a wide array of voluntary clubs and societies, was in fact a distinctive feature of the British World.[57] Although the commercial impact of these associations remains largely undocumented, it is clear that they provided fellowship, mutual support and opportunities for personal advancement for the more upwardly mobile classes of British society. They also developed relations between business, professional and official groups in the colonies, and circulated ideas about commerce, technology and trade.[58]

The rest of this chapter, however, turns from the informal to the more formal commercial structures of the British World: professional

A. Tyrrell, 'A Business of Philanthropy: The Montserrat Company, 1856–1961', *The Journal of Caribbean History* 38 (2004), 184–212; I. Williams, *The Firm of Cadbury, 1831–1911* (London: Constable, 1931).

[53] P. J. Rich, *Elixir of Empire: The English Public Schools, Ritualism, Freemasonry and Imperialism* (London: Regency, 1989), pp. 82–100.
[54] J. L. Harland-Jacobs, *Builders of Empire: Freemasonry and British Imperialism, 1717–1929* (Chapel Hill: University of North Carolina Press, 2007), p. 208.
[55] *Ibid.*, p. 244.
[56] *Ibid.*, p. 6. For a fascinating account of how Cornish freemasonry aided both the migration of Cornish miners and mine managers and the dissemination of mining information around the (mainly British) world, see R. Burt, 'Freemasonry and Business Networking during the Victorian Period', *EcHR* 56 (2003), pp. 657–88.
[57] P. Clark, *British Clubs and Societies, 1580–1800: The Origins of an Association World* (Oxford: Oxford University Press, 2000), pp. 388–429.
[58] *Ibid.*, pp. 452–3.

organisations, patent systems, Chambers of Commerce and international exhibitions. These 'arteries of empire' expanded rapidly after 1850, facilitating the spread of business information, consumer fashions and technological know-how.

Professional diasporas

Professional people were highly mobile across an English-speaking world. Their mobility was, however, less a by-product of imperial policy, and more the result of individuals acting on their own initiative to build careers abroad.[59] At home, expanding education coupled with relatively inexpansive professions ensured that there was keen competition for jobs; many people therefore turned to the colonies instead. Professional knowledge and skills were readily transferred to the dominions, which had yet to train their own citizens in sufficient numbers to supply a growing demand for chemists, doctors, engineers, patent agents, lawyers, teachers and the like. Some of the professionals who left Britain were peripatetic, moving around (and sometimes beyond) the British World, while others settled permanently in their new place of abode. Nor is it simply a case of professional people contributing to, and gaining greatly from empire.[60] In Britain itself, key characteristics of professionalism – trained expertise, disinterested public service and selection by merit – were developed and defined through empire; the aspirations and agendas of professional bodies increasingly reflected their overseas colonial membership; and the voluntary activity of the professional classes was readily transferred on to an imperial stage, deepening its sense of purpose and enhancing its prestige in the process.

Take, for example, engineering. Victorian notions of technological development were closely tied to ideas of moral progress. Armed with a 'civilising' ideology, and sensing economic opportunity, increasing numbers of British engineers ventured abroad from the 1840s, without the

---

[59] For the imperial reach of British scientists, see, for example, the meetings of the British Association for the Advancement of Science, which spread to the settler empire in Montreal (1884), Toronto (1897), South Africa (1905), Winnipeg (1909) and Australia (1914); J. Morrell, *Gentlemen of Science: Early Years of the British Association for the Advancement of Science* (Oxford: Oxford University Press, 1981), pp. 412, 493; B. Marsden and C. Smith, 'Introduction: Technology, Science and Culture in the Long Nineteenth Century', in Marsden and Smith (eds.), *Engineering Empires: A Cultural History of Technology in Nineteenth-Century Britain* (Basingstoke: Palgrave Macmillan, 2005), p. 231.

[60] A. S. Thompson, *The Empire Strikes Back? The Impact of Imperialism on Britain from the Mid-Nineteenth Century* (Harlow: Pearson Education, 2005), pp. 17ff.

need of government support.[61] The first markets for their expertise were in Europe and the USA, but these countries were anxious to build industries and infrastructures of their own. It was in the colonies that British engineers had their greatest impact. Projects ranged from the mining of minerals, to railway, harbour and canal construction, to bridge and dam building. By the turn of the century, the two main professional bodies of engineers had a fifth of their membership – over a thousand people – based in the colonies.[62]

We can explore the experience of engineers by honing in on two important branches of the profession – railways and mining. The importance of the engineering profession rose to new heights during the railway 'boom' or 'mania' of the 1840s. The main lines of Britain's railway system were mostly complete by the 1870s, after which British engineers became increasingly occupied with constructing and promoting railways in Britain's expanding empire.[63] 'Overseas, almost all of the early railways relied on British engines and expertise; conceived in the interests of trade, railways themselves became the great British export.'[64] Orders piled in for equipment and stores – coal, rails, spikes, signals, iron for bridges, pumps, rolling stock and locomotives; even basic items – picks, hammers, buckets, wheelbarrows and small tools – were exported from Britain.

The majority of the railway engineers who supervised construction had received their training in England and Scotland. It was they who surveyed the terrain, drew up drawings and specifications for bridges and stations, liaised with contractors and ensured that work was done according to their requirements. Crucially, it was they who decided where the materials for the railways should be procured, and they naturally favoured familiar products. Railway locomotives, for which the settler colonies provided a major export market, are a case in point.[65] Several large locomotive firms

---

[61] See, especially, the work of R. A. Buchanan: 'The Diaspora of British Engineering', *Technology and Culture* 27 (1986), 501–24; *The Engineers: A History of the Engineering Profession in Britain, 1750–1914* (London: Kingsley, 1989); and *The Life and Times of Isambard Kingdom Brunel* (London: Continuum International Publishing, 2002), pp. 83–102.

[62] T. Johnson, 'The State and the Professions: The Peculiarities of the British', in A. Giddens and G. Mackenzie (eds.), *Social Class and the Division of Labour: Essays in Honour of Ilya Neustadt* (Cambridge: Cambridge University Press, 1983), p. 199.

[63] A. Burton, *The Railway Empire* (London: John Murray, 1994), p. 249; N. Faith, *The World the Railways Made* (London: Bodley Head, 1990), p. 146.

[64] S. Garfield, *The Last Journey of William Huskisson* (London: Faber, 2003), p. 211.

[65] Thompson and Magee, 'A Soft Touch?', p. 698. The exception here is Canada, where the big Montreal foundries, which had grown up on the demand for marine engines, had little difficulty making new steam engines. Already, by the 1850s, the Kingston works were building engines, as was James Good of Toronto. See Bliss, *Northern Enterprise*, p. 239.

in Britain benefited from colonial demand, the most important being the North British Group, which built locomotives 'for the entire empire', a connection 'proudly displayed' in its histories.[66] British superintending engineers were tough taskmasters, however. They designed precisely what they wanted, visited suppliers prior to their departure from the UK to approve designs and to place provisional orders, and were not slow to relay their views on the shortcomings of existing engines to British manufacturers.[67] Engines were often substantially modified to meet the requirements of colonial topography and climate.

The early history of railway building in Australia is instructive here.[68] Largely built by British engineers, it was not surprising that Australia's first railways used British practices and British equipment. In 1854, the first steam-operated railway opened in Victoria. It ran a distance of two-and-a-half miles from Flinders Street to Port Melbourne. Owned and operated by the Melbourne and Hobson's Bay Railway Company, the railway placed orders for locomotives, rolling stock and other equipment with Robert Stephenson and Company in England, although exceptionally, and owing to a delay on delivery, a locally built engine had to be ordered from Robertson, Martin and Smith of Melbourne. This engine was delivered in ten weeks with the help of Langland's Port Phillip foundry, which constructed the boiler.[69] For the most part, however, the materials required for railways in Australia, including iron and steel rails, were shipped from Britain – Australia lacked the manufacturing capacity to cope with large orders. John Whitton, for example, arrived in 1856 as chief engineer for the New South Wales lines.[70] Born in Yorkshire, the son of a Wakefield land agent, he gained his experience working on the Manchester, Sheffield and Lincolnshire railways, and then on the Oxford, Worcester and Wolverhampton line. During his thirty-two year term of office in New South Wales 2000 miles of track were laid down. These included two remarkable zig-zags by which the main line westwards from Sydney crossed the Blue Mountains and the great Hawkesbury River Bridge, opened in 1889. To build at this rate, Whitton turned to Thomas

---

[66] J. M. MacKenzie, 'The Second City of the Empire: Glasgow – Imperial Municipality' in F. Driver and D. Gilbert (eds.), *Imperial Cities: Landscape, Display and Identity* (Manchester: Manchester University Press, 1999), p. 223.
[67] For example, see J. Brunton, *John Brunton's Book: Being the Memories of John Brunton* (Cambridge: Cambridge University Press, 1939), pp. 82–3.
[68] See especially here Burton, *The Railway Empire*, pp. 226–48.
[69] R. Testro, *A Pictorial History of Australian Railways, 1854–1970* (Melbourne: Lansdowne Press, 1971), pp. 16–17.
[70] I. Brady, G. Johnson, S. Sharp, G. Smith, R. Taaffe and A. Watson, *New South Wales Railways: The First Twenty-Five Years, 1855–1880* (Broadmeadow, NSW: Australian Railway Historical Society, 1980).

Brassey for skilled railway labourers, and to a variety of British companies for cheap and reliable equipment and supplies.

Certainly, the colonial construction of goods vehicles was encouraged early on. Yet not until the 1880s did New South Wales railways begin to look to a mix of locally manufactured and British engines. Even then, imported engines remained cheaper, and the larger works in Britain maintained the upper hand over local manufacturers because of their economies of scale. The same was true of rolling stock. The construction of the first passenger vehicles for New South Wales was entrusted to the prolific rolling stock manufacturer, Wright and Son of Birmingham. It was not until 1877, when a series of longer-term contracts were introduced, that local builders of rolling stock were able to establish a secure base for their business. The experience of South Australia was very similar.[71] During the first decade of the Southern and Western line – the 'Pony railway', as it was sarcastically called by its critics – seven types of engine were tried, all of which were ordered from British firms, among them Avonside (Bristol), Neilson (Glasgow), Cross (St Helens) and Kitson (Leeds). Only in 1876 were instructions issued to build a locomotive locally at the Ipswich government shops – a further five were constructed there the following year.

Overseas mining enterprises also created lucrative opportunities for British engineers and major markets for British firms. Melbourne, for example, became a boom-town during the gold rush of the 1850s, the base for many mechanical engineers 'who established flourishing enterprises in Australia'.[72] Some of the business these engineers generated went the way of local firms. But expatriate mine managers and engineers put considerable amounts of business the way of companies 'back home'. In South Africa, as we have seen, there were a large number of Cornish miners, engineers and mine managers employed on the Rand. They opened up opportunities for Cornish engineering companies to sell rock drills, beam engines, compressors, pumping and lift equipment, and a whole variety of other goods. Yet rather than encouraging complacency, Cornwall's close links to South Africa frequently led to technical innovation and better design. A good example would be Holman Brothers – 'the Camborne firm that laid the foundations for Cornwall's world class export market in mining machinery'.[73] Holmans had stores in

[71] J. Armstrong, *Locomotives in the Tropics*, 2 vols., Vol. I: *Queensland Railways, 1864–1910* (Brisbane: Australian Railway Historical Society, 1985).
[72] R. A. Buchanan, 'The British Contribution to Australian Engineering: The Australian Dictionary of Biography Entries', *Historical Studies* 20 (1993), 401–19 (quote from p. 406). See also G. Blainey, *The Rush that Never Ended: A History of Australian Mining* (Melbourne: Melbourne University Press, 1963).
[73] S. P. Schwartz, 'Cornish Migration to Latin America: A Global and Transnational Perspective', unpublished Ph.D. thesis, University of Exeter (2003), pp. 231–2. On

Johannesburg, British Columbia and Coolgardie in Australia. Facing considerable competition from American manufacturers in South Africa,[74] the company's directors travelled between Cornwall and Johannesburg on a regular basis, meeting mine managers and supervisors. They were well aware of the different working conditions in the Transvaal mines, and well acquainted with the important figures in the mining industry. The free flow of people and information between Cornwall and the Rand helped to build the experience and expertise of Cornish engineering firms that was crucial to their success. Although Holmans exported mining machinery around the world, the goldmines of the Witwatersrand remained among its best customers; the company's rock drills won several competitions there, and employees at its 'No. 3 factory' could often be seen working overtime to meet South African orders.

If the situation in South Africa was different from Britain's other dominions it was partly because of the way in which imperial patriotism intruded into debates about manufacturing as a result of the South African War (1899–1902). Alfred Milner's drawing of the Transvaal more firmly into Britain's orbit led to the imposition of a special 'permit system' on interior travel for non-British citizens, one effect of which was to impede the return of American mining engineers and entrepreneurs to the Rand. The permit system helped to stem the expansion of American trade in South Africa, as did strict inspections of incoming American products, delays to and cancellations of official contracts, a lack of local credit, high freight rates (combined with the rebates to British shipping firms mentioned previously), and new preferential customs duties.[75]

American exports to South Africa had grown at an alarming rate in the later nineteenth century, especially stores and equipment for the extractive industries. Although in 1870 America's trade with the region was meagre, this changed with the discovery of gold. By 1896, American mining managed approximately half of all mines on the Rand. Like the British engineers, they tended to direct contracts for equipment to their

Holman's involvement in South Africa, see C. Carter Holman, *Cornish Engineering, 1801–2001: Two Centuries of Industrial Excellence in Camborne* (Camborne: CompAir, 2001), pp. 29, 30–3, 41–9.

[74] Many of the capital goods required by the growing mining industry (including elevators, skips and stamp batteries) came from the United States, which provided keen competition in the sales of rock drills too. See J. T. Campbell, 'The Americanization of South Africa', in R. Wagnleitner and E. T. May (eds.), *'Here, There and Everywhere': The Foreign Politics of American Popular Culture* (Hanover, NH: University Press of New England, 2000), p. 39.

[75] A few US firms were able to by-pass these measures by incorporating themselves in Canada. See Campbell, 'The Americanization of South Africa', p. 40; R. W. Hull, *American Enterprise in South Africa: Historical Dimensions of Engagement and Disengagement* (New York: New York University Press, 1990), pp. 70–7.

own nationals, with the Ingersoll Drill Company a leading beneficiary.[76] Thus, by the end of the century, America had become the largest supplier of heavy equipment and electrical equipment to South Africa's goldmines, and the second largest supplier of all South African imports.

All this revived British fears of American economic influence. In the words of Henry Birchenough, a special British commissioner sent to report on South Africa, 'America is undoubtedly our most formidable rival present and future.'[77] Three influential books appeared during the South African War to alert people to the threat, one by Stafford Ransome (a former British mining engineer in South Africa), one by F. A. Mackenzie (*The American Invaders*), and another by W. T. Stead (*The Americanization of the World*). These publications set the scene for a campaign to weaken American commerce. After 1903, there were far fewer American mining engineers employed on the Rand. 'Even those who retained their positions lost their powers of purchase and control of personnel.'[78] By the end of 1904 American imports to South Africa had halved, and the decline continued for four more years. The winner was Britain, whose exports increased throughout this period, amounting to some 60 per cent of the total South African market by 1913.

British firms did not have it all their own way, however. Of particular interest is the Transvaal's electricity industry, where pro-British sentiment was vigorously asserted during and after the reconstruction era.[79] By 1907, the three main power companies operating on the Rand had been consolidated into a new operation, the Victoria Falls Power Company. The German banks and the German industrial giant Allgemeine Elektrizitäts-Gesellschaft (AEG) bought their way into a British colony by paying a British-controlled 'African Concessions Syndicate' an exorbitant price for its shares.[80] Their clear intention was to monopolise the South African market for steam-powered electricity-generating machinery. Predictably, the Transvaal Institute of Mining Engineers protested strongly against AEG's tactics. On two separate occasions the Institute's British professionals drew on deep-seated anti-German sentiment among

---

[76] T. J. Noer, *Briton, Boer and Yankee: The United States and South Africa, 1870–1914* (Kent, OH: Kent State University Press, 1978), pp. 30–2; Campbell, 'The Americanization of South Africa', pp. 38–9.

[77] Quoted in Campbell, 'The Americanization of South Africa', p. 93.

[78] *Ibid.*, p. 98.

[79] Our analysis of this industry draws on N. L. Clark, *Manufacturing Apartheid: State Corporations in South Africa* (New Haven: Yale University Press, 1994); R. Christie, *Electricity, Industry and Class in South Africa* (Oxford: Oxford University Press, 1984).

[80] For the role of German entrepreneurs, bankers and industrialists in the economic development of modern South Africa, see J. D. F. Jones, *Through Fortress and Rock: The Story of Gencor, 1895–1995* (Johannesburg: Jonathan Ball, 1995).

English-speakers in the Transvaal to bolster their opposition, only to be rebuffed by the mining magnates and the government. The mining magnates seemed interested only in mechanising their industry, increasing productivity and reducing reliance on black labour. The government, meanwhile, insisted that the Transvaal's economy was benefiting greatly from increased supplies of cheap electricity, so that there was no need to put contracts for machinery out to open tender. In this instance, at least, the 'buy-British' argument had little purchase in business or official circles. In 1911, the Victoria Falls Power Company's new Vereeniging station came into operation. Sammy Marks likened it to a 'South African *Sheffield* on the Rand'. In truth, it would have been better likened to Berlin – the industrial heartland of AEG.

Patents systems

Technological convergence was not restricted to the railway and mining sectors; nor was it the product of professional mobility alone. The emergence of colonial patent systems and professional patent agencies had an integral role to play.[81]

In most countries there was a long tradition of granting patents; Australians, Canadians, New Zealanders and other nationals were all well accustomed to their use. The evolution of affordable and enforceable patent protection was in fact central to the development of a modern market for technological ideas. Patents worked because they offered a sensible compromise between the competing interests of the owners of the new technology, who wished to protect their intellectual property by controlling its use, and society at large, whose interests were obviously best served by the widespread adoption of new, more efficient technology. Both parties could clearly benefit, and once this was realised and the systems issuing them trusted, there was a strong incentive to extend the arrangement to as many jurisdictions as possible. Successful inventors, such as Thomas Edison (1847–1931), therefore took the patenting of their inventions in non-American patents systems, including colonial ones, very much as a matter of course.[82]

Reflecting this willingness to patent across national boundaries was the fact that patent offices and agents in every system worked to establish

---

[81] The section draws from G. B. Magee, *Knowledge Generation: Technological Change and Economic Growth in Colonial Australia* (Melbourne: Australian Scholarly Publishing, 2000), esp. pp. 138–80, 208–14. Unless otherwise stated, this is the source of the material cited.

[82] P. Israel and R. Rosenberg, 'Patent Office Records as a Historical Source: The Case of Thomas Edison', *Technology and Culture* 32 (1991), pp. 1094–101; Magee, *Knowledge Generation*, p. 83.

contacts and to exchange relevant information and publications with their counterparts elsewhere. As a result, by the latter half of the nineteenth century British and Colonial Patent Offices held vast libraries containing reports and specifications of the patents that had been issued in various parts of the world. The richest information in their collections, however, inevitably related to colonial and British patenting. Moreover, from 1864 the British *Commissioner of Patents' Journal* published and circulated booklets, which furnished information on how prospective patentees could protect their inventions in each of the settler colonies.

Patent agents also contributed to this pro-colonial informational asymmetry. By selling their specialist knowledge on the acquisition and management of patent protection, they were crucially placed to influence the dissemination of information and technological knowledge. So important had their role become in the patent system that, as early as 1851, the progress of approximately 90 per cent of all patent applications in Britain was directed by a patent agent. In the colonies, too, patent agents quickly became important to the running of the local patent systems.[83]

In Australia, for example, the first practising patent agent appears to have been William Henry Ritchie, who began operating out of an office in Melbourne from about 1857. He was soon followed by others, many of whom had prior experience as lawyers, engineers or even patent agents back in Britain. The profession actively sought to preserve these ties to Britain, and it was not uncommon for patent agents from the colonies to visit and interact with like-minded colleagues in London. The Melbourne-based patent agent Edward Waters, for example, visited and presented a paper on Australasian patents to the Chartered Institute of Patent Agents in London in 1885, an interest in Australia and the empire that the organ of the British Institute followed up subsequently with articles on patenting law and practice in the colonies. These visits and various exchanges of information appeared to have had the desired effect. A manual compiled by two leading British patent agents in 1905 listed the relatively small Australian system among the twenty or so in which it was worthwhile for inventors to seek patent protection.[84] Australia, like the other dominions, was therefore clearly part of an international patenting network, albeit one centred in London.

The footprint of Australia's imperial status is clearly evident in the records of the Colony of Victoria's patent system. Established in 1857, the Victorian system was without doubt the largest, the most modern

[83] H. I. Dutton, *The Patent System and Inventive Activity during the Industrial Revolution, 1750–1852* (Manchester: Manchester University Press, 1984), pp. 86–96.
[84] E. Edwards and A. E. Edwards, *How to Take Out Patents in England and Abroad* (Edwards and Co., 1905).

and the most effective in pre-Federation Australia.[85] It was popular with local and overseas inventors alike. Not only did non-Australians, predominantly Americans and Britons, manage to lodge approximately a third of all applicants between 1857 and 1903 (when the Victorian system was superseded by that of the Australian Commonwealth), their patents related to all areas of the economy, not just the primary and mining sector. Indeed, the strengths of their patenting overwhelmingly lay in the manufacturing and service sectors. That said, it can hardly be claimed that the Victorian system was a truly level playing field for most international inventors. Given its grounding in British patent law, the Victorian Patent Office practices and procedures were bound to be more familiar – and hence accessible – to British inventors and their agents. Thus, British World connections – personal, professional and official – made the typical British inventor more aware of Australia than foreign counterparts. This is why in most years British patent applications there outnumbered even American ones, despite the amazing scale of American inventive activity that was taking place at this time.

Chambers of Commerce

If trans-national history is conceived as 'the study of the ways in which past lives and events have been shaped by processes and relationships that have transcended the borders of nation states',[86] then business networks should be seen as a primary manifestation of it. As one scholar observes, 'businessmen in regional industries in different countries sometimes had more in common with each other, through the mutually dependent demands of a shared trade, than they had with their fellow citizens operating in other spheres of interest'.[87]

Something of the significance of these business networks can be seen from the colonial Chambers of Commerce. By the second half of the nineteenth century these chambers were well established in settler societies. They were also increasingly well networked with each other. Cape Town's Chamber, for example, was founded in 1861. With the encouragement of its first president, the merchant, financier and politician John Ebden (1787–1873), it rapidly established itself as an important civic institution. Although many of the matters it dealt with were of local significance

[85] B. Hack, *A History of the Patent Profession in Colonial Australia* (Melbourne: Clement Hack and Co., 1984), pp. 11–15; Magee, *Knowledge Generation*, pp. 16–19.
[86] A. Curthoys and M. Lake, 'Introduction', in Curthoys and Lake (eds.), *Connected Worlds: History in Transnational Perspective* (Canberra: Australian National University Press, 2005), pp. 5–20 (p. 5).
[87] B. M. King, *Silk and Empire* (Manchester: Manchester University Press, 2005), p. 85.

only, the Cape Chamber exchanged information on markets and prices with other colonial Chambers, and sent representatives to commercial gatherings in London and Canada – practices that gained momentum over time.[88] Similarly, the Melbourne Chamber of Commerce, founded the previous decade in 1851, was an influential force in the city's history. Its first president, William Westgarth (1815–89), was another merchant, financier and politician, one of the most respected men in the infant colony of Victoria. Westgarth formed the Melbourne Chamber almost single-handedly, and later helped to found the London Chamber of Commerce in 1881. He was well-known for his support of good causes, his advocacy of manhood suffrage, the secret ballot and state education, and the quality of his writings on early Australia. Following his return to England to establish a stockbroking firm in 1857, he was an influential adviser to those Australian colonies trying to float loans and strengthen their City borrowing credentials.[89] Like the Cape Chamber, the Melbourne Chamber was very much outward-looking. Imperial communications were a consistent concern.[90] The Chamber campaigned vigorously for a fortnightly mail service with Europe, for the extension of the telegraph from Ceylon to Australia, and for an imperial postal union, arguing that the progress and development of colonial trade were being retarded for want of such things. It also pressed for the formation of a Colonial Wool Merchants' Association in London to improve the mode of warehousing Australian wools in the United Kingdom – this was eventually set up in 1868–9.

British and Colonial Chambers of Commerce were first brought together in London in 1886 for the Congress of Chambers of Commerce of the Empire (CCCE).[91] This self-declared 'true Parliament of British Commerce' met again in London in 1892, 1896 and 1900, and then in Montreal in 1903. In 1911, the Federation of Chambers of Commerce of the British Empire was formed. The Federation's headquarters were

[88] R. F. M. Immelman, *Men of Good Hope: The Romantic Story of the Cape Town Chamber of Commerce, 1804–1954* (Cape Town: Cape Town Chamber of Commerce, 1955), pp. 179–86, 259–62.
[89] W. Westgarth, *Personal Recollections of Early Melbourne and Victoria* (Sydney: G. Robertson and Co., 1888). See also J. B. Cooper, *Victorian Commerce, 1834–1934* (Melbourne: Robertson and Mullens, 1934); and G. Serle, 'Westgarth, William (1815–89)', in H. C. G. Matthew and B. Harrison (eds.), *The Oxford Dictionary of National Biography* (Oxford: Oxford University Press, 2004).
[90] See especially the memoir of its long-standing secretary, B. Cowderoy, *Melbourne's Commercial Jubilee: Notes from the Records of Fifty Years' Work of the Melbourne Chamber of Commerce* (Melbourne: Mason, Firth and M'Cutcheon, 1901), pp. 12–23, 34–43, 61–75, 97–8, 133, 143.
[91] B. H. Brown, *The Tariff Reform Movement in Great Britain, 1881–95* (New York: Routledge, 1943), pp. 92–3.

in London. It organised biennial conferences, held alternately in London and the dominions.[92] Intent upon improving commercial relations across the empire, the Federation's proceedings make it clear that it was nonetheless primarily concerned with settler states. So much is apparent from the many resolutions it passed on preferential trade. Opinion was divided as to their desirability, with Canadian delegates coming out strongly in favour, and Manchester delegates remaining resolutely opposed. This stand-off highlighted the starkly differing perspectives between cotton manufacturers tied predominantly to the Indian market, and other sections of the business community with commercial interests stretching across the self-governing dominions. The latter tended to feel more threatened by Germany and the United States, and were thus more sympathetic to measures calculated to protect colonial markets from foreign competition.

The majority of delegates, however, adopted a pragmatic position on the subject of preferential tariffs: namely, that whatever their pros and cons, there was little mileage in a policy of fiscal reform until all the settler colonies could confidently subscribe to it. Indeed, although the Federation provided a major forum for the business community to debate tariffs, much more of its time was spent discussing a raft of more practical and pressing commercial questions. These ranged from the codification of commercial law and procedures for bills of exchange; to postal and telegraphic facilities, routes and rates; to the liability of shipowners for damage to cargo; to charges for maintaining lighthouses, buoys and beacons (and who should bear them); to questions of labour conciliation and arbitration (where advances in Australia and New Zealand were of particular interest to delegates); to emigration (where government was encouraged to use every means available to encourage people to go to the colonies); to the need to adopt more uniform (metric) systems of weights, measures and currency. Significantly, the majority of the resolutions on these subjects were co-sponsored by British and dominion delegates, and virtually all were adopted unanimously after they had been carefully and constructively examined.[93] It would take a much longer and more intensive study of the Federation to evaluate its contribution to commercial reform across the British World, but the evidence adduced here suggests that it played a major, if hitherto neglected, role.

Among the glaring omissions in the proceedings of the Federation is that of the impact of colonisation upon 'coloured' or indigenous

---

[92] Copies of the *Official Reports* of the Congress can be consulted at the Guildhall Library, London, MS 18.278/1.

[93] For a flavour of the topics and the discussion surrounding them, see, for example, *Official Report of the 3rd Congress of the Chambers of Commerce of the British Empire, 9–12 June 1896* (1896), MS 18.278/1.

peoples. Indeed, if racial exclusion has been an 'inevitable counterpart' of globalisation,[94] then the Chambers of Commerce offer insights into how imperial networks, while linking up markets through the spread of information and technology, marginalised particular subordinate groups by depriving them of access to the very structures that might have helped to empower them.

The moment one begins to think of the British World as a series of over-lapping networks through which knowledge and ideas were exchanged, goods traded and people travelled, then questions of who belonged to them and who did not, and of the implications of being included or excluded, need to be addressed. South Africa provides a useful case study. The Cape Town Chamber excluded people on grounds of wealth, status and colour. Unlike Nigeria, where Africans were not excluded from commer-cial life until after 1897, Cape merchants were predominantly white and European for most of our period, allowing perhaps for a small number of individuals who may have been light-skinned descendants of white slave-owners and probably non-African slaves.[95] The Cape Chamber consisted of an established mercantile elite (or 'grand bourgeoisie') with a long history of engagement with the imperial economy and personal links with metropolitan capital: sixty or so men who would all have known (or known of) each other.[96] They can be contrasted with the less prosper-ous and colonially oriented middle-class businessmen, retailers and mer-chants (English- and Dutch-Afrikaans-speaking) who looked instead to municipal institutions to establish their identity and press their claims.[97] Initially, therefore, there does not appear to have been any active racial exclusion on the part of the Cape Chamber. Rather, in keeping with many 'elite' civic institutions of this period, it was not felt necessary to stipulate that blacks could not be members. There was an annual sub-scription of £5, which was high enough to have put off small traders of whatever ethnic background.[98] In general, it seems to have been more a question of Africans preferring accumulation in cattle and land, while lacking access to the necessary credit (provided on the basis of social class as much as colour) and transportation to engage in mercantile activity. In

[94] A. Hoogvelt, *Globalisation and the Postcolonial World: The New Political Economy of Development*, 2nd edn (Basingstoke: Palgrave Macmillan, 2001), p. 130.
[95] We are grateful to Vivian Bickford-Smith for steering us through the complexities of commercial life in the nineteenth-century Cape and African involvement in it.
[96] Immelman, *Men of Good Hope*, pp. 178, 184.
[97] T. Keegan, *Colonial South Africa and the Origins of the Racial Order* (Cape Town: New Africa Books, 1996), pp. 164–7.
[98] Racial exclusion may have been more apparent in the Eastern Cape where Chambers were formed in Port Elizabeth in 1864, East London in 1873 and Graaff-Reinet in 1875, but further research is required to confirm whether this was so.

those places where indigenous entrepreneurs did gain a foothold – such as the Eastern Cape where transport riding became a field for coloured and Black enterprise, especially among the Khoikhoi who fell under missionary influence – technological development (in this case, the railways) destroyed livelihoods, as did lack of access to credit and the ability to buy land outside cramped reserve areas.[99] What is not in doubt is that, for a small number of affluent and privileged Europeans, membership of the Cape Chamber brought the benefits of access to commercial bodies in Britain promoting Cape trade,[100] of contact with other colonial Chambers, and, from 1879, of representation at the regular collective gatherings of the empire's Chambers of Commerce in London.

Meanwhile, in Natal, there was a sizeable and successful Indian merchant community.[101] It was made up partly of the larger and wealthier Muslim merchant groups, originating from Surat and Porbandar, and joined together by family and kinship ties. These merchants defended their privileges and status as 'British Indians' and enjoyed relatively good trading relations with white wholesale merchants and retail customers who valued their business and reputation for punctual payment. The other section of Natal's Indian merchant community, the so-called 'dukawallahs', were small storekeepers or shopkeepers, either ex-indentured Hindu labourers or Muslim 'passenger Indians', operating in semi-urban and rural areas. They were resented by the smaller English shopkeepers, who later began to rail against the entire Indian merchant class. After the grant of responsible government to Natal in 1893, pressure upon parliamentarians mounted from white residents and businesses to pass discriminatory legislation. The bigger Indian merchants and storekeepers were forced out of Durban's commercial district, licence-renewal applications were refused and the number of Indian-owned shops on West Street fell dramatically. Faced by such pressures, Natal's Indian merchants felt compelled to organise commercially to defend their interests. Whereas previously they had formed themselves into associations for the purpose of protecting and celebrating their religious, cultural and social distinctions, they now initiated political campaigns to protest against discrimination in trade. This culminated in the formation of a

---

[99] See here R. Bouch, 'Mercantile Activity and Investment in the Eastern Cape: The Case of Queenstown, 1853–1886', *South African Journal of Economic History* 6 (1991), 18–37; A. Muller, 'The Economic History of the Port Elizabeth–Uitenhage region', *South African Journal of Economic History* 15 (2000), 20–47.

[100] For example, the Cape of Good Hope Trade Society, the South African Association, and the South African Merchants Committee.

[101] See especially V. Padayachee and R. Morrell, 'Indian Merchants and Dukawallahs in the Natal Economy, *c.* 1875–1914', *JSAS* 17 (1991), 71–102, from which the rest of this paragraph is drawn.

separate Indian Chamber of Commerce in 1908 during the depths of a severe depression in Natal, exemplifying the racial boundaries that, by this time, had developed around the colonial Chambers.

Exhibitions

Exhibitions, international and imperial, grew in popularity in the second half of the nineteenth century. Only a small percentage of the 14,000 exhibitors at the Crystal Palace (1851) were colonial, and foreign countries were allocated more space than the empire in its official catalogue. Subsequently, however, explicitly imperial events were organised, most notably the Indian and Colonial exhibition of 1886.[102] In addition to the exhibitions staged in Britain, which tended to present the 'metropole' as the hub of the 'imperial economy', there were many inter-colonial events, and these had a different dynamic.

Melbourne staged six such exhibitions in 1854, 1861, 1866, 1872, 1875 and 1880–1. Together they attracted hundreds of thousands of visitors, and paved the way for the city's more elaborate Centennial Exhibition of 1888–9, which was probably witnessed by more Australians than any other single event before the First World War.[103] Each exhibition was designed to encourage trade (import and export) and to attract new capital into the colony. The exhibition of 1880–1 was intended to stimulate a recovery from the economic and political turmoil of the late 1870s, while the exhibition of 1888–9 promoted Melbourne as a sophisticated, industrialising city that symbolised the ideals of a manufacturing age. Indeed, by the 1880s it was noticeable how a previously strong prejudice against colonial-made goods had begun to dissipate,[104] as the products of other countries had to make way for those of Victoria, aided of course by the colony's introduction of tariffs, which not only raised revenue but helped

---

[102] In London, there was also a 'Greater Britain' exhibition in 1899, and a 'South African Products' exhibition in 1907, plus several provincial exhibitions focusing on empire. For an overview, see P. Greenhalgh, *Ephemeral Vistas: The Expositions Universelles, Great Exhibitions and World's Fairs, 1851–1939* (Manchester: Manchester University Press, 1988); and P. H. Hoffenberg, *An Empire on Display: English, Indian and Australian Exhibitions from the Crystal Palace to the Great War* (Berkeley: University of California Press, 2001).

[103] *Official Record of the Centennial International Exhibition, Melbourne, 1888–89* (Melbourne, 1890), pp. 124–7; G. Davison, 'Festivals of Nationhood: The International Exhibitions', in S. L. Goldberg and F. B. Smith (eds.), *Australian Cultural History* (Melbourne: Australian Academy of Humanities, 1988), pp. 158–77 (p. 172). For the full range of inter-colonial exhibitions, see J. E. Findling (ed.), *Historical Dictionary of World's Fairs and Expositions, 1851–1988* (New York: Greenwood, 1990).

[104] *Official Record of the Centennial International Exhibition*, p. 124.

to foster an economically and politically significant manufacturing base by the end of the century.[105]

The displays of locally and British-manufactured goods at these colonial exhibitions provided a focus for negotiations to open up new channels of trade, as did their official catalogues (which contained large amounts of information on exhibits, the contact details of organisers and even prices of displayed merchandise) and the private advertising distributed by companies. The fact that companies often redesigned products for exhibitions in the hope of additional sales is significant. Williamson's, a leading British manufacturer of printed and patterned floorcloths and linoleum, provides an example of the benefits that could flow from exhibitions. In the twentieth century, Australia was one of the company's most important markets. The springboard for its sales to Australia was the Melbourne Centennial Exhibition of 1888–9. After this, Williamson's products drew widespread interest and the major retail emporiums of Australia added them to their catalogues.[106] A marked surge in export orders from Australia is reported to have followed.

Melbourne was not unique in staging exhibitions that stimulated imperial trade. New Zealand's Chambers of Commerce organised similar events, filling their displays with local, Australian and British products. Dunedin was first off the mark in 1865 (it subsequently staged another exhibition in 1889–90) and Christchurch followed suit in 1882 and 1906–7.[107] Every effort was made to link the colony's social and material progress. In the words of James Cowan, official historian of the Christchurch exhibition of 1906–7:

[it was] a solid advertisement for New Zealand products and manufactures, as a trade-bringer and a means for fixing, if only for a brief period, the attention of the outside world upon the individuality, the ego of this new country, the special trend of genius that animates its people, and the expression in concrete form of its progress in useful industries and the amenities that soften life and sweeten man's feelings towards man.[108]

---

[105] For the importance of manufacturing interests as protagonists for these exhibitions, see J. Parris and A. G. L. Shaw, 'The Melbourne International Exhibition 1880–81', *Victorian Historical Journal* 51 (1980), 238–49. For Victoria's protective policies, see Cain and Hopkins, *British Imperialism*, p. 224.

[106] Historical Houses Trust of New South Wales, *Floorcoverings in Australia, 1800–1950* (Glebe, NSW: Historical Houses Trust, 1997), pp. 48–51.

[107] G. McLean, 'The Colony Commodified: Trade, Progress and the Real Business of Exhibitions', in J. M. Thomson (ed.), *Farewell Colonialism: The New Zealand International Exhibition, Christchurch 1906–7* (Palmerston North: University of Auckland, 1998), pp. 27–38.

[108] Quoted in *ibid.*, p. 35.

Indeed, these exhibitions were commercial opportunities in their own right. They brought business into local economies: for transport, hotels, restaurants and cafes; for publishers and printers (biographical compilations were produced for an elite market); and for a range of firms manufacturing commemorative goods.[109]

To form a clearer view of the perceived value of these exhibitions to British and colonial business it is necessary to look more closely at a particular event – the Colonial and Indian Exhibition of 1886 and, specifically, Canadian participation in it. Canada had been actively promoting the possibilities of immigration, investment and trade for some time beforehand.[110] At the Great Exhibition in 1851 it had sought through its displays, which ranged from raw minerals to industrial and craft products, to point to the growing diversity of its produce.[111] Subsequently, emigration agents in Britain had taken up the work of publicising Canadian goods.[112] The Colonial and Indian Exhibition at South Kensington was one of the first to focus on the empire. While much attention has been paid to the propagandist functions of such gatherings, including their trumpeting of the economic advantages of empire to the populace, much less notice has been taken of the opportunity they provided to colonial producers and consumers to take the measure of the British market.

Canada was the most economically developed self-governing colony at this time. It occupied the largest exhibition space (some twenty-eight times as large as that allotted to it in 1851) and sent the greatest number of exhibitors.[113] The Canadian Federal Government encouraged Canadian

---

[109] J. R. Gold and M. M. Gold, *Cities of Culture: Staging International Festivals and the Urban Agenda, 1851–2000* (Aldershot: Ashgate, 2005), p. 68.

[110] But Canada was by no means the only colony to see the exhibition's commercial potential. Australian wines received a lot of attention at this event – George Francis Morris, a Lancashire-born emigrant-turned-goldfields-grocer, who then turned his hand to winemaking in Rutherglen, made contacts with potential buyers, and within a few years his property at Fairfield was one of the world's largest vineyards and wineries. His exports to the UK were helped by the rationalisation of duties at this time: imports of Australian wine increased by almost 150 per cent from 60,000 gallons in 1885 to 145,000 gallons in 1886. Several English merchants were also inspired to start, or stick to, the Australian wine trade as a result of the exhibition, including the buyer, Peter Bond Burgoyne, who later established his own winery at Mt Ophir, and Walter Pownall, whose company became a major purchaser from South Australia. See D. Dunstan, 'A Sobering Experience: From "Australian Burgundy" to "Kanga Rouge": Australian Wine Battles on the London Market, 1900–1981', *Journal of Australian Studies* 17 (2002), 179–210.

[111] S. Murray, 'Canadian Participation and National Representation at the 1851 London Great Exhibition and the 1855 Paris *Exposition Universelle*', *Histoire sociale/Social History* 32 (1999), 1–22.

[112] H. Gordon Skilling, *Canadian Representation Abroad: From Agency to Embassy* (Toronto: Ryerson Press, 1945), p. 47.

[113] We have drawn mainly on the work of one of our MA students here: J. Fukushi, 'Canada and the British Imperial Economy in the Late Nineteenth Century: A Case of the

exhibitors to display at South Kensington by carrying their products to London free of charge, installing their displays in the Canadian court and maintaining them during the exhibition, and returning them to Canada if they so wished. It also appointed a large team of agents for each province to visit leading industrial establishments and to persuade them to participate. For example, A. W. Wright, the agent for Ontario, emphasised to Canadian manufacturers and merchants the value of the reports of the exhibition carried in the English newspapers in opening up new markets for their goods – a form of free advertising not to be missed. The Canadian display at South Kensington was organised under different headings, one of which was entirely devoted to Canadian manufacturing. Other colonies exhibited relatively few machines, most of which were for mining, whereas Canada exhibited over a hundred. It was especially proud of its agricultural implement displays.

Canada, in fact, led the world in labour-saving farm machinery.[114] It is hardly surprising, therefore, that Canadian manufacturers of agricultural implements and tools saw the exhibition as an ideal opportunity to develop their presence overseas. There were forty-four of them in total, many from Ontario, and they eagerly targeted potential business partners, pursuing their benefit in spite of criticism from the London press that Canadian exhibits were 'too shoppy'.[115] They had already successfully driven American manufacturers out of their domestic market, and now sought to expand overseas – the best markets were in England, Australia and Argentina. The lightness and durability of their products was the chief selling point. They were also able to gain valuable insights into the special requirements of British farmers – harvesting machines, for example, had to be adapted to break up straw into larger pieces. In some cases, enquiries about Canadian products led directly to overseas orders. Cockshutt's secured a large contract for its ploughs, and opened an agency in England after the exhibition closed, while the Hart Emery Wheel Company started to export to Queensland soon after. Indeed, the exports of Canadian agricultural implements to Britain more than doubled the year following the exhibition, and it would seem surprising if there were no connection.[116]

Colonial and Indian Exhibition in 1886', unpublished M.A. thesis, University of Leeds (2005). See also C. Tupper, *The Colonial and Industrial Exhibition: Official Catalogue of the Canadian Section* (1886); and W. G. Phillips, *The Agricultural Implement Industry in Canada: A Case Study of Competition* (Toronto: University of Toronto Press, 1956).
[114] For a discussion of the Canadian agricultural machinery industry, see Bliss, *Northern Enterprise*, pp. 241–2, 244, 306–8.
[115] *Toronto Globe*, 1 May 1886, p. 6.
[116] They amounted to £3,539 in 1886, and continued to grow thereafter to £347,996 at the end of the century: *Statistical Abstract for the Several Colonial and Other Possessions of the United Kingdom in Each Year from 1886 to 1900* (1901), Cmd 751, pp. 122–3.

What was true for Canadian exporters was true for British and other colonial producers. If they were to compete on quality as well as price, they had to get the measure of empire markets, and to understand the specific needs of the customers to whom they wished to sell. Imperial exhibitions greatly facilitated this process by bringing both parties into closer contact at venues purposely designed to promote long-distance trade. The fact that these exhibitions spread so rapidly to the dominions, and were even staged multiple times in a single place, further speaks of the importance that colonial as well as British businessmen attached to them. None of this is to deny their propagandist functions – the visual imagery of empire had a strength and immediacy that the written word often lacked – but we need equally to be alert to their commercial and financial motivations and effects.[117]

Britishness: cultures of consumption

The study of material culture is a vibrant field of research.[118] What we consume, and the way we consume it, is widely recognised as a marker of identity. By exploring tastes in food, furniture and fashion scholars have sought to understand how people in the past perceived themselves and were in turn perceived by others. Commodities, it is argued, were culturally specific: they took on a symbolic value from the environment in which they were produced.

After 1850 consumerism intensified across the English-speaking world.[119] The rise of bourgeois society in Britain, the United States and the settler colonies saw a language of 'needs' increasingly displaced by a language of 'wants', particularly in the sphere of household goods. Women led the way in forging this expressive genteel culture, its values and practices. Notions of gentility surrounding the nineteenth-century household fuelled the demand for certain types of goods, and shaped the meaning attached to them.

The question of how far British habits of consumption, as well as marketing and advertising practices, were shaped by the colonial encounter is a complex one.[120] Certainly, by the end of the nineteenth century, several leading British companies were actively, even aggressively, exploiting imperial sentiment in selling their products at home. But British firms

---

[117] Thompson, *The Empire Strikes Back?*, pp. 84–8.
[118] For a key study, see Young, *Middle Class Culture in the Nineteenth Century*.
[119] P. N. Stearns, *Consumerism in World History: The Global Transformation of Desire*, 2nd edn (London: Routledge, 2006), pp. 30, 47.
[120] For references and a commentary on the recent literature, see Thompson, *The Empire Strikes Back?*, pp. 44–9.

also found themselves at an advantage in responding to colonial consumer preference. They were often the first to establish distribution networks in the colonies, and they were in a good position therefore to try to inculcate, as well as to exploit, 'British' tastes. This is not to deny that colonial South Africans, Canadians, New Zealanders and Australians ate, drank, dressed and generally behaved in distinctive ways: they did, and colonial preferences did not slavishly follow imported British (or European) styles. People in the colonies lived differently, and so, even when goods were imported from Britain, the use to which they were put, and the meanings they acquired, could change.

There was not always a need for product differentiation between Britain and its colonies. Thus in the case of the serialised fiction syndicated to colonial weekly newspapers by Lancashire's provincial press (Australia and New Zealand proved its most durable market), rather than targeting particular kinds of client or consumer, it was assumed that a single, standardised list, based around sensational novels, would appeal equally to overseas settlers and people in the provinces in Britain. 'Syndication amounted to an imposition of the metropolis's cultural machinery on that of the (settler) colonies, since it cramped literary production, or at least opportunities for publication, in the colonies.'[121]

The same is true of many so-called 'comfort' foods and drinks. 'We are what we eat' is a popular refrain, and food is said to be 'loaded with cultural meaning and value' – a crucial element in defining national identity.[122] The fact that 'British' food was widely consumed in the dominions partly reflects a preference for the familiar, partly a residue of earlier eating habits, and partly perhaps a desire to sustain cultural and historical bonds.[123] For example, long after their arrival, middle-class colonists continued to rely on British cookery books and household guides. Not until the end of the century did they begin to be locally produced. The most famous is Mrs Beeton's skilfully marketed *Book of Household Management* (1859–61), a major publishing success story of the Victorian era.[124] Such guides played an important role in acculturation. To be sure, much of the food derived from their recipes was locally grown, and merely took on

---

[121] C. Hilliard, 'The Provincial Press and the Imperial Traffic in Fiction: 1870s–1930s', *JBS* 48:3 (July 2009), 653–73. The colonies' share of provincial newspapers' fiction department revenue was approximately 20 per cent from the 1870s through to the 1920s.

[122] P. Manning, *Migration in World History* (New York: Routledge, 2005), p. 127.

[123] A. Wessel, 'There's No Taste Like Home: The Food of Empire', paper presented at the British World Conference, University of Melbourne, July 2003.

[124] N. Humble (ed.), *Mrs Beeton's Book of Household Management: Abridged Edition* (Oxford: Oxford University Press, 2000); and K. Hughes, *The Short Life and Long Times of Mrs Beeton* (London: Random House, 2007).

British trademarks. Yet some of it was actually imported from Britain. By contrast, there is little evidence of indigenous foods from the dominions being exported back to the 'mother country'; in fact, colonists tended to overlook such foods, or regarded them as inedible. Interestingly, this situation was different from that of the Victorian Raj. In their letters to the editors of British magazines, memsahibs proffered Indian recipes – those for curry were especially popular, as such dishes were regarded as a relatively easy way for housewives in Britain to use up leftovers.[125]

Usually, however, British products had to be adapted for colonial tastes. Alcoholic drinks are an example. The three leading Scotch whisky blenders – Buchanan, Dewar's and Walker's – all developed major markets in Australia, Canada and South Africa. The whisky industry boasted an above average export performance, and its products tended to follow the flag. But the preferences of colonial consumers were distinct. On the South African Rand and in the Australian Outback it was strong-flavoured, fiery whiskies that were most prized, so much so that a much higher proportion of grain whisky had to be put into colonial blends.[126]

The case of Australia is worth exploring a little further here.[127] It was once claimed that 'no people on the face of the earth ever absorbed more alcohol per head of population'.[128] Yet the reality was somewhat different. Tea was a better thirst quencher and was consumed in large quantities in Australia, even when compared to Britain. The drinking of alcohol peaked in periods of economic prosperity during the 1830s, 1850s, 1870s and 1880s, and then slumped during depressions. During the convict years, when rum and brandy were favoured spirits, alcohol seems to have offered migrants an opportunity (temporarily) to escape the harsh realities of settler life. Subsequently, from the mid century, the consumption of alcohol reflected the growing prosperity and security felt by many settlers. Whisky grew in popularity during these years: by the 1890s, more of it was drunk than all of other spirits combined. However, during the nineteenth century there was a long-term decline in spirit drinking, and a gradual shift from spirits to beer. Unlike whisky, imported beer faced stiff domestic competition. Beer was expensive to transport and deteriorated rapidly with age. This encouraged local production. Australian breweries already accounted for 80 per cent of total consumption by the late 1880s,

[125] N. Chaudhuri, 'Shawls, Curry, and Rice in Victorian Britain', in N. Chaudhuri and M. Strobel (eds.), *Western Women and Imperialism: Complicity and Resistance* (Bloomington: Indiana University Press, 1992), pp. 231–46.
[126] Thompson and Magee, 'A Soft Touch?', pp. 699, 708.
[127] Our analysis is based on A. Dingle, '"The Truly Magnificent Thirst": An Historical Survey of Australian Drinking Habits', *Historical Studies* 19 (1980), 227–43.
[128] R. Ward, *The Australian Legend* (Melbourne: Oxford University Press, 1966), p. 35.

albeit that local production developed more rapidly in New South Wales than it did in Victoria, which was more dependent on British imports. From the early 1900s, a lighter chilled Australian beer, different in style from English ales, was introduced by the New York brothers W. R. & M. Foster. On the back of this new, 'lager style' of beer, which was better suited to a hot climate, Fosters greatly increased production.[129]

Fashions in clothing and home decoration also provide insights into the spread of consumer culture across the British World. Among middle-class emigrants – an 'Anglo' bourgeoisie, as they have been called – there is evidence that, as early as the 1830s and 1840s, women were recreating changing metropolitan tastes in clothes and furnishings.[130] The maintenance of such connections demonstrated their determination to stay in touch with friends and family back home through correspondence and, later, through the reading of British magazines. Dresses, tablecloths, curtain fabrics and other domestic items were either requisitioned from relatives or ordered directly from British firms; the poor quality and expense of locally available goods helps explain why. Because many early settlers relied on parcels sent by their families back home this transfer of goods does not show up in export statistics, although relatives may well have been reimbursed by remittances (see Chapter 3).

Such consuming habits need to be set in the context of colonial cultural sensitivities. There was a widespread fear of being labelled 'provincial', 'unfashionable' or 'backward' by metropolitan visitors to the colonies; strongest in the early-to-mid 1800s, it persisted into the second half of the nineteenth century. More generally, there was the bourgeois desire to assert social status – a desire that intensified later in the century as a result of the rise of home ownership, the growth of suburban living, and the widening range of domestic furnishings and other household goods. A study of household inventories in Edinburgh, Delaware and Sydney shows how there were marked continuities across English-speaking societies in terms of the ownership of commodities through which the rising middle-classes sought to establish a sense of identity: drawing and dining room tables, bedroom wardrobes, bathroom equipment, china services and pianos. Consumers in these cities purchased similar goods and used them in similar ways, a practice reinforced by the fact that their codes of etiquette were derived from the same body of texts. On this basis, it

---

[129] D. Dunstan, 'Boozers and Wowsers', in V. Burgmann and J. Lee (eds.), *Constructing a Culture: A People's History of Australia since 1788* (Fitzroy, Victoria: Penguin, 1988), pp. 96–123 (pp. 108–10), and 'A Sobering Experience', pp. 179–81.

[130] A. Lester, *Imperial Networks: Creating Identities in Nineteenth Century South Africa and Britain* (London: Routledge, 2001), p. 74; M. Weidenhofer (ed.), *Colonial Ladies* (South Yarra, Victoria: Gordon and Gotch, 1985), p. 14.

is possible to speak of a 'transnational Anglo culture', which was less a case of pale imitation and more of an authentic cultural continuity across 'Greater Britain'.[131]

Three case studies will help us to establish how far these bourgeois household and consumer goods were actually exported from Britain. The first is decorative tiles. Marketed to colonial consumers as high-status goods that could not be purchased locally, decorative ceramic tiles represented the cutting edge in British aesthetic fashion.[132] They gained in popularity from the 1850s, and the two biggest tile producers were Maw and Co., and Minton's. Both companies were successful exporters, with expertise in handling large overseas contracts. They faced relatively little competition from foreign manufacturers until the end of the century. Tile exports to Australia, New Zealand and Canada accounted for a large share of their overseas orders, and lavish catalogues were produced specifically for colonial markets. For a while British-manufactured tiles were also in demand in the United States. But after the 1876 Centennial Exhibition in Philadelphia an American tile industry emerged; American consumers tended to prefer classical styles, while colonial consumers favoured pictorial and ornamental designs. Ceramic tiles were expensive. Hence they were purchased mainly by wealthy emigrants, or to adorn prestigious public buildings. For example, the Scottish decorators Daniel Cottier and John Lyon, who opened a branch of their firm in Sydney in 1873, decorated many big private houses 'in the latest London style', while public commissions included St Anne's Chapel in Fredericton; the Calgary Herald Building; the Canadian Pacific Railroad Hotel in Vancouver; St John's Cathedral in Saskatoon; St Paul's Cathedral in Melbourne; St Andrew's Cathedral in Sydney; and the Parliament House buildings in Queensland, Perth and Melbourne.

A second case study is floor and table coverings. The later nineteenth and early twentieth centuries saw the launch of linoleum as a household word.[133] Linoleum's appeal was strongly linked to middle-class concerns about cleanliness and home-making – Mrs Beeton's manual provided two recipes for polishing linoleum floors. The main centres of production were London, Lancaster and Kirkaldy, and the industry grew rapidly from

---

[131] Young, *Middle Class Culture in the Nineteenth Century*.

[132] The rest of this paragraph draws on L. Pearson, 'The World at Their Feet: Decorative Tile Exports by British Manufacturers, 1850–1910', paper given at *Imperial Globalisation? Trade, Technologies, and Transnationalities within the British Empire, c. 1800–2000*, 10–11 September 2004, British Empire and Commonwealth Museum, Bristol. We are grateful to Dr Pearson for discussing the implications of her research with us during the conference.

[133] P. J. Gooderson, *Lord Linoleum: Lord Ashton, Lancaster and the Rise of the British Oilcloth and Linoleum Industry* (Keele: Keele University Press, 1996), pp. 17, 25–6, 30–51, 107, 113.

the 1890s to 1914. Williamson's was a leading manufacturer. Benefiting from rising living standards and an increased demand for house decoration and furnishings, the firm specialised in printed and patterned floorcloths at the cheaper end of the market, and higher-quality cork linoleum for wealthier consumers. Steam-powered rotary printing techniques allowed Williamson's to produce a variety of designs more quickly and cheaply than its rivals. Australia was a key market. First displayed at the Melbourne exhibition in 1888–9, linoleum was then actively marketed through the catalogues of retail emporiums.[134] A marked surge in export orders to Australia was recorded in 1904. By 1913, the empire as a whole was taking 58 per cent of exported floorings from Britain. There was a steady growth of demand from South Africa, New Zealand and Canada, while Australia continued to account for the largest share.

Musical instruments, including the organ, were likewise exported all over the British World.[135] Compared to the piano, national schools of organ building differed widely. Moreover, unlike pianos, organs were a community's possession, purchased for town halls and churches by civic or congregational effort. At the forefront of Victorian music technology, organs attracted a lot of public attention at international exhibitions, and provided the basis for a flourishing export business for firms such as William Hill and Sons and Henry Willis and Sons. Missionaries were the first carriers. The Reverend Henry Williams received a mechanical barrel organ in New Zealand in 1830, one that apparently still survives. After this date, the estimate books for organ manufacturers contain a steady stream of empire references. Australia and New Zealand proved the best customers, although in South Africa both Afrikaans and English churches ordered organs from Britain up to 1914, as did many town halls.[136] British organs were popular because British-trained organists saw them as world leading in terms of quality and reliability. The colonies welcomed the instruments and, up to a point, the people who played them, although they did not always favour British music.

No discussion of material culture would be complete without reference to clothing and fashion. As early as the 1840s, following the sharp fall in prices of cotton fabrics in Britain, the export of clothes to the

---

[134] Historical Houses Trust of New South Wales, *Floorcoverings*, pp. 48–51.

[135] The key study is by Stephen Banfield, 'Towards a History of Music in the British Empire: Three Export Studies', in K. Darian-Smith, P. Grimshaw and S. Macintyre (eds.), *Britishness Abroad: Transnational Movements and Imperial Cultures* (Melbourne: Melbourne University Press, 2007), pp. 63–90. The rest of this paragraph is drawn from this source.

[136] Canada, by contrast, does not appear to have imported many organs from Britain. The United States was a leading supplier, and French-speaking Canada had a first-rank company of its own, Casavant Frères of St-Hyacinthe, established in Québec in 1879.

Cape and Australia had become a lucrative business. For example, the London family firm, E. Moses and Son, which specialised in cut-price, ready-made clothing, profited from a surge in Australian orders during this decade.[137] After 1850, stylish dress became a sign of social status and moral worth among middle-class settlers. Developments in the production and marketing of clothing, and the rise of the modern department store, laid the foundations of the modern fashion industry.[138] Complete outfits were offered to migrants, as well as bedding, washing and eating gear, and a chest to contain them. By the 1860s, Moses and Son had opened several branches throughout the settler empire.

Australia boasts some of the best research into clothing habits and fashions.[139] Australia's manufacturing of cloth was at first limited: the severe depression of the 1840s stifled expansion, as did the outpouring of good-quality textiles from Britain. The same was true of footwear, where a lack of local tradesmen fostered a dependence on imported goods. The British company, C. and J. Clark, opened up a lucrative market in the colony of Victoria during the gold rush, although it faced considerable competition from America later in the century.[140] From the mid century, the migrants who poured into Australia were consumers as well as producers, and relatively prosperous ones too. The total value of imports per head expanded accordingly. Wealthier settlers even sometimes ordered their clothes direct from England. The slower economic expansion of the late 1860s, and the implementation of tariffs in Victoria in 1867, subsequently saw a fall in imported clothing and footwear.[141]

Much colonial urban dress was modelled on European styles. If not imported, it was made up with overseas patterns. In their quest for respectability, the merchants and businessmen of Victoria and New South Wales adopted the British preference for dark-coloured outfits, consisting of frockcoats, trousers and waistcoats, often offset with a tall top hat. Men in Queensland were understandably more reluctant to follow this sartorial trend, which was hardly suited to its tropical climate. (Even in

[137] S. Chapman, 'The Innovating Entrepreneurs in the British Ready-Made Clothing Industry', *Textile History* 24 (1993), 5–25, esp. pp. 14–22.

[138] See, for example, R. Ross, *Status and Respectability in the Cape Colony, 1750–1870: A Tragedy of Manners* (Cambridge: Cambridge University Press, 1999), pp. 85–6, and, more generally, 'Cross-Continental Cross-Fertilisation in Clothing', *European Review* 14:1 (2006), 135–47 (p. 119).

[139] See especially the seminal study by M. Maynard, *Fashioned from Penury: Dress as Cultural' Practice in Colonial Australia* (Cambridge: Cambridge University Press, 1994), from which the rest of this paragraph is drawn.

[140] G. B. Sutton, 'The Marketing of Ready-Made Footwear in the Nineteenth Century', *Business History* 6:2 (1964), 93–112 (pp. 99–102, 109).

[141] K. Buckley and T. Wheelwright, *No Paradise for Workers: Capitalism and the Common People in Australia, 1788–1914* (Oxford: Oxford University Press, 1988), p. 99.

Melbourne and Sydney lighter clothing was favoured during the sum-
mer.) Meanwhile, the quality garments worn by middle-class Australian
women were usually imported. Australian women admired the styles of
dress from Paris as well as London, and social refinement in female clothing was European rather than exclusively British. In Australia's sunny climate, women, moreover, preferred boldly designed garments in brighter
colours. That said, Australian women wishing to adopt a genteel lifestyle paid close attention to codes of social practice in Britain, including
dress. Indeed, for much of the nineteenth century what was on offer to
them locally was limited and more expensive. Hence the tendency for
Australian department stores to combine the retailing of imported British
goods with local garment production. While dependence on British garment manufacturers varied over time, and was possibly more pronounced
for high-quality goods, British producers made deep inroads into the
Australian market from the 1840s.

Indigenous peoples adopted European styles of clothing, too. However,
when non-Europeans did don western garments they mostly did so voluntarily (rather than because they were required to do so), and they
invested them with their own symbolic meanings.[142] In South Africa the
first people to take on such clothing were male converts to Christianity
in the 1860s and 1870s.[143] As the Comaroffs have argued, 'clothing was
a morally charged medium for missionaries'; the naked or semi-clad,
'native' body evoked degeneracy and disorder, and the campaign to
clothe Africans 'was inseparable from other aspects and axes of the civilising mission'.[144] Thus visitors to mission stations on the Eastern Cape
commented approvingly on how Africans wore English (or English-style)
clothing, such as frock-coats, suits, ties, socks and shoes. Yet there were
limits to what whites thought acceptable, and Africans pushed right up
against them. While missionaries desired that their flocks should be covered, and saw clothing as a part of their civilising offensive on African manners, they became increasingly concerned with Africans' use of European
dress. They felt such dress was often worn immodestly to display wealth
and status, or even to express opposition to white supremacy.

How much of this clothing would have been imported from Britain?
The question is hard to answer. During the period 1835–70 we know

---

[142] H. Hendrickson (ed.), *Clothing and Difference: Embodied Identities in Colonial and Post-
Colonial Africa* (Durham, NC: Duke University Press, 1996), p. 2.

[143] See here Ross, 'Cross-Continental Cross-Fertilisation in Clothing'; and K. Ruether,
'Heated Debates over Crinolines: European Clothing on Nineteenth-Century Lutheran
Mission Stations in the Transvaal', *JSAS* 28 (2002), 359–78.

[144] J. L. Comaroff and J. Comaroff, *Of Revelation and Revolution*, 2 vols., Vol. II: *The
Dialectics of Modernity on a South African Frontier* (Chicago: University of Chicago Press,
1997), pp. 218–73 (quotations from pp. 229, 236).

that Britain's share of the Cape's imports fluctuated between 60 and 80 per cent, and that textiles and clothing in particular made up the largest part of these goods.[145] However, traders at this time passed infrequently through the interior of the Cape, and Africans largely lacked the means to purchase their wares. Mission societies had therefore to appeal to the generosity of the British public. Used apparel, collected for the poor and needy at home, was also sent abroad. Meanwhile, missionaries and their wives gathered old clothes whilst on furlough and carried them back to the Cape on their return to their station.[146]

Subsequently, mineral discoveries, labour migrancy and urbanisation made European clothing more widely available.[147] On the diamond fields of Kimberley, the inflow of migrants led to a rapid rise in purchasing power from the early 1880s. For black workers clothing formed an important marker of their passage into a new community. On either side of Du Toitspan Road were shops that were emporiums for imported and colonial goods, where migrants were introduced to the wonders of consumerism. Some of this clothing was plain working garb: so-called 'oilman's clothing', such as hats, boots, shirts and the like. Yet fancy and luxury attire was also on sale. To impress their peers, Christian converts wore trousers and tails at weekends, the accessories of a civilised existence; other mineworkers wore a variety of more garish garments, including cast-off military tunics from imperial regiments. Labour migrants took European clothes home for their families, or to sell, as well as purchasing imported cloth, which their wives then used to make clothing for themselves. Similarly, it was social standing rather than a desire to conform to European norms that influenced the dress codes of African miners on the Witwatersrand. Here well-stocked shops, catering specifically for black labour migrants, grew up next to the compounds on the Reef. Popular items of clothing included leather boots, hats, frock- and waistcoats, jackets, shirts, socks, belts, canes and umbrellas. 'European clothing that was rare and exotic at home marked a man as a *gayisa*' (a man returned from wage work).[148] It is probable that much of this clothing was second-hand: sent to South Africa from Britain when new, and then later sold on to so-called 'smouse'. These were Jewish traders, mostly from eastern Europe, who were famous throughout southern Africa for

---

[145] J. Inggs, 'Port Elizabeth's Response to the Expanding Economy of Europe, 1820–1870', *South African Journal of Economic History* 3 (1988), 61–84 (pp. 71–5).

[146] Comaroff and Comaroff, *Of Revelation and Revolution*, p. 237.

[147] See P. Harries, *Work, Culture, and Identity: Migrant Labourers in Mozambique and South Africa, c. 1860–1910* (Portsmouth, NH: Heinemann, 1994), pp. 60, 101–2, 124, 173.

[148] *Ibid.*, p. 173.

retail and wholesale trading, and who took goods into the interior to sell from their wagons or to rural traders.[149]

Perhaps the major item of clothing imported from England for indigenous Africans, however, was the woollen blanket.[150] Blankets were an integral part of the costume of many ethnic groups during the second half of the nineteenth century, replacing skin cloaks, and worn in both ritual and everyday contexts.[151] Recommended by their versatility, blankets could be secured at the shoulder, or pinned around the waist; they could cradle babies; and they provided bedding. The demand from Basotho people, for example, was such that the company of Wormald and Walker of Dewsbury in Yorkshire began designing blankets for Basutoland (today's Lesotho) well before the turn of the century. Blankets were sold through the rural trading stores. The famous merchant firm, Fraser Limited, founded in the 1870s by the Ipswich immigrants Donald and Douglas, and based in Wepener in the Orange Free State, generated large profits by importing blankets into southern Africa, paying particular attention to this branch of merchandise.[152] The blanket, however, had to be designed to suit African tribal fabric and design preferences, not to reflect European ones, even if the names given to particular styles sometimes reflected their British origins.[153] Indeed, to protect market share, and guard against heavy losses, it was vital to keep abreast of (shifting) African tastes. The 'Victoria' line, depicting the 'beloved' British Queen, and produced during her Jubilee Year of 1897, was probably the best-known blanket. Sixty years later one of Wormald and Walker's agents

[149] For a contemporary fictional account of eastern European Jews, who had fled the pogroms for South Africa, at first to trade from a mule-drawn buggy, and later from a local store, see Pauline Smith's *The Beadle* (London: Jonathan Cape, 1927), pp. 13–17. Smith was born in 1882 in Little Karoo in the Cape colony; her father, a doctor, was an Englishman born in China; her mother was a Scottish nurse from Aberdeenshire. Her novels depict isolated, resourceful, conservative colonists (Dutch, English and Scots), and are memorable for their fine evocations of the place and people of the Little Karoo. See D. Driver (ed.), *Pauline Smith* (Johannesburg: McGraw-Hill, 1983); and G. Haresnape, *Pauline Smith* (Berkeley: University of California Press, 1969). See also C. Van Onselen, *The Fox and the Flies: The World of Joseph Silver, Racketeer and Psychopath* (Richmond: University of Virginia Press, 2007), p. 272.
[150] C. Danziger, *A Trader's Century: The Fortunes of Frasers* (Cape Town: Purnell, 1979), pp. 45–7.
[151] Comaroff and Comaroff, *Of Revelation and Revolution*, pp. 263–7.
[152] T. Keegan, 'The Making of the Rural Economy from 1850 to the Present', in Z. A. Konczacki (ed.), *Studies in the Economic History of Southern Africa*, 2 vols., Vol. II: *South Africa, Lesotho and Swaziland* (London: Cass, 1991), pp. 36–63 (p. 44).
[153] Hence J. Prestholdt's observation that consumer tastes and demand on the [African] 'periphery' were often more significant in the formation of global economic systems than commentators allow: 'On the Global Repercussions of East African Consumerism', *AHR* 109 (2004), 775–83 (pp. 755–60).

could still remark that 'the Victoria is ... the hallmark of the well-dressed Basotho'.[154]

Australia's Aboriginal population present an equally fascinating case.[155] Ignoring the importance of codes of bodily decoration to Aborigines, British settlers regarded their nakedness as a sign of inherent inferiority. From the first moments of settlement, Aborigines were given European clothing and encouraged to dress in ways that conformed to western habits. As in South Africa, this was often at the instigation of missionaries, with posed photographs of Aborigines wearing frock-coats and holding Bibles up as evidence of the soundness of their conversion. That said, Aborigines often discarded government or missionary-issued clothing when they returned to the bush, or sold or exchanged such garments for liquor.

During the 1840s and 1850s, men's trousers and shirts, and women's petticoats, were worn by Aborigines mostly when they were in direct contact with settlers, either in their employment as stockmen or domestic servants, or when they ventured into towns. During these decades it became more common to see Aborigines dressed like Europeans. The policy of encouraging Aborigines to settle on supervised mission or government reserve stations accelerated the process of acculturation. On Victoria's reserves, Aborigines were given a clothing ration each year, or cloth to make clothes. They also bought clothing from travelling hawkers (usually Indians), or from mail order catalogues. The *Illustrated Australian News* of 25 August 1865 remarked on how Aborigines on the Coranderrk reserve were 'all dressed in European clothes, not received in charity, but acquired by the earnings of their own industry'.[156] Indeed, surviving photographs show how elegantly Aborigines on reserves were dressed, a fact remarked on by many of the visitors to these stations.[157]

While some of the European clothing worn by Aborigines may have been imported from Britain, such as that purchased by mail order from department stores, more of it (especially of the hardwearing variety) was probably manufactured locally – the clothing industry of Victoria gained in strength from the mid century and became a large employer

---

[154] *Ibid.*, p. 46.
[155] On Aboriginal dress, see R. Broome, *Aboriginal Victorians: A History since 1800* (Crows Nest, NSW: Allen and Unwin, 2005), pp. 113, 137, 140–2, 149; A. Massola, *Coranderrk: A History of the Aboriginal Station* (Kilmore: Lowden Publishing, 1975), especially the photographs in this collection; and Maynard, *Fashioned from Penury*, pp. 59–72. We are also grateful to Richard Broome for guiding us through the complexities of this subject.
[156] Quoted in Massola, *Coranderrk*, p. 64.
[157] D. E. Barwick, 'And the Lubras are Ladies Now,' in F. Gale (ed.), *Women's Role in Aboriginal Society* (Canberra: Australian Institute of Aboriginal Studies, 1994), pp. 51–63 (p. 57).

of labour.[158] More likely still, Aborigines on reserves made the clothes themselves, as during the 1860s and 1870s Aboriginal women had rapidly acquired sewing skills. Neither should we see western dress as a sign of the erosion of Aboriginal identity or self-esteem. As Richard Broome explains, Aborigines tended to adopt British culture voluntarily and only in so far as it suited them to do so. Like their fight for equal wages, clothing offered Aborigines an opportunity to assert their equality with British settlers.

The same desire can be observed off the reserves. For instance, when the Daisy Hill people from the Maryborough region of Victoria found surface gold nuggets during the 1860s 'they spent the money on clothing, dressing themselves in black suits, bell toppers and crinolines ... cutting such airs as to greatly amuse everyone who chanced to see them'.[159] Such behaviour can just as plausibly be read as an act of cultural defiance as imitation. Indeed, the rather stark distinction made by officials on the Royal Commission on the Aborigines (1877) between 'necessary' and 'ornamental' dress suggests white disapproval of Aboriginal peoples wearing anything other than the most basic and functional articles of clothing.[160] In this light, it is interesting to read a report on the Coranderrk station published five years later. It was littered with complaints from Aboriginal witnesses that they had been given insufficient clothing by its superintendent, who then struggled to explain to officials why his order books contained so many items of more expensive clothing.[161]

Consumption, therefore, was a rather blunt tool of conquest. If the civilising mission in the settler colonies was founded on an assumption that western commodities, especially clothing, could bring about a revolution in the habits of Africans or Aborigines, the reality proved different. Limited access to such goods and the people who traded them, low purchasing power, the resilience of local costume, the ridicule sometimes directed at those wearing European garb, the fear of missionaries that those who did wear it would become puffed up with their own self-importance, and the syncretic clothing styles that emerged – all these things

---

[158] Cooper, *Victorian Commerce*, pp. 135–6; Cowderoy, *Melbourne's Commercial Jubilee*, p. 61. In 1868, as much as 24.2 per cent of Victoria's industrial workforce (some 4,347 people), was already employed in the colonies' clothing and footwear factories; this figure continued to grow over the latter half of the century, reaching 27.2 per cent (12,941 employees) by 1882–3 and 30 per cent (19,265 employees) by 1900. These data come from C. J. R. Linge, *Industrial Awakening: A Geography of Australian Manufacturing, 1788 to 1890* (Canberra: Australian National University Press, 1979), p. 744

[159] Quoted in Broome, *Aboriginal Victorians*, p. 149.

[160] *Royal Commission on the Aborigines: Report of the Commissioners*, Vol. I (1877), p. 47.

[161] *Report of the Board Appointed to Enquire into the Present Condition and Management of the Coranderrk Aboriginal Station*, Vol. II (1882).

stood in the way of implanting new cultures of consumption among indigenous peoples.

Among Europeans, by contrast, commodities, and the specific ways in which they were used, were emblematic of British culture – especially bourgeois culture. Much of the economic power that derived from 'Britishness' was tied to its associations with bourgeois consuming culture. Middle-class women played a particularly important role here. As we have seen, their concerns, tastes and buying power were formative in terms of colonial demand. In this way, it is possible to conceive of the growth of branches of trade in the colonies as an essentially 'domestic' expansion process that was driven by middle-class female desires.

Increasingly, merchants and manufacturers from Britain seized upon the settler colonies to expand markets for their products. Their branding of British goods – for example, the way they were linked to particular towns or cities – often evoked the proximity, familiarity, and even romance, of the 'mother country'. Moreover, the fact that these goods were widely advertised in colonial newspapers, displayed at colonial exhibitions and agricultural shows, and (later) featured in newsreels, documentaries and films further worked to the advantage of British exporters who had a sharp eye for consumer preferences and how to exploit them. This continued to be true right up to the First World War, at which point the Americanisation of consumer society in some parts of the British World began to gather pace.[162]

Conclusions

If the phenomenon of globalisation is that of 'a world of things in motion', then the logic of the market has been central to it.[163] During the nineteenth century, the effects of falling transport costs, tariff liberalisation and mass migration intensified the integration of global commodity, capital and labour markets.[164] Yet these global markets were embedded in complex cultural matrices.[165] Co-ethnic networks, in particular, played a

[162] Campbell, 'The Americanization of South Africa', pp. 41ff.
[163] A. Appadurai, 'Grassroots Globalisation and the Research Imagination', in A. Appadurai (ed.), *Globalisation* (Durham, NC: Duke University Press, 2001), pp. 1–22 (p. 5).
[164] D. K. Das, *The Economic Dimensions of Globalization* (Basingstoke: Palgrave Macmillan, 2004); D. Held, A. McGrew, D. Goldblatt and J. Perraton, *Global Transformations: Politics, Economics and Culture* (Oxford: Oxford University Press, 1999); O'Rourke and Williamson, *Globalization and History*.
[165] J. Brewer and F. Trentmann, 'Introduction: Space, Time and Value in Consuming Cultures', in J. Brewer and F. Trentmann (eds.), *Consuming Cultures: Global Perspectives, Historical Trajectories, Transnational Exchanges* (Oxford: Oxford University Press, 2006), pp. 1–17 (p. 13); P. du Gay and M. Pryke (eds.), *Cultural Economy: Cultural Analysis and Commercial Life* (London: Sage, 2002).

key role in overcoming obstacles to the circulation and exchange of economic knowledge. 'As commodities travel greater distances, knowledge about them tends to become partial, contradictory, and differentiated.'[166] By building trust and reciprocity, co-ethnic networks in the British World broke down barriers to long-distance trade, and thus helped to match consumer tastes to producer knowledge and skills. They also helped to spread new scientific and technological ideas, to facilitate the transfer of labour, to develop commercial facilities, and to improve transport and communications infrastructure. In short, they were instrumental in expanding British World trade.

The irony here, of course, is that for a long time empire markets were perceived not as an engine of economic convergence and modernity but exactly the reverse – a form of economic escapism. Reliance on 'safe', 'soft' or 'sheltered' colonial markets supposedly debilitated British manufacturing by depriving it of the competitive stimulus that would have come from fuller participation in European and American trade. By retreating into the empire, industry in Britain is said to have managed (for a while) to hold at bay the globalising forces of commodity market integration, only eventually to pay the price for failing to invest in new technologies, or to renovate and restructure their business organisation.

However, recent scholarship has become more mindful of the relationship between group values and beliefs and levels of economic performance, and the capacity of culture to promote (as well as retard) economic growth.[167] Ethnic affiliation, in particular, is understood to have influenced trading patterns, present and past. Whether it be Chinese business networks in South East Asia during the late twentieth and early twenty-first centuries,[168] or the networks forged by Maghribi traders in the eleventh century Mediterranean, it is now clear that such networks could either facilitate trade by deterring opportunistic behaviour, or hinder it by becoming too exclusive in their membership.[169] A key conclusion drawn from these examples is that trade can often develop more readily, and effectively, among people sharing a common identity, whether that identity is ethnic, religious or political.

[166] A. Appadurai, 'Introduction: Commodities and the Politics of Value', in A. Appadurai (ed.), *The Social Life of Things: Commodities in Cultural Perspective* (Cambridge: Cambridge University Press, 1986), pp. 3–64 (p. 56).

[167] M. C. Casson and A. Godley, 'Cultural Factors in Economic Growth', in Casson and Godley (eds.), *Cultural Factors in Economic Growth* (Berlin: Springer, 2000), pp. 1–43; D. S. Landes, *The Wealth and Poverty of Nations: Why Some Are So Rich and Some So Poor* (London: W. W. Norton, 1999), esp. pp. 516–18.

[168] Menkhoff and Gerke (eds.), *Chinese Entrepreneurship*; and Haley, Tan and Haley (eds.), *New Asian Emperors*.

[169] Grief, 'Contract Enforceability'.

In the British World of the 'long' nineteenth century, the information, trust and reciprocity flowing through co-ethnic networks created value for those lucky enough to participate in them, yet further marginalised and impoverished those who were not. In this sense, 'imperial globalisation' was far from being truly global in its reach. The business and commercial networks upon which this first 'wave' of modern globalisation was built not only exhibited a strong bias towards the empire's Anglophone societies, they exposed the marked social and ethnic prejudices within those societies.

To what extent were these powerful exclusionary tendencies offset, or at least concealed, by Britain's dogged pursuit of tariff liberalisation before 1914? Unlike the English-speaking world's other major power, the United States, Britain did not seek to shelter its own industries behind tariff walls, nor did it favour a view of the international order based around exclusive economic zones. This policy ensured a degree of openness in the world economy, and helps to explain why Britain's commercial and financial relationships with the dominions mapped so easily on to its relationships with foreign states, and why the two sets of relationships often strengthened and reinforced each other. To be sure, the economy of the British World had its own cultural dynamic. Yet this dynamic did not prevent Britain, or the dominions, from engaging with, and expanding into, the wider world economy.

However, the conspicuous failure of the United States to subscribe to this heady vision of 'free trade, empire and universalism',[170] increasingly pushed politicians and businessmen in Britain to reconsider the relationship between tariffs and trade loyalties. While subject to ebbs and flows, the level of media and political attention to American competition in trade grew steadily throughout these years. According to one commentator, 'America loomed larger than any other foreign nation as a commercial or emotional force in many portions of the Empire, especially in Canada'.[171] Thus, in the sphere of trade, the Anglo-American relationship took a different course from that of migration (Chapter 3) and finance (Chapter 5). Much of what people consumed in the colonies, and the way they consumed it, was a marker of identity. In choosing what

[170] See here A. Howe, 'From Pax Britannica to Pax Americana: Free Trade, Empire and Globalisation, 1846–1948', *Bulletin of Asia-Pacific Studies* (2003), 137–59.

[171] Heindel, *The American Impact on Great Britain, 1898–1914: A Study of the United States in World History* (New York: Octagon Books, first published 1940, reprinted 1968), p. 163. America traded four or five times as much with Canada as with all the other British dominions combined, so there is no surprise that the proposed Canadian–American Reciprocity Agreement of 1910 provoked such heated political controversy; see B. Perkins, *The Great Rapprochement: England and the United States, 1895–1914* (New York: Atheneum, 1968), pp. 124–30.

to eat, wear or drink, or how to furnish their homes, people made statements about themselves, and these statements frequently expressed how they perceived their role in, and relationship to, the colonising process. Yet this 'cross-fertilisation' in consumption[172] was increasingly squeezed in the case of the United States by its move from revenue-raising to protectionist tariffs, and by the rapid growth of its domestic industries. It is only evident with respect to genteel habits of consumption.[173] High tariffs actually helped British migrants to transfer their skills and technology to the United States, and to develop new crafts and industries there – the 2,000 or so Staffordshire potters who poured into Ohio from the mid century eventually broke Britain's virtual monopoly over the production of earthenware.[174] Fast becoming its greatest trade rival, America's relationship to the British World was decidedly, and increasingly, ambiguous.

[172] For this term, see Ross, 'Cross-Continental Cross-Fertilisation in Clothing'.
[173] The similarities in English and American consumer behaviour were much stronger in the seventeenth and eighteenth centuries, both in terms of the consumption of groceries (tobacco, sugar products and tea) and durables (haberdashery, clothing and tableware); see C. Shammas, 'Changes in English and Anglo-American Consumption from 1550 to 1800', in J. Brewer and R. Porter (eds.), *Consumption and the World of Goods* (London: Routledge, 1993), pp. 177–205.
[174] W. E. Van Vugt, *British Buckeyes: The English, Scots, and Welsh in Ohio, 1800–1900* (Kent, OH: Kent State University Press, 2006), pp. 135–7.

5 Information and investment

Introduction

So far we have examined the overseas movement of British people and British goods. This chapter concerns itself with Britain's other great export of the pre-First World War period: its capital. We seek to uncover the key relationships and mechanisms that made possible a massive and rapid movement of money across borders. For many scholars, it is this 'runaway quality of global finance' that lay at the very heart of the forces integrating the world economy in the nineteenth and twentieth centuries.[1] Certainly, it had a profound and lasting effect, in its wake opening up new regions of the world, delivering efficiency gains from improved transport and communication, and widening the scope of the multi-lateral payments system.[2] Britain's imperial and financial pre-eminence are, moreover, traditionally understood to have been two sides of the same coin.

Yet appearances can be deceptive. While the empire was at times prized by British investors, these same investors also freely sank even larger sums of money outside it. 'Imperial piety' or 'British traditions', of themselves, could not and did not replace the profit motive. Rather, it was the attractions of the rapidly expanding temperate regions of recent settlement – political stability, economic security and protection within the law – that mattered. These attractions were not confined to the British World, even if they manifested themselves most strongly there. Argentina enjoyed a place in the affections of the British investor; for a relatively brief period before the war, in terms of portfolio investment, it may even have been 'more popular with the British investor than Canada, itself the most popular of the British Dominions'.[3]

---

[1] A. Appadurai, 'Grassroots Globalisation and the Research Imagination', in A. Appadurai (ed.), *Globalisation* (Durham, NC: Duke Universitiy Press, 2001), pp. 1–21 (p. 4).
[2] J. Darwin, 'Globalism and Imperialism: The Global Context of British Power, 1830–1860', in S. Akita (ed.), *Gentlemanly Capitalism: Imperialism and Global History* (Basingstoke: Palgrave Macmillan, 2002), p. 49.
[3] D. C. M. Platt, 'Canada and Argentina: The First Preference of the British Investor, 1904–14', *JICH* 13 (1985), 77–92.

On what basis, then, did British investors make their decisions? More particularly, how, if at all, did the ties of social interaction predispose them to provide greater support to investment projects within the British World than outside it? This question can be approached from several angles: by studying the coverage of investment opportunities as reported by the popular and financial presses, by exploring and detailing the rich social and financial networks that underpinned Britain's capital markets, and by investigating the investment patterns of some of London's leading financial institutions.

We will see how dominion securities were indeed treated differently by British investors in the decades prior to the First World War, and, as a result, were usually financed in the City at lower rates of interest than similar assets from other nations. This situation stemmed not so much from 'imperial piety', as from the way the British World's institutions, press and networks gave rise to a distinct and potent informational asymmetry within capital markets. As a consequence, people found themselves having to make choices not just without a complete set of information before them, but on the basis of a stock of knowledge that was heavily biased in favour of the British World. Simply put, British investors were just better informed about, and better placed to act upon, investment opportunities in the dominions than elsewhere. Understood in this way, it is hardly surprising that dominion securities were among the first overseas assets to catch their eye. This state of affairs was in many ways the natural by-product of the global expansion of British human and social capital in the nineteenth century. Thus, just as the bonds of trust and reciprocity promoted British trade (Chapter 4), so too, it is contended, did they exert influence over the course and direction of British overseas investment.

The pattern of British overseas investment, 1865–1914

An overview

Throughout the nineteenth and early twentieth centuries, London was the undisputed financial capital of the world. From its famous Stock Exchange and financial houses, historically unprecedented volumes of external capital – some £4.1 billion of money calls for new overseas issues between 1865 and 1914 – flowed to all corners of an ever-expanding global economy.[4] It was a development that bound Britain's ongoing

---

[4] For an excellent account of the City of London in the nineteenth century, see D. Kynaston, *The City of London*, 3 vols., Vols. I and II (London: Pimlico, 1995).

prosperity more tightly and deeply to the success of economies in other parts of the world. Whereas £1 in every £48 earned by Britons in the 1850s was invested overseas, between 1870 and 1914 the proportion had grown to £1 in every £23; in some years, it was substantially greater. The investment surge of the Edwardian period, for example, saw as much as £1 in every £16 of the nation's domestic income end up as net foreign investment. As a consequence, Britain's net overseas assets, which comprised approximately 7 per cent of the stock of its national wealth in 1850, had risen to just over 32 per cent by 1913.[5]

Britain's overseas investment was truly a global affair. Over 170 countries and colonies benefited from this outpouring of capital.[6] As Table 5.1 illustrates, though, not all were to share the benefits equally. Most British investment funds found their way to the temperate, settler societies of the 'New' world. Six of these societies alone – the USA, Argentina and the four self-governing dominions – received more than half (56 per cent) of all British overseas investment. Significant amounts of capital also flowed to India, Russia and Brazil. Tropical and European countries on the whole fared less well, together accounting for only a third of total British overseas investment in this period.

As Table 5.2 demonstrates, these proportions were not static. At the beginning of our period, European countries were the main recipients of British capital. From the second half of the 1870s, however, Europe's dominance steadily declined, and by the turn of the century Europe accounted for only 5 per cent of total British overseas investment. The United States, by contrast, although subject to considerable year-on-year variation, remained an important destination for British capital throughout the period under consideration. Likewise, Latin America, in particular Argentina, was an important outlet for British investment, with significant surges in the flow of capital experienced in the late 1880s and between 1904 and 1914.[7]

The composition of British investment in the empire underwent profound changes. Before 1870 India held sway with the British investor, although its share of capital, which peaked in the 1860s and 1870s, declined slightly thereafter, except for a sharp spike at the end of the century. As Figure 5.1 shows, from the 1870s the dominions emerged as

---

[5] M. Edelstein, 'Foreign Investment, Accumulation and Empire, 1860–1914', in R. Floud and P. Johnson (eds.), *Cambridge Economic History of Modern Britain*, 3 vols., Vol. II: *Economic Maturity, 1860–1939* (Cambridge: Cambridge University Press, 2004), pp. 191–6.

[6] L. Davis, 'The Late Nineteenth-Century British Imperialist: Specification, Quantification and Controlled Conjectures', in R. E. Dumett (ed.), *Gentlemanly Capitalism and British Imperialism: The New Debate on Empire* (Basingstoke: Palgrave Macmillan, 1999), pp. 82–112 (p. 99).

[7] For more on the popularity of Argentine securities, see Platt, 'Canada and Argentina'.

Table 5.1. *Recipients of British capital exports, 1865–1914 (capital called).*

	£1,000	%
USA	836,371	20.5
Canada	412,283	10.1
Argentina	349,243	8.6
Australia	339,001	8.3
India	317,174	7.8
South Africa	262,233	6.4
Dependent British colonies	199,644	4.9
Brazil	172,742	4.2
Russia	138,695	3.4
Mexico	81,585	2.0
New Zealand	84,495	2.1
Chile	61,818	1.5
France	57,920	1.4
Turkey	42,268	1.0
Peru	37,173	0.9
Uruguay	30,678	0.8
Other	655,931	16.1
Europe	488,158	12.0
North America	1,399,841	34.3
South America	686,332	16.8
Africa	430,738	10.6
Asia	570,423	14.0
Oceania	503,762	12.3
Empire	1,614,830	39.6
Dominions	1,098,012	26.9
Total	**4,079,254**	

Source: I. Stone, *The Global Export of Capital from Great Britain, 1865–1914* (London: St Martin's Press, 1999).

the primary destination for British investment. From then on, other than for a short spell in the 1890s, these colonies experienced a faster growth in investment than anywhere else, an apt reflection of their increasingly important economic role within the empire. The vast majority of British investment in Canada arrived after 1904, while Australia's investment boom occurred between the 1870s and the early 1890s. Table 5.2 also shows that Britain's dependent colonies (excepting India) did not figure prominently in its overseas investment. Even when aggregated, these colonies together typically accounted for less than 4 per cent of all British capital sent abroad.

Table 5.2. *British overseas investment by destination, 1865–1914 (annual average capital called; as a percentage of all overseas investment).*

	USA £1,000	USA %	Canada £1,000	Canada %	Australia £1,000	Australia %	India £1,000	India %	South Africa £1,000	South Africa %
1865–9	2,231	8.2	695	2.6	1,644	6.0	6,421	23.6	232	0.9
1870–4	16,755	24.3	3,607	5.2	1,954	2.8	3,513	5.1	159	0.2
1875–9	4,449	14.1	3,092	9.8	4,677	14.8	3,733	11.8	1,885	6.0
1880–4	15,682	25.5	2,872	4.7	9,933	16.1	5,005	8.1	3,719	6.0
1885–9	14,412	16.0	6,841	7.6	13,320	14.7	8,108	9.0	2,318	2.6
1890–4	15,531	26.3	5,287	9.0	,8731	14.8	4,608	7.8	3,490	5.9
1895–9	12,028	15.6	2,762	3.6	9,655	12.5	10,705	13.8	9,096	11.8
1900–4	16,872	23.5	3,599	5.0	4,259	5.9	4,732	6.6	16,773	23.3
1905–9	27,058	20.7	15,386	11.8	4,382	3.4	9,310	7.1	9,026	6.9
1910–14	42,257	21.4	38,315	19.4	9,244	4.7	7,,300	3.7	5,748	2.9

	Europe £1,000	Europe %	New Zealand £1,000	New Zealand %	Latin America £1,000	Latin America %	Dependent colonies £1,000	Dependent colonies %
1865–9	7,200	26.4	604	2.2	4,231	15.5	907	3.3
1870–4	24,757	35.9	1,076	1.6	13,479	19.6	819	1.2
1875–9	5,621	17.8	2,712	8.6	2,866	9.1	889	2.8
1880–4	9,262	15.1	2,147	3.5	8,892	14.5	2,040	3.3
1885–9	7,701	8.5	2,532	2.8	28,946	32.0	1,543	1.7
1890–4	3,987	6.8	1,147	1.9	11,084	18.8	2,139	3.6
1895–9	6,264	8.1	1,822	2.4	8,855	11.5	6,828	8.8
1900–4	3,638	5.1	913	1.3	8,745	12.2	5,536	7.7
1905–9	9,187	7.0	709	0.5	30,297	23.2	7,703	5.9
1910–14	20,016	10.1	3,237	1.6	44,862	22.7	11,524	5.8

Source: Stone, *Global Export of Capital.*

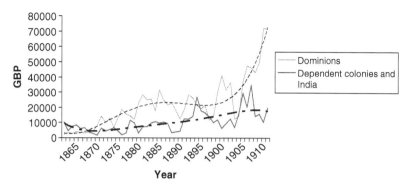

Figure 5.1 British investment to the empire, 1865–1914 (£1,000).

To a large extent, the intensification of British investment in the regions of recent settlement after 1870 was related to their inherent development potential. These were new, rapidly growing and resource-rich societies, which shared a common problem: a transport and communications infrastructure that could not cope with the export-led expansion they were pursuing. Incomplete integration into the global marketplace threatened that process of development. To remedy this, they recognised that essential building blocks had to be put in place: efficiently run and adequately equipped ports to despatch exports without delay, railroads to link the agricultural and mining hinterlands with the coast, tramways to convey the swelling numbers of urban dwellers to work, and modern postal and telegraphic systems to facilitate the freer flow of information both internally and externally. With few sources of capital of their own, these societies instinctively turned to the UK for assistance. The consequences are readily evident in the statistics – almost 70 per cent of all funds leaving Britain went into the construction of infrastructure in regions of recent settlement.[8] Of the different types of infrastructural projects dependent on British capital, the railways were the hungriest: as many as 71.4 per cent of all railway securities issued in London in the latter half of the nineteenth century were for lines located in regions of recent settlement.[9] By contrast, only 12 per cent of British funds went into agriculture and mining, and a meagre 4 per cent into manufacturing.

[8] M. Simon, 'The Pattern of New British Portfolio Foreign Investment, 1865–1914', in J. H. Adler (ed.), *Capital Movements and Economic Development* (London: Macmillan, 1967), pp. 33–70.
[9] I. Stone, *The Global Export of Capital from Great Britain, 1865–1914* (London: St Martin's Press, 1999), p. 414.

The significance of these so-called 'social overhead' projects had major implications for the structure of British investment. The finance of such projects is notoriously 'lumpy'. Building roads, bridges and ports is horrendously expensive, requiring huge up-front injections of capital. Profits from these ventures cannot be realised for a number of years until the project is completed and the desired services are up and running. It was thus not possible to rely on the direct investment of the wealthy few to finance these ventures. Instead what was needed was the capital of large numbers of investors who would be content with a steady rate of return from an asset rather than its outright ownership. The thousands of small-scale, middle-class savers dotted across the UK were the obvious target; the debenture and fixed-term security were the financial mechanisms that could attract them. Given the pervasiveness of these 'lumpy' social overhead projects, the preponderance of indirect, or portfolio, investment among late-nineteenth-century British investors (some 70 to 80 per cent of all investment) is hardly surprising.[10]

What encouraged British investors to underwrite overseas development? Quantitative analysis has shown that, even after due allowances have been made for risk, British investment in this period did not appear to exhibit any overt irrational bias towards or against any particular type of project; rather, individual investor behaviour was governed by a calculated reading of comparative rates of return. On the whole, Britons invested overseas at the end of the nineteenth century primarily because, on comparable types of assets, such securities tended to perform better. Looking at first- and second-class investments in the period from 1870 to 1913, Edelstein thus found that on average overseas securities attracted a realised return of 5.72 per cent compared to the 4.60 per cent offered by domestic issues.[11] These rates suggest that if British investors exhibited any bias at all, it was one that favoured the making of more money over less.[12]

An imperial subsidy?

Did the same hold true for the empire? Davis and Huttenback's econometric analysis of a sample of domestic, colonial and foreign government securities, as well as Edelstein's dataset of first- and second-class

[10] Edelstein, 'Foreign investment', pp. 194–5.
[11] The disparity was even greater for those varieties of stock central to Britain's nineteenth-century capital export. Thus, debentures earned 3.21 per cent at home and 4.92 per cent overseas, whereas in railway securities the differential was even more marked: 3.74 per cent in the UK, 6.03 per cent in the USA, 5.33 per cent in Latin America and 5.33 and 5.28 per cent in eastern and western Europe respectively.
[12] Edelstein, 'Foreign investment', pp. 196–200.

Table 5.3. *Yields on colonial and foreign government securities, 1882–1912 (as percentage points above the UK municipal government rate).*

	1882–1912	1882–1900	1901–12
Dominions	1.14	0.99	1.55
Dependent colonies	0.85	0.90	1.19
India	0.64	0.25	1.12
Independent developed countries	2.04	2.37	1.97
Independent undeveloped countries	4.26	4.24	4.53

Source: L. E. Davis and R. A. Huttenback, *Mammon and the Pursuit of Empire: The Poltical Economy of British Imperialism, 1860–1912* (Cambridge: Cambridge University Press, 1986), p. 173.

securities, suggest not.[13] Rather, British investors do appear to have discriminated between foreign and colonial stock. So much is evident from the average interest rates charged in London on public loans raised by different countries. Table 5.3 presents the key findings – the figures are expressed in terms of the spread: that is, the difference between the rates of interest charged on loans raised by certain types of countries and those floated by UK municipalities. What the table vividly shows is that, over the period 1882 to 1912, colonial governments consistently paid lower interest rates on capital raised in the UK than other governments. The effect was most marked before 1900, when the Indian government, for example, paid on average 4 per cent less on a loan than similarly underdeveloped nations outside the empire. Although India was the biggest beneficiary of these lower rates, the dominions also gained.[14] Relative to comparably developed nations outside the empire, dominion governments were able to raise public loans at a noticeably discounted rate: 1.25 per cent and 0.42 per cent lower on either side of 1900 respectively. A similar picture emerges from analysis of the funding of social overhead securities. As Table 5.4 shows, the average realised returns on various colonial debentures and stocks lay significantly below comparable foreign assets.

Ferguson and Schularick also provide quantitative evidence for an 'empire effect' in the British capital market. Using an even broader base of securities, and separating out the impact of monetary, fiscal and commercial policies, they place the average yield of colonial borrowers at 3.89 per cent compared to 6.30 per cent for those in independent

[13] L. E. Davis and R. A. Huttenback, *Mammon and the Pursuit of Empire: The Political Economy of British Imperialism, 1860–1912* (Cambridge: Cambridge University Press, 1986).
[14] The dominions gained by about 3.3 per cent between 1882 and 1900.

Table 5.4. *Average annual realised returns on various types of stock, 1870–1913.*

	Railway debentures	Railway equities	Other infrastructure equities
UK	3.77	4.41	5.22
Colonial	4.48	5.00	7.50
Foreign	5.72	7.70	8.13

Source: Davis and Huttenback, *Mammon and the Pursuit of Empire*, p. 81.

countries. In other words, colonials paid on average 2.41 per cent less on capital raised in London than those of other nationalities. Once again, the biggest beneficiaries were the dependent colonies and India, whose membership of the British empire, it is contended, reduced their risk premiums by as much as 60 per cent between 1890 and 1913.[15]

Taken together, these econometric analyses provide strong evidence that colonial securities were treated differently by British investors in the later Victorian and Edwardian era, typically being financed in London at significantly lower rates of interest than comparable assets from independent foreign countries at similar levels of development. Contemporaries appear to have been well aware of this phenomenon. For example, Robert Benson, the Chairman of the Merchants' Trust, exclaimed in 1906 that 'the sentiment of the Mother Country predisposes the public to lend capital to our colonies at lower rates of interest and with less security than we exact from borrowers elsewhere'.[16]

It is therefore possible to speak of, and even to quantify, a 'British subsidy' to the colonies: relatively cheap capital from London gave a significant spur to their development. For the period 1882 to 1912, Davis and Huttenback estimate that, per capita, this gift amounted annually to £0.17 in the dominions, £0.04 in the dependent colonies, and £0.01 in India. Alternatively, the subsidy on public borrowing represented a transfer of £216,091,000 from the UK to the Empire, of which 39.7 per cent was received by the dominions, 41.4 per cent by India and 18.9 per cent by the dependent colonies.[17]

---

[15] N. Ferguson and M. Schularick, 'The Empire Effect: The Determinants of Country Risk in the First Age of Globalization, 1880–1913', *Journal of Economic History* 66 (2006), pp. 290–312.

[16] 'Merchant Trust AGM', *The Economist*, 10 March 1906.

[17] Davis and Huttenback, *Mammon and the Pursuit of Empire*, pp. 175–6. For further evidence of contemporary recognition of this subsidy, see George Paish's comments quoted

Who was this investing public that so favoured colonial borrowers? By the end of the nineteenth century, stock market participation in Britain had widened well beyond the privileged few. Promoters of colonial investments targeted a much wider range of individuals who were willing to sink smaller sums of money either into the relative safety of government securities, or, conversely, into more speculative private stocks in the hope of making spectacular gains; mining markets, in particular, had few equals as an arena for speculation. Yet, while savers from all parts of British Isles invested in the empire, it was in London, the Home Counties, Scotland and the rural east of England that colonial securities were preferred. Socio-economically, the most committed empire investors were elites and peers (who invested heavily in banks; breweries; financial trusts; tea and coffee plantations; some heavy industries; and public utilities, like telephonic and telegraphic networks, and gas and light production and distribution) and the London-based businessmen (whose portfolios normally contained a healthy share of colonial financial and land development companies, as well as mining, railroads, canals, docks, trams, omnibuses and waterworks stock).[18]

Given there are no grounds to believe that the British investor at this time acted irrationally or was prepared to place imperial piety above profit, why, then, was he or she willing to accept a lower rate of return? Part of the answer may lie in the parliamentary guarantees that Indian government bonds attracted.[19] Yet this alone cannot be the full story, since from the late 1870s dominion loans were freely raised without such guarantees. Similarly, direct Treasury control and scrutiny of colonial finances may have swayed investor perceptions but, once again, not in the dominions, where, with the advent of responsible government, the scope for such control was dramatically curtailed.

Another commonly cited explanation for an 'empire effect' in capital markets relates to the Trustee Acts, the legislation that regulated the types of assets that could be purchased by trustees in the UK. Prior to 1889 the list of assets that could be legally acquired was restricted to consols, Bank of England and East India stock, and the mortgages of freehold and copyhold in England and Wales. The Trustee Acts of 1889 and 1893, however, extended the range of acceptable assets to include the debentures of British and guaranteed Indian railways and a number of other

---

in A. R. Dilley, 'Gentlemanly Capitalism and the Dominions: London Finance, Australia and Canada', unpublished D.Phil. thesis, University of Oxford (2006), p. 148.

[18] Davis and Huttenback, *Mammon and the Pursuit of Empire*, pp. 211–17.

[19] J. M. Hurd, 'Railways', in D. Kumar (ed.), *The Cambridge Economic History of India*, 2 vols., Vol. II: c. *1757–1970* (Cambridge: Cambridge University Press, 1983); W. J. Macpherson, 'Investment in Indian Railways, 1845–75', *EcHR* 8 (1955), 177–86.

securities. This approved list was further broadened by the Colonial Stock Act of 1900, which legally cleared the way for British trust funds to invest for the first time in the registered and inscribed stock of colonial governments.

From their inception, the Trustee Acts proved controversial. One of their most vehement critics, John Maynard Keynes, found them doubly pernicious: first, because they provided 'an artificial stimulus on a great scale to foreign investment within Empire'; second, because they lulled 'trustees and others into a false sense of security' by making them feel 'that all such investments are, in a sense, beyond criticism'.[20] Yet Keynes was overly pessimistic. By 1900 the list of approved assets was already quite extensive and not in itself sufficiently restrictive to create the type of bias claimed by its opponents.[21] Nor can it be convincingly argued that the inclusion of colonial stock on approved trustee lists profoundly altered general investor perception of such assets: colonial securities were already extremely well-known to and popular with British savers by the time these Acts came into being. What the Acts did do, though, was to strengthen this existing perception of the safety of colonial stock and incorporate it within the law. Thus the impact of the Trustee Acts on colonial securities, while certainly positive, was in all probability rather small. Davis and Huttenback estimate, for example, that between 1882 and 1912 they lowered the interest rate on listed colonial securities by only 0.16 per cent, an amount that leaves the vast majority of the interest rate differential unaccounted for.[22]

What, then, is the missing piece in the puzzle? In 1986, Davis and Huttenback were unsure: 'Nor does the distance of a century make the explanation of the British investor's willingness to underwrite these activities any more apparent. One can never be certain what it was that motivated the investors to act as they did, but the explanation cannot lie in legal guarantees nor in effective Treasury control.'[23] Subsequent work by Davis and others on the evolution of financial markets and institutions, however, points a way forward.[24] In particular, this research ascribes a major role

---

[20] J. M. Keynes, 'Foreign Investment and the National Advantage', *The Nation and the Athenaeum* 35 (9 August 1924), 585–6.

[21] A. K. Cairncross, *Home and Foreign Investment* (Cambridge: Cambridge University Press, 1953); A. R. Hall, *The London Capital Market and Australia, 1870–1914* (Canberra: Australian National University Press, 1963), p. 58; D. N. McCloskey, 'Did Victorian Britain Fail?', *EcHR* 23 (1970), 446–59; and Dilley, 'Gentlemanly Capitalism', pp. 157–61.

[22] Davis and Huttenback, *Mammon and the Pursuit of Empire*, pp. 171–4.

[23] *Ibid.*, p. 170.

[24] See for example Davis, 'Late-Nineteenth-Century British Imperialist'; L. E. Davis and R. E. Gallman, *Evolving Financial Markets and International Capital Flows: Britain, the Americas, and Australia, 1865–1914* (Cambridge: Cambridge University Press, 2001);

to institutional innovation in improving the dissemination of information. Since rational choice operates according to the quality and quantity of data available to decision-makers, the continued development of financial institutions is understood to have been an important factor in the emergence of ever more efficient and encompassing capital markets. As W. Hayes Fisher explained in his investment manual of 1912, 'the effective supervision of investments demands a knowledge of how all investments of each class held are progressing, for without such information the requisite system of comparison between actual and possible results cannot be maintained'.[25]

In other words, for investors to judge the merits of investment projects, adequate and reliable information was (and remains) vital – information not just about the safety and likely profitability of an investment, but about the financial instruments through which their claims on assets could be established. Left unknown or misunderstood, even the most promising of investment opportunities were likely to attract a very high uncertainty discount. Hence the choices made by investors, and the ability of certain investment projects and countries to mobilise sufficient quantities of capital cheaply, were heavily influenced by the nature of informational flows at particular points in time.[26]

Much investment-related information in the nineteenth century came through personal experience, word of mouth, or from what was published in the local and specialist press. In his analysis of the behaviour of late-nineteenth-century British savers, Davis noted that:

not everyone received the same information; savers were more confident about the information they received about investments in places and industries with which they were more familiar ... As a result, *ceteris paribus*, when the British saver calculated the potential gains from each of a set of alternative investment choices, he or she applied a lower uncertainty discount to information about the better-known alternatives.[27]

---

and B. DeLong, 'Did Morgan's Men Add Value?', in P. Temin (ed.), *Inside the Business Enterprise: Historical Perspectives on the Use of Information* (Chicago: University of Chicago Press, 1991), pp. 205–49.

[25] W. Hayes Fisher, *Investing at Its Best and Safeguarding Invested Capital* (London: Financial Review of Reviews, 1912), p. 23.

[26] In *Evolving Financial Markets*, Davis and Gallman argue persuasively that the different information sets possessed by each variety of saver can explain both the existence of a 'dual capital market' in the UK (where a domestic market provided safe investments for the middle class and an international market catered for the needs of the nation's merchants, financiers, gentlemen and peers) and the varying timing and rates of financial development (and need for institutional innovation) experienced by different nations in the long nineteenth century. See also Davis, 'Late-Nineteenth-Century British Imperialist', p. 109 for discussion of the role played by information in financial development.

[27] Davis, 'Late-Nineteenth-Century British Imperialist', p. 107.

Such informational asymmetry could have important international dimensions too:

a British country gentleman might have thought he was better informed about investments in Delhi, where his cousin worked, than about ... Midland textile firms; and a London merchant may have felt more confident about commercial investments in Buenos Aires, where his firm had an office, or about the bonds of the Grand Trunk Railway – his City-based broker, partner in Baring Brothers and fellow club member, had told him that those bonds had some (explicit or implicit) government guarantee – than about coal mines in Scotland.[28]

What needs to be emphasised here is that modern capital markets and the information required to make them function do not appear *ex nihilo*. Rather, they evolve gradually in response to current perceived needs and failings. Thus, the emergence of the Anglo-American investment banks, which came to dominate the foreign and domestic financing of railroad construction in the second half of the nineteenth century, had their origins in the earlier need of British merchant banks for more on-the-spot information on American issues. Similarly, the bond houses, whose imprimatur of quality from the end of the nineteenth century convinced both Canadian and British savers of the merits of unguaranteed local government securities, emerged as a creative solution to the initial difficulties that communities such as Saskatoon, Calgary and Edmonton experienced in securing financial backing for their public works.[29]

How does the British World fit into this story of steadily improving capital markets? For one thing, we know from the 1870s that the majority of British investors regarded colonial securities as safe bets. Protected by the Royal Navy and governed by British laws and standards, they were 'on a different plateau of reliability' from most foreign countries.[30] Indeed, for the most part, colonial securities did prove reliable: there was little question – and even less experience – of default by a colonial government.[31] From the investor's perspective, they were a known quantity. Well-informed of the borrower's track record and trustworthiness, even the most risk-averse middle-class investor could confidently take the plunge. As a result, by the latter half of the nineteenth century these

---

[28] *Ibid.*, p. 107.
[29] Davis and Gallman, *Evolving Financial Markets*, pp. 333–4, 459–60, 814–17.
[30] A. J. Purkis, 'The Politics, Capital and Labour of Railway Building in the Cape Colony, 1870–1885', unpublished D.Phil. thesis, University of Oxford (1978), p. 268.
[31] The only instance of an empire issue going into default between 1870 and 1914 was the New Zealand Harbour Loan; Davis and Huttenback, *Mammon and the Pursuit of Empire*, p. 171.

'gilt-edged' colonial 'consols', as they were called, had become a mainstay of the investment portfolio of many British savers and institutions.[32]

The ease with which investors underwrote colonial assets was partly a product of the comparative abundance of information that they had at their disposal.[33] At a time when capital markets still had limited global reach, and were subject to significant informational asymmetries, the familiarity of colonial securities offered British savers a sense of relative security.[34] Although there were always exceptions, from the perspective of the British investors, the effects of informational asymmetry were generally felt most acutely in comparisons between projects in the British World and those outside it. *Ceteris paribus*, savers were more likely to know and invest in railroad construction in Canada than in a similar plan proposed by promoters in China. The choice of the Canadian project could be more readily made on the basis of a well-informed analysis of probable rates of return, with much less regard for the trustworthiness of the borrowers. So well-endowed with information about the British World was the British investor that it has been suggested that in the half century preceding the First World War 'there was little need for Anglo-Australian or Anglo-Canadian institutions to solve problems of asymmetric information'.[35]

---

[32] Hall, *London Capital Market*, pp. 6–7; Purkis, 'Politics', p. 264; and *Investors Monthly Manual*, 1873, p. 411.

[33] A. Offer, 'Costs and Benefits, Prosperity and Security', in A. N. Porter (ed.), *The Oxford History of the British Empire*, 5 vols., Vol. III: *The Nineteenth Century* (Oxford: Oxford University Press, 1999), pp. 690–711 (pp. 700–1). Similarly, in A. G. Ford, *The Gold Standard, 1880–1914: Britain and Argentina* (Oxford: Oxford University Press, 1962), p. 86, it is argued that a lot of the British investment in Argentina at the end of the nineteenth century was due to the accumulation of first-hand knowledge of conditions there by British businessmen. This information made them more aware of the prospects for profits. The role of informational asymmetry finds a parallel in contemporary finance literature, where it is contended that in many stock markets 'foreign' investors incur higher trading costs than 'domestic' because of the informational disadvantages they face. See H. Choe, H. Kho and R. Stulz, 'Do Domestic Investors Have an Edge? The Trading Experience of Foreign Investors in Korea', *Review of Financial Studies* 18:3 (2005), 795–829; T. Dvorak, 'Do Domestic Investors Have an Information Advantage? Evidence from Indonesia', *Journal of Finance* 60:2 (2005), 817–39; and H. Hau, 'Location Matters: An Examination of Trading Profits', *Journal of Finance* 56 (2001), 1951–83.

[34] This informational asymmetry was probably less marked for direct investment, since such projects placed more onus on investors having detailed knowledge of the specifics of the investment in question. While widespread belief in the inherent safeness of colonial debentures may have been sufficient knowledge for many investors to acquire a particular security, they presumably would have needed to have more first-hand knowledge of the firm or project seeking their direct investment (than would have been typically available to them) before committing their savings to it. Such considerations also partly explain why direct investment assumed such a low proportion of all British overseas investment at this time.

[35] Davis and Gallman, *Evolving Financial Markets*, p. 765.

How did such a situation arise? The answer lies in the manner in which information was created and diffused in the later Victorian and Edwardian era. The British World, by availing the British investor of rich streams of information about the nation's overseas possessions and investment opportunities therein, afforded colonial borrowers distinct advantages in their search for external development capital. Such informational asymmetries stemmed from occupational background (peers and gentlemen, wherever they lived, showed a preference for empire investment, sometimes because they themselves or a family member were in colonial or military employment); region of residence (London businessmen were much more likely to invest in the formal empire than provincial businessmen – the latter had plenty of domestic opportunities and did not need to send their capital abroad); mobility and migration (people recognised profitable openings for capital on their travels); and social or kinship 'webs' and the shared values and expectations that these engendered (as we shall see, such webs played a major if not always acknowledged role in the buying of stocks and shares).

These informational advantages enabled financial institutions and individual investors wishing to diversify their portfolios to turn first to colonial stock, then to US securities, and finally to other foreign stock some time later when knowledge of these unfamiliar markets was more broadly available in the UK. This process of portfolio diversification played itself out over decades rather than years, and was made possible by two inter-related developments: greater awareness of a wider range of investment opportunities, and the emergence of a better functioning capital market.[36] As Davis and Gallman noted, in the 1860s and 1870s 'no one, not even well established merchant bankers, knew if there were *any* sound American, let alone Argentine railroads'.[37] While this state of affairs was not to endure, initially it enhanced the status and appeal of colonial securities. Moreover, given the intrinsic 'public good' properties of knowledge (which once available can be relatively costlessly utilised by other potential investors), there is a potential for such informational asymmetries in favour of empire investments to intensify with the passing of time. After all, the very act of investing in the empire ensured that a further influx of colony-specific information would be forthcoming.[38]

---

[36] R. C. Michie, 'The Social Web of Investment in the Nineteenth Century', *Revue internationale d'histoire de la banque* 18 (1979), 158–61.

[37] Davis and Gallman, *Evolving Financial Markets*, p. 756.

[38] In other words, once individuals choose to invest in a colony, they acquire as a by-product deeper experience and knowledge of that location. In turn, some of that experience and knowledge would be passed on to other potential investors, who as a result become better informed. In a world of imperfect information, such streams of feedback about the merits and potential of a certain place or type of asset tend to sharpen, rather than reduce, informational asymmetry.

For a while, then, imperial relations in the latter half of the nineteenth century acted to accentuate the perceived benefits of investing in the British World.

Investors and the press

So far we have established that information – its quality and supply – is central to decision-making and the efficient workings of financial markets.[39] In the nineteenth century, that supply of information was, at least by today's standards, limited. While technological change over the preceding century had already started to increase the speed and volume of international knowledge transfer, from many parts of the world the flow of information remained scarce and unreliable. Other than commodity prices, interest rates, exchange rates and some data on public debt, the nineteenth-century investor was still short of the knowledge required to discriminate between rival investments. Consequently, their attitudes to projects, indeed entire countries, was to a large extent inferred from whatever news was available to them either through the emerging mass media or direct personal contact and experience.[40] And they could respond with alacrity. For example, reports of rising land prices in Argentina, a signal to many of good times, tended to encourage further investment; the slightest whiff of financial or political crisis engendered a flow of capital in the opposite direction.[41] Precisely how information flowed to investors in the decades prior to the First World War was therefore a matter integral to the unfolding pattern of British overseas investment in this period.

Information reached investors from various sources, most obviously, the published media. Victorian daily newspapers devoted relatively little space to detailed financial analysis and comment. What we today might recognise as financial journalism only appeared in the years immediately prior to the First World War. This is not to say, of course, that financial matters were totally ignored by the mainstream press. From the 1890s, *The Times* regularly printed in its pages three financial columns: 'Money Matters', 'Stocks and Shares' and 'Railway and Other Companies'.

---

[39] As McMillan explains, 'information is the lifeblood of markets. Knowledge of what is available where, and who wants it, is crucial. A market works badly if information does not flow through it.' J. McMillan, *Reinventing the Bazaar: A Natural History of Markets* (New York: Norton, 2002), p. 44. Information, of course, can be explicit or tacit. It is also context-dependent. What is not said or known can often reveal as much as what is. Thus, in certain circumstances, ignorance of a particular subject can in itself be a state of affairs heavily laden with information. It may even be taken to imply the opposite of ignorance: that *there is in fact nothing more* to be known.

[40] N. Ferguson, 'Political Risk and the International Bond Market between the 1848 Revolution and the Outbreak of the First World War', *EcHR* 59 (2006), 70–112 (p. 79).

[41] Ford, *Gold Standard*, pp. 129–31.

As their headings suggest, these sections focused primarily on reporting broad economic and financial indicators, such as prevailing interest and exchange rates, the movements of share prices in the London Stock Exchange, and dividends paid out by public companies. Typically, this material was simply listed with little by way of comment. Since the intended readership was clearly the financially initiated, discussion and explanation of the data were deemed unnecessary.[42]

The broadsheets offered the growing number of investors in the latter half of the nineteenth century little direct information or advice on how best to utilise their savings. Nor can it be said that these newspapers informed their readers particularly well of events taking place in the colonies. Indeed, prior to the South African War, coverage of imperial matters, relative to the space devoted to European and American news, was limited. Dominion news represented a small proportion of the cable news that appeared in the British press. While the South African War nurtured an interest in the empire among the British public that was actively exploited by propagandists within the press, everyday coverage of the dominions remained scant.[43] Certainly, major events, such as the Québec Tercentenary celebrations in 1908, Indian protests in Natal in 1913 and gold discoveries in South Africa received significant attention. But once such events had ended, coverage of the region concerned rapidly returned to previous low levels. Between 9 and 14 March 1903, for example, only 2.9 per cent of the columns of cable news printed in the *Daily Telegraph* came from the dominions. By contrast, news from Europe and the United States accounted respectively for 57.6 and 25.7 per cent of all news reported during this period.[44]

Cable news data need to be read with caution, though. After all, the greater volume of cable news coming from Europe and the United States

---

[42] O. R. Hobson, 'The Financial Press', *Lloyd's Bank Limited Monthly Review* 5 (1934), 1–10 (p. 3); N. Grieser, 'The British Investor and His Sources of Information', unpublished M.Sc. dissertation, University of London (1940), p. 93. Hobson described *The Times*' coverage of financial matters as 'a medley of information without classification and without cross-headings, the reader of which was given no visual help in selecting the important events of the day, and very little help in the shape of editorial comment'.

[43] *The Standard* is a case in point. The politics of its editor (H. Gwynne) and the hope of securing lucrative advertisements from dominion governments, banks, railways and land companies encouraged it consciously to incorporate more colonial content in its news. For more details, see S. J. Potter, 'Nationalism, Imperialism and the Press in Britain and the Dominions *c.* 1898–1914', unpublished D.Phil. thesis, University of Oxford (2001), pp. 200–7.

[44] S. J. Potter, 'Empire and the English Press, 1857–1914', in Potter (ed.), *Newspapers and Empire in Ireland and Britain* (Dublin: Four Courts Press, 2004ᵃ), pp. 39–61; and *News and the British World: The Emergence of an Imperial Press System, 1876–1922* (Oxford: Oxford University Press, 2003), p. 111.

Table 5.5. *News coverage in* The Times, *selected countries, 1870–1913.*

	Average annual number of news items (of all types)	Ratio of good to bad economic news reported
Queensland	23	5.70
Canada	343	4.90
Sweden	29	3.66
Mexico	50	3.32
Turkey	517	2.53
Greece	148	2.37
Argentina	56	2.05
Brazil	74	1.98
Uruguay	25	1.91
Colombia	10	1.87
Hungary	42	1.67
Japan	56	1.66
Egypt	446	1.51
Chile	36	1.43
Costa Rica	2	1.28
China	193	1.17
Portugal	102	1.12
Russia	515	0.90

Note: Bad economic news includes not only adverse commentary on commercial and business affairs but also reports of political instability, violence and war.

Source: Data taken from P. Mauro, N. Sussman and Y. Yafeh, *Emerging Markets and Financial Globalization: Sovereign Bond Spreads in 1870–1913 and Today* (Oxford: Oxford University Press, 2006), p. 93.

might have simply reflected the fact that less of what was deemed of general interest to the reading public – wars, scandals, disasters and the like – occurred in the dominions. Indeed, from an investor's perspective the *absence* of such cable news in itself may have spoken volumes. What really mattered to the investor was the volume of *investment-related* information available, not information per se. Since the dailies did not directly provide news on available investment projects in different countries, their influence on investors must have been primarily exerted through their coverage of other aspects of those countries' experiences. The reporting of negative political news, in particular, appears to have shaped investment behaviour adversely.[45]

[45] P. Mauro, N. Sussman and Y. Yafeh, *Emerging Markets and Financial Globalization: Sovereign Bond Spreads in 1870–1913 and Today* (Oxford: Oxford University Press, 2006), p. 61; Ferguson, 'Political Risk', p. 79.

Table 5.5 provides an overview of *The Times*' coverage of a selection of countries between 1870 and 1913. It shows how colonies such as Queensland received little mention – about twice a month on average – despite the fact that *The Times* had the most extensive network of correspondents in the empire of all British papers. Part of the problem, of course, was the expense of sending cables from such 'remote' parts of the world.[46] Canada fared better in terms of coverage, but most of its 343 items occurred after 1900 when relatively dense cable networks with North America had already been laid. Even so, Turkey, Russia and Egypt were all seemingly regarded as more newsworthy, as indeed would have been the United States and most western European countries.

Yet, as mentioned before, from the investor's perspective the type of news offered mattered just as much as, if not more than, the volume. Table 5.5 shows how the ratio of good to bad economic news varied significantly between countries. Russia, for example, received more negative press than positive, whereas Portugal and China furnished marginally more good economic news than bad. At the other extreme, Queensland, Canada and Sweden were very positively portrayed in Britain's main daily newspaper.[47] Not without reason could the Earl of Grey write with satisfaction to Moberly Bell in March 1910 that Canada's advantages had been so well covered in the media that for the time being 'she may count on remaining the Belle of the Ball in the London Stock Exchange without resorting to expensive advertisements'.[48]

The case of Queensland is also informative. What would a *Times*-reading investor have made of the paper's coverage of this distant northern Australian colony? Presumably, he or she would have observed that Queensland was a place bothered by few dramatic, newsworthy events, untouched by war and serious political instability, and blessed by healthy economic prospects (since it received nearly six times as much good economic news as bad). In other words, Queensland would have seemed an attractive and safe place for investment, at least relative to other major capital-seeking locations, such as Chile, Brazil or even Argentina.

While positive reporting of the dominions may have often simply reflected the reality that they were safe places to invest, the 'imperial' nature of information flows certainly reinforced this perception. Official mechanisms were often exploited to a colony's advantage. Dominion

---

[46] Potter, *News and the British World*, p. 111.
[47] Sweden's positive image is not surprising given its average debt per capita was just £3.38 and that from 1898 it was awarded the Credit Lyonnais highest credit rating. See Mauro, Sussman and Yafeh, *Emerging Markets*, pp. 93, 99.
[48] Quoted in Potter, *News and the British World*, p. 131.

agents in London, for example, were not averse to using their contacts in the City and the media to propagate information beneficial to their interests. Charles Mills, the Cape Colony's agent in 1885, informed the Cape government that in regard to raising loans he had 'personally seen the editors of the leading journals' and that 'the following papers will give us their unqualified support, whatever your course of action is decided on – *The Times – Daily News – Morning Post – The Standard – Pall Mall Gazette – St James – The Economist – Statist – Money*, and *Railway Times* … With such support we need not fear failure, in whatever steps you may choose to take.'[49]

With respect to cable news, meanwhile, what the British public read about the Empire was largely determined by a single agency, Reuters. Indeed, by the 1870s, Reuters had acquired a virtual news monopoly of the colonies and Far East, a state of affairs that, according to the news agency's official historian, made it a 'semi-official institution of the British Empire'.[50] While Reuters asserted its independence, its stances, conscious or otherwise, were pro-British and, by extension, pro-British World. As the editor of *The Nation* rather frankly admitted to his readers on the occasion of the fiftieth anniversary of Reuters Company, at heart the agency 'stood for British interests as the Foreign Office sees them, and in reporting the internal affairs of foreign countries, its bias was usually governmental … It was bound to reflect the views here of "official circles", there of colonists' clubs, and everywhere of the mercantile or governing class'.[51] As a consequence, British colonies were likely to be presented more favourably in despatches than were foreign nations.

Such advantages were amplified by Reuters' assessment of what news was fit to be telegraphed back to London. As an 1883 circular to agents and correspondents made clear, because of the 'increased attention paid by London and English provincial press to disasters &c., of all kinds … all occurrences of the sort' should be telegraphed 'with the utmost promptitude'.[52] The content of cable news was driven as much (or more)

---

[49] Quoted in Purkis, 'Politics', p. 303. Colonial governments and companies were also wont to supplement this behind-the-scenes influence with overt advertisement in the press, publicity that it was felt would help to attract both capital and labour their way. Twenty-one Australasian banks, thus, advertised their deposits in *The Scotsman* alone in November 1890. See Potter, *News and the British World*, p. 107; Potter, 'Nationalism', pp. 204–5; and J. D. Bailey, 'Australian Company Borrowing, 1870–1893: A Study in British Overseas Investment', unpublished D.Phil. thesis, University of Oxford (1958), p. 123.

[50] D. Read, *The Power of News: The History of Reuters 1849–1989* (Oxford: Oxford University Press, 1992), p. 49.

[51] Quoted in *ibid.*, p. 94.

[52] The circular went on to list the types of events that should be brought to London's notice: 'fires, floods, inundations, railway accidents, destructive storms, earthquakes, shipwrecks attended with loss of life, accidents to British and American war vessels and

by the desire to provide sensational, entertaining news that might boost
newspaper circulation (and hence demand for their cables) than by a
desire to help the British investor make their investment decisions.[53]
Given such priorities, it is hardly surprising that increasingly prosper-
ous, growing and politically stable colonies such as Victoria, New South
Wales and South Australia failed to generate much cable traffic for most
of the nineteenth century. Other than the escapades of bush-rangers,
which might have temporarily titillated the British public, and tours by
English cricket teams, Reuters' correspondents in these locations typically had little material that their editors back in London would have
deemed worthy of telegraphic transmission.[54] From the perspective of
the investor, of course, no such news is in fact good news.

Reuters also provided an additional service that facilitated the spread
of information within the empire: the private telegram. Established in
1871, this service was subsequently extended to include the Far East,
Australasia and South Africa. Its users were wealthy individuals and
companies, and by 1881 Reuters had established standard codes aimed
to reduce wordage. Single word codes for common phrases such as 'market rising' or 'market falling' betray the fact that the service was heavily used for commercial purposes. Of all of the lines on offer, the most
popular service was the Eastern Private Telegram, which linked Britain
to the merchants and businessmen of India and the Far East. In 1875,
approximately 4,000 telegrams were being sent on these lines; by 1912,
this number had risen to 276,195.[55]

The daily newspapers, of course, were not the only source of investment-related news. Around the turn of the century, a number of periodicals were established that focused on imperial issues, such as *The Empire
Review* (founded 1901), *Colonial Quarterly* (1906), *Standard of Empire*
(1908) and *Round Table* (1910). These journals complemented a series
of other publications, which appeared from the 1880s, and whose subject matter related exclusively to one specific colony.[56] Typical of these
was the *British Australasian*, the creation of the eminent London banker,
R. H. Inglis Palgrave, and the financial journalist, Robert Lucas Nash.

to mail steamers, street riots of a grave character, disturbances arising from strikes, duels
between, and suicides of persons of note, social or political, and murders of a sensational
or atrocious character'. See Read, *The Power of News*, p. 106.
[53] For the contrary (unsubstantiated) view that newspapers were primarily catering for the
interests of the investors, see Mauro, Sussman and Yafeh, *Emerging Markets*, p. 18.
[54] Read, *The Power of News*, p. 102. It is worth noting in this regard that the onset of depression and the growth of a strong labour movement in Australia from the end of the nineteenth century attracted adverse press coverage that undermined its reputation as a 'safe
haven' for investors for a while. See Hall, *London Capital Market*, pp. 190–1.
[55] Read, *The Power of News*, pp. 79–80.
[56] Potter, *News and the British World*, pp. 107–8; and 'Nationalism', pp. 202–7.

Both men had had prior editorial experience at *The Economist*, and, when the first edition of the newspaper appeared in October 1884, Nash assumed its editorship. In 1888 the paper merged with the *Anglo-New Zealander and Australian Times*, which had been founded in August 1884 by a London-based *Argus* employee, Charles Short.[57] Its immediate competitor was the *Australian Trading World* (founded 1886). Although the *British Australasian* acted as a general storehouse of information on Britain's antipodean colonies and, as such, provided much news on sporting, social and political events, not to mention colonial gossip, it also explicitly projected itself as 'A Newspaper for Merchants, Shareholders, Land Selectors, and Emigrants'.[58] Through its pages, readers could familiarise themselves with the great land companies of Australia, the state of the New South Wales wool industry, the capital requirements of Melbourne's metropolitan tramways and the promising mining opportunities in Western Australia, as well as more mundane information on prevailing prices, dividends and shipping to and from Australasia. At times, the newspaper felt confident enough to counsel its readers on which Australian stocks were worth holding on to and which should be liquidated. From the early 1900s, the paper operated a bookshop and information centre in central London, 'The Rendezvous', in which interested parties could buy or simply browse through materials and government publications pertaining to Australia and New Zealand.[59]

Australia and New Zealand were by no means unique in having such publications. *The Canadian Mail* (founded 1909) aimed to keep the British investor informed of developments and investment opportunities, whereas British interests in southern Africa were ably advertised in London by Edward P. Mathers' *South Africa*.[60] Mathers provides an excellent example of an individual whose imperial connections acted to tie the British press to its colonies.[61] Born in Edinburgh, Mathers worked as a journalist on several provincial papers before heading off to South Africa in 1878. He settled in Durban, where he founded the Natal Caledonian Society, covered the Zulu War of 1879 for the *Scotsman* and other papers, and later became editor of the *Natal Advertiser*. Fascinated by the discovery of gold in the 1880s, he made numerous treks through South Africa and Rhodesia, journeys that he subsequently recounted in a series of

---

[57] S. Sleight, 'Reading the British Australasian Community in London, 1884–1924', mimeo of paper delivered at the Australian diaspora conference held at the Menzies Research Centre, University of London, 2005, p. 2.
[58] *Ibid.*, pp. 6–7.   [59] *Ibid.*, pp. 3, 6–8, 18–19.
[60] Potter, *News and the British World*, p. 108.
[61] See especially anon., *The Story of* South Africa *Newspaper and Its Founder (Edward P. Mathers): Told by Others* (London, 1903).

popular travel books, such as *A Trip to Moodie's* and *Zambesia*. These treks also led him to be recognised as an early authority on the subject of the Witwatersrand goldfields. Author of several standard works – including *Golden South Africa*, *A Glimpse of the Goldfields* and *Goldfields Revisited* – he was reputed to be a shrewd judge of the economic potential of South Africa, and an independent commentator on its political situation. Thus while generally supportive of the claims of the Uitlanders, and critical of Kruger for 'dragging his country through the mire of misery and possible bankruptcy', he nonetheless took Rhodes to task in 1898–9 for putting his friendship to Jameson above his patriotic duty towards South Africa.

In 1889, Mathers returned to London determined to provide better news coverage of South Africa, which he described as the 'Cinderella of the Empire'. He set up a journal to promote British trade with and investment in the region, and to report on its general progress. Published weekly, and copiously illustrated, *South Africa* described itself as a 'Home-Colonial' journal 'for all those interested in South African affairs'. The diamond and gold mining industries were particularly well covered, but agriculture, commerce, politics and social affairs also received attention. The paper was very much aligned to the cause of promoting 'British freedom in South Africa', yet did its best to eschew party politics. As a prominent daily London newspaper claimed in 1889, 'Journals like *South Africa* play an important part in strengthening the federal bond between various portions of the Empire by diffusing a knowledge of their requirements, achievements, aims, purposes, and progress throughout the lands occupied by teeming millions of English-speaking people.'

South Africa was a commercial success, building up a buoyant advertising income from South African companies, and widely (and favourably) quoted in the provincial and national British press. Its offices were situated in the City close to the Stock Exchange and Bank of England. To raise its profile, interviews were secured with notable figures in South African society – in addition to Kruger and Rhodes, Alfred Beit, Lionel Phillips, Abe Bailey and George Farrar from the mining industry, and John Merriman, James Rose Innes, Henry Loch, Alfred Milner, Jan Smuts and Gordon Sprigg from the world of government and politics. Special supplements (for example, on emigration) were also issued from time to time.

Mathers was acutely aware of the number of fraudulent companies pushing puffed-up prospectuses at British investors in the 1890s, and the damage they were inflicting on the reputation of South Africa in the London money market. Hence he did not shrink from exposing bogus firms trying to float themselves in the City, and, to this end, enlisted the help of the Chambers of Mining and Commerce on the Rand. Some members of the Chambers were supportive of his move, while others proved reluctant to break with the practice of not commenting on such matters. Mathers also organised the annual South African dinner for South Africans living in or visiting the UK. The first occasion in 1889 was chaired by the shipping magnate, Sir Donald Currie, and attended by prominent business and financial interests. It aimed to foster public awareness and interest in South Africa.[62]

Another source of published news for investors was the growing number of specialist journals and newspapers concerning themselves with financial matters. A burgeoning financial press had its origins in the investor's hunger for more information on the plethora of shares that appeared on the market during the great railway speculations of the 1840s. By 1845, in excess of twenty papers and periodicals, such as the *Quarterly Railway Intelligence* and *The Daily Railway Share List*, had emerged.[63] From the 1870s, these industry-specific publications were joined by a raft of papers and journals devoted exclusively to questions of investment. The most notable of these were *The Financier* (founded March 1870) and *The Financial and Mining News* (founded January 1884). Unlike the financial sections of mainstream dailies, these publications did not target the initiated, seasoned investor with a sophisticated understanding of financial markets, but the emerging market of small-scale, middle-class and relatively uninformed investors. These 'new' investors sought easily intelligible information on investment prospects, as well as editorial opinion and guidance. Journals and newspapers such as the *Daily Stock Exchange*, *The Money Market Review* and the *Investor's Gazette* and numerous others arose to cater precisely for their demands.[64]

The information and advice proffered by such publications was not always accurate, nor indeed well intentioned. The practice of 'puffing' – the advertising and fraudulent endorsement of doubtful investments – was a problem that troubled the financial press. Ostensibly reputable publications were created by promoters in a thinly veiled attempt to lend respectability to dubious projects they were pushing, while the placement of prominent advertisements for an investment alongside an editorial that brazenly sung its praise (often secretly written and paid for by its promoter) was commonplace. These practices were felt to be sufficiently

[62] E. Rosenthal (ed.), *Southern African Dictionary of National Biography* (n.p., 1966), p. 243.
[63] A. Preda, 'The Rise of the Popular Investor: Financial Knowledge and Investing in England and France, 1840–1880', *Sociological Quarterly* 42 (Sociological Quarterly 2001), 205–32 (p. 212).
[64] Hall, *London Capital Market*, pp. 46–7; Hobson, 'Financial Press', p. 6; Preda, 'Rise of the Popular Investor', p. 212; Grieser, 'British Investor', pp. 119–25.

widespread for *The Statist* to openly condemn them in an article published on 9 April 1887 entitled 'The Sham Financial Press'.[65]

The quality and reliability of the information supplied aside – and it must not be forgotten that much of the financial press was bona fide – these publications indubitably influenced the investment choice of many in the latter half of the century. The precise extent to which they mattered is, of course, hard to establish. It clearly varied considerably between individuals and different classes of investors. Nonetheless, in Hall's view there could be 'little doubt that by making information simultaneously available to a wider public, it [the specialised financial press] magnified any trends that did occur' both in terms of the 'short-term speculative movements' and 'longer-term biases favouring investment in a particular area that were ... a feature of this period'.[66]

How far did the financial press really engender such alleged investment biases? The range and type of information published in *The Economist* (founded 1844) and the *Investor's Monthly Manual* (hereafter *IMM*) between 1880 and 1905 support Hall's claim. Both papers were well-respected, and not vulnerable to the blatant manipulation of some of their lesser regarded competitors. The *IMM*, a monthly supplement produced by *The Economist*, enjoyed that publication's high esteem.[67] Table 5.6 provides an overview of their geographical coverage towards the end of the nineteenth century. Observed and expected[68] frequencies of coverage of various parts of the world are presented. The figures from *The Economist* relate to the number and percentage of articles on a particular region that appeared in that period. More information, however, can be gleaned from the *IMM*. In addition to the usual listing of share prices and dividends and reporting of AGMs, it published two sections entitled 'Notes upon Investments' and 'Incidents Tending to Affect the

---

[65] Examples and discussions of such deceptions can be found in Hall, *London Capital Market*, p. 77; Hobson, 'Financial Press', p. 4; Grieser, 'British Investor', pp. 126–9; C. C. Spence and M. Casson, *British Investments and the American Mining Frontier, 1860–1901* (Ithaca, NY: Taylor and Francis, 2000), pp. 17–18. Another source of a successful 'puff' was the swindler like Horatio Bottomley, Whitaker Wright or Perry Tarbutt, who seemed to have the charisma to induce many a naïve investor to sink his or her capital into the most suspicious of ventures. For examples of such scams, see J. Mouat and I. Phimister, 'Mining, Engineers and Risk Management: British Overseas Investment, 1894–1914', *SAHJ* 49 (2003), 5–18; and R. P. T. Davenport-Hines and J. J. Van Helten, 'Edgar Vincent, Viscount D'Abernon, and the Eastern Investment Company in London, Constantinople and Johannesburg', in R. P. T. Davenport-Hines (ed.), *Speculators and Patriots: Essays in Business Biography* (London: Routledge, 1986), pp. 35–62 (p. 35).

[66] Hall, *London Capital Market*, p. 47. For another favourable assessment of the role of the press in providing information, see Potter, 'Nationalism', p. 41.

[67] Grieser, 'British Investor', p. 144; Preda, 'Rise of the Popular Investor', p. 212.

[68] On the basis of investment shares.

Table 5.6. *Observed and expected geographical coverage of* The Economist *and the* Investor's Monthly Manual, *1880–1905 (percentage of total in brackets).*

	Observed frequency of coverage in The Economist	Expected frequency of coverage in The Economist (based on its investment share)	Observed frequency of reports in IMM 'Notes'	Expected frequency of reports in IMM 'Notes' (based on its investment share)	Observed frequency of 'incidents' in the IMM	Expected frequency of 'incidents' in the IMM (based on its investment share)	Expected frequency of 'incidents' in the IMM (based on its share of reports in IMM 'Notes')
Dominions	152 (26.4)	158.1	56 (29.0)	53.0	102 (16.1)	174.3	184.3
India	65 (11.3)	49.0	23 (11.9)	16.4	17 (2.7)	54.0	75.7
Dependent colonies	18 (3.1)	28.1	4 (2.1)	9.4	16 (2.5)	30.9	13.2
Europe	141 (24.5)	53.7	19 (9.8)	18.0	255 (40.2)	59.2	62.5
Asia	26 (4.5)	53.7	8 (4.2)	18.0	55 (8.7)	59.2	26.4
Latin America	49 (8.5)	79.3	38 (19.7)	26.6	70 (11.0)	87.4	125.0
USA	125 (21.7)	139.7	45 (23.3)	46.8	96 (15.1)	154.1	148.1
Other	0 (0.0)	121.7	0 (0.0)	40.8	24 (3.8)	134.2	0.0

Notes: This table gives the number of articles on each of these regions that appeared in the 'Business Notes' section of *The Economist* in 1880, 1890 and 1900 as well as in the 'Notes upon investments' ('Notes') and 'Incidents tending to affect the money market' ('Incidents') sections of the *IMM* in 1881, 1885, 1890, 1895, 1900 and 1905. Expected frequency is calculated on the assumption that the amount of coverage a region attracted was proportional to the share of British overseas investment it received (or, in the case of the last column, its share of coverage in the 'Notes' section of the *IMM*) in those same years.

Sources: The Economist *and the* Investor's Monthly Manual. Investment data come from Stone, *Global Export of Capital.*

Money Market' (hereafter referred to as 'Notes' and 'Incidents' respectively). The monthly 'Notes' section appeared at the front of the publication and consisted of what was perceived to be the most important news and developments from the world of investment. The returns and prospects of specific investment projects (or types of investment) were discussed, and an editorial opinion frequently offered. The 'Notes' section therefore was the part of the publication where true financial journalism was practised. By contrast, the 'Incidents' section, which appeared in each December edition, carried no analysis or discussion, but merely listed in tabular form international and domestic events that over the past year had impacted on the money market. For example, in 1890, incidents such as four days of rioting in Buenos Aires, the financial crisis in Uruguay, the course of a US Tariff Bill, the illness of the infant King of Spain and the partial outbreak of a London dock strike merited mention. The information presented thus sheds light on contemporaneous perceptions of the relative uncertainties of investing in different locations. It seems reasonable to presume that such perceptions, as they appeared in the *IMM*, true or otherwise, provided much of the information available to the less informed British investor.[69]

Statistical analysis of Table 5.6 confirms that these two sections of the *IMM* imparted different types of information: the 'Notes' section informed readers of current developments and opportunities, whereas 'Incidents' warned them, albeit indirectly and possibly unintentionally, of societies where the safety of their capital was more likely to be put in jeopardy. Overall, the geographical spread of *The Economist*'s news coverage was different from Britain's pattern of overseas investment over the corresponding period.[70] Nor did the pattern of reporting in the 'Notes' and 'Incidents' sections conform to that which one might expect on the basis of investment shares.[71] Moreover, the regional coverage of the *IMM*'s 'Incident' section differed statistically from the patterns observed in its 'Notes' section.[72] An important implication of each of these findings

[69] Such an interpretation of the *IMM* 'Incidents' section is also employed by Mauro, Sussman and Yafeh, *Emerging Markets*, p. 28.

[70] More formally expressed, the *chi*-squared statistic of 300.197, generated by a comparison of the first two columns, allows us with 99 per cent confidence to reject the hypothesis that the observed regional coverage did not differ significantly from that expected on the basis of investment share. For details of the *chi*-square test, see M. Hamburg, *Basic Statistics* (London: R. D. Irwin, 1985), pp. 233–60.

[71] The *chi*-squared statistics of 57.3 and 826.6 respectively for the 'Notes' and 'Incidents' comparisons permits us with 99 per cent confidence to reject the hypothesis that the observed coverage did not differ significantly from that expected on the basis of investment share.

[72] The *chi*-squared statistic of 749.7 generated permits us with 99 per cent confidence to reject the null hypothesis that the 'Incidents' section's observed coverage did not differ significantly from that expected on the basis of the 'Notes' section's coverage.

is that the pattern of reporting in both publications did not merely reflect Britain's current investment behaviour. Rather, other factors, such as opinion, conjecture and actual on-the-ground developments, shaped the density of information flows. Of further note is the fact that the *IMM*'s coverage of financially significant events was independent not only of prevailing investment patterns, but of the periodical's own policies as to what was newsworthy enough to cover in its 'Notes' section.

Table 5.6 also reveals significant variation between regions in terms of the different types of information reported. The dominions enjoyed a high level of coverage (over a quarter of all articles published) consistent with their importance as major recipients of British capital, whilst receiving relatively few reported episodes (about 16 per cent) that threatened capital. Like Table 5.5, this finding again highlights the perception of safety that the press coverage of the dominions projected to British investors. Thus *The Economist*'s 1880–1 survey of Britain's colonies could confidently conclude: 'we regard these possessions of ours as a first-rate field, if properly cultivated, for the utilisation of British surplus capital and population, and it is the main object of these comments to direct both where they may be employed to their best advantage'.[73] Over the coming years, the paper's coverage of dominion affairs expanded markedly to include accounts of speeches by leading colonials visiting London and even the placement of their own correspondents in a number of colonies.[74]

What of the coverage of Britain's other colonies? India tended to be over-reported and the dependencies under-reported in the news. Like the dominions, though, all these colonies were significantly under-represented in the 'Incidents' section of the *IMM*. For one reason or another, membership of the empire appeared to coincide with lower investment uncertainty. Such security, however, was not a uniquely imperial experience. The British financial press coverage of the USA closely paralleled that of the dominions, namely a large allocation of space, as consistent with its share of British investment, and relatively few reports of events that might have upset the money markets.

In marked contrast, Europe was heavily reported, and a more uncertain prospect for investors. Given that much of what was reported about Europe concerned war, political instability or scandal, such a pairing of characteristics is hardly surprising. Comparatively speaking, news from Asia (other than India) tended to be ignored, even though it endured only marginally more worrying 'Incidents' than might have

---

[73] 'Our Colonial Possessions', *The Economist*, 1881, p. 1075.
[74] For examples, see Hall, *London Capital Market*, pp. 162–3.

been expected. Finally, Latin American affairs were under-reported by *The Economist* (though, interestingly, the region was over-reported in the more investment-focused 'Notes' section of the *IMM*) and slightly under-represented in the 'Incidents' section.

Financial networks

The media were not the only source of information on investment opportunities. Nor was the individual investor the only actor making decisions and, hence, in need of information. The reality, then as now, was that many of the most important investment decisions, such as those relating to the raising of government and company loans, were taken within the financial sector *prior* to the individual saver ever becoming involved. How financial institutions arrived at decisions could thus impact significantly on subsequent investment flows.

In dealing with money matters, financiers, of course, had many advantages not available to the lay investor. These included experience of reading markets, a detailed understanding of financial mechanisms and the ability to make sense of an array of pertinent, if potentially confusing, information. Personal relationships with and connections to other financiers, officials and businessmen also gave them a competitive edge. As Grieser explains, 'through the channels of business friendships, less puzzling information than that contained in balance sheets and statistical reports is whispered and telephoned throughout the City'.[75] In an uncertain world, the information from such human interaction was often invaluable. Coming from individuals who were known and trusted, it acted to reduce the risk and cost of investing.[76] Typically, the most successful networkers were those who concentrated on the quality, rather than quantity, of their contacts. Of itself, a large network could simply lead to a plethora of competing signals and information; it could even prove inimical to the establishment of the intimacy upon which trust was founded. Hence getting to the important 'players' was the key to success. Effective networking was ultimately a matter of building tight and reliable relationships *with the right people*.

The challenge for the would-be networker was that the *right people* were usually few in number. For those attempting to influence the investment policies of a nineteenth-century bank, for instance, the key players were its

---

[75] Grieser, 'British Investor', p. 73. See also Davenport-Hines and Van Helten, 'Edgar Vincent', p. 35.

[76] M. C. Casson, 'An Economic Approach to Regional Business Networks', in J. F. Wilson and A. Popp (eds.), *Industrial Clusters and Regional Business Networks in England, 1750–1970* (Aldershot: Ashgate, 2003), pp. 19–44 (pp. 21–2, 28, 31).

directors. This small group of individuals held the ultimate power in determining how their institutions would utilise the capital at their disposal.[77]
For governments wishing to raise loans on the London capital market,
there were in fact very few banks and brokerage firms with which they
could deal. Indeed, well-defined, almost exclusive relationships emerged
between colonies and specific banks and stockbrokers. Thus, the London
and Westminster Bank, and R. Nivison and Co. catered for much of the
capital needs of the dominions, particularly Australia, whereas Barings
Brothers and Messrs Scrimgeour and Co. were the preferred financiers of
Canada, and, until the mid 1880s, the Cape Colony.[78]

For the dominions, personal connections could mean the difference
between financial embarrassment and security. In 1883, the Cape Colony,
facing a budgetary crisis, sought reprieve by seeking a temporary loan from
the City. When the colony's bank, Barings, declined to support such a
loan, its government broke its long-standing relationship with Barings and
its preferred broker, Scrimgeours, and searched for an alternative backer.
This proved problematic. The financial sector was predictably reluctant
to upset the modus vivendi, while Barings and Scrimgeours threatened to
'bear' any loan raised through a rival bank and brokerage firm (by dump-
ing large volumes of the Cape securities they still retained on the market just before the issuance of the new loan). Not until December 1883
did the Cape secure the backing of the London and Westminster Bank,
which agreed to accept responsibility for both the short-term loan and
the floating of a new permanent £5 million loan. In return, the London
and Westminster was guaranteed a monopoly of all of the Cape's future
financial business. The successful denouement of the crisis owed much
to personal connections. Particularly influential was Sir Penrose Julyan,
Crown Agent for the Cape until 1878 but now, crucially, a director of the
London and Westminster Bank. It was he who not only managed to persuade his fellow directors to support the Cape's loan, but also used the
considerable sway and reputation in the City that he had acquired over
his years as Crown Agent to encourage others to take up the new issue. In
the words of one scholar, 'his experience – he had floated 92 loans by late
1883 – and his influence with the London and Westminster, were working
to help the Cape avoid "disaster and discredit"'.[79]

[77] G. Jones, *British Multinational Banking, 1830–1990* (Oxford: Oxford University Press,
1993), p. 43; D. T. Merrett, *ANZ Bank: A History of the Australia and New Zealand
Banking Group Limited and Its Constituents* (Sydney: Allen and Unwin, 1985), p. 25.
[78] T. Suzuki, *Japanese Government Loan Issues on the London Capital Market, 1870–1913*
(London: Athlone, 1994), pp. 33–7; Purkis, 'Politics', p. 292.
[79] Julyan's cause was also undoubtedly advanced by the presence on the board of the
London and Westminster of Sir Henry Barkly, a former Governor of the Cape. See

The professional relationship between broker and client – whether Agent-General, Crown Agent, company or, simply, investor – was a close and personal one. A common practice of nineteenth-century brokers was to keep clients informed by sending out monthly or weekly circulars listing securities deemed worthy of investment. Stamped application forms for these securities were enclosed in the envelope. Typically, such lists were kept very short and were sparse on detail. This brevity reflected not the slackness of brokers, but the esteem that they commanded from their customers. For an established broker, if a security merited a place on his list, his clients could – and often did – take that as a strong endorsement.[80] Successful brokers therefore had considerable influence on their clientele and, if their customer base was large enough, this degree of influence could in turn grant power over those attempting to raise loans in London; all the more so if the broker was regarded by his colleagues as a market leader.

The classic example of a broker whose support of a colonial loan was integral to its success in London is Robert Nivison (later Lord Glendyne). Beginning his career at the London and Westminster, Nivison, having acquired an extensive understanding of the capital market, left the bank in 1886 to establish his own brokerage firm, R. Nivison and Co. It was an immediate success. Exploiting his contacts in the London and Westminster, Nivison became the bank's main broker, taking responsibility for the floating of various colonial government and municipal loans with which his firm had been entrusted. He took an innovative approach to the job and pioneered a new financial instrument, the underwriting syndicate.[81] Above all, he became the City's expert on Australian issues; by the 1890s the fate of antipodean finances was heavily dependent upon his skills, judgement and goodwill. No wonder the *Banker's Magazine* felt it apposite to anoint him the Australian colonies' 'special confidant'.[82]

Purkis, 'Politics', pp. 307–17. The quotation comes from Purkis, 'Politics', p. 315. For an account of how the personal links of the Scottish emigrant residing in Ballarat could lubricate the flow of investment from Scotland to Australia by securing a deposit agency in Edinburgh for the Commercial Bank of Australia, see Bailey, 'Australian Company Borrowing', pp. 127–9.

[80] Grieser, 'British Investor', pp. 70–3; Suzuki, *Japanese Government*, p. 46.

[81] The underwriting syndicate was a group, usually of banks or brokerages, that came together to underwrite (guarantee to take the unsubscribed portion of) a large loan issue in return for a commission. Such syndicates helped spread the inherent risk of large financial undertakings and thereby made them more likely to eventuate. See Suzuki, *Japanese Government*, p. 28.

[82] For more on Nivison, see Hall, *London Capital Market*, pp. 103–5; R. S. Gilbert, 'London Financial Intermediaries and Australian Overseas Borrowing, 1900–1929', *Australian Economic History Review* 11 (1971), pp. 39–47; R. P. T. Davenport-Hines, 'Lord Glendyne', in R. T. Appleyard and C. B. Schedvin (eds.), *Australian Financiers: Biographical Essays* (Melbourne: Macmillan Co. of Australia, 1988), pp. 190–205;

Nivison's strengths were twofold: his detailed knowledge of the small-scale investors and trustees' demand for Australian securities, and his unmatched access to the brokers and jobbers who had the task of managing the accumulated funds of such savers. His method emphasised the personal. Davenport-Hines' succinct description of his modus operandi is worth recounting:

Glendyne devised his own rules for issuing colonial loans in London. He discussed terms with prospective borrowers without consulting institutions, judged what the market would take, and on the day of issue walked around the City institutions offering them an opportunity to participate ... If any institution said that it disliked the terms and was not interested in sub-underwriting at the price offered, it was permanently removed from Nivison's list, and was never again offered an opportunity to participate in an issue made by the firm.[83]

Nivison's methods were thus uncompromising, perhaps even arrogant. But his style spoke of his authority and the respect he commanded in the marketplace. Moreover, it worked. As A. A. Grainger, the South Australian Agent-General in London, observed in 1908, whenever a new Australian issue appeared potential sub-underwriters (the jobbers and brokers of the London Stock Exchange) always inquired if Nivision were involved and 'if he is not they will not touch it'.[84]

Colonial governments complained that these dense networks of connections that lay at the heart of the City impeded their freedom of action. Yet the reality, grudgingly conceded, was that these relationships granted privileged access to British investment funds. Indeed, foreign governments and businesses, as City outsiders, were not so blessed and frequently struggled to make the right contacts.[85]

In addition to the presence of colonial representatives in London, many of whom were directly involved in raising capital, several other factors worked to cement the colonies' advantages there. Colonial financial institutions drew their staff from the same pool of people that worked in the

---

Suzuki, *Japanese Government*, pp. 46–7; Kynaston, *City of London*, Vol. II., p. 49; and Jones, *British Multinational Banking*, pp. 123–4.

[83] Davenport-Hines, 'Lord Glendyne', p. 199.

[84] Quoted in Gilbert, 'London Financial Intermediaries', p. 42.

[85] See, for example, Suzuki, *Japanese Government*, p. 44. The exception to the case was the United States. Close links between the so-called 'London Yankee' investment houses and British merchant bankers and individuals like Robert Fleming proved an effective conduit through which British capital could flow into American railway companies. Yet again, in many ways aspects of the USA's experience with British investors was closer to that of the dominions than other foreign countries. See D. R. Adler, *British Investment in American Railways, 1834–1898* (Charlottesville: University Press of Virginia, 1970), pp. 145–8, 171–6; and Davis and Gallman, *Evolving Financial Markets*, pp. 300–5 for more detailed discussion of this 'transatlantic partnership'.

joint stock banks of England and Scotland as well as the imperial banks. The movement of these professionals around the British World, which developed apace in the second half of the nineteenth century, fostered personal connections. The role of Scottish bankers in this movement was particularly marked, such that by 1900 it has been estimated that as many as two-thirds of all Canadian bankers came from Scotland.[86]

Typical of this trend was Falconer Larkworthy. Born in Weymouth in 1833, but raised in Scotland, he began his banking career as a clerk with the Oriental Bank Corporation in London in 1852. He quickly demonstrated his talents. After a spell in Mauritius, the Oriental sent him to Melbourne in 1855. Soon afterwards he became manager of the bank's branch in Beechworth situated on the goldfields of Victoria. In 1861 he moved once again, this time to Auckland, and while there played an instrumental role in establishing the Bank of New Zealand (BNZ). In August 1862, he returned to London as the inaugural managing director of the BNZ's London branch, retaining this role until 1888. While in London, he helped establish and became the first director in 1865 of the New Zealand Loan and Mercantile Company Ltd, a position he held until 1890. At that time he joined the Court of Directors of the Ionian Bank, and assumed its chairmanship in 1900. As a Fellow of the Institute of Bankers, Larkworthy's position in the City and vast first-hand knowledge of many of the colonies, in particular New Zealand, made him a valuable source of information and contacts for colonial governments and companies seeking credit in London.[87]

A further advantage the colonies enjoyed in London emanated from the system of interlocking directorships favoured by imperial and colonial banks from the mid nineteenth century. This was a practice that made it commonplace for leading bankers and financiers to be seated on the boards of a variety of banks and financial institutions. Oliver Farrer, for example, concurrently held directorships in the Provincial Bank of Ireland, the Bank of Australasia, the Ionian Bank, the Mediterranean Bank and the Bank of British North America. This system of interlocking directorships facilitated the flow of information, and allowed colonial interests to forge fruitful relationships stretching right across the British financial world.[88] Imperial and colonial banks were aware of this

[86] S. Jones, 'The Imperial Banks in South Africa, 1861–1914', *South African Journal of Economic History* 11(1996), 5–57 (p. 28); and Bailey, 'Australian Company Borrowing', p. 108.

[87] F. Larkworthy, *Ninety-One Years: Being the Reminiscences of Falconer Larkworthy* (London: Mills and Boon, 1924); N. M. Chappell, *New Zealand's Banker's Hundred: A History of the Bank of New Zealand, 1861–1961* (Wellington: Bank of New Zealand, 1961), pp. 14, 29, 74, 112, 114; Bailey, 'Australian Company Borrowing', pp. 109–10; and Kynaston, *City of London*, Vol. II, p. 315.

[88] A. S. J. Baster, *The Imperial Banks* (London: P. S. King, 1929), p. 120.

advantage and consciously sought to place well-connected members of English establishment families on their boards. Having such people on the board, it was thought, would lend one's bank credibility and provide it with an entrée to elite financial circles in London. Certainly, this was the rationale that lay behind the Bank of Australasia's decision to invite Alban George Gibbs, the second Lord Aldenham, onto its Court of Directors in 1887. He accepted and retained his seat until his death in 1936.[89]

Of course, the colonies' access to London financial networks was a gift not entirely free of conditions. One of these conditions was that colonial governments and financial institutions had to have a permanent physical presence in the City, if they were to tap the potential there on offer. Without it, they could not hope either to acquire an informational advantage or exert an influence over events, something of which imperial and colonial banks were clearly cognisant. Although imperial banks typically did not take direct responsibility for colonial loan issues, given their presence in London and the position of many of their directors in the City's important financial circles, they were nonetheless often well placed to influence the outcome of particular floats. Being in London really did matter.[90]

A further condition was that colonials tapping into British financial networks, like their British counterparts, had to play by the 'rules of the game'.[91] A high standard of morality and propriety, as in all 'good' society, went without saying.[92] The restrictions, however, extended beyond the merely personal. Certain types of behaviour either in the public domain or the business arena were also deemed unacceptable. First, colonists should not intentionally promote 'unpatriotic' investments, an unwritten rule that led London's main financial houses to ostracise those who had imprudently chosen to underwrite the so-called German 'war loan' issue of July 1908.[93] Second, the integrity of the system or its main institutions should never be publicly questioned. As Queensland discovered in 1891, such behaviour could have disastrous consequences. Running a debt, the government of the Colony of Queensland instructed the Queensland National Bank to cover the shortfall by raising a new loan by the usual

[89] Merrett, *ANZ Bank*, pp. 25–33; Jones, *British Multinational Banking*, pp. 92–3; Baster, *Imperial Banks*, pp. 244–5.
[90] Jones, *British Multinational Banking*, p. 46; Baster, *Imperial Banks*, p. 243–4; R. J. Wood, *The Commercial Bank of Australia Limited: History of an Australian Institution, 1866–1981* (North Melbourne: Hargreen Publishing Company, 1990), pp. 93–9; and Merrett, *ANZ Bank*, pp. 26–33.
[91] P. J. Cain and A. G. Hopkins, *British Imperialism, 1688–2000* (Harlow: Longman, 2001), pp. 215ff.
[92] Grieser, 'British Investor', p. 30.
[93] Davenport-Hines, 'Lord Glendyne', p. 194.

means in London. The Bank of England was engaged to assist in the floating of the proposed loan. But with investors still shell-shocked by the Baring crisis, these were anything but usual times. The issue failed and only £300,000 worth of the £1 million issue was subscribed. The expectation, at least on the part of the Queensland government, was that the Bank of England would now step in and take up a further £500,000 of the loan. Queensland believed that such an undertaking had indeed been agreed with the Bank prior to the float. The Bank of England, however, refused, pointing out that even if it did oblige it would still leave the issue significantly undersubscribed. Instead the Bank arranged a new private subscription where £100 debentures were effectively sold for less than £90. On hearing what had happened in London, the Treasurer of Queensland, Sir Thomas McIlwraith, exploded and publicly lambasted the Bank of England for its blatant dishonesty and breach of promise. William Lidderdale, the Governor of the Bank of England, unimpressed by the outburst, demanded a prompt, direct and unreserved apology from Queensland's Griffith government. When no such apology was forthcoming, Lidderdale wrote to Queensland's Agent-General in London, with whom he had previously negotiated the disputed details of the loan, and informed him that 'the relations between your Government and the Bank are at an end'. Lidderdale's words impacted immediately on Queensland's reputation. Concerned British investors began withdrawing capital from the colony, while the Queensland National Bank reported greater difficulty moving the colony's Treasury Bills in the City. Common sense (and self interest) eventually prevailed. In April 1892, McIlwraith, by then elevated to the premiership of Queensland, provided the requisite apology, opening the way for a resumption of normal relations with the Bank, itself now under the new Governorship of David Powell. Financial calamity had been averted and a lesson learned.[94]

Social webs

Those directly connected to the financial sector were not the only parties to benefit from the workings of networks. The presence of significant numbers of colonials in nineteenth-century London – engaged both inside and outside the City – also had a role to play in augmenting the volume and quality of information about different parts of the empire that circulated through British society. This colonial presence mirrored

---

[94] G. Blainey, *Gold and Paper: A History of the National Bank of Australasia Limited* (Melbourne: Georgian House, 1958), pp. 208–11. The quotation comes from J. Clapham, *The Bank of England: A History*, 2 vols., Vol. II: *1797–1914* (Cambridge: Cambridge University Press, 1970), p. 400. See also Kynaston, *City of London*, Vol. II, pp. 48–9.

and reinforced the links that existed between London and the empire, particularly its self-governing components. Both sides benefited. The nexus was vital for the colonies, whose economies, lacking not just capital and labour but the specialised expertise necessary to marshal them, were reliant for their continued development on privileged access to the rich array of financial networks operating in Britain.[95] From the British perspective, these connections offered the entrepreneur, the financier and the official regular opportunities to interact with prominent colonials, who were not only well-informed about their homelands, but well-practised in the ways of the City. It was a state of affairs that fostered mutual confidence and trust, reaffirming the belief in British minds that their investments were safe with their brethren in the colonies.[96]

The Canada Club in London was typical of the type of institution that promoted such social and economic links between British and colonial elites. Founded in 1810, the club provided a venue throughout the nineteenth century for prominent Canadians and British to meet and discuss the issues of the day, including those pertaining to finance. It was an important port-of-call for visiting Canadian dignitaries. Politicians passing through London often scheduled functions within its walls. At other times, local expatriates, involved in raising British capital for Canada, like Joseph Colmer, J. H. Dunn and Arthur Grenfell, entertained at the club. Having so many financially and politically connected Canadians in London proved advantageous in securing investment. As Michie observes, the result was that 'both government and the railways could raise capital more easily and cheaply in London than in either Toronto or Montreal and, as the British investors' knowledge of Canada continued to improve, so could increasingly smaller concerns'.[97]

Social contacts, sometimes far removed from the concerns of capital, could likewise provide an important source of information for investors. The power of gossip, word of mouth and personal experience in determining individual investment behaviour is easily overlooked. Yet its importance could be considerable, especially for the wealthy. Such individuals knew (or were related to) others who had first-hand experience of particular parts of the empire, or who had enjoyed success with a certain type of investment, or just had germane, 'insider' knowledge about the potential

---

[95] On the theoretical importance of such connections between regional economies and the metropolis, see Casson, 'Economic Approach', pp. 20, 40–1.

[96] Dilley, 'Gentlemanly Capitalism', p. 168.

[97] R. C. Michie, 'The Canadian Securities Market, 1850–1914', *Business History Review* 62 (1988), 35–73 (pp. 49–50). The Congress of Chambers of Commerce of the Empire, first established in 1886, was another forum for the social interaction of British and colonial businessman. For a discussion of the Congress, see Dilley, 'Gentlemanly Capitalism', pp. 172–4.

of a particular stock or project. Thus, as early as 1824–5, on the basis of his brother-in-law, W. S. Davidson's advice, the Aberdeenshire landowner, William Leslie, purchased shares in the Australian Agricultural Company. Davidson lived in London and had based his tip on his own interactions with the company.[98]

By the last quarter of the nineteenth century, these social links between the aristocracy and the big financiers had grown closer, as the landed interest sought higher yielding uses for their capital and as bankers in turn looked for ways to become more deeply integrated into Britain's social elite.[99] It was these 'social webs', to use Ranald Michie's term, which often drew members of the aristocracy to particular financial opportunities. Investment advice could be imparted on the most inconspicuous of occasions such as during a hunting party, a family get-together or a society function. Public school and university networks were also potential sources of information, while personal travel and the emigration of family members sometimes provided the necessary stimulus for an investment plunge. Colonial correspondence with friends at home often became, as *The Economist* noted as early as 1860, 'the channel through which British capital ... more freely embarked in the colonies than in foreign countries'.[100]

Retired imperial officials could be a further source of information. Many ex-governors retained interest in the lands over which they had presided and could provide useful connections to aristocratic investors back in the UK. Victor Villiers, the Earl of Jersey and Governor of New South Wales between 1891 and 1893, for example, freely offered his services and City contacts to the state on raising a loan in 1904.[101] Sir Albert Henry George Grey, the Fourth Earl of Grey, Administrator of Rhodesia (1896–7) and Governor of Canada (1904–11), was similarly active in promoting and investing in imperial projects. He held a diverse portfolio of assets, especially in Canada and Rhodesia. He was a consummate

---

[98] Michie, 'Social Web', p. 163.
[99] J. Harris and P. Thane, 'British and European Bankers, 1880–1914: An Aristocratic Bourgeoisie?' in P. Thane, G. Crossick and R. Floud (eds.), *The Power of the Past: Essays for Eric Hobsbawm* (Cambridge: Cambridge University Press, 1984), pp. 215–34 (pp. 221–7). For the preceding period, see, especially, Cain and Hopkins, *British Imperialism*, pp. 105–202.
[100] Quoted in H. J. Habakkuk, 'Free Trade and Commercial Expansion, 1853–1870', in J. Holland Rose, A. P. Newton and E. A. Benians (eds.), *The Cambridge History of the British Empire*, 5 vols., Vol. II: *The Growth of the New Empire, 1783–1870* (Cambridge: Cambridge University Press, 1940ª), pp. 797–8. For more on the social webs of investment, see Michie's seminal article, 'Social Web', pp. 158–75. Grieser, 'British Investor', p. 30 also discusses how educational networks were an important source of information (and recruitment) for brokerage firms.
[101] Dilley, 'Gentlemanly Capitalism', pp. 169–70.

networker, with an impressive array of well-placed family, business and governmental contacts that spanned the British World. In part, this was a product of extensive travel and work experience in the colonies, but intermarriages with the 'right' families played their role too. All of his sisters had married into the aristocracy; and his own daughters had wed the sons of two prominent City families. Thus he included among his friends and confidants the likes of Cecil Rhodes, Alfred Beit, Sir John Willoughby, the Duke of Abercorn, R. Maguire, H. W. Fox, S. Neumann, J. Werner, L. S. Jameson and L. L. Michell. Nor was he shy of using these connections to get or pass on investment-related information.[102] The constant stream of information he received from these contacts clearly influenced his investment choices. A skilful statistical analysis of Grey's southern African investment portfolio between 1885 and 1917 reveals that his share selection did not appear to have been made 'at random ... but on the basis of asymmetric information provided by his business and social connections whose judgement he trusted. His investments in the [gold] mania were broadly profitable as would be expected if someone had insider information.'[103]

Extended family was a fruitful source of 'inside information'. Grey's closest advisers, at least with respect to his investments, were two merchant bankers who also happened to be family members: R. H. Benson (his wife's brother-in-law) and Arthur Grenfell (his son-in-law). Their opinions were highly regarded. In 1895, Grey acquired 400 shares in the Trust and Mortgage Company of Iowa on the strength of Benson's advice alone. Similarly, he took heed of Grenfell when he told Grey in 1911 to replace some of his stock in Rand Mines and Rhodesian Railways with a selection of Canadian industrial and land companies.[104]

Grenfell's information was derived from his own extensive networks. These intersected with the world of Robert Nivison, with whom Grenfell collaborated in floating western Canadian securities in the period between 1909 and 1914. Grenfell was the brother-in-law of Nivison's business partner Guy St Aubyn (who also was related to Lord Galloway and Lord St Levan).[105] Grenfell appears to have worked assiduously to

---

[102] Michie 'Social Web', pp. 164–5; S. M. Nollan, 'A Gentlemanly Capitalist at Home and Abroad: The 4th Earl of Grey, 1885–1917', unpublished M.A. thesis, University of Durham (2004), pp. 11, 12, 52.

[103] Nollan, 'Gentlemanly Capitalist', p. 56.

[104] Of course, information flowed both ways. Grey, using knowledge acquired in his role as a director of the British South Africa Company (1898–1904), advised his uncle, Lord Wantage, in 1899 to buy certain southern African mining and railway securities with which he was familiar. Wantage complied. See Michie, 'Social Web', pp. 7–10.

[105] Nivison had his own social web that complemented his City networks. See Davenport-Hines, 'Lord Glendyne', pp. 191, 194.

keep Grey and others informed of developments in Canada. As his letter to Grey of 8 August 1906 states, he saw himself as 'an information bureau – distributing such information as I receive from Canada to the London and especially provincial newspapers'.[106]

Another financial promoter who effectively exploited these social webs of investment was Edgar Vincent, the first Viscount D'Abernon. A protégé of the Gladstone family and of George Goschen, his gregarious nature endeared him to many. His range of influential friends and acquaintances – including the Marchioness of Crewe, Arthur Balfour and the South African mining magnate Sir Julius Wernher (many of whom he could call on for capital) – was his greatest asset. Indeed, his biographer observes that 'as a financier he had little intrinsic ability, but through his cosmopolitan connections [he] was able to carry a glittering range of investors in sometimes bizarre schemes'.[107] First-rate establishment links were to bring him early career success. He became the financial adviser to the Khedive of Egypt (1883–9), and then Director General of the Imperial Ottoman Bank (1889–97), at the young ages of 26 and 32 respectively. In the 1890s, he was involved through the auspices of the Eastern Investment Company in southern African mining ventures. Such stock operated at the highly speculative end of the market, notorious for its potential for manipulation and overblown claims. While on paper the stock promised high rates of return, the prudent investor tended to stay clear. Yet, drawing upon his network of influential people in London, Johannesburg and Paris, Vincent was able to sell his securities with relative ease, even to the more cautious investor like the German-Jewish banking family, the von Bleichroeders. More than anything else, it was the eminence of the people in his network that lent him the credibility and stamp of trustworthiness he required.[108]

While opportunities for profitable networking were greater among the wealthy and privileged, the elite were not the only segment of British society who could avail themselves of its benefits. Investment-related networks could equally be erected upon ethnic or cultural foundations. Schmitz, for example, has neatly demonstrated how the choice of nineteenth-century Scottish investors could be informed, and hence influenced, by 'the strong cultural and commercial bonds which seemingly linked the capital markets of Edinburgh, Glasgow, Dundee and Aberdeen with a far-flung network of expatriate Scots around the globe': a series of personal

---

[106] Quoted in Davis and Gallman, *Evolving Financial Markets*, p. 767.
[107] Davenport-Hines and Van Helten, 'Edgar Vincent', p. 56.
[108] *Ibid.*, pp. 35–61; and Kynaston, *City of London*, Vol. II, pp. 106–9.

connections that worked to identify and unlock 'a host of foreign investment opportunities'.[109]

Similarly, skilled migrant workers were also at the cutting edge of
private information flows. Often the information flowing homeward
pertained to job opportunities and the potential for immigration. But
investment-relevant news could be – and was – transmitted along these
trans-national lines of communication. A case in point is the growing
British community located in the American West during the late nineteenth century. Most of this community had been attracted to the West
by its burgeoning mining industry. Between 1860 and 1890, the number of British-born residents in the West rose from 10,391 to 84,652,
with Colorado witnessing the most spectacular growth. Despite their
distance from the UK, many of these skilled British migrants retained
close ties with friends and associates back home. Their experience and
observations often eventually made their way, either in print or by word
of mouth, into the public domain and did much to alert British investors
to the great mining potential of the American West.[110] Moreton Frewen,
a visitor to the United States in 1899, for example, wrote back to the Earl
of Grey from Denver informing him that 'times are very good here and
there is lots of money to be made'. He promised to find profitable assets
with which they could both make money. True to his words, he returned
home with an interest in a Utah silver mine and plans to float the Denver
Street Railway Company in London.[111]

Britishness

So far our emphasis has been on what may be called *project-specific*
investment-related information: that is, data, news or opinion that were
directly related to the likely returns on a specific (or specific types of)
investment project. Whether the information pertained to a company's
balance sheet, market prices or merely the possibility of the economic
life of a particular location being disrupted by political strife, the unifying
feature of this knowledge was its ability to shape an investor's perception
of the likely profitability of a certain investment. Yet not all information
at the investor's disposal was project-specific. Context clearly mattered
too. Norms, conventions and beliefs acted to filter and give 'meaning'
to information. Then as now, investors, like traders and businessmen,

---

[109] C. Schmitz, 'The Nature and Dimensions of Scottish Foreign Investment, 1860–1914',
Business History 39 (1997), 42–68 (pp. 60–1).
[110] Spence, *British Investments*, pp. 13–15.
[111] Michie, 'Social Web', p. 170.

preferred to operate in environments where the rules of behaviour, law and etiquette were familiar and compatible with their own. In such contexts, misunderstandings, unexpected responses and conflict were less likely to occur; trust, as a result, was more easily and firmly established. Hence what might be called *context-specific* information could also have a bearing on investment behaviour.[112]

Contemporary testimony affirms that many people found investing in the dominions appealing. The lure of these regions of settlement was twofold. First, and most obviously, they promised considerable pecuniary rewards. But, as a secondary consideration, there was the fact that they were self-proclaimed 'British' societies; in many ways, therefore, investing in them was like investing at home. Indeed, the two characteristics were closely related: the dominions, for their part, were acutely aware of the financial benefits of their distinctive 'Britishness'. They knew, for example, that UK investors were highly sensitive to uncertainty about the future of their imperial connection with Britain. Thus, following the first Anglo-Boer War (1880–1), widely circulated rumours about the possibility of Britain giving way to the Transvaal's demands, and thereby cutting off the Cape colony's road to the north, coupled with fears of the Afrikaner Bond emerging victorious from the next general election, jeopardised the colony's credit. The value of Cape securities in London, it was (correctly) claimed, had already depreciated as a result. With the colony's ability to finance its economic development in doubt, its Agent-General, Charles Mills, noted that merely 'to mention the possibility of [the British flag] being in danger of coming down would be most embarrassing if not fatal to our financial and other business transactions in [the UK]'.[113] Just over a year later, with rumours about the colony's future still pervasive, Mills added that 'the idea of a Dutch Republic is indeed the *bête noire* of the English capitalist with respect to investment in our securities'.[114]

Why did 'Britishness' matter so much to the investor? Like all issues of identity, this is a complicated question. The most commonly advanced explanation finds its answer not so much in what it meant to be 'British' but rather in *what the United Kingdom did for the colonies*: most crucially, provide defence, law and order, justice, a sound political and monetary

---

[112] D. C. North, *Understanding the Process of Economic Change* (Princeton: Yale University Press, 2005), pp. 135–6; E. L. Jones, *Cultures Merging: A Historical and Economic Critique of Culture* (Princeton: Yale University Press, 2006), pp. 259–60; L. Guiso, P. Sapienza and L. Zingales, 'Does Culture Affect Economic Outcomes?', *Journal of Economic Perspectives* 20 (2006).

[113] Mills to Merriman, 13 April 1883, quoted in Purkis, 'Politics', p. 304.

[114] Mills to Sprigg, 15 May 1884, quoted in Purkis, 'Politics', p. 306. The whole episode is recounted in *ibid.*, pp. 304–6.

system, and the basics of good governance.[115] A tradition of political stability and a thriving market economy were the empire's most enduring legacies. As the most recent advocates of this view contend: 'The Victorians imposed a distinctive set of institutions that was very likely to enhance their appeal to investors. These extended beyond the Gladstonian trinity of sound money, balanced budgets and free trade to include rule of law (specifically, British-style property rights) and relatively non-corrupt administration – among the most important "public goods" of late-nineteenth-century liberal imperialism.'[116] The importance of stable property rights and sound, predictable government to capital accumulation and mobilisation cannot be denied. There is considerable historical evidence to support such a contention.[117] But was the institutional structure that Britain imposed on its colonies the key element of what it meant to be 'British'? After all, did not the United States and the Dutch have their own strong tradition of liberal institutions? Neither nation in this period can be said to have been countries that wantonly trampled on investors' rights. The fact that the British had a record of rich interaction with them reinforces the point. There must be a deeper issue here, therefore: namely, was the existence of British institutions in itself enough to elicit a healthy flow of external development capital?

'Good' institutions can work their putative 'economic magic' if, and only if, they are endowed with substance. In other words, what matters is whether the institutions were in practice merely facades, perhaps even cynically created to attract the gullible foreign investor, or whether they did what they were supposed to. An institutional framework out of kilter with its society's underlying belief structure is unlikely to perform in ways its designers intend – a cursory glance at the traumatic experience of most post-Soviet societies shows this is so.[118]

What really mattered, then, for one to have faith that one's rights as an investor would be recognised, respected and strongly enforced, was the actual behaviour, rather than the surface appearance, of institutions. A recent econometric study of interest rate spreads for securities from 'emerging' nineteenth-century markets emphasises this point. It finds that British investors in the short term actually tended not to

---

[115] See Ferguson, *Empire: The Rise and Demise of the British World Order*, pp. xix–xxvi; Edelstein, 'Foreign Investment', p. 217; and Dilley, 'Gentlemanly Capitalism', pp. 151–68. Ford, *Gold Standard*, p. 20 also highlights the extension of the English Monetary Area beyond the British Isles as one of the empire's institutional achievements.

[116] Ferguson and Schularick, 'Empire Effect', p. 6.

[117] A fascinating introduction to this historical literature is E. L. Jones, *The European Miracle: Environments, Economies and Geopolitics in the History of Europe and Asia* (Cambridge: Cambridge University Press, 1981).

[118] North, *Understanding the Process of Economic Change*, pp. 1–8, 65–80.

respond positively to the appearance of liberal institutions in a country, 'either because it took years for new institutions to attain the necessary credibility, or because their establishment was followed by renewed turbulence'.[119] Adoption of the gold standard is a case in point. Although Argentina formally re-joined the gold standard in 1883, before 1914 the landed and export-producing oligarchy, according to Ford, 'willingly abandoned or adopted the gold standard whenever it was to their benefit and profit'. As a consequence, investors could never be sure of the true extent of Argentina's commitment to exchange rate stability. By contrast, Australia's and New Zealand's adherence to the international monetary order never appeared as anything other than exemplary.[120] These findings suggest that a key part of what was distinctively 'British' about Britain's settler colonies was the ease with which they could credibly operate the institutions they had imported from 'home'.

But where did that perception of credibility come from? For Platt, the answer lay in the bonds of 'race and tradition' that Britain and the dominions enjoyed.[121] After all, these colonies were part of a larger British community; they were brethren who shared the same norms, conventions and values. The foundations of trust were already in place. As *The Times* informed its readers in 1901, 'the people of these colonies, brought up in a sound school of self-government and inheriting the best traditions of the mother country, may be trusted to work out their own destiny in a manly spirit and with the practical sagacity that marks the British race'. Such a view was far from uncommon in Victorian and Edwardian Britain, and J. W. Taverner, Victoria's Agent-General, was merely drawing out one of its most obvious implications when he noted that 'surely a country, in which 97 per cent are British – your flesh and blood, your language, and under one flag – is a safe spot to invest British capital'.[122]

It is worth teasing out these quotations a little further. The underlying message seems to be that the dominions were regarded as 'safe' precisely because the British investor knew what type of behaviour to expect from both the borrowers and the state apparatus that ultimately guaranteed their capital's security. For the British, therefore, 'Britishness' connoted not their parliamentary or legal systems per se, but all the virtues they saw in themselves and that breathed life into their institutions: fairness, justice, reliability, technical competence, accountability, individual freedom and respect for private property.[123] Whether or not such virtues were

[119] Mauro, Sussman and Yafeh, *Emerging Markets*, p. 6.
[120] Ford, *Gold Standard*, pp. 133, 169.
[121] Platt, 'Canada and Argentina', p. 81.
[122] Both quotations come from Dilley, 'Gentlemanly Capitalism', pp. 176–7.
[123] For the concept of 'character', and its imperial connotations, see P. J. Cain, 'Character and Imperialism: The British Financial Administration of Egypt, 1878–1914', *JICH* 34

peculiar to the British character – and many non-British people would have undoubtedly begged to differ – it was this perception of themselves, and by extension those in their colonies, that influenced, at both the conscious and sub-conscious levels, the attitudes of investors. As Ranald Michie astutely observes, 'the Empire found it easier, and less expensive, to borrow in Britain than foreign countries, as the British investor was more inclined to trust those who belonged to the wider British community though the actual security offered might be identical'.[124]

For their part, colonial and imperial banks and companies wore the 'British' tag with pride (and for gain). The Bank of Australasia and the Union Bank of Australia openly proclaimed both their 'Britishness' and their place at the heart of the British banking system.[125] Every effort was taken to cultivate such branding. Australian financial institutions consciously (and as a result of inherited banking traditions) packaged their products in a manner that appealed and was instantly recognisable to British savers.[126] Representatives regularly visited British cities and towns to demonstrate their British credentials and in the process drum up more deposits. British-based borrowing agents – bankers, brokers, solicitors, accountants – were employed on commission to interact with the public and put a local face on the colonial bank or finance company. So widespread was the practice that the *British Economist* in 1888 commented that there was 'hardly an influential firm of lawyers in the city which does not hold an agency for one or other of those [colonial investment companies]'.[127]

Railway companies, including American ones, likewise saw it opportune to trumpet their British credentials in the latter half of the nineteenth century. They certainly marketed their shares on such a basis.[128] Yet, even if only partially true, it was not a hard claim to sustain. Keynes could look back on Britain's splurge of investment in 'New World' railways in the decades before the First World War and claim that 'we did not, as a rule, lend the money to foreign corporations or Governments. We built the railways ourselves with British engineering skill, with our own iron and steel, and rolling stock from our own workshop.'[129] Armed

(2006), 177–200; and S. Collini, *Public Moralists: Political Thought and Intellectual Life in Britain, 1850–1930* (Oxford: Oxford University Press, 1991), pp. 91–118.
[124] Michie, 'Social Web', p. 170.
[125] Merrett, *ANZ Bank*, pp. 12–14.
[126] For instance, the maturing debenture stock popular with Scottish investment trusts was adopted by many Australian investment companies; see Bailey, 'Australian Company Borrowing', p. 15.
[127] Davis and Gallman, *Evolving Financial Markets*, pp. 815–17. For a detailed discussion of Australian companies' use of Scottish agencies, see Bailey, 'Australian Company Borrowing', pp. 107–39. The quotation comes from p. 122.
[128] Davis and Gallman, *Evolving Financial Markets*, p. 832.
[129] Keynes, 'Foreign Investment', p. 584. For a similar view, see Habakkuk, 'Free Trade', pp. 797–8.

with such assurances from promoters, British investors might have been excused for thinking the tracks were going to be laid in, say, Berkshire, England rather than Berkshire, Massachusetts. American railway companies worked hard to build British confidence in their creditworthiness. To that end, a number of organisational innovations were employed, all of which in some manner shored up the firm's British connections. Some negotiated long-term partnerships with leading British financial houses. In return for their capital, these arrangements typically allowed the British house to monitor the railway firm's finances, offer advice, and act as an almost-silent partner. Other American railway companies opted to appoint or elect prominent British shareholders (usually financiers and aristocrats) onto their board and create shareholders' committees – organisational features that were designed to safeguard the British investors' interests, or at least to give that impression. Finally, direct British ownership of the railway could be assumed. One way this could be achieved was for an existing American company to be bought out, reconfigured as a freestanding company, and then re-floated as a new, purely British enterprise. From the 1880s a number of entirely British lines were constructed and operated on such a basis.[130] Being seen to be British paid dividends.

Institutional investment

For many investors the world of high finance was bewildering and alien: a world about which they knew little and to which they had had limited direct exposure. Interaction with the capital market was normally conducted through the agency of a financial institution. The large merchant banks, such as Barings, Kleinworts, Brown Shipley, Morgans, Schroders, Rothchilds and Hambros, were the most ostentatious of these institutions, each with its own long history of financing public loans both inside and outside the empire.[131] Yet, by the latter half of the nineteenth century, other institutions, most importantly the commercial banks and insurance companies, had begun to move to the fore. They operated by consolidating the savings of thousands of individuals into a single fund, which they then invested on the behalf of the contributors. The advantage of this arrangement was that it enabled the individual saver to benefit from the higher returns that the financial expertise and experience of the institution could bring. Moreover, when thousands of savers joined together,

---

[130] Adler, *British Investment*, Chapter 8; Davis and Gallman, *Evolving Financial Markets*, p. 332.
[131] Kynaston, *City of London*, Vol. II, p. 9. For an account, for example, of Hambros' and Rothchilds' involvement in the Transvaal government loan of 1891, see pp. 62–4.

both economies of scale and a degree of financial clout were obtained. In normal times, it was a 'win–win' situation, for even after the institution had extracted its portion of the capital gain, the contributor was left with a satisfactory return (without actually having to manage their capital personally). At any rate, the amounts of capital available from tapping the savings of the small-scale British investor were more than sufficient to whet the interest of the biggest players in the market. Between 1870 and 1914, for example, Britain's insurance companies alone invested around £250 million in securities listed on the Stock Exchange.[132]

Given the prominent place of institutional investors in the capital market, it is worth considering how they made their investment decisions. In particular, did the pattern of their investment mirror that of the elite and other types of investors who have thus far been considered in this chapter? Did they treat colonial securities differently, and how exactly did they manage their investment portfolios? The next section looks to the experiences of two of the most important institutional investors in later Victorian and Edwardian Britain – the commercial banks and insurance companies – for answers.

Commercial banks

From the early nineteenth century, Britain's joint stock banks asserted a right to operate an investment portfolio; by 1903, around £145 million was held in such accounts.[133] These investment portfolios served a dual function as both a reserve fund and as an income-earning asset for the bank. Until the turn of the twentieth century, however, the reserve function of the bank's investment portfolio predominated. Consequently, British banks sought, above all else, to place their funds in negotiable liquid assets. The question of returns, if considered at all, was secondary. This desire for liquidity gave rise to an extremely conservative investment policy that saw banks investing almost exclusively in safe and reliable British government securities and consols. Industrial and foreign shares were eschewed.[134] This orthodoxy was enshrined in the banker's code

---

[132] Hall, *London Capital Market*, p. 51.

[133] Not all banks had investment funds, however. In 1880, the Liverpool Union and Bradford Bank Company, for example, reported no investment securities at all among their assets. See M. Baker and M. Collins, 'English Bank Investment Portfolios, 1880–1910', unpublished working paper, University of Leeds School of Business, 2007, pp. 3–6. We are very grateful to Professor Collins and Dr Mae Baker for their insightful comments on this section and for allowing us to see a draft version of their new and important paper on bank investment in England.

[134] C. A. E. Goodhart, *The Business of Banking, 1891–1914* (London: London School of Economics, 1972), pp. 127–9; A. R. Holmes and E. Green, *Midland: 150 Years*

of practice. The Midland's deed of settlement, for instance, expressly limited the bank's investment activity to a narrow range of securities that included government stock, Navy and Exchequer Bills, Bank of England or East India Company bonds, and annuities.[135] Similarly, the by-laws of the London Joint Stock Bank (hereafter LJSB) prohibited it from investing in foreign issue, irrespective of their rate of return.[136] As Charles Gow, the General Manager of the LJSB, explained to the US National Monetary Commission in 1910, from the bank's point of view, the interest any security bore was of 'secondary importance to their negotiability'.[137]

Such disregard for the rate of return was not simply a norm for the industry, but in time became a shibboleth with which the financial prudence of an institution was established. As such, a policy that openly sought to maximise the bank's return from its investments came to be regarded as a sure sign of profligacy and, consequently, was frowned upon by all 'right-minded' bankers. Take the case of the Westminster Bank, whose board in 1852 had just voted to deviate from this orthodoxy. Sir David Salomons, an absent member of the erring board (and Alderman of the City of London and Middlesex), wrote with notable disgust to the bank on 1 September:

I am sorry to learn that at a small Board today a resolution was come to that we should take a line in the new loan for the Turkish Bank. This seems to me so great a departure from our usual principle of business that I do think it ought not be acted on till the Board should have had an opportunity of considering whether they will so far relax their usual course of conduct in respect to foreign speculations. I do not discuss whether this new stock be or be not an eligible general investment of money. I am, however, quite sure that an application from the Bank will become a subject of conversation for the purposes of giving the new security a character and we shall possibly be judged as paying out high dividends from these speculative things rather than from the scrapings of slow and less adventurous business.[138]

Over the second half of the nineteenth century such conservatism among British banks with regard to investment gradually broke down.

of Banking Business (London: Batsford, 1986), p. 49; and M. Collins and M. Baker, *Commercial Banks and Industrial Finance in England and Wales, 1860–1913* (Oxford: Oxford University Press, 2003), pp. 63–4.

[135] Holmes and Green, *Midland*, p. 49.
[136] Suzuki, *Japanese Government*, p. 31.
[137] National Monetary Commission, *Interviews on the Banking and Currency Systems of England, Scotland, France, Germany, Switzerland and Italy* (Washington, DC, 1910), p. 68.
[138] T. E. Gregory, *The Westminster Bank through a Century* (Oxford: Oxford University Press, 1936), p. 265 n. 2.

By the beginning of the new century, the investment portfolios of many banks were beginning to be managed in a very different manner.[139] While there was considerable variation in practice between banks, these changes manifested themselves in two main ways.[140]

First, an increasingly broad range of assets was deemed acceptable investments by the banks. This process began with colonial government securities, which, from the 1870s, steadily came to be seen as safe and liquid enough assets for even the most traditional of banks. From the 1890s, they were joined by colonial and domestic municipal stock as well as Canadian and, then, eventually American railway bonds. As the First World War approached, a limited number of foreign and other securities started to appear in some banks' portfolios.[141] The converse side of this broadening of investment was that the proportion of the portfolio devoted to traditional assets, most particularly consols, declined, though it is noteworthy that public sector securities overall (either British or colonial in origin) continued to predominate.[142]

Typical of this changing investment composition was the experience of the Metropolitan Bank. Figure 5.2 provides snapshots of its investments between 1880 and 1913. Beginning in 1880 with a portfolio almost completely dominated by UK government stock, by 1913 it included a wide variety of assets from across the globe. The first step in the internationalisation of its portfolio, however, had been its embrace of empire stock. It was not till the second decade of the twentieth century that assets from

---

[139] It is worth noting that the proportion of assets banks were devoting to investments at this time also declined from about 21 per cent on average in 1890 to about 15 per cent by 1913. The 1913 percentage, however, was still significantly above that of 1860, when only about 11 per cent of bank assets were invested. See Collins and Baker, *Commercial Banks*, pp. 75–6. If the percentage is calculated so that each bank's contribution counts the same irrespective of size, then it does not decline, but remains fairly constant after 1900. These figures are, of course, averages: individual bank investment ratios could vary considerably and in ways unrelated to bank size. See Baker and Collins, 'Investment Portfolios', pp. 3–6.

[140] Some banks continued to adopt a very traditional approach to investment well into the twentieth century. The Lincoln and Lindsay Bank, and the Union Bank of London, for instance, continued to invest purely in consols and other government annuities right up until the First World War. See Baker and Collins, 'Investment Portfolios', p. 16. For other examples, see Goodhart, *Business of Banking*, p. 135; National Monetary Commission, *Interviews*, pp. 179–85.

[141] Industrial shares, however, never figured prominently in the banks' investment portfolios prior to the First World War; Collins and Baker, *Commercial Banks*, p. 67.

[142] Hall, *London Capital Market*, pp. 7–15; Collins and Baker, *Commercial Banks*, pp. 63–8; and Goodhart, *Business of Banking*, pp. 130–41. With respect to the public sector's continued dominance, Baker and Collins, 'Investment Portfolios', pp. 12–13 show that between 76 per cent and 87 per cent of bank investments between 1880 and 1910 went to public sector securities.

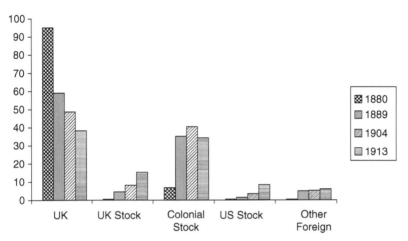

Figure 5.2 The Metropolitan Bank of England and Wales'
investment portfolio, 1880–1913 (share of total investments).

outside the empire, including *inter alia* Brazilian, Chinese and Danish
bonds, made their presence felt. Even then, a third of all Metropolitan
Bank investment were still based in the empire.

The second change, which underpinned the transformation in the composition of the banks' investment, was a subtle shift in the management,
and indeed rationale, of their investment funds. As Charles Goodhart
notes, there was at this time a change in the importance of the earning
capacity of assets relative to their desirability as reserves. As a result,
greater attention began to be focused on the fund's rate of return.[143]

What drove this change in banks' investment behaviour? The most
common explanation is the steady, late-nineteenth-century decline in
the interest rates on consols, which slowly but surely tarnished their
reputation as a reserve asset. Holding on to large volumes of consols no

---

[143] Goodhart, *Business of Banking*, p. 134. This view has recently been challenged. Baker
and Collins, 'Investment Portfolios', p. 22, contend that the change in investment patterns was less to do with the banking sector's increasing use of its investment funds as
sources of income and more the result of the wider range of public sector stock available
on exchanges towards the end of the nineteenth century. Given the fact that the banks
at this time did not embrace large amounts of high-yielding foreign or industrial shares,
but merely came to hold a more diverse portfolio of public sector securities, such a
view is certainly plausible. Yet, from the perspective of the argument advanced in this
chapter, it matters little why this diversification occurred. If British banks in this period
chose to acquire more colonial stock, they must have done so because they were now
better aware of the advantages of holding such stock. Therefore, it still comes back to
the question of the timing and availability of information. Colonial securities became
popular because the banks steadily learned that they were negotiable liquid assets *and*
that they brought decent returns.

longer guaranteed protection for the banks against runs: the very opposite, in fact, for as their price diminished, so did the security they could
offer. Banks had no other option but to look further afield to regain that
sense of safety. It was a long-term search. No revolution in behaviour
occurred, just a gradual, though perceptible, move towards a new pattern
of investment.[144]

That bankers readily responded to market incentives in altering their
investment behaviour is hardly surprising. Yet, while the banks' new
behaviour may have had its origins in a fundamental transformation in
the relative rates of return and liquidity of the different assets available
to them, such an explanation cannot in itself account for the actual pattern and timing of the diversification in portfolios. Specifically, it leaves
unanswered the question of why the banks first turned to colonial, then
US, and finally to foreign stock. The answer cannot simply lie in the relative rates of return, for highly profitable foreign ventures continued to be
ignored by banks well into the twentieth century.

Bankers tend to be conservative creatures, arguably not given to great
turns in either thought or deed. As such, it is unlikely that, when confronted by altered circumstances, they would have instantly rejected an
orthodoxy that had served them so well in the past. Instead, they were
more likely to have made piecemeal accommodations to prevailing conditions; in other words, change would have come as an evolutionary process that, over time, and almost unwittingly, transformed the basis of the
investment strategy of banks. Given this gradualist approach, how does
this process of change start: where, if you like, would have banks looked
first for their new investment opportunities? It seems in areas they knew
best. Thus, when the Imperial Bank of Persia began diversifying its portfolio in the 1890s, its first recourse was to turn heavily towards Persian
government stock, only later broadening out to include colonial and then
some Chinese, Japanese, US, Mexican and Russian government stock.
Similarly, nearly 40 per cent of the African Banking Corporation's investments in 1913 were in South Africa, mostly in government securities.[145]

Thanks to the informational asymmetries inherent in the capital market in the latter half of the nineteenth century, British banks knew and
trusted best colonial securities. Moreover, once a decision to branch into
a new type of stock had been taken, banks had an incentive to continue
to support that stock, so as to retain their negotiability. This obligation
drew banks closer and closer to certain types of securities and helped
to foster the special relationships that some had begun to establish with

---

[144] Goodhart, *Business of Banking*, pp. 130–3; Jones, *British Multinational Banking*, p. 93.
[145] Jones, *British Multinational Banking*, pp. 93–4.

specific colonies. The case of the London and Westminster Bank is illustrative. Having assumed responsibilities for the underwriting of Western Australian colonial loans, they now held a large number of Western Australian securities in their portfolio. To protect the value of those assets, the Bank determined in June 1910 that it would take up as much as £100,000 worth of any Western Australian stock that appeared on the market.[146]

In its initial stages, the pattern of portfolio diversification often closely correlated with the personal connections of senior bank personnel. These connections tended to be heavily biased towards the British and Anglophone worlds. As better information on other markets became available, this bias gradually diminished. Despite its importance, this networking left relatively few traces in the written records of banks. It was, after all, an unofficial, almost invisible, activity. A rare yet excellently documented example of the role of personal contact in banking can however be pieced together from the archives of the Midland Bank.

In the mid nineteenth century, the Midland, like most British banks, managed its portfolio in a rather unsophisticated manner. Lacking much first-hand knowledge and experience with securities, it typically opted to accept the recommendations of its London agent. Detailed discussion of investment choices at the board level rarely took place, and independent advice from brokers or other financial intermediaries was not sought. Decisions about investments were uncomplicated and involved few people. Adherence to the accepted canons of banking practice, of course, obviated the need for much deliberation.[147] Nevertheless, the nature of the process placed great emphasis on the personal contacts, experiences and preferences of those whose duty it was to manage the bank's investment funds. Individuals, therefore, were well placed to influence the bank's investment behaviour, particularly when portfolio diversification became a priority. For the Midland, Edward Holden, its Managing Director between 1898 and 1919 (and Chairman between 1908 and 1919), played such a role.[148]

From its inception, the investment portfolio of the Midland was managed as a reserve fund very much in accordance with the canons of British banking practice. It is therefore telling that when the Midland Bank departed from this conservative investment strategy during the 1870s and 1880s, it did so first and foremost by diversifying into colonial issues, most prominently Canadian, Australian and Indian railway stock. So dramatic was the shift that, by early December 1888, colonial stock

[146] Goodhart, *Business of Banking*, p. 138.
[147] Holmes and Green, *Midland*, p. 50.   [148] *Ibid.*, p. 141.

alone already constituted no less than 46 per cent of the bank's entire investment portfolio. This choice was driven not only by a desire for higher yields, but by the availability of reliable information about such stock that was readily obtainable from the bank's London agents and increasingly from its manager's own correspondence with and travels to overseas branches.[149]

From 1904, Holden made a number of trips to the USA and Canada in order to acquire first-hand knowledge of business practices and opportunities on the other side of the Atlantic. He hoped that this knowledge could be used to expand the bank's business there. Holden kept a fascinating diary of his first eight-week journey to North America (10 September to 5 November 1904), in which he detailed all of his meetings and impressions. His trip took in New York, Toronto, Niagara and Chicago. In each location he met leading bankers, manufacturers and politicians; delivered speeches to various business communities; and toured prominent industrial sites. It was, by all accounts, a life-changing experience for Holden and he was noticeably impressed by what he had witnessed. Canada was, in his words, 'a grand country' ripe with opportunity, where, if only British capital could be delivered in sufficient quantity, 'the wealth that will come out of the land ultimately will also be enormous'. He was particularly struck by the Power Company at Niagara and the new lines being built by Canadian railway companies, the bonds of which he regarded as 'good investments'. In the United States, he was amazed by the slaughter and stripping houses of Morris Beef in Chicago, an establishment that he described at great length in his diary. Holden returned to Britain eager to utilise the knowledge he had gleaned from his trip. Above all else, through the trip he had succeeded in establishing a number of North American business contacts for the bank.[150]

Holden cultivated those links and soon found himself at the centre of a transatlantic network that was largely of his own making. He was regularly called upon by North American businessmen who valued his advice and input. On 27 May 1909, for example, a Mr J. Child paid Holden a visit at the bank. Child, it turns out, was a client of the Traders Bank of Toronto and had arrived at the Midland with a personal introduction from the Traders Bank's manager, Mr E. W. Strathy, whom Holden had met back in 1904. Child represented a syndicate, which had obtained a large land grant from the Canadian government to establish a paper-pulp

[149] *Ibid.*, pp. 49–51, 80, 141.
[150] Hongkong and Shanghai Banking Corporation Archives (hereafter HSBC Archives): ACC 150/2, 'Mr Holden's Report on his Visit to America, 10 September to 5 November, 1904'.

concern, and was now intending to buy out the Spanish Pulp and Paper Co. Ltd of Espanola, Ontario. The funds for the purchase were to come from a $4 million bond issue to be underwritten by the UK company, United Mining and Finance Corporation. Child sought Holden's advice both about the reputation of United Mining and Finance and the prudence of the financial measures proposed. Holden promised to make enquiries for Child.[151]

Similarly, Mr Crichton, a barrister from Winnipeg, saw Holden in September 1909, to ask his advice about placing some (unspecified) Canadian securities on the British market. Holden recommended that he advertise his requirements and take a room at a hotel so as to carry out negotiations with interested parties. Holden further advised him to emphasise to potential backers the fact that there was no income tax in Canada.[152]

Sometimes these inquiries led to more business for the bank. The President of the Robert Simpson Department store (founded 1872) in Toronto called on Holden on 31 July 1907. Some of Robert Simpson's directors sat on the board of the Canadian Bank of Commerce, which Holden had visited three years earlier. The store sourced material from Britain and continental Europe and hoped that, on the basis of the initial contact that had been made in 1904, the Midland would agree to take the company on as a customer and handle all of its European banking requirements. Holden obliged, and a long-term relationship was established between Simpsons and the Midland. When, in 1910, the company expanded its Toronto store and acquired a branch in Montreal (operating under the name of John Murphy and Co.), it sought and received detailed advice from Holden on how to finance the expansion. Two years later, when a further £900,000 was sought by Simpsons, Holden again offered his assistance, recommending that the funds be raised by a mixture of an issue of preference shares and bonds. He further promised that his bank would provide guidance on the correct pricing of the issue.[153]

But Holden was not always so supportive of North American companies. His interest in Canada was always based on hard, commercial realties. In August 1909, for example, Mr E. Jackson of the Midland Railway Carriage and Wagon Company called to see him about work that his company had been offered in Canada. The Hudson Bay and Pacific Railway and Development Company had requested £100,000 worth of railroad materials from his company. However, it had come

[151] HSBC Archives: E. H. Holden Diary, ref 26/7 (Midland Bank Papers), 27 May 1909.
[152] *Ibid.*
[153] HSBC Archives: E. H. Holden Diary, ref 26/7 (Midland Bank Papers), 31 October 1907, 24 May 1910, 13 March 1912.

with a condition: that the British company deposit a sum of money as an investment with them. Concerned, Jackson canvassed Holden for his views. Holden informed him that he had had reports from the American bankers, the Kountze brothers (whom he had met in 1904) on the company in question and that these were anything but favourable. He read the reports he had received to Jackson and advised him to keep out of the whole business.[154] Once again, information gleaned from financial and social networks appears to have exerted an influence over commercial and financial decision-making. Personal contacts and experience mattered. The case of the Midland simply illustrates that this was no less true for banks than it was for individual investors.

Insurance companies

A profound transformation of the investment practices of British insurance firms took place in the latter part of the nineteenth century. Like the commercial banks, the insurance industry had its own orthodoxy with regard to the management of investment portfolios. First annunciated by A. H. Bailey in 1861, these 'principles' governed how life assurance funds were invested. In a way, the principles reversed the priority set by the banks. Beyond a very small amount to be set aside as a reserve, insurance firms aimed to invest in assets that would provide a regular flow of income and could guarantee timely repayment of the principal. Liquidity was not such a concern. Indeed, the favourite of the commercial banks – the consol – was frowned upon because of its variable rate of return and declining market price. Similarly, the uncertainty of stock exchange securities was to be avoided. Instead, insurers were actively encouraged to prefer fixed-term securities, whose maturities were well defined in advance and enforceable before the law. Thus, since the mid century, the great preponderance of insurance funds tended to be invested in UK mortgages and real estate, particularly agricultural land. As late as 1880, just under £71 million – about 46 per cent of the industry's assets – was tied up in funding mortgages in the UK.[155]

As Table 5.7 demonstrates, this situation was about to change. Over the following three decades, mortgages' share of total industry assets fell to less than a quarter (and the majority of these mortgages in 1913

---

[154] HSBC Archives: E. H. Holden Diary, ref 26/7 (Midland Bank Papers), entry for 24 August 1909.

[155] M. Baker and M. Collins, 'The Asset Portfolio Composition of British Life Insurance Firms, 1900–1965', *Financial History Review* 10 (2003), 137–64 (pp. 137, 143–4); Hall, *London Capital Market*, p. 52; and C. Trebilcock, *Phoenix Assurance and the Development of British Insurance*, 2 vols., Vol. II: *The Year of the Insurance Giants, 1870–1914* (Cambridge: Cambridge University Press, 1998), pp. 63–5.

Table 5.7. *The value and distribution of UK life insurance companies' assets, 1870–1913 (in £1,000; share of total assets in brackets).*

Types of assets	1870	1880	1885	1890	1895	1900	1905	1910	1913
Mortgages	48,183 (44.3)	70,787 (46.1)	75,039 (42.9)	82,808 (41.7)	85,143 (36.8)	85,174 (27.4)	91,833 (26.0)	103,293 (23.1)	113,852 (21.5)
Securities									
British government	7,455 (6.9)	4,887 (3.2)	5,343 (3.1)	5,915 (2.9)	5,502 (2.4)	7,718 (2.5)	9,673 (2.7)	7,307 (1.6)	5,314 (1.0)
Indian and colonial government	3,952 (3.6)	7,059 (4.6)	10,705 (6.1)	12,696 (6.3)	15,818 (6.8)	19,330 (6.2)	19,713 (5.6)	20,321 (4.5)	19,728 (3.6)
Indian and colonial municipal	—	—	—	—	—	—	—	—	22,712 (4.3)
Foreign governments	1,323 (1.2)	4,412 (2.9)	3,898 (2.2)	3,534 (1.8)	4,162 (1.8)	10,865 (3.5)	10,507 (3.0)	17,358 (3.9)	24,635 (4.7)
Foreign municipal	—	—	—	—	—	—	—	—	14,718 (2.8)
Debentures	10,565 (9.7)	10,570 (6.9)	12,623 (7.2)	21,857 (10.8)	28,770 (12.4)	51,995 (16.7)	63,147 (17.9)	99,485 (22.2)	132,357 (24.9)
Shares and stock	3,276 (3.0)	7,939 (5.2)	10,398 (6.0)	12,931 (6.4)	14,435 (6.2)	35,111 (11.2)	39,900 (11.3)	44,614 (10.0)	49,056 (9.3)
Total securities	26,571 (24.4)	34,867 (22.7)	42,972 (24.6)	56,933 (28.2)	68,687 (29.7)	125,019 (40.2)	142,940 (40.5)	189,085 (42.3)	268,520 (50.5)
Mortgages and securities	74,754 (68.7)	105,654 (68.8)	118,011 (67.5)	139,741 (69.9)	153,830 (66.5)	210,193 (67.6)	234,773 (66.5)	292,378 (65.4)	382,372 (72.0)
Total assets	**108,825**	**153,403**	**174,757**	**201,603**	**231,362**	**311,084**	**352,613**	**447,343**	**530,112**

Notes: This table includes some companies that also engaged in general, non-life insurance business. Only the main asset types are included. The figures for debentures and shares in 1870 are tentative owing to classification problems in that return. Similarly, the cited figures for total securities up to 1910 are probably slightly underestimated because until then some colonial and municipal securities appear to have been recorded under other categories of assets. For further details, see A. R. Hall, *The London Capital Market and Australia, 1870–1914* (Canberra: Australian National University, 1963), p. 53.

Sources: Annual returns of the life assurance companies to the Board of Trade, *British Parliamentary Papers.*

were on properties outside the UK, whereas in 1880, non-UK mort-gages were of negligible importance).[156] A variety of securities rose in their place. Given the preference for fixed-term securities recommended by Bailey's principles, foreign and colonial stock – in particular muni-cipals and debentures – grew in importance from about 7 per cent of investments in 1880 to 30 per cent in 1913.[157] Thus, by the outbreak of the First World War, debenture stock figured more prominently than mortgages in the industry's investment portfolios. Stock and shares pur-chased off the London Exchange – usually domestic, US and colonial railway shares – also grew in importance from about 3 per cent in 1870 to approximately 10 per cent by the turn of the century; and the propor-tion of industry's assets invested in colonial government bonds also rose over the late Victorian period, reaching its apogee at around 7 per cent in the late 1890s. This percentage, though, almost certainly underesti-mates the empire's importance in the portfolios of insurance companies, since the data on debentures and mortgages reported in Table 5.7 cannot be analysed by country of origin. Given the prevalence and attractiveness of social overhead and land development projects in the dominions at this time, it would not be unreasonable to presume that a considerable proportion of the debentures and mortgages acquired were colonial in origin.[158]

For many insurance companies, the transformation in investment behaviour followed a pattern not dissimilar to that being taken at the same time by the commercial banks: diversify first towards local govern-ment stock, then colonial and US, and finally towards securities that lay beyond the British World. It was a strategy based on investing in what one

[156] The stimulus for the transformation in investment practice appears to have originated in alterations in the returns of different types of assets. Differences in the rates of return of comparable assets in the UK and overseas also drove the changes. See J. H. Treble, 'The Pattern of Investment of the Standard Life Assurance Company, 1875–1914', *Business History* 22 (1980), 170–88 (pp. 170–1). See also Trebilcock, *Phoenix Assurance*, p. 74.

[157] Colonial municipals were not separated in the return from other colonial debentures or government securities until 1913. It is worth noting that part of the rise of foreign and colonial stock can be explained by the fact that North American authorities compelled insurance companies to acquire some of this stock as insurance guarantee. This was the price of doing business there. In 1909, for example, in order to expand its insurance business in North America, Phoenix Assurance was required to purchase $160,000 of US securities and $150,000 of Canadian securities at prices above par. Such pur-chases, of course, reinforced a trend that was happening naturally. Indeed, at least in this case, they may have accelerated that trend, since compulsory purchases inadvert-ently brought Phoenix greater familiarity with North American securities, prompting it in just a few years' time in 1913 to invest heavily in the municipal stock of the cities of Christiania, Port Arthur, Victoria, Winnipeg, Regina and Moose Jaw. See Trebilcock, *Phoenix Assurance*, pp. 70, 75.

[158] Hall, *London Capital Market*, p. 54.

knew best, and that reveals itself clearly in company records.[159] As Phoenix Assurance's historian notes about that company's investment history:

the purchase of colonial government stock – from the Cape and from Victoria and South Australia in 1878, and from New South Wales, Queensland, Tasmania and New Zealand in 1889 … represented the first *willed* diversifications of the portfolio towards major foreign opportunities. This opened a path that was to become much more heavily trodden in the 1900s, especially in relation to American railway stock.[160]

Further insight into the changing investment behaviour of the insurance industry can be gleaned from another prominent firm, the Standard Life Assurance Company, which was founded in 1825. Standard Life was a pillar of the British life assurance establishment. It operated offices all over the world, often in support of Scottish expatriate communities involved in the engineering, construction and oil industries. By the early twentieth century, one-third of the company's new business came from within Britain, a further third came from professionals in the British empire and the remainder came from a miscellany of 'foreign' countries (including Hungary, Argentina, Uruguay, China and Egypt). It was William Thomson, the Manager of Standard Life, who first pressed for life cover to be available to those who lived and worked overseas. Thomson was quick to appreciate the security that well-to-do emigrants craved. To this end, a new company was created in 1845 – Colonial Standard Life – with four regions earmarked for initial operation: Australia, North America, Ceylon and the West Indies.[161]

The first Colonial Standard Life policy was issued to George Smith on 6 November 1846 for £1,000. Smith was a twenty-eight-year-old merchant in Ceylon. It was Canada, however, that was the company's main target for this business. Standard Life already had a number of policy-holders in the dominion, and within a few years a network of twenty-six agents had been established there.

---

[159] Take the case of Phoenix Assurance. For the period between 1880 and 1910, it can be seen that the proportion of Phoenix's investment in UK stock rose from 25 per cent in 1880 to 43.7 per cent in 1890, before declining to 21.8 per cent and 11.7 per cent in 1900 and 1910 respectively. Colonial and US stock's share rose from 27.5 per cent in 1880 to 32.4 per cent in 1890 and 36.0 per cent in 1900, before it too fell to 21.1 per cent in 1910. By contrast, the proportion of its investment devoted to foreign stock remained low (1.2 per cent in 1880, 2.9 per cent in 1890) until around the turn of the century, when it became steadily more important, accounting for 17 per cent of the company's investments in 1900 and as much as 42.7 per cent in 1910. See Trebilcock, *Phoenix Assurance*, pp. 73, 82.

[160] *Ibid.*, p. 70.

[161] The new company was dissolved in 1866, its activities having been taken over by Standard Life.

Standard Life also had premiums to invest; indeed, the company's assets were approximately £13 million by 1910. Table 5.8 details how these funds were disbursed between 1870 and 1910. In the face of the downward movement of UK interest rates, Standard Life began restructuring its portfolio from the 1870s. Colonial property markets, Indian and colonial government securities, and especially colonial municipal bonds all became attractive options, as did railways and debenture stock after 1900. Mortgages on UK property, which in 1870 constituted almost two-thirds of its assets, steeply declined, while mortgages on property outside the UK rose. By 1910, 30 per cent of the company's assets were invested in mortgages, of which two-thirds were on foreign, mostly colonial, property.

In shifting its investment strategy, Standard Life was assisted by the presence of salaried staff in the colonies who monitored economic trends and gauged prospective investment yields. It was to Australia and New Zealand that the company's attention first turned. In 1881, Standard Life took £20,000 of debenture stock from the recently reconstructed New Zealand and Australian Land Company. Two large advances on the security of freehold property in New South Wales and Queensland followed in 1883. Many of its antipodean loans were made to sheep farmers, with sureties provided by partners in Scottish Borders textile mills (who had switched to buying wool from Australian and New Zealand producers). Rates of interest in the colonies were much higher than those prevailing at home during this decade. Not until the financial crises of the mid 1890s, which brought the land boom in Australia to an end, did Standard Life begin to look further afield. Thereafter Canadian municipal bonds and high-yielding urban and farm mortgage transactions, such as the £18,000 lent on the property at the corner of St James and Victoria Square and the £300,000 advanced to the Roman Catholic Church in Montreal in 1895, were the favoured investments; they, in turn, stimulated new business in life assurance in the dominion from 1913 to 1914.[162]

Company rules further encouraged investment in the dominions. These rules insisted that for a mortgage to be provided on non-UK property two non-negotiable conditions had to be met: that the borrower hold sufficient collateral in the UK, and that interest payments on the loan be fully guaranteed by a UK-based mercantile firm or bank. In other words, tapping Standard Life's funds required a potential mortgagee to have significant prior roots in the UK: something, it can be assumed, that

[162] J. M. Atkin, *British Overseas Investment, 1918–1931* (New York: Arno Press, 1977), p. 120; Hall, *London Capital Market*, pp. 53–4; Treble, 'Pattern of Investment', pp. 170–88; M. Moss, *The Building of Europe's Largest Mutual Life Company: Standard Life, 1825–2000* (Edinburgh: University of Edinburgh Press, 2000), pp. 112–20.

Table 5.8. *The value and distribution of the Standard Life Assurance Company's assets, 1870–1910 (share of total assets in brackets).*

Types of assets	1870	1875	1880	1885	1890	1895	1900	1905	1910
Mortgages on UK property	2,769,730 (63.7)	3,371,831 (69.9)	4,077,396 (71.6)	3,914,561 (59.4)	3,341,144 (44.6)	2,537,088 (31.1)	2,089,873 (21.0)	1,871,771 (16.2)	1,311,587 (10.0)
Mortgages on non-UK property	35,816 (0.8)	52,811 (1.1)	221,049 (3.9)	505,075 (7.7)	1,279,531 (17.1)	2,632,686 (32.3)	1,670,367 (16.8)	2,257,672 (19.5)	2,645,555 (20.3)
Loans on surrender value of policies	209,346 (4.8)	241,633 (5.0)	274,788 (4.8)	313,178 (4.8)	355,539 (4.8)	402,280 (4.9)	466,189 (4.7)	679,224 (5.9)	940,529 (7.2)
British government securities	79,060 (1.8)	40,742 (0.9)	38,242 (0.7)	39,810 (0.6)	37,790 (0.5)	29,218 (0.4)	80,638 (0.8)	191,058 (1.7)	138,765 (1.1)
Indian and colonial government securities	72,630 (1.7)	199,682 (4.1)	281,552 (4.9)	636,134 (9.7)	402,469 (5.4)	300,152 (3.7)	186,313 (1.9)	142,703 (1.2)	11,396 (0.1)
Indian and colonial municipal bonds	—	—	—	—	457,991 (6.1)	292,336 (3.6)	2,093,759 (21.1)	1,963,007 (17.0)	2,028,668 (15.5)
Railway and other debenture stock	81,500 (1.9)	82,623 (1.7)	—	102,578 (1.6)	199,115 (2.7)	331,143 (4.1)	889,094 (8.9)	1,775,347 (15.3)	2,810,029 (21.5)
Loans on shares with collateral security	—	—	—	—	—	—	70,553 (0.7)	150,058 (1.3)	336,181 (2.8)
House property – freehold	77,603 (1.8)	116,605 (2.4)	139,946 (2.5)	257,949 (3.9)	334,631 (4.5)	435,814 (5.4)	857,755 (8.6)	856,659 (7.4)	776,400 (6.0)
Total assets	**4,346,028**	**4,821,005**	**5,693,150**	**6,592,974**	**7,488,625**	**8,146,519**	**9,943,490**	**11,574,556**	**13,058,045**

Notes: Only the main asset types, together accounting for over three-quarters of the total, are included. See also the notes to Table 5.1.

Sources: Annual returns of the life assurance companies to the Board of Trade, *British Parliamentary Papers*, and Treble, 'The Pattern of Investment of the Standard Life Assurance Company, 1875–1914', *Business History* 22 (1980), 170–88 (pp. 173–4).

was more common among colonists than peoples from elsewhere in the world. Such a preference for colonial investments was further reinforced by the provision passed by the firm's shareholders in July 1891 that permitted it to acquire debentures and preference shares, but only, it went on to stipulate, from companies located in the 'United Kingdom, India, or any British Colony or Dependency'. Later the provision was extended to include the United States and a number of other foreign countries, but the way 'reliable' investments were identified continued to afford distinct advantages to colonial assets.[163] Like the commercial banks, therefore, Britain's insurance companies maintained a strong and active interest in colonial securities right up until the First World War.

Conclusions

This chapter has examined the pattern and behaviour of British overseas investment between 1870 and 1914. Most historical analyses of investment behaviour take it as given that capital markets function purely on the basis of a hard-nosed rationality that leaves little scope for either sentimentality or imperial piety. At first sight, the data appear to back up this view. As we have seen, the geographical distribution of British capital in the later Victorian and Edwardian era did not map neatly at all onto imperial boundaries. The United States, after all, was the biggest recipient of British funds, with Latin America not far behind. Nor can it be accurately claimed that access to the financial resources of the City was in any way contingent upon acceptance of British-style political and economic institutions. China and Japan, for example, were granted entrance on far less exacting terms.

Finding an imperial dimension to Britain's investment history is not therefore a straightforward task. We have argued that attention should focus less on formal institutions and political boundaries and more on the substance that underpinned these things; that is, for guidance, one should look first and foremost to the behaviour of those directly engaged in the investment of capital overseas. Consequently, the focus of our enquiry has been on the informal aspects of the British World economy, the social and organisational networks (that thickened and multiplied during the later Victorian and Edwardian era), and the quality and

---

[163] Moss, *Standard Life*, pp. 116–19; Treble, 'Pattern of Investment', p. 179. Standard Life's investment in the USA was delayed by its negative experiences there earlier. In the 1870s, it had lent money on some high-quality property in New York, only to find itself subjected to fraudulent behaviour from its American solicitor that cost the company over £30,000 in losses. It was an episode that deterred Standard Life from investing in the USA for a generation. For details, see Treble, 'Pattern of Investment', pp. 180–1.

quantity of information flowing through them. These networks afforded Britain's colonies, and especially the dominions, informational advantages that enhanced their attractiveness to British investors; at any rate at least until better information about the investment opportunities on offer elsewhere in the world became more readily available. Positive British press coverage vis-à-vis the rest of the world reinforced this advantage.

Another key, albeit less apparent, component of the British World's informational advantage was cultural. This is not to proffer a culturally deterministic approach. Culture was one of several factors determining how knowledge was created, disseminated and consumed. Thus, perceptions of the inherent 'Britishness' of the dominions, actual or imagined, are regarded here as something that played favourably 'back home' with British savers. A combination of rich, context-specific and project-specific information, provided to investors by personal and co-ethnic networks, made the security offered by the dominions appear all the more safe a bet.

Yet the benefits of dominion status for borrowers proved transient. With time, the British World's informational advantages in London subsided. As the nineteenth century approached its end, the knowledge and information available to the typical investor was in the process of expanding rapidly, and in its wake both the variety of outlets and intensity of competition for British capital increased. At any rate, by the early 1900s the global integration of capital markets had progressed sufficiently to ensure that the dominions could not monopolise the British investor's attention. None of this, of course, means that imperial considerations ceased to figure – right through to the First World War they still made their presence felt, as this chapter has shown – but, as the decades passed, the frequency and extent with which the British World impinged on investment decisions declined.

Economists typically view informational asymmetries unfavourably. Markets with informational deficiencies, we are told, work badly. Yet, it is worth pausing here to contemplate in what sense these information-deprived markets 'underperform'. Economics provides a clear answer: analytically speaking, it is only relative to markets that have no (or significantly fewer) informational deficiencies that asymmetric ones are seen to be poorly performing. But beyond showing the existence of a hypothetical optimal, how useful is such abstract analysis to the explanation of actual historical events? No doubt, it would be convenient to live in a world of complete or near-complete information. The reality, however, is that past worlds, even more so than our own, were not so information-rich.

Taking a broader historical perspective, informational asymmetries may be seen as a positive, rather than negative, force that promoted global integration: an early, certainly partial, yet nonetheless still crucial, step towards full globalisation. Modern globalisation, of course, had to start somewhere. That its first phase was nurtured within the confines of the British World does not necessarily imply that the forces that drove those events must have been morally benighted. That said, the flow of British capital to the dominions did play an instructive role by accustoming British savers to take a more global perspective, to perceive the benefits of overseas investments, and thereby gradually to open their minds to the prospects of even more 'alien' or 'foreign' ventures. By exploiting their networks and aligning their institutions towards the needs of the British capital market before anyone else, Britain's settler colonies from the mid century were able to engender – for a time – an ever-greater bias in the direction of international capital flows. Bias, of course, is a word heavily laden with negative, even pejorative connotations. Yet sometimes biases can yield positive results. Such was the case with much British investment in the dominions in the latter half of the nineteenth century, a period in which the only real alternative on offer was a choice between a world of informational asymmetry and one of virtually no information at all.

Thus 'imperial globalisation', as presented in this analysis of capital markets, was not truly global in its reach. Rather, the British World economy, in the realm of finance, as in that of migration and trade, was strongly skewed towards Anglophone societies. The sense of connectedness that influenced the information flows that were so crucial to investor behaviour was not only present in the case of the dominions but also in the United States, and even perhaps in some Latin American societies, like Argentina, albeit to a lesser degree. Moreover, the way in which globalisation unfolded financially before the First World War may help to explain why Britain's imperial economic relationships sat relatively comfortably with its global economic relationships, and why the two sets of relationships could draw strength from each other. To be sure, the British World economy had its own (cultural) dynamic, yet this dynamic did not prevent Britain from expanding economically into a wider world.

Conclusion

This book has brought together new research in the field of cultural history with long-standing debates about the economics of imperialism. By combining approaches from the humanities and social sciences we have explored the relationship between two key features of the later-nineteenth and early-twentieth-century world: empire and globalisation. On the face of it, the division of the world into rival empires and the processes of closer international integration would appear to be inherently in conflict. To the extent that rivalry between empires, and violence and oppression within them, have pitted cultures and peoples against each other, this is true. Yet preceding chapters have also shown how the British empire, or more precisely the British World, promoted greater economic and social integration – a force for globalisation, in fact. Such a finding may seem surprising, especially when viewed through the lens of contemporary experience and national sovereignty. We are accustomed to perceive most political phenomena, including globalisation itself, through the framework of the nation state. From that perspective, closer international integration is largely a product of the interplay of different national policies.[1] The unspoken assumption is clear: a society's freedom to make its own way in the global marketplace is contingent upon a prior ability to gain and exert its independence. If we accept this proposition, then such freedom of action cannot be attained within the structures of empire.

We should not, however, underestimate the historic role of geo-politics in providing momentum to the process of globalisation, however segmented and uneven the results may have been.[2] Thus, in the nineteenth

---

[1] For the independent nation state as 'the paradigmatic form through which globalization … proceeded' in the later half of the twentieth century, see B. Axford, *The Global System: Economics, Politics and Culture* (Oxford: Polity, 1995), p. 29.

[2] For the dangers of globalisation silencing the past, see M.-R. Trouillot, 'The Perspectives of the World: Globalisation Then and Now', in E. Mudimbe-Boyi (ed.), *Beyond Dichotomies: Histories, Cultures and the Challenge of Globalization* (Albany: SUNY Press, 2002), esp. pp. 5–6. For the view, from a contemporary theorist of globalisation, that the expansion of European power was central to connections of global production and finance, and to the spread of communications technology and political systems of sovereign states,

century, the British empire (at the time the world's pre-eminent power) willingly utilised its military might and economic influence to advance its interests – interests that included the global expansion of free trade. In so doing, of course, it was not unique. Hegemonic relationships have always been used to push through broader agendas, irrespective of opposition and resistance. Indeed, in our own time there are those who attribute a similar driving role in the global economy to America and its 'empire'.[3] A priori, then, the proposition that an empire promoted globalisation is clearly within the realms of possibility.

Nor should we succumb to the temptation to focus overwhelmingly on modern technologies and their role in initiating and accelerating the process of globalisation, whether they be high-speed transportation, the Internet or telecommunications. In this view, globalisation is depicted as belonging to the later twentieth and early twenty-first centuries, and, moreover, as being largely a culturally blind, technology-driven phenomenon. This book reminds us that globalisation belongs to the past as well as to the present, and that it is as much about people as technology. In particular, it has shown how the culturally shaped networks built by migrants played crucial roles in forging the increasingly globalised world of the half-century prior to the First World War.

Central to the whole process of nineteenth-century globalisation was migration.[4] By its very nature, migration is transformative. It changes the perceptions and outlook of individuals and communities, teaching them to look beyond the inhibiting parochialism of former generations. In the case of the British World, it also changed the way in which individuals – and the families whom they left behind – imagined their social and political spaces, thereby making their migration a defining aspect of their identity. By encouraging people to see themselves as part of a global chain of kith and kin, who shared common standards, forms of communication and expectations, the exodus of people from the British Isles during the 'long' nineteenth century turned national (and indeed regional) identities into trans-national ones.[5]

---

see N. Bisley, *Rethinking Globalization* (Basingstoke: Palgrave Macmillan, 2007), p. 34. For two key detailed historical studies of the relation between empires and globalisation, and how earlier episodes of globalisation have been reworked and reproduced today, see J. Darwin, *After Tamerlane: The Global History of Empire* (London: Allen Lane, 2007); and A. G. Hopkins (ed.), *Globalization in World History* (London: Pimlico, 2002).

[3] N. Ferguson, *Colossus: The Rise and Fall of the American Empire* (London: Penguin, 2004).

[4] For the neglect of migrant diasporas in globalising processes, see J. Nederveen Pieterse, *Globalization and Culture: Global Mélange* (Lanham, MD: Rowman and Littlefield, 2003), pp. 4, 32.

[5] See for example S. J. Potter, 'Webs, Networks, and Systems: Globalization and the Mass Media in the Nineteenth- and Twentieth-Century British Empire', *JBS* 46 (July 2007), 621–46 (pp. 621–2).

The story of this British diaspora (or 'ethnic group in dispersal') with all its fateful implications, merits a more prominent place in global histories.[6] Alongside this massive out-migration of people there emerged a more expansive, even cosmopolitan, sense of 'Britishness' that overlapped, and was able to co-exist, with a range of other forms of identity. This 'imperial' Britishness was not just a form of belonging, but a set of widely shared and strongly felt (albeit sometimes vigorously contested) values, attitudes and beliefs. These attributes in turn impacted on religious, social and, less obviously but no less importantly, economic life. As we have seen, whether with respect to remittance activity, consumer choice or investment decisions, culture and ethnicity could be key determinants of economic behaviour and performance.

This does not, of course, mean that Britishness was homogenised or static. For reasons of both class and gender, the proletarian forms of Britishness we have identified around peripatetic skilled labour (which tied working-class emigrants to their homeland) were different from the bourgeois forms of Britishness derived from middle-class values, saving and consumerism (from which much of Britishness' trans-national economic power derived). Meanwhile rapid advances in communication – which had major repercussions for travel, correspondence and the media – meant that interactions between the different parts of the British World were more frequent and intense at the end of our period than they had been at its beginning. Moreover, it was also at the end of our period, around the time of the South African War (1899–1902), that an increasingly defensive language of 'race nationalism' came to the fore. Immigration policy, and the ambitions of rival European colonial powers, contributed to the growing appeal of ethnic nationalism in the settler colonies, while racial sensibilities were also sharpened by the fears surrounding an 'awakening Asia', and by the insecurities resulting from the redeployment of much of the Royal Navy from the Pacific to the Mediterranean.[7]

Thus, as well as showing how a developing sense of global Britishness aided, rather than thwarted, economic and social integration in the half-century before the First World War, this book also highlights how this

---

[6] Robin Cohen notes how the original Greek word 'signified expansion and settler colonisation' and can thus 'best be compared to the European (especially British, Portuguese, and Spanish) settlements of the mercantile and colonial period'; see Cohen 'Diasporas, the Nation-State, and Globalization' in W. Gungwu (ed.), *Global History and Migrations* (Boulder, CO: Westview Press, 1997), pp. 117–44 (pp. 139–40).

[7] For a perceptive commentary on the language and rhetoric of Britishness in the settler colonies, see especially S. Ward, 'Imperial Identities Abroad', in S. Stockwell (ed.), *The British Empire: Themes and Perspectives* (Oxford: Blackwell, 2008), pp. 226–34. For the racialisation of immigration policy and practice, see A. Bashford, *Medicine at the Border: Disease, Globalisation and Security, 1850 to the Present* (Basingstoke: Palgrave Macmillan, 2006).

process had its limits. The globalisation of the period on which we focus did not encompass all parts of the world and all races equally; it did not lend itself to the creation of the type of supra-national institutions that have helped to co-ordinate the modern global economy; it was not official policy; nor did it always receive the imprimatur of the great and mighty of its time. That said, this limited, culturally and regionally focused globalisation of the late nineteenth century did promote economic integration of a like hitherto not witnessed.[8] Above all else, it was an informal, grass-roots phenomenon. There was no grand design here: almost by stealth, the workings of a multitude of trans-national networks by-passed national boundaries and unwittingly took large and historically important steps towards the emergence of a truly global market.[9] While Britain was often the hub of these networks through which people, capital and goods moved, Canada, Australia, New Zealand and South Africa were rapidly evolving and maturing societies and economies in their own right, remarkably open to the world beyond their shores, and each thus contributing distinctively to, as well as feeding off, the trans-national networks under consideration.

The United States, too, fed into these networks, although its place in the British World of the long nineteenth century was markedly more ambiguous, and hence is far more difficult to isolate. Again, however, the fact that the USA played such a role at all was in large part due to a shared heritage and the bonds of language that arose from mass emigration. Together, these factors fostered ties to, as well as a much deeper awareness and knowledge of, America in British society than scholars have typically acknowledged.[10] As previous chapters have detailed, the impact of these connections was most evident in activities where transatlantic ties were at their strongest: *inter alia* the workings of financial networks, the destination choices of prospective emigrants (and their inclination to send part of their wages back 'home') and the consumption habits of the middle classes.

While this book has squarely focused on the networks forged by British migrants across the British imperial world,[11] it is important to

---

[8] For the argument that much of contemporary globalisation is regional rather than truly 'global' in nature, see A. Rugman, *The End of Globalization: Why Global Strategy Is a Myth and How to Profit from the Realities of Regional Markets* (New York: AMACOM, 2001), pp. 1–12; and U. Beck, *What Is Globalization?* (Malden, MA: Polity, 2000), pp. 119–20.

[9] For an historical perspective on the trans-national networks forged by migrants, see S. Vertovec, 'Transnationalism and Identity', *Journal of Ethnic and Migration Studies* 27 (2001), 573–82 (pp. 576–7).

[10] For a recent overview, see K. Burk, *Old World, New World: The Story of Britain and America* (London: Little Brown, 2007).

[11] For the significance of 'micro level networks of information and assistance' to transatlantic migrations from Europe, see E. Morowska and W. Spohn, 'Moving Europeans in the Globalizing World', in Gungwu (ed.), *Global History and Migrations*, pp. 23–62 (pp. 46ff).

remember that there were, of course, other co-ethnic entities contributing to nineteenth-century economic integration – most notably the French, German, Spanish, Portuguese, Italian and Jewish diasporas, which partly or largely lay beyond the boundaries of the formal British empire, and the Chinese and Indian diasporas, which largely lay within it. The substantial emigration from India and China, which followed the abolition of slavery, and which was discussed in Chapter 3, was indispensable to the workings of global (and colonial) capitalism. It comprised approximately 14.5 million people in the century after the 1830s, was spread across Asia and the Pacific rim, and mostly took the form of colonially regulated indenture and associated forms of labour, recruited by family and group networks forged in the nineteenth century. Chinese and Indian migration is a salutary reminder that not all the processes of globalisation were rooted in Europe.[12] This Asian migration included people who settled in other parts of the empire – the Caribbean, the Pacific and southern Africa – as well as those who moved to other parts of Asia, such as Ceylon, Malaya and Burma.[13] While these flows may not always have been especially demographically significant for the 'exporting' societies, they were, as we have seen, of greater importance for the recipient countries, not least in terms of the increasingly hostile reactions from their burgeoning 'home-grown' labour movements to imported or indentured workers.[14]

Patterns of global migration were profoundly shaped by these Asian and European diasporas, and they would certainly benefit from being studied in a more explicitly comparative framework. Yet, given its economic, financial and imperial dominance in the nineteenth century, it was Britain's diaspora that left the largest single impression. The economic globalism wrought by British migrants took early root in capital markets, but also became evident in the 'real' economy of commodities

---

[12] A point well made with respect to migration by Adam McKeown in 'Periodizing Globalization', *HWJ* 63 (2007), 218–30 (pp. 226–7); and further elaborated with respect to consumer cultures by J. Prestholdt in 'On the Global Repercussions of East African Consumerism', *AHR* 109 (2004), 755–83, and *Domesticating the World: African Consumerism and the Genealogies of Globalization* (Berkeley, CA: University of California Press, 2008). For a succinct summary of the special place of Africa in the world history of migration, see P. D. Curtin, 'Africa and Global Patterns of Migration', in Gungwu (ed.), *Global History and Migrations*, pp. 63–94. For the impact of, and responses to, the Indian and Chinese diasporas across the British empire and the United States, see A. R. Zolberg, 'Global Movements, Global Walls: Responses to Migration, 1885–1925', in Gungwu (ed.), *Global History and Migrations*, pp. 287–93.

[13] See especially A. McKeown, 'Global Migration, 1846–1940', *Journal of World History* 15 (2004), 155–89.

[14] R. Findlay and K. H. O'Rourke, *Power and Plenty: Trade, War, and the World Economy in the Second Millennium* (Princeton: Princeton University Press, 2007), pp. 407–8.

and manufactured products. Yet, although driven by profit, the networks forged by these migrants retained throughout a persistent bias towards Anglophone societies, in which British exporters found ready and expanding markets precisely because British settlers tended to have tastes that were more similar to than different from those of people back home. Free migration, too, followed patterns that saw certain 'British' destinations preferred to others.[15] Even in the City of London, the residual effects of a culturally created informational asymmetry were reflected in the choice of projects favoured by investors right up until the First World War. Thus, while the markets for many nineteenth-century Britons many have been increasingly global, their 'Britishness' remained both palpable and, no doubt, decidedly welcoming.

How could a series of distinct co-ethnic networks possibly have fostered a process of broader globalisation? British World networks offered unique opportunities for enrichment and advancement. In the period covered by this book, they tended to be expansionary, and, to the extent that they flourished, they did so by actively building bridges – not only between the metropolitan elite of the United Kingdom and privileged parts of settler society in the colonies, but between an ever more dynamic 'provincial' Britain, and its various overseas contacts, communities and spheres of interest. Sometimes they also built bridges across class and religious divides, so that people who were not bourgeois, or Protestant, or born in the British Isles – the pervasive appeal of ethnic identification meant that they normally had to be 'white' – were to varying degrees accepted as part of this broader 'British' community. Put simply, the information, trust and reciprocity (or 'social capital') engendered by these networks created value,[16] and the British migrants who enjoyed privileged access to them became adept at exploiting them for their own gain.[17] It is said that membership has its rewards, and, in this case, it was often true. Participation brought benefits, not least in terms of one's admission (even if only partially) to an economic club that was relentlessly expanding its global reach.

---

[15] This was not just a feature of British emigration; see F. Cooper, *Colonialism in Question: Theory, Knowledge, History* (Berkeley: University of California Press, 2005), p. 95.

[16] The concept of trust as a 'public good' rather than a mere regulatory mechanism, and the conditions under which such trust is created and can thrive, have become increasingly prominent subjects in debates about modern society; see B. A. Misztal, *Trust in Modern Societies: The Search for the Bases of Social Order* (Cambridge: Cambridge University Press, 1996).

[17] See for example M. Boyd, 'Family and Personal Networks in International Migration: Recent Developments and New Agendas', *International Migration Review* 23 (1989), 638–70.

Looking back, the way in which British World networks readily took root and thrived in the Victorian and Edwardian era gives this process almost an aura of inevitability. Indeed, it could be argued that had the First World War not intervened, British 'imperial globalisation' might well have continued, and even deepened. Yet care is needed here. Extrapolation is a dangerous practice. Just as the sub-prime crisis has revealed the fatal errors of those who believe that housing prices only go up, the notion that co-ethnic networks always promote economic activity, simply because they did so for a while in the nineteenth century, is illusory. The harsher reality is that, when forcefully challenged in the inter-war period, the inclusiveness of nineteenth-century British World networks proved remarkably fragile, so much so that, under examination, their earlier inclusiveness looks less like an intrinsic quality or characteristic and more like a product of the relatively benign economic conditions of the period. After all, for many involved, their enthusiasm for closer economic integration was not ideological; instead their support was predicated on the ability of the process to generate continuing prosperity.[18] In a sense, therein lay the weakness of 'imperial globalisation'. Success encouraged openness and further expansion; failure saw the door slam shut. The problem was built-in. The *raison d'être* of networks, it should be recalled, is to promote the interest of insiders – at the expense of others, if need be. When economic opportunities dry up, as they did in the wake of the First World War, networks have a natural inclination to turn inwards, and to become shields for their members against the outside world. If, in the good times, networks can look to each other for synergies, in harder times they can come to regard each other as rivals. The results could be paradoxical. Networks that had formerly championed globalisation could, and did, when circumstances altered, become instruments of its rollback. Indeed, the common cultural identity and racial ideology that underpinned these networks now acted to facilitate this transition. More than that, culture and race provided a potent vehicle, by which ethnic, inter-racial and class tensions could be parleyed into protectionism, extreme nationalism and even xenophobia – with baleful domestic and international consequences.[19]

---

[18] As Frieden has opined: 'History showed that support for international economic integration depended on prosperity.' See J. A. Frieden, *Global Capitalism: Its Fall and Rise in the Twentieth Century* (New York: W. W. Norton, 2006), p. 172. See also David Singh Grewal's assessment that network power grows because of the increasing size of a network, rather than because of any intrinsic value: *Network Power: The Social Dynamics of Globalisation* (New Haven: Yale University Press, 2008).

[19] L. Barrow, 'White Solidarity in 1914', in R. Samuel (ed.), *Patriotism: The Making and Unmaking of British National Identity*, 3 vols., Vol. I: *History and Politics* (London: Routledge, 1989), pp. 275–87; Bisley, *Rethinking Globalization*, pp. 32–4; H. James, *The End of*

The hostile geo-political considerations that determined the fate of globalisation during the inter-war period were responsible for breeding a form of what has been labelled 'insular capitalism'.[20] By the later Victorian and Edwardian era, however, the potential for such a turn was already evident.[21] Witness, *inter alia*, the adverse reaction of British financiers to those wishing to invest in the German 'war loan' issue of July 1908,[22] the mounting opposition to non-white immigration and calls for greater protectionism in settler colonies, or the deepening racial and ethnic exclusiveness of masonic and commercial, and various types of professional networks.[23] In each case, the role of non-Anglophone groups in British imperial networks was to become more curtailed, even if one effect of this exclusionary tendency was to spur indigenous subjects to create and maintain counter-networks of their own, some of which fostered anti-colonial resistance, while others laid claim to inclusion in the colonial state.[24]

Racial exclusionism and protectionism were therefore a very common reflex of the imperial networks we have been examining. Even those networks that started out relatively open and outward looking often became more restrictive over time. This is because access to networks was ultimately a matter of power: not just the formal political power of the colonial state, but the informal cultural power conferred by membership of an imperial community that was becoming ever more skewed along ethnic and racial lines. The inward retreat of networks was in part the flipside of British, and indeed all ethnic (trans)-nationalism. While such a retreat cannot alone account for the dark days of the inter-war years, the growing culturally and racially based insularity of the period was nurtured,

Globalization: Lessons from the Great Depression (Cambridge, MA: Harvard University Press, 2001), p. 13; D. Held and A. McGrew, 'The Great Globalization Debate: An Introduction', in Held and McGrew, *The Global Transformations Reader: An Introduction to the Globalization Debate* (Cambridge: Cambridge University Press, 2000), pp. 1–50 (p. 4); Zolberg, 'Global Movements, Global Walls'.

[20] M. Daunton, 'Britain and Globalisation since 1850, II: The Rise of Insular Capitalism, 1914–1939', *TRHS* 17 (2007), 1–30.

[21] James, *End of Globalization*, pp. 200–1.

[22] R. P. T. Davenport-Hines, 'Lord Glendyne', in R.T. Appleyard and C.B. Schedvin (eds.), *Australian Financiers: Biographical Essays* (Melbourne: Macmillan Co. of Australia, 1988), pp. 190–205 (p. 194).

[23] For an informative study of networks among freemasonry, see J. L. Harland-Jacobs, *Builders of Empire: Freemasons and British Imperialism, 1717–1927* (Chapel Hill: University of North Carolina Press, 2007), pp. 10–13, 23, 216–22, 232.

[24] C. A. Bayly, 'Informing Empire and Nation: Publicity, Propaganda and the Press 1880–1920', in H. Morgan (ed.), *Information, Media and Power through the Ages* (Dublin: University College Dublin Press, 2001), pp. 179–98 (pp. 197–8); R. Holton, 'The Inclusion of the Non-European World in International Society, 1870s–1920s: Evidence from Global Networks', *Global Networks* 5 (2005), 239–59.

and even amplified, by networks, and, along with the changing economic fundamentals of the New and Old Worlds, gave rise to the political movements that dealt a death blow to the first phase of modern globalisation initiated in the nineteenth century.[25]

We began this book with definitions. We set out the range and diversity of opinion about the true character of globalisation – its origins, nature, scope and impact. We noted how globalisation has become one of the single most important concepts in the social sciences (and arguably in the humanities too),[26] and how it has both its champions and its critics. We also referred to the danger of globalisation becoming little more than a glib polysyllable – a word widely bandied around, and of which everyone assumes they know the meaning, yet which on closer inspection actually turns out to be rather ill-defined. In the pages that followed, we then sought to show how an historical perspective can help not only to shed light on the origins of globalisation in its more modern forms, but also on the way in which earlier episodes of globalisation have in turn left their mark on the global forces at work today. In particular, we have argued that it is in the relationships between Britain, the settler societies of its empire and the United States that the early stages of modern globalisation can most clearly be seen. This British World was among the first and most powerful sponsors of globalisation as we recognise it today. Indeed, several of the characteristics of the global economy and society talked about so frequently in the early twenty-first century – 'semi-globalisation',[27] 'regionalised globalisation',[28] the notions of 'network

[25] On the role of changing relative factor prices on the political economy of different regions of the world in the late nineteenth and early twentieth centuries, see K. O'Rourke and J. G. Williamson, *Globalization and History: The Evolution of a Nineteenth-Century Atlantic Economy* (Cambridge, MA: Harvard University Press, 1999), pp. 269–87.

[26] M. Shrivastava, 'Globalising "Global Studies": Vehicle for Disciplinary and Regional Bridges?', *New Global Studies* 2 (2008), 1–20 (pp. 1–5).

[27] The emphasis here tends to be either on the fact that globalisation has advanced more rapidly in some sectors of the economy than others, or that even in those sectors where it has rapidly advanced (e.g. financial markets) it is still more unstable than commentators often assume. See Bisley, *Rethinking Globalization*; Darwin, *After Tamerlane*, pp. 502–3; and M. Veseth, *Selling Globalization: The Myth of the Global Economy* (London: Lynne Reinner, 1998).

[28] As Patrick Manning asks, is what we are witnessing 'a world-encompassing global economy or a global economy made up of distinct regional systems?'; see P. Manning, *Navigating World History: Historians Create a Global Past* (Basingstoke: Palgrave Macmillan, 2003), p. 19. For the debate surrounding 'regionalised globalisation' – including the argument that what we have witnessed is 'economic internationalisation, not globalisation' – see Beck, *What is Globalization?*, pp. 119–21; F. Halliday, *The World at 2000: Perils and Promises* (Basingstoke: Palgrave Macmillan, 2000), pp. 60–1; Held and McGrew, *Global Transformations Reader*, pp. 4, 20–5, 39; Rugman, *End of Globalization*, pp. 1–15.

power' and the 'networked society',[29] and the centrality of international migration to the globalisation process – stem in part from the historical experience of the British imperial (and wider Anglophone) World. The reason why the above characteristics are so significant may be precisely because they are so deeply rooted.

How far can a greater awareness of previous experiences or episodes of globalisation help governments to manage its consequences today? The British World economy that lay at the heart of the first great wave of modern globalisation from the 1850s to 1914 was an ethnically based trans-national rather than fully global phenomenon; the sense of trust that was so crucial to its working was partly a matter of ethnic self-recognition, and partly of the exercise of the real sinews of imperial power, including the naval-based *Pax britannica*. History shows how such trans-national forms of identity, based around cultural and ethnic groups – Anglophone, Francophone, Lusophone – have formed much more readily than concepts of global citizenship, which, however desirable, have in reality been much slower to emerge. History also reveals the fragility of this first wave of modern globalisation, which came crashing down on the rocks of war in Europe in 1914 and the devastation that followed. The Great War not only stopped but actually reversed integration. Afterwards, the world gradually divided into regional economic blocs, 'each aiming to shrink its trade with the others'.[30]

Two of the main contemporary challenges currently recognised in the literature on globalisation arguably have their roots in the half-century prior to 1914. The first challenge arises from the sheer scale of global mobility: the explosion of diasporic cultures (whereby many more people now imagine themselves as part of a nation beyond a homeland), and the resulting question of how to extend economic relations across cultural and ethnic boundaries. In short, how successfully can economic interdependence co-exist with cultural diversity? The second challenge arises from the contingent nature of globalisation: the varying nature of its openness over time, and its almost self-destructive capacity to produce the very circumstances – economic nationalism, trade protection and tight immigration controls – in which it is likely to break down.[31] This set

[29] M. Castells, *The Information Age: Economy, Society and Culture*, 3 vols., Vol. I: *The Rise of the Network Society* (Oxford; Malden, MA, Blackwells 2000); Cooper, *Colonialism in Question*, pp. 107–10; Potter, 'Webs, Networks, and Systems'; G. F. Thompson, 'Is All the World a Complex Network?', *Economy and Society* 33 (2004), 411–24.
[30] Darwin, *After Tamerlane*, p. 503.
[31] See, for example, Morowska's and Spohn's observations on the 'discordant tendency' of past and contemporary phases of globalisation to produce, as a reaction to swelling migration, restrictive immigration policies by receiver countries 'confronted with a

of circumstances has been called the 'globalization backlash'.[32] Is such a backlash (and the de-globalisation that ensues) sooner or later inevitable, or can it be avoided?

In view of these challenges, it is perhaps not surprising that the focus of recent writing has shifted away from the capacity of specific, high pro-file international organisations – the International Monetary Fund and the World Trade Organization, for example – to resolve the resentments against globalisation in favour of exploring more broadly the role of trans-national social networks, especially migrant networks, in reorganising spatial rela-tions. How do such networks make connections across national borders? How is power distributed across them? What are the limits to the resulting linkages? Particular attention has been paid to the type of networks required to sustain a global economy and to prevent its component parts from turn-ing inward and sealing themselves off from each other. Social scientists have highlighted the need to cultivate more open and inclusive forms of social capital that can better foster cross-cultural entrepreneurial activities.[33] Such an aspiration entails a rather different mindset from that of the imperial past. In a postcolonial and multi-cultural world, integration, as one scholar has shrewdly observed, is predicated on a view of social relations 'founded on a belief in equality': indeed, the view of social relations 'governed by a racial hierarchy' is precisely the reason why 'imperial systems are incompat-ible with the process of globalization' as it unfolds today.[34]

Maintaining the degree of openness and interconnectedness (widely felt to be the sine qua non of positive globalisation) requires us to take

deluge of foreign residents'; 'Moving Europeans in the Globalizing World', p. 51. It is a moot point as to how far we today may be witnessing an era of resurgent nationalism, depending upon how one reads the complex and shifting political landscapes of Russia, China, the Indian subcontinent and Latin America.

[32] O'Rourke and Williamson, *Globalization and History*, pp. 286–7.

[33] Nederveen Pieterse, *Globalization and Culture*, pp. 35–8. See also the conclusion to Paul James' thoughtful essay, 'Globalisation and Empires of Mutual Accord', *Arena Magazine* 85 (October–November 2006), 41–6.

[34] A. G. Hopkins, 'Rethinking Decolonization', *Past & Present* 200 (2008), 211–47 (p. 242). For a similar line of reasoning, see also Charles Maier, *Among Empires: American Ascendancy and Its Predecessors* (Cambridge, MA: Harvard University Press, 2006); and N. Kirk, *Comrades and Cousins: Globalization, Workers and Labour Movements in Britain, the USA and Australia from the 1880s to 1914* (London: Merlin Press, 2003). Maier claims that 'Territorial fron-tiers are not the only boundaries that empires establish. Crucial, too, for the structure of an empire is the stratification within each of its political units ... Empires seek to defend internal socio-political frontiers as well as external boundaries ... extending their gradients of privilege and participation outward through space and downward into society' (p. 10). Meanwhile, Kirk argues for the importance of a 'strategy of [labour] inclusiveness under the conditions of capitalist globalization', in particular, as a counterpoint to growing social inequalities and the divisive effects of globalisation in national and international labour movements (p. 221).

account of its cultural as well as economic dynamic.[35] As we move in the early twenty-first century into a period of fundamental economic change, with the effects of a world financial crisis ever more widely felt, globalisation looks decidedly less irreversible than it once did. It would, however, be a mistake to focus exclusively on the immediate manifestations of that crisis – the complex financial instruments, such as credit-fault swaps, hedge funds, sub-prime mortgages and the like – which have exposed virtually all of the major banks' shareholders and customers to dizzying levels of risk, and which have been so corrosive of confidence precisely because they are so little understood. Globalisation is, after all, as much about people as it is about institutions or infrastructure, all the more so at a time when we are witnessing a worldwide increase in mobility for virtually all categories of migrants – legal and illegal, refugees and asylum-seekers, people in search of employment, temporary guest workers and permanent residents – and not only from the developing to the developed world, but from one developing country to another.[36]

To the extent that the *Pax britannica* of the past promoted a more 'globalised' world economic system, it was, to be sure, a vertical and hierarchical process that relied heavily upon the imposition of the British law necessary to open up trade routes, accelerate capital flows and encourage the mobility of people. Law and order, however, were insufficient in themselves. As we have seen, the growth and integration of markets relied equally on a plethora of dense, everyday social networks that straddled national borders, linked migrants in their places of settlement to their places of origin, generated trust and solidarity, improved the quality and quantity of information flows, and combined cultural and economic pursuits.[37] What they did not – and perhaps never could – succeed in doing was to transcend the culture from which they had emerged. Inclusive networks, then as now, proved very difficult to construct, all the more so when questions of race and ethnicity came into play. At a time when we are grappling with our own 'global migration crisis', and emigrants are more likely to be regarded as a threat than an opportunity for receiving

---

[35] See for example C. Hay and D. Marsh, 'Introduction: Demystifying Globalization', in Hay and Marsh (eds.) *Demystifying Globalization* (Basingstoke: Palgrave Macmillan, 1999), pp. 12–13; and S. D. Sharma, 'The Many Faces of Today's Globalization: A Survey of Recent Literature', *New Global Studies* 2 (2008), 1–27 (p. 20).

[36] M. Weiner, 'The Global Migration Crisis', in Gungwu (ed.), *Global History and Migrations*, pp. 96, 98.

[37] A. Portes, 'Globalization from Below: The Rise of Transnational Communities', in W. P. Smith and R. P. Korczenwicz (eds.), *Latin America in the World Economy* (Westport: Greenwood Publishing Group, 1996), pp. 151–68.

states,[38] this is a lesson that the *Pax americana* – and those now calling for a worldwide community of English-speaking states (or 'Anglosphere') to provide international leadership in the twenty-first century[39] – would do well to learn.

[38] D. S. Massey, J. Arango, G. Hugo, A. Kouaouci, A. Pellegrino and J. Edward Taylor (eds.), *Worlds in Motion: Understanding International Migration at the End of the Millennium* (Oxford: Oxford University Press, 1998), pp. 6–7.

[39] For a leading example, see James C. Bennett, *The Anglosphere Challenge: Why the English-Speaking Nations Will Lead the Way in the Twenty-First Century* (Plymouth: Rowman and Littlefield, 2007). For another call for English-speaking peoples to join together, see Robert Conquest's *Reflections on a Ravaged Century* (London: John Murray, 1999). For an encomium to the history of the English-speaking world, see Andrew Roberts' *A History of the English-Speaking Peoples since 1900* (London: Weidenfeld and Nicolson, 2006).

Bibliography

UNPUBLISHED PRIMARY SOURCES

THE BRITISH POSTAL MUSEUM AND ARCHIVE, FREELING HOUSE, PHOENIX PLACE, LONDON

51st Report of the Post Master General on the Post Office (1905).
52nd Report of the Post Master General on the Post Office (1906).
53rd Report of the Post Master General on the Post Office (1907).
54th Report of the Post Master General on the Post Office (1908).
55th Report of the Post Master General on the Post Office (1909).
56th Report of the Post Master General on the Post Office (1910).
Annual Reports of the Money Orders Office (1899–1908).
'Report on the Imperial Postal Order Scheme Two Years after Its Commencement', in *Imperial Postal Order Service: Heads of Arrangement, 11/7/1904*.

HSBC ARCHIVES

ACC 150/2, 'Mr Holden's Report on his Visit to America, 10 September to 5 November, 1904'.
E. H. Holden Diary, ref. 26/7 (Midland Bank Papers), 31 October 1907.
E. H. Holden Diary, ref. 26/7 (Midland Bank Papers), 27 May 1909.
E. H. Holden Diary, ref. 26/7 (Midland Bank Papers), 24 August 1909.
E. H. Holden Diary, ref. 26/7 (Midland Bank Papers), 24 May 1910.
E. H. Holden Diary, ref. 26/7 (Midland Bank Papers), 13 March 1912.

PARLIAMENTARY COMMAND PAPERS AND OTHER OFFICIAL REPORTS (BRITISH)

Annual Returns of the Life Assurance Companies to the Board of Trade, 1890–1914.
BME Remittance Survey, Research Report, prepared for the Department of International Development by ICM, 27 July 2006.
Report from the Select Committee on Colonisation, Sessional Papers, Vol. X (1889).
Statistical Abstract for the Several Colonial and Other Possessions of the United Kingdom in Each Year from 1886 to 1900 (1901), Cmd 751.

PARLIAMENTARY COMMAND PAPERS AND OTHER OFFICIAL REPORTS
(AUSTRALIA)

Report of the Board Appointed to Enquire into the Present Condition and Management of the Coranderrk Aboriginal Station, Vol. II (1882).
Royal Commission on the Aborigines: Report of the Commissioners, Vol. I (1877).

PUBLISHED PRIMARY SOURCES

BRITISH CHAMBER OF COMMERCE REPORTS, GUILDHALL
LIBRARY, LONDON

National Monetary Commission, *Interviews on the Banking and Currency Systems of England, Scotland, France, Germany, Switzerland and Italy*, Washington, DC: 1910.
Official Report of the 3rd Congress of the Chambers of Commerce of the British Empire, 9–12 June 1896 (1896), MS 18.278/1.

BRITISH EMPIRE CHAMBER OF COMMERCE REPORTS,
GUILDHALL LIBRARY, LONDON

Official Record of the Centennial International Exhibition, Melbourne, 1888–89, Melbourne, 1890.
Tupper, C., *The Colonial and Industrial Exhibition: Official Catalogue of the Canadian Section* (1886).

BOOKS AND JOURNAL ARTICLES

Anon., *The Story of South Africa Newspaper and Its Founder (Edward P. Mathers): Told by Others*, London: 1903.
Brunton, J., *John Brunton's Book: Being the Memories of John Brunton*, Cambridge: Cambridge University Press, 1939
Bryce, J. *The American Commonwealth*, 2 vols., London: Macmillan, 1888.
Caird, J., *Prairie Farming in America: With Notes by the Way on Canada and the United States*, London: Longman, Brown, Green, Longmans and Roberts, 1859.
Coghlan, T. A., *A Statistical Account of Australia and New Zealand, 1903–4*, Sydney: Government of the State of New South Wales and the Commonwealth of Australia, 1904.
Cooper, J. B., *Victorian Commerce, 1834–1934*, Melbourne: Robertson and Mullens, 1934.
Cowderoy, B., *Melbourne's Commercial Jubilee: Notes from the Records of Fifty Years' Work of the Melbourne Chamber of Commerce*, Melbourne: Mason, Firth and M'Cutcheon, 1901.
Dilke, C. W., *The British Empire*, London: Chatto and Windus, 1899.
Edwards, E. and A. E. Edwards, *How to Take Out Patents in England and Abroad*, London: Edwards and Co., 1905.
Flux, A. W., 'The Flag and Trade: A Summary Review of the Trade of the Chief Colonial Empires', *Journal of the Royal Statistical Society* **62**:3 (1899), 489–533.

Froude, J.A., *The English in the West Indies; or, The Bow of Ulysses*, London: Longmans, 1888.

Gregory, T.E., *The Westminster Bank through a Century*, Oxford: Oxford University Press, 1936.

Hayes Fisher, W., *Investing at Its Best and Safeguarding Invested Capital*, London: Financial Review of Reviews, 1912.

Hobson, J. A., *Canada To-Day*, London: T. Fisher Unwin, 1906.

Immelman, R.F.M., *Men of Good Hope: The Romantic Story of the Cape Town Chamber of Commerce, 1804–1954*, Cape Town: Cape Town Chamber of Commerce, 1955.

Kircaldy, A.W., *British Shipping: Its History, Organisation and Importance*, London: Kegan Paul, Trench, Trübner and Co., 1919.

Lewis Hind, C., *Days in Cornwall*, London: Methuen, 1907.

Robinson, H., *The British Post Office: A History*, Princeton: Greenwood Press, 1948.

Schlote, W., *British Overseas Trade from 1700 to the 1930s*, Oxford: Oxford University Press, 1952.

Seeley, J.R., *The Expansion of England*, ed. and introduction J. Gross, Chicago: Cosimo, 1971.

Sibbett, R.M., *Orangeism in Ireland and throughout the Empire, 1688–1938*, 2 vols., Belfast: Henderson and Co., 1914.

Smith, A., *The Wealth of Nations* [1776], ed., with an Introduction and notes, A. Skinner, Books 1–3, Harmondsworth: Penguin, 1974; Books 4–5, New York: Penguin, 1999.

Smith, P., *The Beadle*, London: Jonathan Cape, 1927.

Westgarth, W., *Personal Recollections of Early Melbourne and Victoria*, Sydney: G. Robertson and Co., 1888.

NEWSPAPERS

The Economist
Financial Review of Reviews
Investor's Monthly Manual (IMM)
Lloyd's Bank Limited Monthly Review
The Standard
The Times
Toronto Globe

SECONDARY SOURCES

Abbott, A.W., *A Short History of the Crown Agents and Their Office*, London: The Crown Agents, 1959.

Adelman, J., *Frontier Development: Land, Labour and Capital on the Wheatlands of Argentina and Canada, 1890–1914*, Oxford: Oxford University Press, 1994.

Adhikari, M., 'Ambiguity, Assimilationism and Anglophilism in South Africa's Coloured Community: The Case of Piet Uithalder's Satirical Writings, 1909–22', *SAHJ* 47 (2002), 115–31.

' "Give us the Benefit of Our British Blood": Changing Perceptions of Coloured Identity in South Africa', paper given at the British World Conference, University of Auckland, July 2005.

Adler, D. R., *British Investment in American Railways, 1834–1898*, Charlottesville: University Press of Virginia, 1970.

Akerloff, G. A. and R. E. Kranton, 'Economics and Identity', *Quarterly Journal of Economics* **115** (2000), 715–73.

Alford, B. W. E., *Britain in the World Economy since 1880*, London: Longman, 1996.

Annen, K., 'Inclusive and Exclusive Social Capital in the Small-Firm Sector in Developing Countries', *Journal of Institutional and Theoretical Economics* **157** (2001), 319–30.

'Social Capital, Inclusive Networks, and Economic Performance', *Journal of Economic Behavior and Organization* **50** (2001), 449–63.

Appadurai, A., 'Grassroots Globalisation and the Research Imagination', in A. Appadurai (ed.), *Globalisation*, Durham, NC: Duke University Press, 2001, pp. 1–22.

'Introduction: Commodities and the Politics of Value', in A. Appadurai (ed.), *The Social Life of Things: Commodities in Cultural Perspective*, Cambridge: Cambridge University Press, 1986, pp. 3–64.

Modernity at Large: Cultural Dimensions of Globalization, Minneapolis: University of Minnesota Press, 1996.

Armstrong, J., *Locomotives in the Tropics*, 2 vols., Vol. I: *Queensland Railways, 1864–1910*, Brisbane: Australian Railway Historical Society, 1985.

Arrow, K., 'Gifts and Exchanges', *Philosophy and Public Affairs* **1** (1972), 343–62.

Arthur Lewis, W., *Growth and Fluctuations, 1870–1913*, London: G. Allen and Unwin, 1978.

Artibise, A. F. J., 'Boosterism and the Development of the Prairie Cities, 1871–1913', in R. D. Francis and H. Palmer (eds.), *The Prairie West: Historical Readings*, Edmonton: Pica Pica Press, 1985, pp. 408–35.

Atkin, J. M., *British Overseas Investment, 1918–1931*, New York: Arno Press, 1977.

Avery, D., *Reluctant Host: Canada's Response to Immigrant Workers, 1896–1994*, Toronto: McLelland and Stewart, 1995.

Axford, B., *The Global System: Economics, Politics and Culture*, Oxford: Polity, 1995.

Bailey, J. D., 'Australian Company Borrowing, 1870–1893: A Study in British Overseas Investment', unpublished D.Phil. thesis, University of Oxford, 1958.

Baines, D., *Emigration from Europe, 1815–1930*, Cambridge: Cambridge University Press, 1995.

Migration in a Mature Economy: Emigration and Internal Migration in England and Wales, 1861–1900, Cambridge: Cambridge University Press, 1985.

'Population, Migration and Regional Development, 1870–1939', in R. Floud and D. N. McCloskey (eds.), *The Economic History of Britain since 1700, 3 vols.*, Vol. II: *1860–1939*, Basingstoke: Palgrave Macmillan, 1991, pp. 25–55.

Baker, M. and M. Collins, 'The Asset Portfolio Composition of British Life Insurance Firms, 1900–1965', *Financial History Review* **10** (2003), 137–64.

'English Bank Investment Portfolios, 1880–1910', unpublished working paper, University of Leeds School of Business, 2007.

Ballantyne, T., *Between Colonialism and Diaspora: Sikh Cultural Formations in an Imperial World*, Durham NC: Duke University Press, 2006.

'Empire, Knowledge and Culture: From Proto-Globalization to Modern Globalization', in A.G. Hopkins (ed.), *Globalization in World History*, London: Pimlico, 2002, pp. 115–40.

Ballara, A., *Iwi: The Dynamics of Maori Tribal Organisation from c. 1769 to c. 1945*, Wellington: Victoria University Press, 1998.

Banfield, S., 'Towards a History of Music in the British Empire: Three Export Studies', in K. Darian-Smith, P. Grimshaw and S. Macintyre (eds.), *Britishness Abroad: Transnational Movements and Imperial Cultures*, Melbourne: Melbourne University Press, 2007, pp. 63–90.

Barman, J., *The West beyond the West: A History of British Columbia*, Toronto: University of Toronto Press, 1996.

Barnett, C., *The Lost Victory: British Dreams, British Realities, 1945–1950*, London: Macmillan, 1995.

Barnett, R.J. and J. Cavanagh, 'A Globalizing Economy: Some Implications and Consequences', in B. Mazlish and R. Buultjens (eds.), *Conceptualizing Global History*, Boulder, CO: Westview Press, 1993, pp. 153–73.

Barrow, L., 'White Solidarity in 1914', in R. Samuel (ed.), *Patriotism: The Making and Unmaking of British National Identity*, 3 vols., Vol. I: *History and Politics*, London: Routledge, 1989, pp. 275–87.

Barwick, D.E., 'And the Lubras are Ladies Now', in F. Gale (ed.), *Women's Role in Aboriginal Society*, Canberra: Australian Institute of Aboriginal Studies, 1994, pp. 51–63.

Bashford, A., *Imperial Hygiene: A Critical History of Colonialism, Nationalism and Public Health*, Basingstoke: Palgrave Macmillan, 2004.

Medicine at the Border: Disease, Globalisation and Security, 1850 to the Present, Basingstoke: Palgrave Macmillan, 2006.

Baster, A.J., *The Imperial Banks*, London: P.S. King, 1929.

Bauman, Z., *Globalization: The Human Consequences*, Cambridge: Cambridge University Press, 1998.

Baumeister, R.F., 'The Need to Belong: Desire for Interpersonal Attachments as a Fundamental Human Motivation', *Psychological Bulletin* **117** (1995), 497–529.

Bayly, C.A., *The Birth of the Modern World, 1780–1914: Global Connections and Comparisons*, Oxford: Oxford University Press, 2004.

'Informing Empire and Nation: Publicity, Propaganda and the Press 1880–1920', in H. Morgan (ed.), *Information, Media and Power through the Ages*, Dublin: University College Dublin Press, 2001, pp. 179–98.

Beck, U., *What Is Globalization?* Malden, MA: Polity, 2000.

Belich, J., 'The Rise of the Angloworld: Settlement in North America and Australasia, 1784–1918', in P. Buckner and D. Francis (eds.), *Rediscovering the British World*, Calgary: University of Calgary Press, 2005, pp. 39–58.

Bell, D. A., 'Dissolving Distance: Technology, Space and Empire in British Political Thought, 1770–1900', *Journal of Modern History* 77 (2005), 523–62.

Bennett, J. C., *The Anglosphere Challenge: Why the English-Speaking Nations Will Lead the Way in the Twenty-First Century*, Plymouth: Rowman and Littlefield, 2007.

Berger, C., *Imperialism and Nationalism, 1884–1914: A Conflict in Canadian Thought*, Toronto: Toronto University Press, 1969.

Berthoff, R. T. *British Immigrants in Industrial America*, New Haven: Harvard University Press, 1953.

Bevir, M. and F. Trentmann (eds.), *Markets in Historical Contexts: Ideas and Politics in the Modern World*, Cambridge: Cambridge University Press, 2004.

Bickers, R. (ed.), *Settlers and Expatriates: Britons over the Seas*, Oxford: Oxford University Press, 2010.

Bickford-Smith, V., 'The Betrayal of Creole Elites, 1880–1920', in P. D. Morgan and S. Hawkins (eds.), *Black Experience and the Empire*, Oxford: Oxford University Press, 2004, pp. 194–227.

'Revisiting Anglicisation in the Nineteenth-Century Cape Colony', in C. Bridge and K. Fedorowich (eds.), *The British World: Diaspora, Culture and Identity*, London: Taylor and Francis, 2003, pp. 82–95.

Bickford-Smith, V. and R. Mendelsohn, *Black and White in Colour: African History on Screen*, Athens, OH: Ohio University Press, 2007.

Bielenberg, A., 'Irish Emigration to the British Empire', in A. Bielenberg, (ed.), *The Irish Diaspora*, Harlow: Longman, 2000, pp. 251–72.

Bisley, N., *Rethinking Globalization*, Basingstoke: Palgrave Macmillan, 2007.

Blainey, G. *Gold and Paper: A History of the National Bank of Australasia Limited* Melbourne: Georgian House, 1958.

The Rush that Never Ended: A History of Australian Mining, Melbourne: Melbourne University Press, 1963.

Bliss, M. *Northern Enterprise: Five Centuries of Canadian Business*, Toronto: University of Toronto Press, 1987.

Bodnar, J. E., *The Transplanted: A History of Immigrants in Urban America*, Bloomington: Indiana University Press, 1985.

Bongiorno, F., 'Fabian Socialism and British Australia, 1890–1972', in P. Buckner and D. Francis (eds.), *Rediscovering the British World*, Calgary: University of Calgary Press, 2005, pp. 209–31.

Borrie, W. D., *Immigration to New Zealand 1854–1938*, Canberra: Australian National University Press, 1991.

Bose, *A Hundred Horizons: The Indian Ocean in the Age of Global Empire*, Cambridge, MA: Harvard University Press, 2006.

Bouch, R., 'Mercantile Activity and Investment in the Eastern Cape: The Case of Queenstown, 1853–1886', *South African Journal of Economic History* 6 (1991), 18–37.

Bourdieu, P., 'The Forms of Social Capital', in J. G. Richardson (ed.), *Handbook of Theory and Research for the Sociology of Education*, New York: Greenwood Press, 1986, pp. 241–58.

Bourdieu, P. and L. Wacquant, *An Invitation to Reflexive Sociology*, Chicago: University of Chicago Press, 1992.

Bowles, S. and H. Gintis, 'Social Capital and Community Governance', *Economic Journal* **112** (2002), 419–36.

Boyce, G. H., *Information, Mediation and Institutional Development: The Rise of Large-Scale Enterprise in British Shipping, 1870–1919*, Manchester: Manchester University Press, 1995.

Boyd, M., 'Family and Personal Networks in International Migration: Recent Developments and New Agendas', *International Migration Review* **23** (1989), 638–70.

Bradbury, B., 'Rethinking Marriage, Civilization and Nation in Nineteenth-Century White Settler Societies', in P. Buckner and D. Francis (eds.), *Rediscovering the British World*, Calgary: University of Calgary Press, 2005, pp. 135–57.

Brady, I., G. Johnson, S. Sharp, G. Smith, R. Taaffe and A. Watson, *New South Wales Railways: The First Twenty-Five Years, 1855–1880*, Broadmeadow, NSW: Australian Railway Historical Society, 1980.

Brah, A., *Cartographies of Diaspora: Contesting Identities*, London: Routledge, 1997.

Brennan, P. H., 'The Other Battle: Imperialist versus Nationalist Sympathies within the Officer Corps of the Canadian Expeditionary Force, 1914–19', in P. Buckner and D. Francis (eds.), *Rediscovering the British World*, Calgary: University of Calgary Press, 2005, pp. 251–65.

Brewer, J. and F. Trentmann, 'Introduction: Space, Time and Value in Consuming Cultures', in J. Brewer and F. Trentmann (eds.), *Consuming Cultures: Global Perspectives, Historical Trajectories, Transnational Exchanges*, Oxford: Oxford University Press, 2006, pp. 1–17.

Bridge, C. and K. Fedorowich, *The British World: Culture, Diaspora and Identity*, London: Taylor and Francis, 2003.

  'Mapping the British World', in C. Bridge and K. Fedorowich (eds.), *The British World: Culture, Diaspora and Identity*, London: Taylor and Francis, 2003, pp. 1–15.

Brocklehurst, H. and R. Phillips (eds.), *History, Nationhood and the Question of Britain*, Basingstoke: Palgrave Macmillan, 2003.

Broeze, F. J. A., 'Private Enterprise and the Peopling of Australia, 1831–50', *EcHR* **35** (1982), 235–53.

Brooking, T., 'Weaving the Tartan into the Flax: Networks, Identities, and Scottish Migration to Nineteenth-Century Otago, New Zealand', in A. McCarthy (ed.), *A Global Clan: Scottish Migrant Networks and Identities since the Eighteenth Century*, London: I. B. Tauris, 2006, pp. 183–201.

Broome, R., *Aboriginal Australians: Black Response to White Dominance, 1788–1980*, London: Allen and Unwin, 1983.

  Aboriginal Victorians: A History since 1800, Crows Nest, NSW: Allen and Unwin, 2005.

Brown, B. H., *The Tariff Reform Movement in Great Britain, 1881–95*, New York: Routledge, 1943.

Buchanan, R. A., 'The British Contribution to Australian Engineering: The Australian Dictionary of Biography Entries', *Historical Studies* **20** (1993), 401–19.

  'The Diaspora of British Engineering', *Technology and Culture* **27** (1986), 501–24.

The Engineers: A History of the Engineering Profession in Britain, 1750–1914, London: Kingsley, 1989.

The Life and Times of Isambard Kingdom Brunel, London: Continuum International Publishing, 2002.

Buck, A.R., J. McLaren and N.E. Wright (eds.), *Land and Freedom: Law, Property Rights and the British Diaspora*, Aldershot: Ashgate, 2001.

Buckley, K. and T. Wheelwright, *No Paradise for Workers: Capitalism and the Common People in Australia, 1788–1914*, Oxford: Oxford University Press, 1988.

Buckley, P. and P.N. Ghauri, 'Globalisation, Economic Geography and the Strategy of Multinational Enterprises', *Journal of International Business Studies* **35** (2004), 81–98.

Buckley, P. and P.N. Ghauri, (eds.), *The Internationalisation of the Firm*, London: International Thomson Business Press, 1999.

Buckner, P., 'Casting Daylight upon Magic: Deconstructing the Royal Tour of 1901 to Canada', *JICH* (2003), 158–89.

Buckner, P. and C. Bridge, 'Reinventing the British World', *The Round Table* **368** (2003), 77–88.

Buckner, P. and Francis, D. (eds.), *Rediscovering the British World: Culture and Diaspora* (London: Taylor and Francis, 2003).

Bumsted, J.M. 'Scottishness and Britishness in Canada, 1790–1914', in M. Harper and M.E. Vance (eds.), *Myth, Migration and the Making of Memory: Scotia and Nova Scotia, c. 1700–1990*, Edinburgh: John Donald, 1999.

Burk, K., *Old World, New World: The Story of Britain and America*, Little Brown Book Company Ltd, 2007.

Burke, P., *History and Social Theory*, Cambridge: Cambridge University Press, 1992.

Burt, R., 'Freemasonry and Business Networking during the Victorian Period', *EcHR* **56** (2003), 657–88.

Burton, A., *The Railway Empire*, London: John Murray, 1994.

Bush, J., *Edwardian Ladies and Imperial Power*, London: Continuum International Publishing Group, 2000.

Cable, V., *The World's New Fissures: Identities in Crisis*, London: Demos, 1994.

Cain, P.J., 'Character and Imperialism: The British Financial Administration of Egypt, 1878–1914', *JICH* **34** (2006), 177–200.

'The Economic Philosophy of Constructive Imperialism', in C. Navari (ed.), *British Politics and the Spirit of the Age: Political Concepts in Action*, Keele: Keele University Press, 1996, pp. 41–65.

Cain, P.J. and A.G. Hopkins, *British Imperialism, 1688–2000*, Harlow: Longman, 2001, pp. 205–42.

Cairncross, A.K., *Home and Foreign Investment*, Cambridge: Cambridge University Press, 1953.

Campbell, J.T., 'The Americanization of South Africa', in R. Wagnleitner and E.T. May (eds.), *'Here, There and Everywhere': The Foreign Politics of American Popular Culture*, Hanover, NH: University Press of New England, 2000.

Campo, J.N.F.M. à, 'Engines of Empire: The Role of Shipping Companies in British and Dutch Empire Building', in G. Jackson and D.M. Williams (eds.), *Shipping, Technology and Imperialism*, Aldershot: Ashgate, 1996, pp. 63–96.

Capie, F., 'Britain and Empire Trade in the Second Half of the Nineteenth Century', in D. Alexander and R. Ommer (eds.), *Volumes not Values: Canadian Sailing Ships and World Trades*, Memorial University Newfoundland: Maritime History Group, 1979, pp. 3–29.

Carey, J., 'Recreating British Womanhood: Ethel Osborne and Melbourne Society in the Early Twentieth Century', in K. Darian-Smith, P. A. Grimshaw, K. J. E. Lindsey and S. F. MacIntyre (eds.), *Exploring the British World: Identity-Cultural Production-Institutions*, Melbourne: RMIT Publishing, 2004, pp. 21–39.

Carrier, N. H. and J. R. Jeffrey, *External Migration: A Study of the Available Statistics 1815–1950* (London: HMSO, 1953).

Carter, M. and J. Maluccio, 'Social Capital and Coping with Economic Shock: An Analysis of Stunting of South African Children', *World Development* **31** (2003), 1147–63.

Carter Holman, C., *Cornish Engineering, 1801–2001: Two Centuries of Industrial Excellence in Camborne*, Camborne: CompAir, 2001.

Casson, M., 'Cultural Determinants of Economic Performance', *Journal of Comparative Economics* (1993), 418–42.

  Enterprise and Competitiveness: A Systems View of International Business, Oxford: Oxford University Press, 1990.

Casson, M. and H. Cox, 'International Business Networks: Theory and History', *Business and Economic History* **22** (1993), 42–53.

Casson, M. and M. B. Rose (eds.), *Institutions and the Evolution of Modern Business*, London: Taylor and Francis, 1993.

Casson, M. C., 'An Economic Approach to Regional Business Networks', in J. F. Wilson and A. Popp (eds.), *Industrial Clusters and Regional Business Networks in England, 1750–1970*, Aldershot: Ashgate, 2003, pp. 19–44.

Casson, M. C. and A. Godley, 'Cultural Factors in Economic Growth', in M. C. Casson and A. Godley (eds.), *Cultural Factors in Economic Growth*, Berlin: Springer, 2000, pp. 1–43.

Castells, M., *The Information Age: Economy, Society and Culture*, 3 vols., Vol. I: *The Rise of the Network Society*, Oxford; Malden, MA: Blackwells, 2000.

Castles, M., *The Rise of Network Society*, Oxford: Oxford University Press, 2000.

Castles, S. and M. Miller (eds.), *The Age of Migration: International Population Movements in the Modern World*, 2nd edn, Guilford Press, 1998.

Castro, D. S., *The Development of Argentine Immigration Policy, 1852–1914*, San Francisco: Mellen Research University Press, 1991.

Chapman, S., 'The Innovating Entrepreneurs in the British Ready-Made Clothing Industry', *Textile History* **24** (1993), 5–25.

Chappell, N. M., *New Zealand's Banker's Hundred: A History of the Bank of New Zealand, 1861–1961*, Wellington: Bank of New Zealand, 1961.

Chaudhuri, N., 'Shawls, Curry, and Rice in Victorian Britain', in N. Chaudhuri and M. Srobel (eds.), *Western Women and Imperialism: Complicity and Resistance* Bloomington: Indiana University Press, 1992, pp. 231–47.

Chilton, L., *Emigrating Women: British Female Migration to Canada and Australia, 1830s–1930*, Toronto: Toronto University Press, 2007.

'A New Class of Women for the Colonies: Female Emigration Societies and the Construction of Empire', *JICH* **31**:2 (May 2003), 36–56.

Choe, H., H. Kho and R. Stulz, 'Do Domestic Investors Have an Edge? The Trading Experience of Foreign Investors in Korea', *Review of Financial Studies* **18**:3 (2005), pp. 795–829.

Christie, R., *Electricity, Industry and Class in South Africa*, Oxford: Oxford University Press, 1984.

Clapham, J., *The Bank of England: A History, 2 vols., Vol. II: 1797–1914*, Cambridge: Cambridge University Press, 1970.

Clark, N. L., *Manufacturing Apartheid: State Corporations in South Africa*, New Haven: Yale University Press, 1994.

Clark, P., *British Clubs and Societies, 1580–1800: The Origins of an Association World*, Oxford: Oxford University Press, 2000.

Codell, J. F. (ed.), *Imperial Co-Histories: National Identities and the British and Colonial Press*, Madison, NJ: Farleigh Dickinson University Press, 2003.

Coetzee, F., *For Party or Country: Nationalism and the Dilemmas of Popular Conservatism in Edwardian England*, Oxford: Oxford University Press, 1990.

Cohen, A., *Customs and Politics in Urban Africa: A Study of Hausa Migrants in Yoruba Towns*, Berkeley: University of California Press, 1969.

Cohen, R., 'Diasporas, the Nation-State, and Globalization', in W. Gungwu (ed.), *Global History and Migrations*, Boulder, CO: Westview Press, 1997, pp. 117–44.

Global Diasporas: An Introduction, London: Routledge, 1997.

Coleman, J. S., *The Foundations of Social Theory*, Cambridge, MA: Harvard University Press, 1990.

'Social Capital in the Creation of Human Capital', *American Journal of Sociology* **94** (1988), 95–120.

Coll, R. *Identity of England*, Oxford: Oxford University Press, 2002.

Colley, L., 'Britishness and Otherness: An Argument', *JBS* **31** (1992), 309–29.

Collini, S., *Public Moralists: Political Thought and Intellectual Life in Britain, 1850–1930*, Oxford: Oxford University Press, 1991.

Collins, M. and M. Baker, *Commercial Banks and Industrial Finance in England and Wales, 1860–1913*, Oxford: Oxford University Press, 2003.

Collins, T., 'Rugby and the Making of Imperial Manhoods', paper given at the British World Conference, University of Auckland, July 2005.

'"We Are Just as British as You Are": Masculinity and Working-Class Imperial Loyalty in Rugby Football', paper given at the British World Conference, Melbourne, July 2004.

Comaroff, J. L. and J. Comaroff, *Of Revelation and Revolution, 2 vols., Vol. II: The Dialectics of Modernity on a South African Frontier*, Chicago: University of Chicago Press, 1997.

Conquest, R., *Reflections on a Ravaged Century*, London: John Murray, 1999.

Constantine, S., 'Britain and Empire', in S. Constantine, M. Kirby and M. Rose (eds.), *The First World War in British History*, London: Edward Arnold, 1995, pp. 268–70.

'British Emigration to the Empire-Commonwealth since 1880: From Overseas Settlement to Diaspora?', in C. Bridge and K. Fedorowich (eds.), *The British World*, Calgary: University of Calgary Press, pp. 16–35.

'Migrants and Settlers', in J. M. Brown and W. R. Louis (eds.), *The Oxford History of the British Empire, 5 vols., Vol. IV: The Twentieth Century*, Oxford: Oxford University Press, 1999, pp. 163–88.

Cooper, F., *Colonialism in Question: Theory, Knowledge, History*, Berkeley: University of California Press, 2005.

'Networks, Moral Discourse and History', in T. Callaghy, R. Kassimir and R. Latham (eds.), *Intervention and Transnationalism in Africa*, Cambridge: Cambridge University Press, 2001, pp. 23–46.

Costa, D. and M. Kahn, 'Cowards and Heroes: Group Loyalty in the American Civil War', *Quarterly Journal of Economics* **118** (2003), 519–48.

Cox, H., *The Global Cigarette: Origins and Evolution of British American Tobacco, 1880–1945*, Oxford: Oxford University Press, 2000.

Cox, L., *Kotahitanga: The Search for Maori Political Unity*, Oxford: Oxford University Press, 1993.

Crouzet, F., 'Trade and Empire: The British Experience from the Establishment of Free Trade until the First World War', in B. M. Ratcliffe (ed.), *Great Britain and Her World, 1750–1914: Essays in Honour of W. O. Henderson*, Manchester: Manchester University Press, 1975, pp. 209–35.

The Victorian Economy, London: Routledge, 1992.

Cryle, D., 'Interdependent or Independent? Australia–British Relations at the Melbourne Imperial Press Conference', in K. Darian-Smith, P. Grimshaw, K. Lindsey and S. McIntyre (eds.), *Exploring the British World: Identity-Cultural Production-Institutions*, Melbourne: RMIT Publishing, 2004, pp. 890–907.

Curthoys, A. and M. Lake, 'Introduction', in A. Curthoys and M. Lake (eds.), *Connected Worlds: History in Transnational Perspective*, Canberra: Australian National University Press, 2005, pp. 5–20.

Curtin, P. D., 'Africa and Global Patterns of Migration', in W. Gungwu (ed.), *Global History and Migrations*, Boulder CO: Westview Press, 1997, pp. 63–94.

Cross-Cultural Trade in World History, Cambridge: Cambridge University Press, 1984.

Daniels, C. and M. V. Kennedy (eds.), *Negotiated Empires: Centers and Peripheries in the Americas, 1500–1820*, New York: Routledge, 2002.

Danziger, C., *A Trader's Century: The Fortunes of Frasers*, Cape Town: Purnell, 1979.

Darwin, J. *After Tamerlane: The Global History of Empire*, London: Allen Lane, 2007.

'The British Empire and the "British World"', keynote lecture at *Defining the British World*, 11–14 July 2007.

'The Descent of Empire: Post-Colonial Views of Britain's Imperial History', annual guest lecture given to the Leeds Institute of Colonial and Postcolonial Studies, University of Leeds, 4 May 2006.

'Globalism and Imperialism: The Global Context of British Power, 1830–1860', in S. Akita (ed.), *Gentlemanly Capitalism: Imperialism and Global History*, Basingstoke: Palgrave Macmillan, 2002.

'A Third British Empire? The Dominion Idea in Imperial Politics', in W. R. Louis and J. Brown (eds.), *The Oxford History of the British Empire, 5 vols., Vol. IV: The Twentieth Century*, Oxford: Oxford University Press, 1999, pp. 64–87.

Das, D. K., *The Economic Dimensions of Globalization*, Basingstoke: Palgrave Macmillan, 2004.

Dasgupta, P., 'Social Capital and Economic Performance: Analytics', Faculty of Economics Working Paper, University of Cambridge, 2002.

Daunton, M., 'Britain and Globalisation since 1850, II: The Rise of Insular Capitalism, 1914–1939', *TRHS* 17 (2007), 1–30.

Daunton, M. J. and R. Halpern (eds.), *Empire and Others: British Encounters with Indigenous Peoples, 1600–1850*, Philadelphia: University of Pennsylvania Press, 1998.

Davenport-Hines, R. P. T., 'Lord Glendyne', in R. T. Appleyard and C. B. Schedvin (eds.), *Australian Financiers: Biographical Essays*, Melbourne: Macmillan Co. of Australia, 1988, pp. 190–205.

Davenport-Hines, R. P. T. and J. Slinn, *Glaxo: A History to 1962*, Cambridge: Cambridge University Press, 1992.

Davenport-Hines, R. P. T. and J. J. Van Helten, 'Edgar Vincent, Viscount D'Abernon, and the Eastern Investment Company in London, Constantinople and Johannesburg', in R. P. T. Davenport-Hines (ed.), *Speculators and Patriots: Essays in Business Biography*, London: Routledge, 1986, pp. 35–62.

Davie, M., *Anglo-Australian Attitudes*, London: Secker and Warburg, 2000.

Davies, N., *The Isles: A History*, Oxford: Oxford University Press, 1999.

Davies, P. N., 'Shipping and Imperialism: The Case of British West Africa', in G. Jackson and D. M. Williams (eds.), *Shipping, Technology and Imperialism*, Aldershot: Scolar Press, 1996, pp. 46–63.

Davies, W. E., *Patriotism on Parade: The Story of Veterans and Hereditary Organisations in America*, Cambridge, MA: Harvard University Press, 1955.

Davis, L., 'The Late Nineteenth-Century British Imperialist: Specification, Quantification and Controlled Conjectures', in R. E. Dumett (ed.), *Gentlemanly Capitalism and British Imperialism: The New Debate on Empire*, Basingstoke: Palgrave Macmillan, 1999, pp. 82–112.

Davis, L. E. and R. E. Gallman, *Evolving Financial Markets and International Capital Flows: Britain, the Americas, and Australia, 1865–1914*, Cambridge: Cambridge University Press, 2001.

Davis, L. E. and R. A. Huttenback, *Mammon and the Pursuit of Empire: The Economics of British Imperialism, 1860–1912*, Cambridge: Cambridge University Press, 1986.

Davison, G., 'Festivals of Nationhood: The International Exhibitions', in S. L. Goldberg and F. B. Smith (eds.), *Australian Cultural History*, Melbourne: Australian Academy of Humanities, 1988, pp. 158–77.

Dawe, R., *Cornish Pioneers in South Africa: 'Gold and Diamonds, Copper and Blood'*, St Austell: Cornish Hillside Publications, 1998.

Dean, W., *Remittances of Italian Immigrants from Brazil, Argentina, Uruguay and the USA*, New York: New York University Press, 1974.

Delaney, E. and D.M. MacRaild, 'Irish Migration, Networks and Ethnic Identities since 1750: An Introduction', *Immigrants and Minorities* **23** (2005), 127–35.

Delheim, C., 'The Creation of a Company Culture: Cadburys, 1861–1913', *AHR* **92** (1987), 13–44.

DeLong, B., 'Did Morgan's Men Add Value?', in P. Temin (ed.), *Inside the Business Enterprise: Historical Perspectives on the Use of Information*, Chicago: University of Chicago Press, 1991.

Denoon, D. *Settler Capitalism: The Dynamics of Dependent Development in the Southern Hemisphere*, Oxford: Oxford University Press, 1983.

'Understanding Settler Societies', *Historical Studies* **18** (1979), 511–27.

Denoon, D. and P. Mein-Smith, *A History of Australia, New Zealand and the Pacific*, Oxford: Oxford University Press, 2000.

Desmond, R.W., *The Information Process: World News Reporting to the Twentieth Century*, Chicago: University of Iowa Press, 1978.

Dickenson, J., ' "Nice Company for Christian Men!" Adela Pankhurst Walsh and the British Empire', in K. Darian-Smith, P. Grimshaw, K. Lindsey and S. McIntyre (eds.), *Exploring the British World: Identity-Cultural Production-Institutions*, Melbourne: RMIT Publishing, 2004, pp. 40–59.

Dilley, A.R., 'Gentlemanly Capitalism and the Dominions: London Finance, Australia and Canada', unpublished D.Phil. thesis, University of Oxford, 2006.

Dingle, A., ' "The Truly Magnificent Thirst": An Historical Survey of Australian Drinking Habits', *Historical Studies* **19** (1980), 227–43.

Drache, D. (ed.), *Staples, Markets and Cultural Change: Selected Essays*, Montreal: McGill-Queen's University Press, 1995.

Driver, D. (ed.), *Pauline Smith*, Johannesburg: McGraw-Hill, 1983.

du Gay, P. and M. Pryke (eds.), *Cultural Economy: Cultural Analysis and Commercial Life*, London: Sage, 2002.

Dubow, S. *A Commonwealth of Knowledge: Science, Sensibility and Colonial Identity in South Africa*, Oxford: Oxford University Press, 2006.

'The Commonwealth of Science: The British Association in South Africa, 1905 and 1929', in S. Dubow (ed.), *Science and Society in Southern Africa*, Manchester: Manchester University Press, 2000, pp. 66–100.

Dunstan, D., 'Boozers and Wowsers', in V. Burgmann and J. Lee (eds.), *Constructing a Culture: A People's History of Australia since 1788*, Fitzroy, Victoria: Penguin, 1988, pp. 96–123.

'A Sobering Experience: From "Australian Burgundy" to "Kanga Rouge": Australian Wine Battles on the London Market, 1900–1981', *Journal of Australian Studies* **17** (2002), 179–210.

Durlauf, S.N. and M. Fafchamps, 'Social Capital', National Bureau of Economic Research Working Paper 10485, 2004.

Dutton, H.I., *The Patent System and Inventive Activity during the Industrial Revolution, 1750–1852*, Manchester: Manchester University Press, 1984.

Dvorak, T., 'Do Domestic Investors Have an Information Advantage? Evidence from Indonesia', *Journal of Finance* **60**:2 (2005), 817–39.

Eddy, J. and D. Schreuder (eds.), *The Rise of Colonial Nationalism*, Sydney: Allen and Unwin, 1988.

Edelstein, M., 'Foreign Investment, Accumulation and Empire, 1860–1914', in R. Floud and P. Johnson (eds.), *Cambridge Economic History of Modern Britain, 3 vols., Vol. II: Economic Maturity, 1860–1939*, Cambridge: Cambridge University Press, 2004, pp. 191–6.

Ehrensaft, P. and W. Armstrong, 'The Formation of Dominion Capitalism: Economic Truncation and Class Structure', in A. Moscovitch and G. Drover (eds.), *Inequality: Essays on the Political Economy of Social Welfare*, Toronto: University of Toronto Press, 1981, pp. 95–105.

Elbourne, E., *Blood Ground, Colonialism, Missions and the Contest for Christianity in the Cape Colony and Britain, 1799–1853*, Montreal: McGill-Queen's University Press, 2002.

'Indigenous Peoples and Imperial Networks in the Early Nineteenth Century: The Politics of Knowledge', in P. Buckner and D. Francis (eds.), *Rediscovering the British World*, Calgary: University of Calgary Press, 2005, pp. 59–85.

Eley, G. 'Historicizing the Global, Politicizing Capital: Giving the Present a Name', *HWJ* **63** (2007), 154–88.

Elkins, C. and S. Pedersen (eds.), *Settler Colonialism in the Twentieth Century*, New York: Routledge, 2005.

Elliott, B. S., D. A. Gerber and S. M. Sinke, 'Introduction', in B. S. Elliott, D. A. Gerber and S. M. Sinke. (eds.), *Letters across Borders: The Epistolary Practices of International Migrants*, Basingstoke: Palgrave Macmillan, 2006, pp. 1–29.

Encaoua, D. and A. Jacquemin, 'Organizational Efficiency and Monopoly Power: The Case of French Industrial Groups', *European Economic Review* **19** (1982), 25–51.

Engerman, S. L., 'Mercantilism and Overseas Trade, 1700–1800', in R. Floud and D. N. McCloskey (eds.), *The Economic History of Britain since 1700*, 3 vols., Vol. I: 1700–1860 Cambridge: Cambridge University Press, 1994.

Erickson, C. (ed.), *Emigration from Europe, 1815–1914: Select Documents*, London: A. and C. Black, 1976.

Erickson, C., *Invisible Immigrants: The Adaptation of English and Scottish Immigrants in Nineteenth Century America*, London: London School of Economics, 1972.

Evans, J., P. Grimshaw, D. Phillips and S. Swain (eds.), *Equal Subjects, Unequal Rights: Indigenous People in British Settler Colonies*, Manchester: Manchester University Press, 2003.

Faith, N., *The World the Railways Made*, London: Bodley Head, 1990.

Fedorowich, K. 'The British Empire on the Move, 1760–1914', in S. Stockwell (ed.), *The British Empire: Themes and Perspectives*, Oxford: Blackwells, 2008.

Feinstein, C. H., *An Economic History of South Africa: Conquest, Discrimination and Development*, Cambridge: Cambridge University Press, 2005.

'The End of Empire and the Golden Age', in P. Clarke and C. Trebilcock (eds.), *Understanding Decline: Perceptions and Realities of British Economic Performance*, Cambridge: Cambridge University Press, 1997.

'Exports and British Economic Growth', in P. Mathias and J. A. Davis (eds.), *International Trade and British Economic Growth from the Eighteenth Century to the Present Day*, Oxford: Oxford University Press, 1996, pp. 76–95.

Fenton, S., *Ethnicity*, Cambridge: Polity, 2004.

Ferenczi, I. and W. F. Willcox, *International Migrations*, 2 vols., Vol. I: *Statistics*, New York: National Bureau of Economic Research, 1929.

Ferguson, N., *Colossus: The Rise and Fall of the American Empire*, London: Penguin, 2004.

Empire: How Britain Made the Modern World, London: Allen Lane, 2003.

Empire: The Rise and Demise of the British World Order and the Lessons for Global Power, London: Basic Books, 2002.

'Political Risk and the International Bond Market between the 1848 Revolution and the Outbreak of the First World War', *EcHR* **59** (2006), 70–112.

'We Must Understand Why Racist Belief Systems Persist', *Guardian*, 12 July 2006, p. 26.

Ferguson, N. and M. Schularick, 'The Empire Effect: The Determinants of Country Risk in the First Age of Globalization, 1880–1913', *Journal of Economic History* **66** (2006), 283–312.

Fershtman, C. and U. Gneezy, 'Discrimination in a Segmented Society: An Experimental Approach', *Quarterly Journal of Economics* **116** (2001), 351–77.

Fieldhouse, D. K., 'For Richer, for Poorer?', in P. J. Marshall (ed.), *Cambridge Illustrated History of the British Empire*, Cambridge: Cambridge University Press, 1996, pp. 110–12.

'The Metropolitan Economics of Empire', in J. M. Brown and W. R. Louis (eds.), *The Oxford History of the British Empire*, 5 vols., Vol. IV: *The Twentieth Century*, Oxford: Oxford University Press, 1999, pp. 88–113.

Findlay, R. and K. H. O'Rourke, *Power and Plenty: Trade, War, and the World Economy in the Second Millennium*, Princeton: Princeton University Press, 2007.

Findling, J. E. (ed.), *Historical Dictionary of World's Fairs and Expositions, 1851–1988*, New York: Greenwood, 1990.

Finn, M., *The Character of Credit: Personal Debt in English Culture, 1740–1914*, Cambridge: Cambridge University Press, 2003.

Fitzgerland, R., *Rowntree and the Marketing Revolution, 1862–99*, Cambridge: Cambridge University Press, 1995.

Fitzpatrick, D., *Oceans of Consolation: Personal Accounts of Irish Migration to Australia*, Ithaca, NY: Cornell University Press, 1994.

'The Orange Order', paper given to *Ireland and Empire* workshop, University of Leeds, March 2006.

Fletcher, I., L. E. Nym Mayhall and P. Levine (eds.), *Women's Suffrage in the British Empire: Citizenship, Nation and Race*, London: Routledge, 2000.

Floud, R., *The People and the British Economy, 1830–1914*, Oxford: Oxford University Press, 1997.

Forbes, J., *Munro, Maritime Enterprise and Empire: Sir William Mackinnon and His Business Network, 1823–93*, Woodbridge: Boydell Press, 2003.

Ford, A. G., *The Gold Standard, 1880–1914: Britain and Argentina*, Oxford: Oxford University Press, 1962.

Frank, J., 'Making Social Capital Work for Public Policy', *Policy Research Initiative* **6** (2003), 2–3. Accessed at http://policyresearch.gc.ca/page.asp?pagenm=v6n3_ art_02 on 10 May 2004.

Fraser, L., 'Irish Migration to the West Coast, 1864–1900', *New Zealand Journal of History* **34** (2000), 317–40.

Frederickson, G. M., 'From Exceptionalism to Variability: Recent Developments in Cross-National Comparative History', *Journal of American History* **82** (1995), 587–604.

Frieberg, A. L., *The Weary Titan: Britain and the Experience of Relative Decline, 1895–1905*, Princeton: Princeton University Press, 1988.

Frieden, J. A., *Global Capitalism: Its Fall and Rise in the Twentieth Century*, New York: W. W. Norton, 2006.

Fukushi, J., 'Canada and the British Imperial Economy in the Late Nineteenth Century: A Case of the Colonial and Indian Exhibition in 1886', unpublished M.A. thesis, University of Leeds, 2005.

Fukuyama, F., *Trust: The Social Virtues and the Creation of Prosperity*, New York: Penguin, 1995.

Gabaccia, D. R., *Italy's Many Diasporas*, London: UCL Press, 2000.

Garfield, S., *The Last Journey of William Huskisson*, London: Faber, 2003.

Garvie, J. 'Globalisation and Its Cures', *Times Literary Supplement*, **18** February 2008.

Gascoigne, J. 'The Expanding Historiography of British Imperialism', *HJ* **49** (2006), 577–92.

Gates, P. W., *The Illinois Central Railroad and Its Colonisation Work*, Cambridge, MA: Harvard University Press, 1934.

Ghosh, B. N., *Dependency Theory Revisited*, Aldershot: Ashgate, 2001.

Gibbs, R. M., *A History of South Australia: From Colonial Days to the Present*, Blackwood: Peacock Publications, 1984.

Giddens, A., *Runaway World: How Globalisation Is Reshaping Our Lives*, New York: Routledge, 2002.

Gilbert, R. S., 'London Financial Intermediaries and Australian Overseas Borrowing, 1900–1929', *Australian Economic History Review* **11** (1971), 39–47.

Glaeser, E. L., D. Laibson and B. Sacerdote, 'The Economic Approach to Social Capital', National Bureau of Economic Research Working Paper 7728 (2000).

Glaisyer, N., 'Networking: Trade and Exchange in the Eighteenth Century British Empire', *HJ* **47** (2004), 451–76.

Glass, D. V. and P. A. M. Taylor, *Population and Emigration*, Dublin: Irish University Press, 1976.

Godfrey, B. and G. Dunstall (eds.), *Crime and Empire, 1840–1940: Criminal Justice in Local and Global Context*, Uffculme: Willan, 2005.

Gold, J. R. and M. M. Gold, *Cities of Culture: Staging International Festivals and the Urban Agenda, 1851–2000*, Aldershot: Ashgate, 2005.

Goldin, C. and L. Katz, 'Human Capital and Social Capital: The Rise of Secondary Schooling in America, 1910–1940', *Journal of Interdisciplinary History* **29** (1999), 683–723.

Gooday, G., *Domesticating Electricity: Technology, Uncertainty and Gender, 1880–1914*, London: Pickering and Chatto, 2008.

Gooderson, P. J., *Lord Linoleum: Lord Ashton, Lancaster and the Rise of the British Oilcloth and Linoleum Industry*, Keele: Keele University Press, 1996.

Goodhart, C.A.E., *The Business of Banking: 1891–1914*, London: London School of Economics, 1972.

Goodman, D., 'Anglophilia and Racial Nationalism in the Debate about US Entry into World War Two', in K. Darian-Smith, P. Grimshaw, K. Lindsey and S. McIntyre (eds.), *Exploring the British World: Identity-Cultural Production-Institutions*, Melbourne: RMIT Publishing, 2004, pp. 107–25.

Gordon Skilling, H., *Canadian Representation Abroad: From Agency to Embassy*, Toronto: University of Toronto Press, 1945.

Graham-Yooll, A., *The Forgotten Colony: A History of the English-Speaking Communities in Argentina*, London: Hutchinson, 1981.

Grant, K., P. Levine and F. Trentmann (eds.), *Beyond Sovereignty: Britain, Empire and Transnationalism, c. 1880–1950*, Basingstoke: Palgrave Macmillan, 2007.

Grant, R.D., *Representations of British Emigration, Colonisation and Settlement: Imagining Empire, 1800–1860*, Basingstoke: Palgrave Macmillan, 2005.

Greaves, I., 'The Character of British Colonial Trade', *Journal of Political Economy* **62** (1954), 1–11.

Green, A.G., M. Mackinnon and C. Minns, 'Dominion or Republic? Migrants to North America from the United Kingdom, 1870–1910', *EcHR* **55** (2002), 666–96.

Green, E.H.H., *The Crisis of Conservatism: The Politics, Economics and Ideology of the Conservative Party, 1880–1914*, London: Routledge, 1995.

'The Political Economy of Empire, 1880–1914', in A. Porter (ed.), *The Oxford History of the British Empire*, 5 vols., Vol. III: *The Nineteenth Century*, Oxford: Oxford University Press, 1999.

Greenhalgh, P., *Ephemeral Vistas: The Expositions Universelles, Great Exhibitions and World's Fairs, 1851–1939*, Manchester: Manchester University Press, 1988.

Gregory, T.E., *The Westminster Bank through a Century*, Oxford: Oxford University Press, 1936.

Grewal, D.S., 'Network Power and Globalization', *Ethics and International Affairs* (2003), 89–98.

Network Power: The Social Dynamics of Globalisation, New Haven: Yale University Press, 2008.

Grey, J., 'War and the British World in the Twentieth Century', in P. Buckner and D. Francis (eds.), *Rediscovering the British World*, Calgary: University of Calgary Press, 2005, pp. 233–50.

Grief, A., 'Contract Enforceability and Economic Institutions in Early Trade: The Maghribi Traders' Coalition', *American Economic Review* **83** (1993), 525–48.

'Cultural Beliefs and the Organization of Society: A Historical and Theoretical Reflection on Collectivist and Individualist Societies', *Journal of Political Economy* **102** (1994), 912–50.

'Reputation and Coalitions in Medieval Trade: Evidence on the Maghribi Traders', *Journal of Economic History* **49** (1989), 857–82.

Grieser, N., 'The British Investor and His Sources of Information', unpublished M.Sc. dissertation, University of London, 1940.

Grove, R., *Ecology, Climate and Empire: Colonialism and Global Environmental History, 1400–1940*, Cambridge: Cambridge University Press, 1997.

Grundlingh, A., ' "Gone to the Dogs". The Cultural Politics of Gambling: Rise and Fall of British Greyhound Racing on the Witwatersrand, 1932–49', paper presented at the British World Conference, University of Cape Town, July 2002.

Guarnizo, L. E. and M. P. Smith, 'The Locations of Transnationalism', in L. E. Guarnizo and M. P. Smith (eds.), *Transnationalism from Below*, New Brunswick: Transaction Publishers, 1998, pp. 3–34.

Guiso, L., P. Sapienza and L. Zingales, 'Does Culture Affect Economic Outcomes?', *Journal of Economic Perspectives* **20** (2006), 23–48.

Habakkuk, H. J., 'Free Trade and Commercial Expansion, 1853–1870', in J. Holland Rose, A. P. Newton and E. A. Benians (eds.), *The Cambridge History of the British Empire*, 5 vols., Vol. II: *The Growth of the New Empire, 1783–1870* (Cambridge: Cambridge University Press, 1940), pp. 797–8.

Hack, B., *A History of the Patent Profession in Colonial Australia*, Melbourne: Clement Hack and Co., 1984.

Hagan, J., MacMillan, R. and Wheaton, B., 'New Kid in Town: Social Capital and the Life Course Effects of Family Migration on Children', *American Sociological Review* **61** (1996), 368–85.

Haley, G. T., C. T. Tan and V. C. V. Haley (eds.), *New Asian Emperors: The Overseas Chinese, Their Strategies and Competitive Advantages*, London: Butterworth Heinemann, 1998.

Hall, A. R., *The London Capital Market and Australia, 1870–1914*, Canberra: Australian National University, 1963.

Hall, C., *Civilising Subjects: Metropole and Colony in the English Imagination, 1830–67*, Cambridge: Cambridge University Press, 2002.
   'Rethinking Imperial Histories: The Reform Act of 1867', *New Left Review* **208** (1994), 3–29.

Hall, S., 'Cultural Identity and Diaspora', in J. Rutherford (ed.), *Identity: Community, Culture, Difference*, London: Lawrence and Wishart, 1998, pp. 222–37.
   'The Local and the Global: Globalisation and Ethnicity', in A. McClintock, A. Mufti and E. Shohat (eds.), *Dangerous Liaisons: Gender, Nation and Postcolonial Perspectives*, Minneapolis: University of Minnesota Press, 1997.

Hall, S. and Gieben, B. (eds.), *Formations of Modernity*, Cambridge: Cambridge University Press, 1992.

Halliday, F., *The World at 2000: Perils and Promises*, Basingstoke: Palgrave Macmillan, 2001.

Hamburg, M., *Basic Statistics*, London: R. D. Irwin, 1985.

Hammerton, A. J., *Emigrant Gentlewomen: Genteel Poverty and Female Emigration, 1830–1914*, London: Croom Helm, 1979.

Hancock, W. K., *Australia*, London: Benn, 1930.
   Survey of British Commonwealth Affairs, 3 vols., Vol. I: *Problems of Nationality, 1918–1936*, Oxford: Oxford University Press, 1937.

Handlin, O., *Boston's Immigrants: A Study in Acculturation*, Cambridge, MA: Harvard University Press, 1959.

Harcourt, F., 'The P&O Company: Flagships of Imperialism', in S. Palmer and G. Williams (eds.), *Charted and Uncharted Waters: Proceedings of a Conference on the Study of British Maritime History*, London: National Maritime Museum, 1981, pp. 6–28.

Haresnape, G., *Pauline Smith*, Berkeley: University of California Press, 1969.

Harland-Jacobs, J. L., *Builders of Empire: Freemasons and British Imperialism, 1717–1927*, Chapel Hill: Univesrsity of North Carolina Press, 2007.

Harley, C. K., 'The World Food Economy and Pre-World War I Argentina', in S. N. Broadberry and N. F. R. Crafts (eds.), *Britain in the International Economy*, Cambridge: Cambridge University Press, 1992, 244–68.

Harper, M., *Adventurers and Exiles: The Great Scottish Exodus*, London: Profile Books, 2004.

'British Migration and the Peopling of the Empire', in A. Porter (ed.), *The Oxford History of the British Empire*, 5 vols., Vol. III, Oxford: Oxford University Press, 1999, pp. 75–88.

Harper, M. (ed.), *Emigrant Homecomings: The Return Movement of Emigrants, 1600–2000*, Manchester: Manchester University Press, 2005.

Harper, M., *Emigration from Scotland between the Wars*, Manchester: Manchester University Press, 1988.

Emigration from North-East Scotland, 2 vols., Vol. II: *Beyond the Broad Atlantic*, Aberdeen: Aberdeen University Press, 1988.

'Transient Tradesmen: Aberdeen Emigrants and the Development of the American Granite Industry', *Northern Scotland* 9 (1989), 53–74.

Harper, M. and S. Constantine, *Migrants and Settlers*, Oxford: Oxford University Press, 2010.

Harries, P., *Work, Culture, and Identity: Migrant Labourers in Mozambique and South Africa, c. 1860–1910*, Portsmouth, NH: Heinemann, 1994.

Harris, J. and P. Thane, 'British and European Bankers, 1880–1914: An Aristocratic Bourgeoisie?', in P. Thane, G. Crossick and R. Floud (eds.), *The Power of the Past: Essays for Eric Hobsbawm*, Cambridge: Cambridge University Press, 1984, pp. 215–34.

Hau, H., 'Location Matters: An Examination of Trading Profits', *Journal of Finance* 56 (2001), 1951–83.

Hawkins, F., *Critical Years in Immigration: Canada and Australia Compared*, Kingston: McGill-Queen's University Press, 1989.

Hay, C., and D. Marsh, 'Introduction: Demystifying Globalization', in Hay and Marsh (eds.), *Demystifying Globalization*, Basingstoke: Palgrave Macmillan, 1999, pp. 1–17.

Headrick, D. R., *When Information Came of Age: Technologies of Knowledge in the Age of Reason and Revolution, 1700–1850*, Oxford: Oxford University Press, 2000.

Hedges, J. B., *Building the Canadian West: The Land and Colonization Policies of the Canadian Pacific Railway*, New York: Read Books, 1939.

'The Colonization Work of the Northern Pacific Railroad', *The Mississippi Valley Historical Review* 13 (1926), 311–42.

Heindel, R. H., *The American Impact on Great Britain, 1898–1914: A Study of the United States in World History*, New York: Octagon Books, first published 1940, reprinted 1968.

Held, D. and McGrew, A., 'The Great Globalization Debate: An Introduction', in D. Held and A. McGrew (eds.), *The Global Transformations Reader: An*

Introduction to the Globalization Debate, Cambridge: Cambridge University Press, 2000, pp. 1–50.

Held, D. and McGrew, A. (eds.), *The Global Transformations Reader: An Introduction to the Globalization Debate*, Cambridge: Cambridge University Press, 2000.

Held, D., A. McGrew, D. Goldblatt and J. Perraton, *Global Transformations: Politics, Economics and Culture*, Oxford: Oxford University Press, 1999.

Helliwell, J., *Globalization and Well-Being*, Vancouver: University of British Columbia Press, 2002.

Hendrickson, H. (ed.), *Clothing and Difference: Embodied Identities in Colonial and Post-Colonial Africa* (Durham, NC: Duke University Press, 1996).

Hilliard, C., 'The Provincial Press and the Imperial Traffic in Fiction: 1870s–1930s', *JBS* 48:3 (July 2009), 653–73.

'The Tillotson Syndicate and the Imperial Trade in Fiction', paper given at the British World Conference, University of Auckland, July 2005.

Hirst, R. and G. Thompson, *Globalisation in Question: The International Economy and the Possibilities of Governance*, Cambridge: Cambridge University Press, 1996.

Historical Houses Trust of New South Wales, *Floorcoverings in Australia, 1800–1950*, Glebe, NSW: Historical Houses Trust, 1997.

Hobsbawm, E. J., *Industry and Empire*, London: Pantheon Books, 1969.

Hobson, J. A., *Imperialism: A Study*, 3rd rev. edn, London: Allen and Unwin, 1938.

Hobson, O. R., 'The Financial Press', *Lloyd's Bank Limited Monthly Review* 5 (1934), 6.

Hoffenberg, P. H., *An Empire on Display: English, Indian and Australian Exhibitions from the Crystal Palace to the Great War*, Berkeley: University of California Press, 2001.

Hofmeyr, I., 'Making Bunyan English via Africa', paper given at the British World Conference, Institute for Commonwealth Studies, London, 1998.

The Portable Bunyan: A Trans-national History of the Pilgrim's Progress, Princeton: Yale University Press, 2004.

Hofstede, G., *Cultures and Organisations: Software of the Mind*, London: McGraw-Hill Professional, 1991.

Holland, R., 'The British Empire and the Great War, 1914–1918', in R. Louis and J. Brown (eds.), *Oxford History of the British Empire*, 5 vols., Vol. IV, Oxford: Oxford University Press, 2001, pp. 125–33.

Holland Rose, J., A. P. Newton and E. A. Benians (eds.), *The Cambridge History of the British Empire*, 5 vols., Vol. II: *The Growth of the New Empire, 1783–1870*, Cambridge: Cambridge University Press, 1940.

Holmes, A. R. and E. Green, *Midland: 150 Years of Banking Business*, London: Batsford, 1986.

Holton, R., 'The Inclusion of the Non-European World in International Society, 1870s–1920s: Evidence from Global Networks', *Global Networks* 5 (2005), 239–59.

'Network Discourses: Proliferation, Critique and Synthesis', *Global Networks* 5 (2005), 209–15.

Hoogvelt, A., *Globalisation and the Postcolonial World: The New Political Economy of Development*, 2nd edn, Basingstoke: Palgrave Macmillan, 2001.

Hopkins, A. G., 'Back to the Future: From National History to Imperial History', *Past & Present* **164** (1999), 198–243.

Hopkins, A. G. (ed.), *Global History: Interactions between the Universal and the Local*, Basingstoke: Palgrave Macmillan, 2006.

Hopkins, A. G. (ed.), *Globalization in World History*, London: Pimlico, 2002.

Hopkins, A. G., 'Rethinking Decolonization', *Past & Present* **200** (2008), 211–47.

Hoppen, K. T., *The Mid-Victorian Generation, 1846–86*, Oxford: Oxford University Press, 1998.

Horn, P., 'Agricultural Trade Unions and Emigration, 1872–1881', *HJ* **15** (1972), 87–102.

Houston, C. J. and W. J. Smyth, *The Orange Order in Nineteenth Century Ontario: A Study of Institutional Cultural Transfer*, Toronto: University of Toronto Press, 1977.

'Transferred Loyalties: Orangeism in the United States and Ontario', *American Review of Canadian Studies* **14** (1984), 193–211.

Howe, A., 'From Pax Britannica to Pax Americana: Free Trade, Empire and Globalisation, 1846–1948', *Bulletin of Asia-Pacific Studies* (2003), 137–59.

Howell, P. A., *South Australia and Federation*, Kent Town, OH: Wakefield Press, 2002.

Hudson, P., 'English Emigration to New Zealand, 1839–50: Information Diffusion and Marketing a New World', *EcHR* **54** (2001), 680–98.

Hudson, P. and D. Mills, 'English Emigration, Kinship and the Recruitment Process: Migration from Melbourn in Cambridgeshire to Melbourne in Australia in the Mid-Nineteenth Century', *Rural History* **10** (1999), 71–4.

Hughes, J. (ed.), *Australian Words and Their Origins*, Oxford: Oxford University Press, 1989.

Hughes, K., *The Short Life and Long Times of Mrs Beeton*, London: Random House, 2007.

Hull, R. W., *American Enterprise in South Africa: Historical Dimensions of Engagement and Disengagement*, New York: New York University Press, 1990.

Humble, N. (ed.), *Mrs Beeton's Book of Household Management: Abridged Edition*, Oxford: Oxford University Press, 2000.

Hurd, J. M., 'Railways', in D. Kumar (ed.), *The Cambridge Economic History of India*, 2 vols., Vol. II: c. 1757–1970, Cambridge: Cambridge University Press, 1983.

Huttenback, R. A., 'No Strangers within the Gates: Attitudes and Policies towards the Non-White Residents of the British Empire of Settlement', *JICH* **I** (1972), 271–302.

Hyslop J. 'The British and Australian Leaders of the South African Labour Movement, 1902–1914: A Group Biography', in K. Darian-Smith, P. Grimshaw and S. Macintyre (eds), *Britishness Abroad: Transnational Movements and Imperial Cultures*, Melbourne: Melbourne University Press, 2007, pp. 90–108.

'Cape Town Highlanders, Transvaal Scottish: Military "Scottishness" and Social Power in Nineteenth and Twentieth Century South Africa', *South African Historical Journal* **47** (2002), 96–114.

'The Imperial Working Class Makes Itself "White": White Labourism in Britain, Australia and South Africa before the First World War', *Journal of Historical Sociology* **12** (1999), 398–424.

The Notorious Syndicalist: J. T. Bain, a Scottish Rebel in Colonial South Africa, Johannesburg: Jacana Media, 2004.

Inggs, J., 'Port Elizabeth's Response to the Expanding Economy of Europe, 1820–1870', *South African Journal of Economic History* **3** (1988), 61–84.

Inglis, K. S., 'Going Home: Australians in England, 1870–1900', in D. Fitzpatrick (ed.), *Home or Away? Immigrants in Colonial Australia*, Canberra: Australian National University (1992), pp. 105–30.

Innis, H. A., *Empire & Communications*, Victoria, BC: University of British Columbia, 1986.

A History of the Canadian Pacific Railway, Toronto: David and Charles, 1971.

On Canada: Essays in Canadian Economic History, Toronto: University of Toronto Press, 1956.

Israel, P. and R. Rosenberg, 'Patent Office Records as a Historical Source: The Case of Thomas Edison', *Technology and Culture* **32** (1991), 1094–1101.

Jackson, M. W., 'A Cultural History of Victorian Physical Science and Technology', *HJ* **50** (2007), 253–64.

James, H., *The End of Globalization: Lessons from the Great Depression*, Cambridge, MA: Harvard University Press, 2001.

James, P., 'Globalisation and Empires of Mutual Accord', *Arena Magazine* **85** (October–November 2006), 41–6.

Jephcott, H., *The First Fifty Years: An Account of the Early Life of Joseph Edward Nathan and the First Fifty Years of His Merchandise Business that Eventually Became the Glaxo Group*, Ipswich: n.p., 1969.

Johanson, G., *A Study of Colonial Editions in Australia, 1843–1972*, Wellington: Monash University Press, 2000.

Johnson, T., 'The State and the Professions: The Peculiarities of the British', in A. Giddens and G. Mackenzie (eds.), *Social Class and the Division of Labour: Essays in Honour of Ilya Neustadt*, Cambridge: Cambridge University Press, 1983.

Johnson, V., 'British Multinationals, Culture and Empire in the Early Twentieth Century', unpublished Ph.D. thesis, University of London, 2007.

Jones, A. and B. Jones, 'The Welsh World and the British Empire, c. 1851–1939: An Exploration', *JICH* **31**:2 (2003), 57–81.

Jones, B., *'Raising the Wind': Emigrating from Wales in the Late Nineteenth and Early Twentieth Centuries*, annual public lecture, Cardiff Centre for Welsh American Studies, Cardiff University, 2003 (Cardiff: Cardiff Centre for Welsh American Studies, 2004). Accessed at www.cardiff.ac.uk/welsh/resources/RaisingTheWind.pdf on 7 September 2009.

'Welsh–Australian Organizations and the Promotion of British and Welsh Identities in the 1930s and 1940s', paper given at the British World Conference, University of Melbourne, July 2004.

Jones, E.L., *Cultures Merging: A Historical and Economic Critique of Culture*, Princeton: Yale University Press, 2006.

The *European Miracle: Environments, Economies and Geopolitics in the History of Europe and Asia*, Cambridge: Cambridge University Press, 1981.

Jones, G., *British Multinational Banking, 1830–1990*, Oxford: Oxford University Press, 1993.

Jones, H.M., *The Age of Energy: Varieties of American Experience, 1865–1915*, New York: Viking Press, 1971.

Jones, J.D.F., *Through Fortress and Rock: The Story of Gencor, 1895–1995*, Johannesburg: Jonathan Ball, 1995.

Jones, M.A., *American Immigration*, Chicago: University of Chicago Press, 1992.

'The Background to Emigration from Great Britain', in D. Fleming and B. Bailyn (eds.), *Dislocation and Emigration: The Social Background of American Immigration*, Cambridge, MA: Harvard University Press, 1974.

Jones, P. Te H., *King Potatau: An Account of the Life of Potatau Te Wherowhero, the First Maori King*, Wellington: Polynesian Society of New Zealand, 1960.

Jones, S., 'The Imperial Banks in South Africa, 1861–1914', *South African Journal of Economic History* 11 (1996), 5–57.

Jones, W.D., *Wales in America: Scranton and the Welsh, 1860–1920*, Cardiff: University of Wales Press, 1993.

Judge, R., 'Social Capital: Building a Foundation for Research and Policy Development', *Policy Research Initiative* 6 (2003), 3. Accessed at http://policyresearch.gc.ca/page.asp?pagenm=v6n3_art_03 on 10 May 2004.

Jupp, J., *The English in Australia*, Cambridge: Cambridge University Press, 2004.

From White Australia to Woomera: The Story of Australian Immigration, Cambridge: Cambridge University Press, 2002.

Kali, R., 'Endogenous Business Networks', *Journal of Law, Economics, and Organization* 15 (1999), 615–36.

Kallinikios, J., ' "An Orgy of Britishness": Soccer in Melbourne in the 1950s', paper given at the British World Conference, University of Melbourne, July 2004.

Karsten, P., *Between Law and Custom: 'High' and 'Low' Legal Cultures in the Lands of the British Diaspora. The United States, Canada, Australia and New Zealand, 1600–1900*, Cambridge: Cambridge University Press, 2002.

Kearney, H., *The British Isles: A History of Four Nations*, Cambridge: Cambridge University Press, 1989.

Kearney, M., 'The Local and the Global: The Anthropology of Globalization and Transnationalism', *Annual Review of Anthropology* 24 (1995), 547–65.

Keck, M.E. and K. Sikkink, *Activists beyond Borders: Advocacy Networks in International Politics*, Ithaca, NY: Cornell University Press, 1998.

Keegan, T., *Colonial South Africa and the Origins of the Racial Order*, Cape Town: New Africa Boooks, 1996.

'The Making of the Rural Economy from 1850 to the Present', in Z.A. Konczacki (ed.), *Studies in the Economic History of Southern Africa*, 2 vols., Vol. II: *South Africa, Lesotho and Swaziland*, London: Cass, 1991, pp. 36–63.

Kennedy, T. C., *British Quakerism, 1860–1920: The Transformation of a Religious Community*, Oxford: Oxford University Press, 2001.

Keynes, J. M., 'Foreign Investment and the National Advantage', *The Nation and the Athenaeum* **35** (9 August 1924), 585–6.

Kindleberger, C. P., 'Foreign Trade and Economic Growth: Lessons from Britain and France, 1850–1913', *EcHR* **14**:2 (1961), 295–300.

King, B. M., *Silk and Empire*, Manchester: Manchester University Press, 2005.

Kirk, N., *Comrades and Cousins: Globalization, Workers and Labour Movements in Britain, the USA and Australia from the 1880s to 1914*, London: Merlin Press, 2003.

Knack, S. and P. Keefer, 'Does Social Capital Have an Economic Payoff? A Cross-Country Investigation', *Quarterly Journal of Economics* **112** (1997), 1251–88.

Knowles, V., *Strangers at Our Gates: Canadian Immigration and Immigration Policy, 1540–1997*, Toronto: Dundurn Press, 1997.

Kogut, B. and H. Singh, 'The Effect of National Culture on the Choice of Entry Mode', *Journal of International Business Studies* **19** (1988), 411–32.

Kranton, R. E., 'Reciprocal Exchange: A Self-Sustaining System', *American Economic Review* **86** (1996), 830–51.

Kubicek, R. 'British Expansion, Empire and Technological Change', in A. Porter (ed.), *The Oxford History of the British Empire*, 5 vols., Vol. III: *The Nineteenth Century*, Oxford: Oxford University Press, 1999, pp. 247–70.

'Economic Power at the Periphery: Canada, Australia and South Africa, 1850–1914', in R. E. Dummett (ed.), *Gentlemanly Capitalism and British Imperialism: The New Debate*, London: Longman, 1999, pp. 113–26.

'The Proliferation and Diffusion of Steamship Technology and the Beginnings of "New Imperialism"', in D. Killingray, M. Lincoln and N. Rigby (eds.), *Maritime Empires: British Imperial Maritime Trade in the Nineteenth Century*, Woodbridge: Boydell Press, 2004, pp. 100–10.

Kynaston, D., *The City of London*, 3 vols., Vols. I and II, London: Pimlico, 1995.

Lack, J. and B. Zino, 'A New Imperialism? The Imperial War Graves Commission and the Great War', paper given at the British World Conference, University of Melbourne, July 2004.

Laidlaw, Z., *Colonial Connections, 1814–45: Patronage, the Information Revolution and Colonial Government*, Basingstoke: Palgrave Macmillan, 2005.

'Integrating Metropolitan, Colonial and Imperial History: The Aborigines [*sic*] Select Committee of 1835–1837', in T. Banivanua Mar and J. Evans (eds.), *Writing Colonial Histories: Comparative Perspectives*, Melbourne: RMIT Publishing, 2002, pp. 75–91.

Lake, M. and H. Reynolds, *Drawing the Global Colour Line: White Men's Countries and the International Challenge of Racial Equality*, Cambridge: Cambridge University Press, 2008.

Lamb, W. K., *History of the Canadian Pacific Railway*, New York: Macmillan, 1977.

Lambert, D. and A. Lester (eds.), *Colonial Lives across the British Empire: Imperial Careering in the Long Nineteenth Century*, Cambridge: Cambridge University Press, 2006.

Lambert, D. and A. Lester 'Introduction: Imperial Spaces, Imperial Subjects', in D. Lambert and A. Lester (eds.), *Colonial Lives across the British Empire: Imperial Careering in the Long Nineteenth Century*, Cambridge: Cambridge University Press, 2006, pp. 1–31.

Lambert, J., '"Munition Factories ... Turning Out a Constant Supply of Living Material": White South African Elite Boys' Schools and the First World War', *SAHJ* **51** (2004), 67–86.

'"Preserving Britishness": English-Speaking South Africa's Patriotic, Cultural and Charitable Associations', paper given to the Jubilee Conference of the South African Historical Association, University of Pretoria, July 2006.

'"An Unknown People": Writing a Biography of White English-Speaking South Africans', unpublished article.

Landes, D. S., *The Wealth and Poverty of Nations: Why Some Are So Rich and Some So Poor*, London: W. W. Norton, 1999.

Langfield, M. and P. Roberts, *Welsh Patagonians: The Australian Connection*, Darlinghurst: Crossing Press, 2005.

Larkworthy, F., *Ninety-One Years: Being the Reminiscences of Falconer Larkworthy*, London: Mills and Boon, 1924.

Laugesen, A., 'Australian Soldiers and the World of Print during the Great War', in M. Hammond and S. Towheed (eds.), *Publishing the First World War*, Basingstoke: Palgrave Macmillan, 2007, pp. 93–110.

Leana, C. R. and F. K. Pil, 'Social Capital and Organizational Performance: Evidence from Urban Public Schools', *Organization Science* **17** (2006), 352–66.

Lenin, V. I., *Imperialism: The Highest Stage of Capitalism*. A Popular Outline by V. I. Lenin, London: Pluto Press, 1917.

Lester, A., 'British Settler Discourse and the Circuits of Empire', *HWJ* **54**:1 (2002), 24–48.

Imperial Networks: Creating Identities in Nineteenth Century South Africa and Britain, London: Routledge, 2001.

Lewis, W. A., *Growth and Fluctuations, 1870–1913*, London: G. Allen and Unwin, 1978.

Li, P. S., *The Chinese in Canada*, Toronto: Canadian Historical Association, 1988.

Limb, P., 'The Ambiguities of British Empire Loyalism and Identities in the Politics and Journalism of Early ANC Leaders', paper given at the British World Conference, Cape Town, 2002.

Lin, N., *Social Capital*, Cambridge: Cambridge University Press, 2001.

Linge, C. J. R., *Industrial Awakening: A Geography of Australian Manufacturing, 1788 to 1890*, Canberra: Australian National University, 1979.

Lipsey, R. E., *Price and Quantity Trends in the Foreign Trade of the United States*, Princeton: Princeton University Press, 1963.

Lochner, K., I. Kawachi, R. Brennan and S. Buka, 'Social Capital and Neighborhood Mortality Rates in Chicago', *Social Science and Medicine* **56** (2003), 1797–1805.

Lorimer, D., 'From Victorian Values to White Virtues: Assimilation and Exclusion in British Racial Discourse, *c.* 1870–1914', in P. Buckner and

D. Francis (eds.), *Rediscovering the British World: Culture and Diaspora*, London: Taylor and Francis, 2003, pp. 109–34.

Loury, G. C., 'A Dynamic Theory of Racial Income Differences', in P. A. Wallace and A. M. LaMond (eds.), *Women, Minorities, and Employment Discrimination*, Lexington: University of Michigan Press, 1977, pp. 153–86.

Lower, J. A., *Western Canada: An Outline History*, Vancouver: University of British Columbia Press, 1983.

Lowry, D., 'The Crown, Empire Loyalism and the Assimilation of Non-British White Subjects in the British World: An Argument against "Ethnic Determinism"', in P. Buckner and D. Francis (eds.), *Rediscovering the British World: Culture and Diaspora*, London: Taylor and Francis, 2003, pp. 158–89.

Macdonald, H., ' "Subjects for Dissection": Regulating Anatomy in a British World', in K. Darian-Smith, P. Grimshaw, K. Lindsey and S. Mcintyre (eds.), paper given at the British World Conference, University of Melbourne, July 2004.

MacGillivray, A., *A Brief History of Globalization: The Untold Story of Our Incredible Shrinking Planet*, London: Carroll and Graf, 2006.

Macintyre, S., 'History Wars and the Imperial Legacy in the Settler Societies', in P. Buckner and D. Francis (eds.), *Rediscovering the British World: Culture and Diaspora*, London: Taylor and Francis, 2003, pp. 381–97.

Mackenzie, G., *Why Patagonia?* Stornoway: Stornoway Gazette, 1996.

MacKenzie, J. with N. R. Dalziel, *The Scots in South Africa: Ethnicity, Identity, Gender and Race, 1772–1914*, Manchester: Manchester University Press, 2007.

MacKenzie, J. M., 'The Second City of the Empire: Glasgow – Imperial Municipality', in F. Driver and D. Gilbert (eds.), *Imperial Cities: Landscape, Display and Identity*, Manchester: Manchester University Press, 1999.

Macpherson, W. J., 'Investment in Indian Railways, 1845–75', *EcHR* **8** (1955), 177–86.

Maddison, A., *Monitoring the World Economy, 1820–1992*, Paris: OECD, 1995.

Magee, G. B., 'The Importance of Being British? Imperial Factors and the Growth of British Imports, 1870–1960', *Journal of Interdisciplinary History* **37** (2007), 341–51.

Knowledge Generation: Technological Change and Economic Growth in Colonial Australia, Melbourne: Australian Scholarly Publishing, 2000.

Magee, G. B. and A. S. Thompson, 'The Global and the Local: Explaining Migrant Remittance Flows in the English-Speaking World, 1880–1914', *Journal of Economic History* **66** (2006), 177–202.

'Lines of Credit, Debts of Obligation: Migrant Remittances to Britain, c. 1875–1913', *EcHR* **59** (2006), 539–77.

Maier, C., *Among Empires: American Ascendancy and Its Predecessors*, Cambridge, MA: Harvard University Press, 2006.

Malchow, H. L., *Population Pressures: Emigration and Government in the Late Nineteenth Century*, London: Sposs, 1979.

Manning, P., *Migration in World History*, New York: Routledge, 2005.

Navigating World History: Historians Create a Global Past, Basingstoke: Palgrave Macmillan, 2003.

Marks, S. and P. Richardson (eds.), *International Labour Migration: Historical Perspectives*, London: Maurice Temple Smith for the Institute of Commonwealth Studies, 1984.

Marquand, D., 'How United Is the Modern United Kingdom?', in A. Grant and K. J. Stringer (eds.), *Uniting the Kingdom? The Making of British History*, London: Routledge, 1995, pp. 277–92.

'The Twilight of the British State? Henry Dubb versus Sceptred Awe', in S. J. D. Green and R. C. Whiting (eds.), *The Boundaries of the State in Modern Britain*, Cambridge: Cambridge University Press, 1996, pp. 57–69.

Marrison, A., *British Business and Protection, 1903–32*, Oxford: Oxford University Press, 1996.

Marsden, B. and C. Smith (eds.), *Engineering Empires: A Cultural History of Technology in Nineteenth-Century Britain*, Basingstoke: Palgrave Macmillan, 2005.

Marsden, B. and C. Smith, 'Introduction: Technology, Science and Culture in the Long Nineteenth Century', in Marsden and Smith (eds.), *Engineering Empires: A Cultural History of Technology in Nineteenth-Century Britain*, Basingstoke: Palgrave Macmillan, 2005.

Marshall, A., *Principles of Economics*, New York: MacMillan, 1948.

Martends, J., 'A Transnational History of Immigration Restriction: Natal, 1896–7', *JICH* **34** (2006), 323–44.

Massey, D., L. P. Goldring and J. Durand, 'Continuities in Transnational Migration: An Analysis of 19 Mexican Communities', *American Journal of Sociology* **99** (1994), 1492–533.

Massey, D. S., J. Arango, G. Hugo, A. Kouaouci, A. Pellegrino and J. Edward Taylor (eds.), *Worlds in Motion: Understanding International Migration at the End of the Millennium*, Oxford: Oxford University Press, 1998.

Massola, A., *Coranderrk: A History of the Aboriginal Station*, Kilmore: Lowden Publishing, 1975.

Mathias, P., 'Risk, Credit and Kinship in Early Modern Enterprise', in J. J. McCusker and K. Morgan (eds.), *The Early Modern Atlantic Economy*, Cambridge: Cambridge University Press, 2000, pp. 15–36.

Mauro, P., N. Sussman and Y. Yafeh, *Emerging Markets and Financial Globalization: Sovereign Bond Spreads in 1870–1913 and Today*, Oxford: Oxford University Press, 2006.

Maynard, M., *Fashioned from Penury: Dress as Cultural Practice in Colonial Australia*, Cambridge: Cambridge University Press, 1994.

Mcaloon, J., 'Scots in the Colonial Economy', in T. Brooking and J. Coleman (eds.), *The Heather and the Fern: Scottish Migration and New Zealand Settlement*, Dunedin: Otago University Press, 2003.

McCall, B. P. and J. J. McCall, 'A Sequential Study of Migration and Job Search', *Journal of Labor Economics* **5** (1987), 452–76.

McCarthy, A., *Irish Migrants in New Zealand, 1840–1937: 'The Desired Haven'*, Woodbridge: Boydell Press, 2005.

'Personal Letters and the Organisation of Irish Migration to and from New Zealand, 1848–1925', *Irish Historical Studies* **33** (2003), 297–319.

McCloskey, D. N., 'Did Victorian Britain Fail?', *EcHR* **23** (1970), 446–59.

McCormack, A. R., 'Cloth Caps and Jobs: The Ethnicity of English Immigrants', in J. M. Bumsted (ed.), *Interpreting Canada's Past*, 2 vols., Vol. II: *After Confederation*, Toronto: University of Toronto Press, 1986.

'Networks among British Immigrants', in H. Tinker (ed.), *The Diaspora of the British, Collected Seminar Papers* 31, Institute of Commonwealth Studies, University of London (1982), pp. 62–4.

McDonald, J. M. and E. Richards, 'The Great Emigration of 1841: Recruitment for New South Wales in British Emigration Fields', *Population Studies* **51** (1997), 337–55.

McDougall, F. L., *The Growing Dependence of British Industry upon Empire Markets*, London: HMSO, 1929.

Sheltered Markets: A Study of the Value of Empire Trade, London: J. Murray, 1925.

McGrath, A., *Entangled Frontiers: Marriage and Sex across Colonizing Frontiers in Australia and North America*, New Haven: Yale University Press, forthcoming.

McKenzie, K., *Scandal in the Colonies: Sydney and Cape Town, 1820–1850*, Melbourne: Melbourne University Press, 2004.

McKeown, A., 'Global Migration, 1846–1940', *Journal of World History* **15** (2004), 155–89.

Melancholy Order: Asian Migration and the Globalisation of Borders, New York: Columbia University Press, 2008

'Periodizing Globalization', *HWJ* **63** (2007), 218–30.

McLaren, J., A. R. Buck and N. E. Wright (eds.), *Despotic Dominion: Property Rights in British Settler Societies*, Vancouver: University of British Columbia Press, 2005.

McLaren, J., A. R. Buck and N. E. Wright (eds.), *Land and Freedom: Law, Property Rights and the British Diaspora*, Aldershot: Ashgate, 2001.

McLean, G., 'The Colony Commodified: Trade, Progress and the Real Business of Exhibitions', in J. M. Thomson (ed.), *Farewell Colonialism: The New Zealand International Exhibition, Christchurch 1906–7*, Palmerston North: University of Auckland, 1998.

McMillan, J., *Reinventing the Bazaar: A Natural History of Markets*, New York: Norton, 2002.

McNeill, W. H., 'Globalization: Long Term Process or New Era in Human Affairs?', *New Global Studies* **2**:1 (2008), 1–9.

Menkhoff, T. and S. Gerke (eds.), *Chinese Entrepreneurship and Asian Business Networks*, London: Taylor and Francis, 2002.

Meredith, D. and B. Dyster, *Australia in the Global Economy: Continuity and Change*, Cambridge: Cambridge University Press, 2000.

Merrett, D. T., *ANZ Bank: A History of the Australia and New Zealand Banking Group Limited and Its Constituents*, Sydney: Allen and Unwin, 1985.

Meyer, F. V., *Britain's Colonies in World Trade*, Oxford: Oxford University Press, 1948.

Michie, H. and R. Thomas (eds.), *Nineteenth Century Geographies: The Transformation of Space from the Victorian Age to the American Century*, Rutgers: Rutgers University Press, 2002.

Michie, R. C., 'The Canadian Securities Market, 1850–1914', *Business History Review* **62** (1988), 35–73.

'The Social Web of Investment in the Nineteenth Century', *Revue internationale d'histoire de la banque* **18** (1979), 158–61.

Milgrom, P. and J. Roberts, *Economics, Organization and Management*, Upper Saddle River, NJ: Prentis Hall, 1992.

Milgrom, P. R., D. C. North and B. R. Weingast, 'The Role of Institutions in the Revival of Trade: The Law Merchant, Private Judges, and the Champagne Fairs', *Economics and Politics* **2** (1990), 1–23.

Miller, K., *Emigrants and Exiles: Ireland and the Irish Exodus to North America*, Oxford: Oxford University Press, 1985.

Misztal, B. A., *Trust in Modern Societies: The Search for the Bases of Social Order*, Cambridge: Cambridge University Press, 1996.

Mitchell, B. R., *British Historical Statistics*, Cambridge: Cambridge University Press, 1988.

Morgan, C., 'Creating Transatlantic Worlds? Aboriginal Peoples in Britain, 1830s–1870s', paper given at the British World Conference, Auckland, July 2005.

Morley, R., 'Dropping Off in the Rounding: The Origins and Significance of Affiliations between British and New Zealand Accounting Partnerships', in K. Darian-Smith, P. Grimshaw, K. Lindsey, and S. Mcintyre (eds), *Exploring the British World: Identity, Cultural Production, Institutions. Proceedings of British World Conference III*, Melbourne: RMIT Publishing, 2004, pp. 1003–21.

Morowska, E. and W. Spohn, 'Moving Europeans in the Globalizing World', in W. Gungwu (ed.), *Global History and Migrations*, Boulder, CO: Westview Press, 1997, pp. 23–62.

Morrell, J., *Gentlemen of Science: Early Years of the British Association for the Advancement of Science*, Oxford: Oxford University Press, 1981.

Morris, J., 'The Assisted Immigrants in New Zealand, 1871–79: A Statistical Study', unpublished M.A. thesis, University of Auckland, 1973.

Moss, M., *The Building of Europe's Largest Mutual Life Company: Standard Life, 1825–2000*, Edinburgh: University of Edinburgh Press, 2000.

Mouat, J. and I. Phimister, 'Mining, Engineers and Risk Management: British Overseas Investment, 1894–1914', *SAHJ* **49** (2003), 5–18.

Moya, J. C., *Cousins and Strangers: Spanish Immigrants in Buenos Aires, 1850–1930*, Berkeley: University of California Press, 1998.

Muller, A., 'The Economic History of the Port Elizabeth–Uitenhage Region', *South African Journal of Economic History* **15** (2000), 20–47.

Munro, J. F. *Maritime Enterprise and Empire: Sir William Mackinnon and His Business Network, 1823–93*, Woodbridge: Boydell Press, 2003.

Murdoch, A., *British Emigration, 1603–1914*, Basingstoke: Palgrave Macmillan, 2004.

Murray, M., 'Prayers, Ploughs and Pastures: Moidart Emigrants in the Western District of Victoria', paper given at the British World Conference, University of Melbourne, July, 2004.

Murray, S., 'Canadian Participation and National Representation at the 1851 London Great Exhibition and the 1855 Paris Exposition Universelle', *Histoire sociale/Social History* **32** (1999), 1–22.

Nederveen Pieterse, J., *Globalization and Culture: Global Mélange*, Oxford: Oxford University Press, 2003.

Nicholas, S. J., 'Locational Choice, Performance and the Growth of British Multinational Firms', *Business History* **31**:3 (1989), 122–41.

'The Overseas Marketing Performance of British Industry, 1870–1914', *EcHR* **37**:4 (1984), 489–506.

Noer, T. J., *Briton, Boer and Yankee: The United States and South Africa, 1870–1914*, Kent, OH: Kent State University Press, 1978.

Nollan, S. M., 'A Gentlemanly Capitalist at Home and Abroad: The 4th Earl of Grey, 1885–1917', unpublished M.A. thesis, University of Durham, 2004.

North, D., *Institutions, Institutional Change, and Economic Performance*, Cambridge: Cambridge University Press, 1990.

Understanding the Process of Economic Change, Princeton: Yale University Press, 2005.

North, D. C., 'The United States Balance of Payments, 1790–1860', in National Bureau of Economic Research, *Trends in the American Economy in the Nineteenth Century: Studies in Income and Wealth*, Princeton: Yale University Press, 1960.

Northrup, D., *Indentured Labour in the Age of Imperialism, 1834–1922*, Cambridge: Cambridge University Press, 1995.

'Migration from Africa, Asia, and the South Pacific', in A. Porter (ed.), *The Oxford History of the British Empire*, 5 vols., Vol. III: *The Nineteenth Century*, Oxford: Oxford University Press, 1999, pp. 88–100.

Nugent, W. T. K., *Crossings: The Great Transatlantic Migrations, 1870–1914*, Bloomington: University of Indiana Press, 1992.

O'Connor, P., 'Keeping New Zealand White, 1908–20', *New Zealand Journal of History* **2** (1968), 41–65.

O'Farrell, P., *The Irish in Australia: 1788 to Present*, Sydney: University of Notre Dame Press, 2000.

Letters from Irish Australia, Kensington, NSW: New South Wales University Press, 1984.

Offer, A. 'The British Empire, 1870–1914: A Waste of Money?', *EcHR* **46** (1993), 215–38.

'Costs and Benefits, Prosperity and Security', in A. N. Porter (ed.), *The Oxford History of the British Empire*, 5 vols., Vol. III: *The Nineteenth Century*, Oxford: Oxford University Press, 1999, pp. 690–711.

The First World War: An Agrarian Interpretation, Oxford: Oxford University Press, 1989.

Oppenheimer, M., 'Women's Movements and the Empire, 1880–1920', paper given at the British World Conference, Institute for Commonwealth Studies, London, 1998.

Orde, A., *The Eclipse of Great Britain: The United States and British Imperial Decline, 1895–1956*, Basingstoke: Palgrave Macmillan, 1996.

O'Rourke, K. and J. G. Williamson, *Globalization and History: The Evolution of a Nineteenth-Century Atlantic Economy*, Cambridge, MA: Harvard University Press, 1999.

Osterhammel, J., *Colonialism: A Theoretical Overview*, Princeton: Markus Wiener Publishers, 1997.

Owen, G., *From Empire to Europe: The Decline and Revival of British Industry since the Second World War*, London: HarperCollins, 1999.

Owen, G. D., *Crisis in Chubut: A Chapter in the History of the Welsh Colony in Patagonia*, Swansea: C. Davies, 1977.

Owram, D., *Promise of Eden: The Canadian Expansionist Movement and the Idea of the West, 1856–1900*, Toronto: University of Toronto Press, 1980.

Padayachee, V. and R. Morrell, 'Indian Merchants and Dukawallahs in the Natal Economy, c. 1875–1914', *JSAS* 17 (1991), 71–102.

Palloni, A., D. S. Massey, M. Ceballos, K. Espinosa and M. Spittel, 'Social Capital and International Migration: A Test Using Information on Family Networks', *American Journal of Sociology* 106 (2001), 1262–98.

Palmer, S., *Politics, Shipping and the Repeal of the Navigation Laws*, Manchester: Manchester University Press, 1990.

Parekh, B., G. Singh and S. Vertovec (eds.), *Culture and Economy in the Indian Diaspora*, London: Routledge, 2003.

Parnaby, O. W., *Britain and the Labor Trade in the South West Pacific*, Durham, NC: Duke University Press, 1964.

Parris, J. and A. G. L. Shaw, 'The Melbourne International Exhibition 1880–81', *Victorian Historical Journal* 51 (1980), 238–49.

Payton, P., *The Cornish Overseas*, Fowey: Alexander Associates, 1999.

Pearson, L., 'The World at Their Feet: Decorative Tile Exports by British Manufacturers, 1850–1910', paper given at *Imperial Globalisation? Trade, Technologies, and Transnationalities within the British Empire, c. 1800–2000*, 10–11 September 2004, British Empire and Commonwealth Museum, Bristol.

Perkins, B., *The Great Rapprochement: England and the United States, 1895–1914*, New York: Atheneum, 1968.

Phillips, W. G., *The Agricultural Implement Industry in Canada: A Case Study of Competition*, Toronto: University of Toronto Press, 1956.

Pickles, K., *Female Imperialism and National Identity: The Imperial Order of the Daughters of Empire*, Manchester: Manchester University Press, 2002.

'Female Imperialism in the British World', paper given at the British World Conference, University of Auckland, July 2005.

One Flag, One Throne, One Empire: Canada's Imperial Order Daughters of the Empire and Women's Part in the Making of the British Imperial Past, Manchester: Manchester University Press, 2002.

Pike, R. M., 'National Interest and Imperial Yearnings: Empire Communication and Canada's Role in Establishing the Imperial Penny Post', *JICH* 26 (1998), 22–48.

Pinchbeck, I., *Children in English Society*, 2 vols., Vol. II: *From the Eighteenth Century to the Children Act of 1848*, London: Routledge and Kegan Paul, 1973.

Pla, J., *The British in Paraguay, 1850–1870*, Richmond: University of West Virginia Press, 1976.

Platt, D. C. M., 'Canada and Argentina: The First Preference of the British Investor, 1904–14', *JICH* 13 (1985), 77–92.

'Trade Competition in the Regions of Recent Settlement', in D. C. M. Platt with A. J. H. Latham and R. Michie (eds.), *Decline and Recovery in Britain's Overseas Trade, 1873–1914*, London: Macmillan, 1993, pp. 91–138.

Platt, D. C. M. and G. di Tella, 'Introduction', in D. C. M. Platt and G. di Tella (eds.), *Argentina, Australia and Canada: Studies in Comparative Development, 1870–1965*, London: Macmillan, 1985, pp. 1–19.

Pocock, J. G. A., 'British History: A Plea for a New Subject', *Journal of Modern History* **47** (1975), 604–5.

'Conclusion: Contingency, Identity, Sovereignty', in A. Grant and K. J. Stringer (eds.), *Uniting the Kingdom? The Making of British History*, London: Routledge, 1995, pp. 292–302.

'History and Sovereignty: The Historiographic Response to Europeanisation in Two British Cultures', *JBS* **31** (1992), 358–89.

'The Limits and Divisions of British History: In Search of the Unknown Subject', *AHR* **87** (1982), 311–36.

Pollard, S., *Britain's Prime and Britain's Decline: The British Economy, 1870–1914*, London: E. Arnold, 1989.

Porter, A. N., *Victorian Shipping, Business and Imperial Policy: Donald Currie, the Castle Line and Southern Africa*, Woodbridge: Royal Historical Society, 1986.

Porter, B., *The Absent-Minded Imperialists: Empire, Society and Culture in Britain*, Oxford: Oxford University Press, 2004.

Portes, A., 'Globalization from Below: The Rise of Transnational Communities', in W. P. Smith and R. P. Korczenwicz (eds.), *Latin America in the World Economy*, Westport: Greenwood Publishing Group, 1996, pp. 151–68.

'Social Capital: Its Origins and Application in Modern Sociology', *Annual Review of Sociology* **24** (1998), 1–24.

Portes, A. and P. Landolt, 'The Downside of Social Capital', *American Prospect* **26** (1996), 1–24.

Portes, A. and M. Zhou, 'Gaining the Upper Hand: Economic Mobility among Immigrant and Domestic Minorities', *Ethnic and Racial Studies* **15** (1992), 491–522.

Potter, S. J., 'Communication and Integration: The British and Dominions Press and the British World, c. 1876–1914', in C. Bridge and K. Fedorowich (eds.), *The British World: Culture, Diaspora and Identity*, London: Taylor and Francis, 2003, pp. 190–207.

'Empire and the English Press, 1857–1914', in S. J. Potter (ed.), *Newspapers and Empire in Ireland and Britain* (Dublin: Four Courts Press, 2004), pp. 39–61.

'Nationalism, Imperialism and the Press in Britain and the Dominions c. 1898–1914', unpublished D.Phil. thesis, University of Oxford, 2000.

News and the British World: The Emergence of an Imperial Press System, 1876–1922, Oxford: Oxford University Press, 2003.

Newspapers and Empire in Ireland and Britain, Dublin: Four Courts, 2004.

'Webs, Networks, and Systems: Globalization and the Mass Media in the Nineteenth- and Twentieth-Century British Empire', *JBS* **46** (2007), 621–46.

Preda, A., 'The Rise of the Popular Investor: Financial Knowledge and Investing in England and France, 1840–1880', *Sociological Quarterly* **42** (2001), 205–32.

Prestholdt, J., *Domesticating the World: African Consumerism and the Genealogies of Globalization*, Berkeley, CA: University of California Press, 2008.
'On the Global Repercussions of East African Consumerism', *AHR* **109** (2004), 755–83.
Prevost, J.-G. and J.-P. Beaud, 'A Study in Failure: The 1920 Imperial Statistical Conference', in K. Darian-Smith, P. Grimshaw, K. Lindsey and S. Mcintyre (eds.), *Exploring the British World: Identity, Culture, Production, Institutions. Proceedings of British World Conference III*, Melbourne: RMIT Publishing, 2004, pp. 869–89.
Price, C., *The Great White Walls Are Built: Restrictive Immigration to North America and Australasia, 1836–1888*, Canberra: Australian National University Press, 1974.
Purkis, A.J., 'The Politics, Capital and Labour of Railway Building in the Cape Colony, 1870–1885', unpublished D.Phil. thesis, University of Oxford, 1978.
Putnam, R., *Bowling Alone: The Collapse and Revival of American Community*, New York: Simon and Schuster, 2000.
Putnam, R.D. and R. Leonardi, *Making Democracy Work: Civic Traditions in Modern Italy*, Princeton: Princeton University Press, 1994.
Rauch, J.E., 'Business and Social Networks in International Trade', *Journal of Economic Literature* **39** (2001), 1177–203.
Ray, L. and A. Sayer (eds.), *Culture and Economy after the Cultural Turn*, London: Sage, 1999.
Read, D., *The Power of News: The History of Reuters, 1849–1989*, Oxford: Oxford University Press, 1992.
Reader, W.J., *Imperial Chemical Industries: A History*, 2 vols., Vol. I: *The Forerunners, 1870–1926*, Oxford: Oxford University Press, 1970.
Rich, P.J., *Elixir of Empire: The English Public Schools, Ritualism, Freemasonry and Imperialism*, London: Regency, 1989.
Richards, E., *Britannia's Children: Emigration from England, Scotland, Wales and Ireland since 1600*, London: Continuum International Publishing Group, 2004.
'The British Diaspora: In Wide Angle', paper given at the British World Conference, University of Melbourne, July 2004.
'How Did Poor People Emigrate from the British Isles to Australia in the Nineteenth Century?', *JBS* **32**:2 (1993), 250–79.
'Immigrant Lives', in E. Richards (ed.), *The Flinders History of South Australia: Social History*, Netley, SA: Wakefield Press, 1986, pp. 143–70.
'Return Migration and Migrant Strategies in Colonial Australia', in D. Fitzpatrick (ed.), *Home or Away? Immigrants in Colonial Australia: Visible Immigrants*, Canberra: Australian National University Press, 1992, pp. 64–104.
'Running Home from Australia: Intercontinental Mobility and Migrant Expectations in the Nineteenth Century', in M. Harper (ed.), *Emigrant Homecomings: The Return Movement of Immigrants, 1600–2000*, Manchester: Manchester University Press, 2005, pp. 77–104.
'Scottish Voices and Networks on Colonial Australia', in A. McCarthy (ed.), *A Global Clan*, London: B. Tauris, 2006, pp. 150–83.

'Voices of British and Irish Migrants in Nineteenth Century Australia', in C. G. Pooley and I. D. Whyte (eds.), *Migrants, Emigrants and Immigrants: A Social History of Migration*, New York: Routledge, 1991, pp. 19–41.

Ridden, J., 'Britishness as an Imperial and Diasporic Identity: Irish Elite Perspectives, *c.* 1820–70s', in P. Gray (ed.), *Victoria's Ireland? Irishness and Britishness, 1837–1901*, Dublin: Four Courts Press, 2004, pp. 88–105.

'Liberal Worlds: Empire, Identity and Citizenship in the Nineteenth Century', paper given at the British World Conference, University of Melbourne, July 2004.

Robbins, K., *Great Britain: Identities, Institutions and the Idea of Britishness*, Harlow: Longmans, 1998.

Nineteenth Century Britain: Integration and Diversity, Oxford: Oxford University Press, 1988.

Roberts, A., *A History of the English-Speaking Peoples since 1900*, London: Weidenfeld and Nicolson, 2006.

Robertson, R., *Globalization: Social Theory and Global Culture*, London: Sage, 1992.

Robertson, R. and J. A. Scholte, *Encyclopedia of Globalization*, 4 vols., Vol. III, New York: Routledge, 2007.

Rose, J., *The Intellectual Life of the British Working Classes*, New Haven: Yale University Press, 2002.

Rosenthal, E. (ed.), *Southern African Dictionary of National Biography*, n.p., 1966.

Ross, R., 'The Battle for Britain in the Cape Colony, 1830–60', paper given at the British World Conference, University of Cape Town, July 2002.

'Cross-Continental Cross-Fertilisation in Clothing', *European Review* 14:1 (2006), 135–47.

Status and Respectability in the Cape Colony, 1750–1870: A Tragedy of Manners, Cambridge: Cambridge University Press, 1999.

Routledge, B. and J. von Amsburg, 'Social Capital and Growth', *Journal of Monetary Economics* 50 (2003), 167–94.

Ruether, K., 'Heated Debates over Crinolines: European Clothing on Nineteenth-Century Lutheran Mission Stations in the Transvaal', *JSAS* 28 (2002), 359–78.

Rugman, A., *The End of Globalization: Why Global Strategy Is a Myth and How to Profit from the Realities of Regional Markets*, New York: AMACOM, 2001.

Russell, L. (ed.), *Colonial Frontiers: Indigenous–European Encounters in Settler Societies*, Manchester: Manchester University Press, 2001.

Samuel, R. (ed.), *Patriotism: The Making and Unmaking of a British National Identity*, 3 vols., London: Routledge, 1989.

Sargent, A. J., *British Industries and Empire Markets*, London: HMSO, 1930.

Sarra-Bournet, M., 'For the Empire … at Last: French Canadians in the Boer War', paper given at the British World Conference, University of Cape Town, July 2002.

Saul, S. B., 'The Export Economy, 1970–1914', *Yorkshire Bulletin of Economic and Social Research* 17:1 (1965), 5–18.

Studies in British Overseas Trade, 1870–1914, Liverpool: Liverpool University Press, 1960.

Schenk, C. R., *Britain and the Sterling Area: From Devaluation to Convertibility in the 1950s*, London: Routledge, 1994.

Schevdin, C. B., 'Staples and Regions of Pax Britannica', *EcHR* **43** (1990), 533–59.

Schmitz, C., 'The Nature and Dimensions of Scottish Foreign Investment, 1860–1914', *Business History* **39** (1997), 42–68.

Schrier, A., *Ireland and the American Emigration: 1850–1900*, Minneapolis: University of Minnesota Press, 1958.

Schwartz, S. P., 'Cornish Migration Studies: An Epistemological and Paradigmatic Critique', in P. Payton (ed.), *Cornish Studies* 10 (2002), 136–65.

'Cornish Migration to Latin America: A Global and Transnational Perspective', unpublished Ph.D. thesis, University of Exeter, 2003.

'Migration Networks and the Transnationalization of Social Capital: Cornish Migration to Latin America', *Cornish Studies* 13 (2005), 256–87.

Schwartz, S. P. and R. Parker, *Tin Mines and Miners of Lanner: The Heart of Cornish Tin*, London: Halsgrove Press, 2001.

Scott, J., *Social Network Analysis: A Handbook*, London: Sage, 1991.

Searle, G. R., *A New England? Peace and War, 1886–1918*, Oxford: Oxford University Press, 2004.

Senior, H., *Orangeism: The Canadian Phase*, Toronto: McGraw-Hill Ryerson, 1972.

Serle, G., 'Westgarth, William (1815–89)', in H. C. G. Matthew and B. Harrison (eds.), *The Oxford Dictionary of National Biography*, Oxford: Oxford University Press, 2004.

Shammas, C., 'Changes in English and Anglo-American Consumption from 1550 to 1800', in J. Brewer and R. Porter (eds.), *Consumption and the World of Goods*, London: Routledge, 1993, pp. 177–205.

Sharma, S. D., 'The Many Faces of Today's Globalization: A Survey of Recent Literature', *New Global Studies* **2** (2008), 1–27.

Shrivastava, M., 'Globalising "Global Studies": Vehicle for Disciplinary and Regional Bridges?', *New Global Studies* **2** (2008), 1–20.

Simon, M., 'The Pattern of New British Portfolio Foreign Investment, 1865–1914', in J. H. Adler (ed.), *Capital Movements and Economic Development*, London: Macmillan, 1967, pp. 33–70.

Simpson, T., *The Immigrants: The Great Migration from Britain to New Zealand, 1830–1890*, Auckland: Godwit, 1997.

Sjaastad, L. A., 'The Costs and Returns of Human Migration', *Journal of Political Economy* **70** (1962), 80–93.

Sleight, S., 'Reading the British Australasian Community in London, 1884–1924', mimeo of paper delivered at the Australian diaspora conference held at the Menzies Research Centre, University of London, 2005.

Smith, D. and P. Buckner, 'The Canadianized Monarchy: The Invention of Tradition? Royal Tours to Canada of 1860 and 1901', paper given at the British World Conference, Institute for Commonwealth Studies, London, 1998.

Smith, M. P. and L. E. Guarnizo (eds.), *Transnationalism from Below*, New Brunswick, NJ: Transaction Publishers, 1998.

Spence, C. C., *British Investments and the American Mining Frontier, 1860–1901*, Ithaca, NY: Cornell University Press, 1958.

Starfield, J., 'A Dance with the Empire: Modiri Molema's Glasgow Years, 1914–21', *JSAS* **27** (2001), 479–503.

Stearns, P. N., *Consumerism in World History: The Global Transformation of Desire*, 2nd edn, London: Routledge, 2006.

Stiglitz, J. E., *Globalization and Its Discontents*, London: W. W. Norton, 2002.

Stoddart, B., 'Sticky Wickets: Cricket, Culture and Imperialism, 1880–1960', paper given at the British World Conference, Institute for Commonwealth Studies, London, 1998.

Stolle, D. and T. R. Rochon, 'Are All Associations Alike?', *American Behavioral Scientist* **42** (1998), 47–65.

Stone, I., *The Global Export of Capital from Great Britain, 1865–1914*, London: St Martin's Press, 1999.

Sturgis, J., 'Temperance Reform in the British World', paper given at the British World Conference, Institute for Commonwealth Studies, London, 1998.

Sugiyama, S. and L. Grove (eds.), *Commercial Networks in Modern Asia*, Richmond, Surrey: Curzon, 2001.

Sunderland, D., *Managing the British Empire: The Crown Agents, 1833–1914*, Woodbridge: Boydell Press, 2004.

Sutton, G. B., 'The Marketing of Ready-Made Footwear in the Nineteenth Century', *Business History* **6**:2 (1964), 93–112.

Suzuki, T., *Japanese Government Loan Issues on the London Capital Market, 1870–1913*, London: Athlone, 1994.

Swain, S., 'Centre and Periphery in British Child Rescue Discourse', paper given at the British World Conference, University of Melbourne, July 2004.

Sweetman, R., 'Towards a History of Orangeism in New Zealand', in B. Patterson (ed.), *Ulster–New Zealand Migration and Cultural Transfers*, Dublin: Four Courts Press, 2006, pp. 154–64.

Sykes, A., *Tariff Reform in British Politics, 1903–13*, Oxford: Oxford University Press, 1979.

Tamarkin, M., *Cecil Rhodes and the Cape Afrikaners: The Imperial Colossus and the Colonial Parish Pump*, London: Routledge, 1996.

Tasiulis, D. and N. Yuval-Davis (eds.), *Unsettling Settler Societies: Articulations of Gender, Race, Ethnicity and Class*, London: Sage, 1995.

Taylor, M., 'The 1848 Revolutions and the British Empire', *Past & Present* **166** (2000), 146–80.

Taylor, P. M., *The Distant Magnet: European Emigration to the USA*, New York: Harper and Row, 1971.

Testro, R., *A Pictorial History of Australian Railways, 1854–1970*, Melbourne: Lansdowne Press, 1971.

Theron, B., 'Challenging Gender Conventions: Some English-Speaking Women in South Africa during the Anglo-Boer War', paper given at the British World Conference, University of Melbourne, July 2004.

Thomas, B., *Migration and Atlantic Growth: A Study of Great Britain and the Atlantic Economy*, Cambridge: Cambridge University Press, 1954.

Thompson, A. S., *The Empire Strikes Back? The Impact of Imperialism on Britain from the Mid-Nineteenth Century*, Harlow: Pearson Education, 2005.

Imperial Britain: The Empire in British Politics, c. 1880–1932, Harlow: Pearson Education, 2000.

'The Languages of Loyalism in Southern Africa, c. 1870–1939', *English Historical Review* **118** (2003), 617–50.

'The Power and Privileges of Association: Co-Ethnic Networks and the Economic Life of the British Imperial World', *SAHJ* **56** (2006), 43–59.

'Tariff Reform: An Imperial Strategy, 1903–13', *HJ* (1997), 1033–54.

Thompson, A. S. and G. Magee, 'A Soft Touch? British Industry, Empire Markets and the Self-Governing Dominions, c. 1870–1914', *EcHR* **56** (2003), 689–717.

Thompson, G. F., 'Is All the World a Complex Network?', *Economy and Society* **33** (2004), 411–24.

Thuernstorm, S. (ed.), *Harvard Encyclopaedia of American Ethnic Groups*, Cambridge, MA: Harvard University Press, 1980.

Timlin, M. F., 'Canada's Immigration Policy, 1896–1910', *The Canadian Journal of Economics and Political Science* **26** (1960), 517–20.

Tinker, H. (ed.), *The Diaspora of the British*, Collected Seminar Papers of the Institute of Commonwealth Studies, London: Institute of Commonwealth Studies, 1982.

Todd, A. C., *The Search for Silver: Cornish Miners in Mexico*, Padstow: Lodenek Press, 1977.

Tomlinson, B. R., *The Economy of Modern India, 1860–1970*, Cambridge: Cambridge University Press, 1993.

Torrance, D., 'Race and the Rhodes Scholarship in America and South Africa', paper given at the British World Conference, University of Melbourne, July 2004.

Trainor, L., *British Imperialism and Australian Nationalism: Manipulation, Conflict and Compromise in the Late Nineteenth Century*, Cambridge: Cambridge University Press, 1994.

Treagus, M., 'Spectacles of Empire: Maori Tours of England in 1863 and 1911', paper given at the British World Conference, University of Melbourne, July 2004.

Trebilcock, C., *Phoenix Assurance and the Development of British Insurance*, 2 vols., Vol. II: *The Year of the Insurance Giants, 1870–1914*, Cambridge: Cambridge University Press, 1998.

Treble, J. H., 'The Pattern of Investment of the Standard Life Assurance Company, 1875–1914', *Business History* **22** (1980), 170–88.

Trevelyan, G. M., *English Social History: A Survey of Six Centuries. Chaucer to Queen Victoria*, London: Longmans, Green and Co., 1944.

Trouillot, M.-R., 'The Perspectives of the World: Globalisation Then and Now', in E. Mudimbe-Boyi (ed.), *Beyond Dichotomies: Histories, Cultures and the Challenge of Globalization*, Albany: SUNY Press, 2002.

Tyrrell, A., 'A Business of Philanthropy: The Montserrat Company, 1856–1961', *The Journal of Caribbean History* **38** (2004), 184–212.

Vahed, G., 'Race, Class and Loyalty to Empire: Durban's Indians during the First World War', paper given at the British World Conference, University of Cape Town, July 2002.

van Dijk, F., *Social Ties and Economic Preference*, London: Springer, 1997.

van Heyningen, E. and P. Merrett, ' "The Healing Touch": The Guild of Loyal Women of South Africa, 1900–1912', paper given at the British World Conference, University of Cape Town, July 2002.

Van Onselen, C., *The Fox and the Flies: The World of Joseph Silver, Racketeer and Psychopath*, Richmond: University of Virginia Press, 2007.

'Jewish Marginality in the Atlantic World: Organised Crime in the Era of the Great Migrations, 1880–1914', *SAHJ* **43** (2000), 96–137.

Van Vugt, W. E., *Britain to America: Mid-Nineteenth Century Immigrants to the United States*, Urbana: University of Illinois Press, 1999.

British Buckeyes: The English, Scots, and Welsh in Ohio, 1700–1900, Kent, OH: Kent State University Press, 2006.

Vaughan, M., 'Africa and the Birth of the Modern World', *TRHS* (2006), 143–62.

Vertovec, S. (ed.), *Migration, Diasporas and Transnationalism*, Cheltenham: Edward Elgar, 1999.

Vertovec, S., 'Transnationalism and Identity', *Journal of Ethnic and Migration Studies* **27** (2001), 573–82.

Veseth, M., *Selling Globalization: The Myth of the Global Economy*, London: Lynne Reinner, 1998.

Voisey, P., 'The Urbanisation of the Canadian Prairies, 1871–1916', *Histoire sociale/Social History* **8** (1975), 77–101.

Walton, J. K., 'Britishness', in C. Wrigley (ed.), *A Companion to Early Twentieth Century Britain*, Oxford: Oxford University Press, 2003.

Ward, P., *White Canada Forever: Popular Attitudes and Public Policy toward Orientals in British Columbia*, Montreal: McGill-Queen's University Press, 1978.

Ward, R., *The Australian Legend*, Melbourne: Oxford University Press, 1966.

Ward, S., 'Echoes of Empire', *HWJ* **62** (2006), 264–78.

'Imperial Identities Abroad', in S. Stockwell (ed.), *The British Empire: Themes and Perspectives*, Oxford: Blackwell, 2008, pp. 226–34.

Waterhouse, R., 'The Yeoman Ideal and the Australian Experience', in K. Darian-Smith, P. Grimshaw, K. Lindsey and S. Mcintyre (eds.), *Exploring the British World: Identity, Cultural Production, Institutions*, Melbourne: RMIT Publishing, 2004, pp. 440–59.

Weaver, J. C., *The Great Land Rush and the Making of the Modern World, 1650–1900*, Montreal and Kingston: McGill-Queen's University Press, 2003

Weidenhofer, M. (ed.), *Colonial Ladies*, South Yarra, Victoria: Gordon and Gotch, 1985.

Weiner, M., 'The Global Migration Crisis', in W. Gungwu (ed.), *Global History and Migrations*, Boulder, CO: Westview Press, 1997, pp. 95–117.

Wellings, B., 'Crown and Country: Britishness and Australian Nationalism since 1788', paper given at the British World Conference, University of Melbourne, July 2004.

Wessel, A., 'There's No Taste like Home: The Food of Empire', paper presented at the British World Conference, University of Melbourne, July 2003.

Wesseling, H. L., *The European Colonial Empires, 1815–1919*, Harlow: Pearson–Longman, 2004.

Wickberg, E., (ed.), *From China to Canada: A History of Chinese Communities in Canada*, Toronto: McClelland and Stewart, 1982.

Williams, G., *The Desert and the Dream: A Study of Welsh Colonisation in Chubut, 1865–1915*, Cardiff: University of Wales Press, 1975.

    The Welsh in Patagonia: The State and the Ethnic Community, Cardiff: University of Wales Press, 1991.

Williams, I., *The Firm of Cadbury, 1831–1911*, London: Constable, 1931.

Williams, R., *Keywords: A Vocabulary of Culture and Society*, Oxford: Oxford University Press, 1976.

Woolcock, M., 'Social Capital and Economic Development: Toward a Synthesis and Policy Framework', *Theory and Society* 27 (1998), 151–208.

Woollacott, A., ' "All This Is the Empire, I Told Myself": Australian Women's Voyages "Home" and the Articulation of Colonial Whiteness', *AHR* **102** (1997), 1003–29.

Wood, R. J., *The Commercial Bank of Australia Limited: History of an Australian Institution, 1866–1981*, North Melbourne: Hargreen Publishing Company, 1990.

Worthy, S., 'Royal Tours, Dominion Identity, and Imperial Competition, 1900–1930', paper given at the British World Conference, University of Auckland, July 2005.

Yarwood, A. T., *Asian Migration to Australia: The Background to Exclusion*, Melbourne: Melbourne University Press, 1964.

Young, L., *Middle Class Culture in the Nineteenth Century: America, Australia and Britain*, Basingstoke: Palgrave Macmillan, 2003.

Young, R. J. C., *The Idea of English Ethnicity*, Oxford: Blackwell, 2007.

Zabiello, D., 'The Role of the Architectural Pattern Book in British Colonial Expansion in the Nineteenth Century', in K. Darian-Smith, P. Grimshaw and S. Macintyre (eds.), *Britishness Abroad: Transnational Movements and Imperial Cultures*, Melbourne: Melbourne University Press, 2007, pp. 854–68.

Zahedieh, N., 'Economy', in D. Armitage and M. J. Braddick (eds.), *The British Atlantic World, 1500–1800*, Basingstoke: Palgrave Macmillan, 2002, pp. 51–68.

Zolberg, A. R., 'Global Movements, Global Walls: Responses to Migration, 1885–1925', in W. Gungwu (ed.), *Global History and Migrations*, Boulder, CO: Westview Press, 1997, pp. 287–93.

Index